Intercultural Competence

Interpersonal Communication Across Cultures

SECOND EDITION

MYRON W. LUSTIG
San Diego State University

JOLENE KOESTER
California State University, Sacramento

 HarperCollins*CollegePublishers*

Acquisitions Editor: Cynthia Biron
Project Coordination and Text Design: Ruttle, Shaw & Wetherill, Inc.
Cover Design: Kay Petronio
Cover Illustration: Zita Asbaghi
Electronic Production Manager: Christine Pearson
Manufacturing Manager: Helene G. Landers
Electronic Page Makeup: Ruttle, Shaw & Wetherill, Inc.
Printer and Binder: R.R. Donnelley & Sons Company
Cover Printer: The Lehigh Press, Inc.

Intercultural Competence: Interpersonal Communication Across Cultures, Second Edition

Library of Congress Cataloging-in-Publication Data

Lustig, Myron W.
    Intercultural competence : Interpersonal communication across cultures / Myron W. Lustig, Jolene Koester. —2nd ed.
        p.   cm.
    Includes indexes.
    ISBN 0-673-99710-3
    1. Intercultural communication.   2. Communicative competence—United States.
3. Interpersonal communication—United States.
I. Koester, Jolene.   II. Title.
HM258.L87   1996
303.48'2—dc20   94-45056
                                                                                   CIP

96 97 98   9 8 7 6 5 4 3

To my mother and *To my father and*
  the memory of my father, *the memory of my mother,*
    who taught me tolerance for cultural differences
      in the midst of cultural absolutes.
        MWL *JK*

Contents

Preface

On this, the threshold of the twenty-first century, competence in intercultural communication is an absolute necessity. In both your private and public lives, in all of your personal and professional endeavors, it is imperative that you learn to communicate with people whose cultural heritage makes them vastly different from you. This book is intended to help you accomplish that goal.

FEATURES OF THIS TEXT

Our perspective differs from that of similar texts in several important ways. We have provided a healthy blend of the practical and the theoretical, of the concrete and the abstract, in order to make the ideas and issues salient and meaningful.

First, we recognize that intercultural communicators need specific suggestions and examples about what they should know, how they should interpret their feelings, and how they ought to behave in order to be competent in a given interaction. Beginning students, in particular, need material at the concrete end of the ladder of abstraction. Consequently, we have chosen an easy and conversational style and have linked the presentation of theories with numerous illustrative examples. The "Culture Connections" boxes, in particular, which were so useful to students in the first edition, are now more sharply focused to allow class discussions that emphasize the affective dimension of intercultural competence.

Second, we are aware of the importance of current and accurate descriptions of intercultural communication theories and the supporting research, which provide powerful ways of viewing and understanding intercultural communication phenomena; indeed, we have incorporated ideas from literally hundreds of sources across a wide spectrum of inquiry. These sources form a solid bibliography for those interested in pursuing specific topics in greater depth. However, we have chosen to maintain the text's readability by placing the citations at the end of the book where they are unobtrusive but available to interested readers.

Third, we recognize the significance and importance of cultural patterns, which provide the underlying set of assumptions for cultural and intercultural communication. The focus on cultural patterns as the lens through which all interactions are interpreted is thoroughly explored in Chapters 5 and 6, and the themes of these two chapters permeate the concepts developed in all subsequent chapters. New to this edition is an extended discussion of Confucian cultural patterns, which provides a non-Western counterpoint to the other taxonomies that are included.

Fourth, we include topics not normally considered in intercultural communication textbooks. For instance, although it is standard fare for most text to emphasize verbal and nonverbal code systems, we also provide a careful elaboration of the nature of differing logical systems, or preferred reasoning patterns, and the consequences for intercultural communication when the expectations for the language in use are not widely shared. Similarly, drawing heavily on the available information about interpersonal communication, we explore the dynamic processes of establishing and developing a relationship between culturally different individuals. New to this edition is an elaboration of issues of "face" in interpersonal relationships, and we highlight three important contexts—health care, education, and business—in which people from many cultures converge and interact.

Fifth, we provide a discussion of important ethical and social issues for intercultural communicators. Ethical issues, for instance, are often inadequately considered; yet, in our view, they are crucial because intercultural competence requires a delicate balancing act on the tightrope between moral certainty and cultural relativism. New to this edition is an extensive treatment of such social problems as stereotyping, prejudice, discrimination, and racism, as well as a revised and updated treatment of acculturation experiences.

Finally, we believe this book is different from others because we, as authors, are aware of and wish to acknowledge the cultural perspective that we bring to its writing.

ACKNOWLEDGMENT OF CULTURAL ANCESTRY

When we first began this book, we thought we understood fully how potent the forces of culture are in shaping world views. Yet, as we stepped back at various points in our writing, we were amazed at how subtly but thoroughly our own cultural experiences had permeated the text. Lest anyone believe that our presentation of relevant theories, examples, and practical suggestions is without the distortion of culture, we would like to describe our own cultural heritage. That heritage shapes our understanding of intercultural communication, and it affects what we know, how we feel, and what we do when we communicate with others.

Our cultural ancestry is European, and our own cultural experiences are those that we refer to in this book as European American. Both of our family backgrounds and the communities in which we were raised have influenced and reinforced our cultural perspectives. The European American cultural experience is the one we know best, simply because it is who we are. Many of our ideas and examples about intercultural communication, therefore, draw on our own cultural experiences.

We have tried, however, to increase the number and range of other cultural voices through the ideas and examples that we provide. These voices and the lessons and illustrations they offer represent our colleagues, our friends, and most important, our students.

IMPORTANCE OF VOICES FROM OTHER CULTURES

Although we have attempted to include a wide range of domestic and international cultural groups, inevitably we have shortchanged some simply because we do not have sufficient knowledge, either through direct experience or secondary accounts, of all cultures. Our errors and omissions are not meant to exclude or discount. Rather, they represent the limits of our own intercultural communication experiences. We hope that you, as a reader with a cultural voice of your own, will participate with us in a dialogue that allows us to improve this text over a period of time. Send us examples that illustrate the principles discussed in the text. Be willing to provide a cultural perspective that differs from our own and from those of our colleagues, friends, and students. Our commitment now and in future editions of this book is to describe a variety of cultural voices with accuracy and sensitivity. We ask for your help in accomplishing that objective.

ISSUES IN THE USE OF CULTURAL EXAMPLES

Some of the examples in the following pages may include references to a culture to which you belong or with which you have had substantial experiences, and our example may not match your personal knowledge. As you will discover in the opening chapters of the book, both your own experiences and the example we recount could be accurate. One of the tensions we felt in writing this book was in making statements that are broad enough to provide reasonably accurate generalizations but specific and tentative enough to avoid false claims of universal applicability to all individuals in a given culture.

We have struggled as well with issues of fairness, sensitivity, representativeness, and inclusiveness. Indeed, we have had innumerable discussions with our colleagues across the country—colleagues who, like ourselves, are committed to making the United States and U.S. colleges and universities into truly multicultural institutions—and we have sought their advice about appropriate ways to reflect the value of cultural diversity in our writing. We have responded to their suggestions, and we appreciate the added measure of quality that these cultural voices supply.

TEXT ORGANIZATION

Our goal in this book is to provide ideas and information that can help you to achieve competence in intercultural communication. Part One, "Communication and Intercultural Competence," orients you to the central ideas that underlie this book. Chapter 1 begins with a discussion of the international and domestic imperatives for attaining intercultural competence. We also focus on the United States as an intercultural community, as we address the delicate but important issue of how to characterize its cultural mix and the members of its cultural groups. In Chapter 2, we define and discuss the nature of communication generally and interpersonal communication specifically. We also introduce the notion of culture. As our concern in this book is with interpersonal communication among people from different cultures, an understanding of these key concepts is critical. In Chapter 3, our focus turns to intercultural communication, and we distinguish that form of communication from others. We also lay the groundwork for our continuing discussion of intercultural competence, explaining what it is, what its components are, and how people can achieve it when they communicate with others.

Part Two, "Cultural Differences in Communication," is devoted to explaining the whys and hows of cultural differences. Chapter 4 explains why cultures differ and analyzes some of the important forces that have the potential to create dissimilarities among cultures. Chapter 5 examines the ways in which cultures differ and emphasizes the importance of cultural patterns in differentiating among communication styles. This chapter also examines the structural features that are similar across all cultures. Chapter 6 offers several taxonomies that can be used to understand systematic differences in the ways in which people in various cultures think and communicate.

In Part Three, "Coding Intercultural Communication," we turn our attention to verbal and nonverbal messages, which are central to the communication process. Chapter 7 examines the coding of verbal languages and the influences of linguistic and cultural differences on attempts to communicate interculturally. As the accurate coding and decoding of nonverbal symbols is also vital in intercultural communication, Chapter 8 discusses the effects of cultural differences on nonverbal codes. Chapter 9 investigates the consequences or effects of these cultural differences in coding systems in face-to-face intercultural interactions. Of particular interest are those experiences involving participants who were taught to use different languages and organizational schemes.

Part Four, "Communication in Intercultural Relationships," emphasizes the associations that form among people as a result of their shared communication experiences. Chapter 10 looks at the all-important issues related to the development and maintenance of interpersonal relationships among people from different cultures. Chapter 11 highlights the processes by which communication events are grouped into episodes and interpreted within such contexts as health care, education, and business.

Part Five, the last section of the book, is devoted to "Becoming an Interculturally Competent Communicator." In Chapter 12 we identify particular obstacles or barriers to achieving intercultural competence. Finally, Chapter 13 focuses on the opportunities and possibilities that are available as people attempt to improve their intercultural competence, and it highlights the ethical choices individuals must face when engaged in interpersonal communication across cultures.

A NOTE TO INSTRUCTORS

Accompanying the text is an Instructor's Manual and a Test Bank, which are available to instructors who adopt the text for their courses. Please contact you HarperCollins representative for these materials. They provide pedagogical suggestions and instructional activities to enhance student's learning of course materials.

Teaching a course in intercultural communication is one of the most exciting assignments available. It is difficult to convey in writing the level of involvement, commitment, and interest displayed by typical students in such courses. These students are the reason that teaching intercultural communication is, quite simply, so exhilarating and rewarding.

ACKNOWLEDGMENTS

Many people have assisted us, and we would like to thank them for their help. Reviewers who contributed detailed comments for the second edition include: Karen Carter, University of Houston; Michael Cornett, Loyola University Chicago; John Miohalski, University of Hawaii: Leeward Community College; Peter Nwosu, California State University, Sacramento; Michelle Petersen, Black Hawk College; Sarah Phaffenroth, County College of Morris; Kara Shultz, Bloomsburg University; and Richard Wiseman, California State University, Fullerton. Reviewers who contributed detailed comments for the first edition include: Christina Gonzalez, Arizona State University; Wen-Shu Lee, San Jose State University; Devorah Lieberman, Portland State University; Vicki Marie, San Joaquin Delta College; Kelly Ott, Winona State University; Frank Owarish, United Nations Institute for Training and Research; William Starosta, Howard University; Chudi Uwazuricke, United Nations Institute for Training and Research; Chris Wagner, Cosumnes River College; and Donald Williams, University of Florida, Gainsville. We are also indebted to the students and colleagues at our respective institutions and to our colleagues throughout the communication discipline for their willingness to share their ideas and cultural voices with us. We would also like to thank our editor, Cynthia Biron, and her staff at HarperCollins for their ongoing help.

Finally, we would like to acknowledge each other's encouragement and support throughout the writing of this book. It has truly been a collaborative effort. We also want to acknowledge a shared responsibility for any remaining errors, omissions, oversights, mistakes, and misstatements that may exist despite our best efforts and intentions to correct them.

Myron W. Lustig
Jolene Koester

PART ONE

Communication and Intercultural Competence

1 CHAPTER

Introduction to Intercultural Competence

We live in remarkable times. All around us, there is a heightened emphasis on culture and a corresponding interplay of forces that both encourage and discourage accommodation and understanding among different people.

Consider the enormous changes that have recently occurred in the coalitions and alliances forged among members of vastly different cultural groups: the formation of the European Economic Community, the negotiation of the North American Free Trade Agreement, the creation of ZOPFAN (Zone of Peace, Freedom, and Neutrality) among Southeast Asian nations, and the optimistic signs of peace in the Middle East. These changes are only a few of the many we could name, and they redirect our attention to the problems and possibilities inherent in all attempts at communication among people from different cultures.

A counterweight to these trends toward unification and accommodation, however, has been equally powerful emphases on cultural uniqueness. The importance of maintaining one's cultural identity—and therefore the need to preserve, protect, and defend one's culturally shared values—often creates a rising tide of emotion that promotes fear and distrust while encouraging

3

cultural autonomy and independence. This emotional tide, whose beneficial elements increase people's sense of pride and helps to anchor a people in time and place, can also be a furious and unbridled force of destruction. Witness the problems in Rwanda, Bosnia, Central Asia, and South Central Los Angeles; in each instance, cultures clash over the right to control resources and ideologies. Yet as Catharine R. Stimpson has said of these clashes,

> the refusal to live peaceably in pluralistic societies is one of the bloodiest problems—nationally and internationally—of the 20th century. No wizard, no fairy godmother is going to make this problem disappear. And I retain a pluralist's stubborn, utopian hope that people can talk about, through, across, and around their differences and that these exchanges will help us live together justly.[1]

These are remarkable times, also, because this heightened emphasis on culture is accompanied by a multitude of opportunities to interact with people from different cultural backgrounds. In virtually every facet of life—in work, play, school, and family—communication with others is marked by cultural differences. Both internationally and domestically, competent intercultural communication has become a necessity. The cultural mix challenges each of us to improve intercultural communication.

Our purpose in writing this book is to provide the conceptual tools for understanding how cultural differences can affect interpersonal communication. We also offer some practical suggestions concerning the adjustments necessary to achieve competence when dealing with cultural differences. We begin by examining the imperative to achieve intercultural communication competence.

THE IMPERATIVE FOR INTERCULTURAL COMPETENCE

Marshall McLuhan coined the term *global village* to describe the consequences of the mass media's ability to bring events from the far reaches of the globe into people's homes, thus shrinking the world. Communication technologies now make it possible to establish virtually instantaneous telephone connections with people in other countries. Modern transportation systems also contribute to the creation of the global village. Instead of the challenge posed in the film *Around the World in 80 Days*, astronauts now circumnavigate the globe in eighty minutes. A visit to major cities such as New York, Los Angeles, Mexico City, London, Nairobi, Istanbul, Hong Kong, or Tokyo, with their multicultural populations, demonstrates that movement of people from one country and culture to another has become commonplace. The need to understand the role of culture in interpersonal communication is growing. Internationally and domestically, in business, in education, in health care, and in personal lives, competence in managing intercultural differences in interpersonal communication will be expected.

CULTURE CONNECTIONS

The world of the next century will be different in profound respects from any that we have ever known before—deeply interdependent economically, closely linked technologically, and progressively more homogenized through the movement of information, ideas, people, and capital around the world at unprecedented speed. At the same time, it will be more multicentric in the devolution of economic, political, and military power to smaller adaptable units. Some nations will undergo a perilous fragmentation, as the centralizing forces that once held people together are pulled apart and traditional concepts of national sovereignty and nationhood are contested, sometimes violently. How these tendencies will be reconciled is far from clear.

Source: David A. Hamburg, "Report of the President/1993" (New York: The Carnegie Corporation of New York, 1993) 11.

The International Imperative for Intercultural Competence

The mass media allow people in the United States and throughout the world to have daily glimpses of the events and lives of people in other countries and cultures. The superficiality of this media exposure belies the significant interdependencies that now link the United States politically, economically, socially, and interpersonally with other countries. At the 1994 Goodwill Games in St. Petersburg, for instance, Russian figure-skating champion Victor Petrenko performed his gold-medal routine to rap music as the hometown crowd enthusiastically clapped in rhythm.

The political and economic effectiveness of the United States in the global arena will depend on individual and collective abilities to communicate competently with people from other cultures. To date, however, U.S. businesspeople who were sent overseas by U.S.-based multinational corporations have not fared as well as their European and Asian counterparts; an estimated 20 to 50 percent of these personnel return home early from their international assignments, often because they were ill prepared for their experiences.[2] As the Presidential Commission on Foreign Languages and International Studies has said,

> Nothing less is at stake than the nation's security. At a time when the resurgent forces of nationalism and of ethnic and linguistic consciousness so directly affect global realities, the United States requires far more reliable capabilities to communicate with its allies, analyze the behaviors of potential adversaries, and earn the trust and sympathies of the uncommitted. Yet, there is a widening gap between these needs and the American competence to understand and deal successfully in a world in flux.[3]

The political connections of the United States to other countries is matched by the global interdependence that characterizes U.S. economic relationships. For instance,

- Thirty-three percent of U.S. corporate profits are generated by international trade.
- The twenty-three largest U.S. banks derive almost half their total earnings overseas.
- Four of every five new jobs in the United States are generated as a direct result of foreign trade.
- The economic well-being of the United States is inextricably linked to the world economy, with current U.S. investments abroad valued at more than $300 billion.
- Foreign individuals and corporations hold investments of $200–300 billion in American manufacturing companies.
- Foreign individuals and corporations are estimated to have invested $1.5 trillion in the United States, most of it since 1974.[4]

The economic growth and stability of the United States are now inextricably linked to world business partners. Consider, as only a single example, the Xerox Corporation, whose DocuTech products can be used to create documents in New York that are instantaneously altered and corrected by teams in Australia, England, Denmark, and Norway, and then simultaneously printed and bound at all five locations.[5]

Diplomatic and economic links are reinforced by the ease with which people can now travel to other countries. United States high-school and university students work, study, and travel abroad in increasing numbers.[6] During the 1993–1994 academic year, for instance, an all-time high of 71,000 U.S. students were enrolled in study abroad programs overseas.[7] Citizens of other countries are also visiting the United States in ever larger numbers; some 438,618 foreign students were enrolled in United States universities in 1992–1993, also an all-time high and an increase of 4.5 percent over the previous year.[8] In 1995, about 49 million international visitors to the U.S.—nearly twice as many as a decade ago—are expected to spend a record $86.6 billion.[9]

The vision of interdependence among cultural groups throughout the world has led Robert Shuter to declare that "culture is the single most important global communication issue in the 1990's."[10] Shuter's argument is also supported by the need for intercultural communication competence that characterizes the U.S. domestic scene.

The Domestic Imperative for Intercultural Competence

Nowhere is the imperative to improve intercultural communication competence stronger than within the borders of the United States. The United States—and the world as a whole—is currently in the midst of what is perhaps the largest and most extensive wave of cultural mixing in recorded history.

CULTURE CONNECTIONS

OUR GLOBAL VILLAGE
If the world was a village of 1,000 people,

In the village would be:

590 Asians

123 Africans

95 Europeans

84 Latin Americans

55 Former Soviet Union Members

53 North Americans

They would speak:

155 Mandarin	31 Portuguese
80 English	26 Malay-Indonesian
63 Hindi	22 Japanese
61 Spanish	22 French
53 Russian	21 German
35 Arabic	398 Other languages
33 Bengali	

There would be:

329 Christians (187 Catholics, 67 Protestants, 75 Others)

178 Muslims

60 Buddhists

301 Nonreligious, Atheists, or others

Source: Adapted from *Information Please Almanac* (Boston: Houghton Mifflin, 1990) and *World Almanac and Book of Facts* (New York: World Almanac, 1991).

In the 21st century—and that's not far off—racial and ethnic groups in the U.S. will outnumber whites for the first time. The browning of America will alter everything in society from politics and education to industry, values and culture.[11]

The most recent census figures provide a glimpse into the shape of the changing demographics of the U.S. population. Between 1980 and 1990, growth in the Latino and Asian populations accounted for more than half of the nation's increase. Although changes in population diversity are most pronounced in Sunbelt states, census figures indicate that such cultural diversification is a nationwide phenomenon. In the 1980s, Rhode Island's Asian population grew by 245 percent, New Hampshire's by 219 percent, and Georgia's by 208 percent. Similarly, Latino growth exceeded 100 percent in such states as Rhode Island, Maryland, Massachusetts, New Hampshire, and Virginia.[12] In

CULTURE CONNECTIONS

I fear that Mexican writer Carlos Fuentes is right when he says: "What the U.S. does best is understand itself. What it does worst is understand others." As Senator Paul Simon has put it, "We Americans simply cannot afford cultural isolation." We need to understand our co-inhabitants on this earth so that we can compete effectively in an increasingly global economy. But we also need to better understand the diverse peoples of our world in the interest of peaceful coexistence.

Source: Johnnetta R. Cole, president of Spelman College, in a speech entitled "International Education: Broadening the Base of Participation" to the 43rd International Conference on Educational Exchange, Charleston, South Carolina, November 1990.

New Mexico, 38 percent of the population is now Latino. African Americans constitute 66 percent of the District of Columbia, and they constitute about 30 percent of the population in the states of Mississippi, Louisiana, and South Carolina. There already are "minority majorities"—populations of African Americans, Native Americans, Pacific Islanders, Latinos, and Asian Americans that, when combined, outnumber the European American population—in cities such as Laredo, Miami, Gary, Detroit, Washington, Oakland, Atlanta, San Antonio, Los Angeles, Chicago, Baltimore, Houston, New York, Memphis, San Francisco, Fresno, and San Jose.

Much of the U.S. population shift is attributed to migration and immigration, with about 10.0 million people immigrating to the United States during the 1980s. The other period in the country's history that saw such a large influx of immigrants was between 1900 and 1910, when 8.8 million new citizens arrived. What distinguishes the immigrants of the 1980s from those of the 1900s, however, is the country of origin. Those arriving just after the turn of the last century were 89 percent European; only 10 percent of those arriving in the 1980s were European.[13]

The 1990 census clearly shows that the United States is now a multicultural society. One in seven speaks a language other than English at home.[14] Recent government projections also suggest that the U.S. population will likely increase from 252 million in 1992 to 383 million by 2050, lead by a continuing boom of Latinos, Asian Americans, and African Americans. Through the first half of the twenty-first century, the United States is expected to gain 57 million Latinos, 33 million Asian Americans, and 32 million African Americans.[15] As Antonia Pantoja and Wilhelmina Perry note,

The complete picture is one of change where large numbers of non-European immigrants from Africa, Asia, South and Central America, and the Caribbean will constitute majorities in many major cities. These immigrants will contribute to existing social movements. Many of these new immigrants are skilled workers and professionals, and these qualities will be highly valued in a changing United States economy. They come from countries with a history of democratic civil struggles and political revolutions. They arrive with a strong sense of cultural and ethnic identity within their intact family and social networks and strong ties to their home countries. At the same time they have a strong determination to achieve their goals, and they do not intend to abandon or relinquish their culture as the price for their success.[16]

The consequences of "this browning of America" can be seen in every major cultural and social institution. Many U.S. schools can now be characterized as "Classrooms of Babel."[17] In the Los Angeles County School District, for example, 108 different languages are spoken; in Hollywood High School alone, there are 85 different first languages for students.[18] Five million children of immigrants are expected to enter U.S. public school systems during the 1990s;[19] in 1995, one-third of the students in U.S. schools came from non-white and Hispanic groups.[20] Nonwhites and Hispanics already make up a

Tourists, their ever-present cameras at the ready, record images of the people and places they have visited. *(Copyright © Myron W. Lustig & Jolene Koester.)*

CULTURE CONNECTIONS

An item from the *New York Times,* June 23, 1983: "At the annual Lower East Side Jewish Festival yesterday, a Chinese woman ate a pizza slice in front of Ty Thuan Duc's Vietnamese grocery store. Beside her a Spanish-speaking family patronized a cart with two signs: 'Italian Ices' and 'Kosher by Rabbi Alper.' And after the pastrami ran out, everybody ate knishes."

On the day before Memorial Day, 1983, a poet called me to describe a city he had just visited. He said that one section included mosques, built by the Islamic people who dwelled there. Attending his reading, he said, were large numbers of Hispanic people, 40,000 of whom lived in the same city. He was not talking about a fabled city located in some mysterious region of the world. The city he'd visited was Detroit.

A few months before, as I was visiting Texas, I heard the taped voice used to guide passengers to their connections at the Dallas Airport announcing items in both Spanish and English. . . .

Shortly after my Texas trip, I sat in a campus auditorium at the University of Wisconsin at Milwaukee as a Yale professor—whose original work on the influence of African cultures upon those of the Americas has led to his ostracism from some intellectual circles—walked up and down the aisle like an old-time Southern evangelist, dancing and drumming the top of the lectern, illustrating his points before some Afro-American intellectuals and artists who cheered and applauded his performance. The professor was "white." After his lecture, he conversed with a group of Milwaukeeans—all of whom spoke Yoruban, though only the professor had ever traveled to Africa. . . .

Such blurring of cultural styles occurs in everyday life in the United States to a greater extent than anyone can imagine. The result is . . . cultural bouillabaisse.

Source: Ishmael Reed, "Writin' Is Fightin'," (Addison-Wesley Publishing Company, 1988).

majority of high school graduates in Hawaii, New Mexico, the District of Columbia, California, and Mississippi.[21]

Institutions of higher education are certainly not exempt from the forces that have transformed the United States into a multicultural society. In 1992, the enrollment of "minority-group" college students exceeded 20 percent in over one-third of the states and was above 10 percent in two-thirds of them.[22] In the decade from 1982 to 1992, the proportion of African Americans increased by 8 percent, Native Americans by 14 percent, Latinos by 57 percent, and Asian Americans by 71 percent.[23]

CULTURE CONNECTIONS

Los Angeles is the second largest Spanish-speaking city in the world (which elicits surprise); that there are presently 25 million Hispanics in the United States (the blunt numbers begin to raise some eyebrows); and that by the middle of the next century, almost half of the US population will be Spanish speaking (it is this figure that causes the students to sit up straight in their small wooden desks and start to gape).

What I want, of course, is to impress upon my students the daily relevance that Spanish will have in their lives. And how the bridge between peoples will begin with simple speech and grow to mutual understanding.

Source: "The Living Drama of Language," *(Christian Science Monitor,* January 5, 1994) 20.

The workplace also reflects increasing cultural diversity. The number of women, African Americans, and Latinos in management positions has quadrupled from 1970 to 1988, and the number of Asians in management positions has increased eightfold during that same period.[24] By the turn of the century, white males are expected to become a minority in a work force that is likely to be 12 percent African American, 11 percent Hispanic, 8 percent Asian American, and 43 percent female.[25] In sum, professional success and personal satisfaction will increasingly depend on the ability to communicate competently with people from other cultures.

THE UNITED STATES AS AN INTERCULTURAL COMMUNITY

A set of complicated issues underlies our discussion about the domestic and international imperatives for intercultural communication. Stated most simply, these issues focus on what it means to be an American and on decisions about how to refer to the various cultural groups that reside within the borders of the United States. In the following sections, we first examine the implications of four metaphors that have been used to describe U.S. cultural diversity. Next, we analyze the question of what to call someone from the United States. Finally, we describe the difficult choices we faced in selecting labels to refer to the domestic cultures within the United States.

Metaphors of U.S. Cultural Diversity

Many cultural groups live within the borders of the United States. When people talk about the blend of U.S. cultural groups, their ideas are often con-

The United States is an intercultural community. Even everyday activities such as office discussions are likely to involve intercultural communication. *(Copyright © Beryl Goldberg Photographer.)*

densed into a few key words or phrases. These summary images, called metaphors, imply both a description of what is and, less obviously, a prescription of what should be. Though we will have much more to say in subsequent chapters about the effects of language and labeling on the intercultural communication process, we would like to focus now on four metaphors that have been used to describe the cultural mix within the United States: a melting pot, a set of tributaries, a tapestry, and a garden salad.

The Melting Pot Metaphor   Perhaps the oldest metaphor for describing multiple cultures in the United States is the melting pot.[26] America, according to this image, is like a huge crucible, a container that can withstand extremely high temperatures and can therefore be used to melt, mix, and ultimately fuse together metals or other substances. This image was the dominant way to represent the ideal blending of cultural groups at a time when the hardened steel that was forged in the great blast furnaces of Pittsburgh helped to make the United States into an industrial power. According to this view, immigrants from many cultures came to the United States to work, live, mix, and blend

Where's my luggage? Travelers to other cultures must cope with jet lag and a swarm of luggage. Such scenes have become commonplace as increasing numbers of people visit other cultures. *(Copyright © P.J. Griffiths, Magnum.)*

together into one great assimilated culture that is stronger and better than the unique individual cultures of which it is composed.

Dynamic as the melting pot metaphor has been in the United States, it has never been an accurate description. The tendency for diverse cultures to melt together and assimilate their unique heritages into a single cultural entity has never really existed. Rather, the many cultural groups within the United States have continuously adapted to one another as they accommodated and perhaps adopted some of the practices and preferences of other groups while maintaining their own unique and distinctive heritages.

CULTURE CONNECTIONS

As my friend Denise and I trudged across the University of Tennessee campus to our 9:05 a.m. class, we delivered countless head nods, "Heys" and "How ya' doin's" to other African-Americans we passed along the way. We spoke to people we knew as well as people we didn't know because it's an unwritten rule that black people speak to one another when they pass. But when I stopped to greet and hug one of my female friends, who happens to be white, Denise seemed a bit bothered. We continued our walk to class, and Denise expressed concern that I might be coming down with a "fever." "I don't feel sick," I told her. As it turns out, she was referring to "jungle fever," the condition where a black man or woman is attracted to someone of the opposite race.

This encounter has not been an uncommon experience for me. That's why the first 21 years of my life have felt like a neverending tug of war. And quite honestly, I'm not looking forward to being dragged through the mud for the rest of my life. My white friends want me to act one way—white. My African-American friends want me to act another—black. Pleasing them both is nearly impossible and leaves little room to be just me.

The politically correct term for someone with my racial background is "biracial" or "multiracial." My mother is fair-skinned with blond hair and blue eyes. My father is dark-complexioned with prominent African-American features and a head of woolly hair. When you combine the genetic makeup of the two, you get me—golden-brown skin, semi-coarse hair and a whole mess of freckles.

Someone once told me I was lucky to be biracial because I have the best of both worlds. In some ways this is true. I have a huge family that's filled with diversity and is as colorful as a box of Crayolas. My family is more open to whomever I choose to date, whether that person is black, white, biracial, Asian or whatever. But looking at the big picture, American society makes being biracial feel less like a blessing than a curse.

One reason is the American obsession with labeling. We feel the need to label everyone and everything and group them into neatly defined categories. Are you a Republican, a Democrat or an Independent? Are you pro-life or pro-choice? Are you African-American, Caucasian or Native American? Not everyone fits into such classifications. This presents a problem for me and the many biracial people living in the United States. The rest of the population seems more comfortable when we choose to identify with one group. And it pressures us to do so, forcing us to deny half of who we are.

Growing up in the small, predominantly white town of Maryville, Tenn., I attended William Blount High School. I was one of a handful of minority students—a raisin in a box of cornflakes, so to speak. Almost all of my peers, many of whom I've known since grade school, were white. Over the years, they've commented on how different I am from other black people they know. The implication was that I'm better because I'm only *half* black. Acceptance into their world has meant talking as they talk, dressing as they dress and appreciating the same music. To reduce tension and make everyone feel comfortable, I've reacted by ignoring half of my identity and downplaying my ethnicity.

My experience at UT has been very similar. This time it's my African-American peers exerting pressure to choose. Some African-Americans on campus say I "talk too white." I dress like the boys in white fraternities. I have too many white friends. In other words, I'm not black enough. I'm a white "wanna-be." The other day, an African-American acquaintance told me I dress "bourgie." This means I dress very white—a pastel-colored polo, a pair of navy chinos and hiking boots. Before I came to terms with this kind of remark, a comment like this would have angered me, and I must admit that I was a little offended. But instead of showing my frustration, I let it ride, and I simply said, "Thank you." Surprised by this response, she said in disbelief, "You mean you agree?"

On more occasions than I dare to count, black friends have made sweeping derogatory statements about the white race in general. "White people do this, or white people do that." Every time I hear them, I cringe. These comments refer not just to my white friends but to my mother and maternal grandmother as well. Why should I have to shun or hide my white heritage to enhance my ethnicity? Doesn't the fact that I have suffered the same prejudices as every other African-American—and then some—count for something?

I do not blame my African-American or white friends for the problems faced by biracial people in America. I blame society for not acknowledging us as a separate race. I am speaking not only for people who, like myself, are half black and half white, but also for those who are half white and half Asian, half white and half Hispanic, or half white and half whatever. Until American society recognizes us as a distinct group, we will continue to be pressured to choose one side of our heritage over the other.

Job applications, survey forms, college-entrance exams and the like ask individuals to check only *one* box for race. For most of my life, I have marked BLACK because my skin color is the first thing people notice. However, I could just as honestly have marked WHITE. Somehow when I fill out these forms, I think the employers, administrators, researchers, teachers or whoever sees them will have a problem looking at my face and then accepting a big x by the word WHITE. In any case, checking BLACK or WHITE does not truly represent me. Only in recent years have some private universities added the category of BIRACIAL or MULTIRACIAL to their applications. I've heard that a few states now include these categories on government forms.

One of the greatest things parents of biracial children can do is expose them to *both* of their cultures. But what good does this do when in the end society makes us choose? Having a separate category marked BIRACIAL will not magically put an end to the pressure to choose, but it will help people to stop judging us as just black or just white and see us for what we really are—both.

Source: Brian A. Courtney, "Freedom of Choice: Being Biracial Has Meant Denying Half of My Identity" (*Newsweek,* February 13, 1995) 16.

CULTURE CONNECTIONS

When people ask me my nationality, I find it difficult to give a sufficient answer.

Who am I really? Am I an Asian-Indian? American? Both? Neither? These are questions that many "bi-cultured" teenagers can't help but ask themselves.

I was born in India, and when I was 2 years old my parents emigrated to the United States. They didn't leave India because of any hardships, but simply because they were curious—curious about what America might hold for them. Their curiosity has led to a unique lifestyle for me, as an Indian-American teenager.

But what kind of lifestyle? Do I really fit in here? Do I fit in India? No, I don't. One adventurous move by my parents has turned me, like many others in my situation, into a misfit. I am a person who doesn't have one nationality. I am a person who doesn't have a conflict-free tradition of my own.

One of the more popular American traditions is dating. Can we "bi-cultured" teenagers participate in this activity? No. Why? Because our parents don't approve. In our original countries, dating is looked upon negatively; therefore, our parents' attitudes toward boy-girl relationships remains negative.

In many of our original countries, the biggest "hobby" of teenagers was studying. Yet, in America we continue to participate in this "hobby," but because we do so we are considered nerds and geeks. Many a time I feel like saying, "Forget it!" But then I remember that "forget it" isn't acceptable at home. We realize that our parents pressure us for our own good but sometimes we'd just like to be like our fun-loving American peers.

Another American teenage activity is to attend and to give parties. But then there's the "no parties" rule imposed by our parents. This rule is to "protect us from the drugs and alcohol which could possibly be there."

For me, dating and parties are minor problems. The biggest problem is finding out who I really am. Our parents want us to be like teens in our original countries; however, we want to stay and fit in here. We want to be like everybody around us, and to most of our parents that's a threat.

So is there a middle ground? Or will our teenage years simply end up being a power struggle—in my case a power struggle between India, America and me?

The Tributaries Metaphor   A currently popular metaphor for describing the mix of cultures in the United States is that of tributaries or tributary streams. America, according to this image, is like a huge cultural watershed, providing numerous paths in which the many tributary cultures can flow. The tributaries maintain their unique identities as they surge toward their common destination.

The view described above is useful and compelling. Unlike the melting

Sure, there are many disadvantages to being from another country, but there are a lot of advantages, too. For one, no one can ever confuse our names for someone else's. Who can mix up a name like Smriti Aggarwal? Or Thu Vu?

Another advantage is that you get to travel more than most Americans. Almost all immigrant parents take their kids "back home" to visit. I can speak from personal experience. I've visited India twice, and on those trips also have been to London, Frankfurt, Paris, Istanbul and Amsterdam. Now how many American teens can say they've traveled to all those places?

Aside from visiting a lot of other places, going "back home" was a treat in itself. I got to meet relatives I had never met before, and I shopped more than I imagined possible. Most important of all, I was able to see where I come from, and that in turn helped me to realize who I am.

I also realized how lucky I am compared to others, and I began to be thankful for the luxuries and opportunities I have here in America.

One of the biggest disadvantages and one of the biggest advantages to being "bi-cultured" is that we live in two cultures at once. You could say that we lead double lives. In school, we act, dress and eat like everyone else, but when we get home life changes.

In my home, my parents usually speak in Hindi, our native language. Dad will say something to me in Hindi, and I'll answer back in a mixture of Hindi and English. When Mom says dinner's ready, I go down and eat a delicious Indian meal that most people never get the opportunity to eat. Mom will say "Get ready for temple," and I'll automatically don a salwar-kameez (an Indian two-piece outfit). How many actually lead a life like mine?

My parents emigrated from India, and they are Indians. My children will be born here, they will be Americans. I was born in India and brought here, I am neither Indian nor American, yet I am both.

My life is and will continue to be a struggle between nationalities, but I'm sure I can face this challenge head on. This determination I get from both of my countries.

Source: Smriti Aggarwal, "Where Do I Fit In?" *Sacramento Bee,* May 10, 1991.

pot metaphor, which implies that all cultures in the United States ought to be blended to overcome their individual weaknesses, the tributary image seems to suggest that it is acceptable and desirable for cultural groups to maintain their unique identities. However, when the metaphor of tributaries is examined closely, there are objections to some of its implications.

Tributary streams are small secondary creeks that ultimately flow into a common stream, where they combine to form a major river. Our difficulty

International business contacts increasingly require business cards to be printed in multiple languages to contend with the multicultural business environment. A polite exchange often requires that the cards be studied carefully. *(Copyright © 1986 by Laimute E. Druskis/Stock Boston.)*

with this notion rests in the hidden assumption that the cultural groups will ultimately and inevitably blend together into a single, common current. Indeed, there are far fewer examples of cultures that have totally assimilated into mainstream U.S. culture than there are instances of cultures that have remained unique. Further, the idea of tributaries blending together to form one main stream suggests that the tributaries are somehow subordinate to or less important than the mighty river into which they flow.

The Tapestry Metaphor   A tapestry is a decorative cloth made up of many strands of thread. The threads are woven together into an artistic design that may be pleasing to some but not to others. Each thread is akin to a person, and groups of similar threads are analogous to a culture. Of course, the types of threads differ in many ways; their thickness, smoothness, color, texture, and strength may vary. The threads can range from gossamer strands to inch-thick yarn, from soft silk to coarse burlap, from pastel hues to fluorescent radiance, and from fragile spiders' webs to steel cables. The weaving process itself can vary from one location to another within the overall tapestry. Here, a wide swatch of a single type of thread may be used; there, many threads might be interwoven with many others, so no single thread is distinguished; and elsewhere, the threads may have been grouped together into small but distinguishable clumps.

Although the metaphor of a tapestry has much to commend it, the image is not flawless. After all, a tapestry is rather static and unchangeable. One does not typically unstring a bolt of cloth, for instance, only to reassemble the threads elsewhere in a different configuration. Cultural groups in the United States are more fluid than the tapestry metaphor might imply; migrations, immigrations, and mortality patterns all alter the cultural landscape. Despite its limitations, however, we find this metaphor preferable to the previous two.

The Garden Salad Metaphor   Like a garden salad made up of many distinct ingredients that are being tossed continuously, some see the United States as made up of a complex array of distinct cultures that are blended into a unique, and one hopes tasteful, mixture. Substitute one ingredient for another, or even change how much of each ingredient is present, and the entire flavor of the salad may be changed. Mix the salad differently, and the look and feel will also differ. A salad contains a blend of ingredients, and it provides a unique combination of tints, textures, and tastes that tempt the palate.

Like the other metaphors, the garden salad is not without its flaws. In contrast to the tapestry image, which implies that the United States is too fixed and unchanging, a garden salad suggests an absence of firmness and stability.

CULTURE CONNECTIONS

I only have one-eighth Shoshone blood, but it shows in my hair color and high cheekbones. I seldom think of myself in terms of either my Indian heritage or the Scotch-Irish blood that makes up the remainder of my genetic composition. My attitude is a symptom of what's happened to ethnic groups in America, and I suppose in some ways the blurring of differences is a good thing. But on the other hand, there's an inherent sadness in the loss of consciousness of our roots, the loss of touch with the history and traditions that make us who we are.

Source: Marcia Muller, *Trophies and Dead Things* (New York: Mysterious Press, 1990) 146.

CULTURE CONNECTIONS

At the bottom of the Spring semester course selection sheet is an optional question: students are requested to supply the college with their ethnicity for federal reporting requirements. Six categories are provided: White non-Hispanic, Black non-Hispanic, Puerto Rican, Hispanic other, Asian/Pacific Islander and Native American/Alaskan. Students must choose only one category, the one that best describes them.

I have always found the restriction to only one choice incredibly frustrating. As someone who describes herself as Black-Puerto Rican, there never seems to be any category that acknowledges the strong African heritage of Hispanic people in the Caribbean and Latin America . . .

My recognition of myself as a Black-Puerto Rican may be facilitated by the fact that my parents come from two different islands. My mother is from Puerto Rico and my father from St. Thomas VI, but I have met many Hispanics who do not have mixed parentage who see themselves as I do. My mother emigrated to this country from Puerto Rico when she was three years old. The economic situation in Puerto Rico during the War was harsh and her family came to find a better life, settling in *El Barrio,* East Harlem. She has always viewed herself as a Black woman, a brave and independent stance to take in the 1940s and 50s. To my mother, separating the communities was a dangerous thing. She believes that it strengthens us to find our commonalities and stand united because the price of separation can be great in the face of racist oppression. . . .

My grandmother lives in Ceiba, a sleepy town near the Navy base in Puerto Rico where all the houses are painted in tropical pastels and one can hear the war games being executed along the coast. I see in her brown face my African heritage. Slaves were imported into Puerto Rico like the other neighboring islands for their cheap labor. They were exploited in the sugar cane fields under the hot sun. They brought with

A typical garden salad has no fixed arrangement; it is always in a state of flux. Cultural groups in the United States, however, are not always moving, mixing, and mingling with the speed and alacrity that the metaphor would suggest. Nevertheless, we recommend this metaphor, and that of the tapestry, as the two images that are likely to be most useful in characterizing the diversity of cultural groups in the United States. Additionally, we encourage you to invent your own metaphors.

What Do You Call Someone from the United States of America?

Many people who live in the United States of America prefer to call themselves American. However, people from Brazil, Argentina, Guatemala, Mex-

them their music, spirit and culture, enriching Puerto Rico. Black people in the Spanish-speaking Caribbean and in Latin America have left us with great legacies: The Quilombo leader Ganga Zambi in Brazil, the African rhythms of the *merengue* and the spiritual influences in our religions. My grandmother would never call herself Black though; she is firstly and lastly Puerto Rican. Most Puerto Ricans describe their country like a rainbow, a mixture and blend of African, European and Indian. The manner in which they view their "blackness" is directly related to their environment and culture.

I have often heard Black Americans alienated by this concept; they see a woman as dark as my grandmother not identifying herself as Black and conclude that "Puerto Ricans don't know what they are" or that they seek to deny their blackness. Sadly enough this is true for some. I certainly don't wish to obscure the issues of race, color and class among Puerto Ricans. We are afflicted by these prejudices, much like Black Americans. It is Puerto Rican to recognize our mixed heritage. It is a mulatto country, not the stark Black and White of the United States.

When I learn about Afro-American history I treat it as my own, as part of my identity as a Black woman. I see the accomplishments and survival as a testimony to all people of color. I hope that Black Americans can find pride and strength in Puerto Rican and other Afro-Latin histories, but I know that will take time for people to see this global Pan-Africanist view. . .

I have been told that it is impossible for me to continue being both Puerto Rican and Black and that I will inevitably need to choose sides, perhaps as a way to show my allegiance to my chosen community. But I, like many other Hispanics, know that the blood I share with Afro-Americans links me to the survival and work necessary in both communities equally.

Source: Vivian Brady, "Black Hispanics: The Ties That Bind," *Race, Class, and Gender in the United States,* ed. Paula S. Rothenberg (New York: St. Martin's, 1992).

ico, and many other Central and South American countries also consider themselves American, as they are all part of the continents known collectively as the Americas. Indeed, people from these countries consider the choice of *American* for those from the United States to be imperialistic and insulting. They resent the implication that they are less central or less important.

An alternative choice for a name, which is frequently selected by those who are trying to be more sensitive to cultural differences, is *North American*. *North American* is the English translation of the Spanish label that is commonly used by people from many Central and South American countries to refer to people from the United States, and the name is widely regarded as far less insulting and imperialistic. However, this label still has the potential for creating friction and causing misunderstanding. *North American* refers to an entire continent, and people from Mexico and Canada are, strictly speaking, also North Americans. Indeed, conversations with Canadians and Mexicans have confirmed for us that *North American* is not the ideal term.

One possibility that is often overlooked is to refer to people from the United States as *United Statians* or *United Staters*. These labels have the obvious advantage of being unambiguous, as they specifically identify people from a single country. Realistically, however, these are not labels that citizens of the United States would regard as comfortable and appropriate, and we agree that they are artificial and unlikely to be widely used.

Our preference is the label *U.S. Americans*. This referent retains the word American but narrows its scope to refer only to those from the United States. The term retains the advantages of a name that is specific enough to be accurate, yet it does not resort to a form of address that people would be unlikely to use and would regard as odd.

Cultural Groups in the United States

It is also important to select terms that adequately and sensitively identify the variety of cultural groups that make up the U.S. citizenry. As the population of the United States becomes increasingly more varied culturally, it is extremely urgent that we find ways to refer to these cultures with terms that accurately express their differences but avoid negative connotations and evaluations.

Some of the terms used in the past have negative associations, and we, as authors, have struggled to find more appropriate alternatives. For example, earlier writings about intercultural communication often referred to the culture associated with white U.S. Americans as either the "dominant" culture or the "majority" culture. The term *dominant* usually suggested the economic and political power of white U.S. America, referring to the control of important sources of institutional and economic power. The term often conveyed a negative meaning to members of other cultural groups, as it suggested that white U.S. Americans were somehow better or superior. It also implied that people from nondominant cultures were somehow subordinate or inferior to the dominant group. As more and more cultural groups have gained political and economic power in the United States, *dominant* no longer accurately reflects the current reality.

An alternative label for white U.S. Americans was *majority culture*. This term was intended to reflect a numerical statement, that the majority of U.S. Americans are from a particular cultural group. Majority was often coupled with the term *minority*, which also had negative connotations for many members of other cultural groups: It suggested to some people that they were not regarded as important or significant as members of the majority. In addition, as previously suggested, nonwhite cultural groups now make up a sufficient proportion of the total population; so white U.S. Americans no longer constitute an absolute majority in many places. Thus, we prefer to avoid such emotionally charged words as *majority, minority, dominant, nondominant,* and *subordinate* when we discuss the cultural groups residing in the United States.

We have also elected not to use the term *white* in all subsequent discussions about a specific cultural group of U.S. Americans. *White* is a synonym for *Caucasian* and refers to a particular race. As we discuss in greater detail in Chapter 2, a racial category does not necessarily identify and distinguish a particular culture. Though the census data reported previously use the term *white*, we think it is inaccurate to refer to a cultural group in the United States by a term that denotes race. Consequently, because their common cultural heritage is predominantly European, we have chosen to describe white U.S. cultural members as European Americans.

Recently, many black Americans have also chosen to be identified by a term that distinguishes them by their common cultural characteristics rather than by their racial attributes. *African American* recognizes the effects of traditional African cultural patterns on U.S. Americans of African heritage, and it acknowledges that African American cultural patterns are distinct from those of European Americans. Because it denotes a cultural rather than a racial distinction, we will use the latter term in this book.

Another set of terms is usually applied to those residents of the United States whose surname is Spanish. *Hispanic*, *Chicano*, *Mexican American*, and *Latino* are often used interchangeably, but the distinctions between the terms can be quite important.[27] *Hispanic* derives from the dominant influences of Spain and the Spanish language, but many shy away from this term because it tends to homogenize all groups of people who have Spanish surnames and who use the Spanish language. *Chicano* (or *Chicana*) refers to the "multiple-heritage experience of Mexicans in the United States" and speaks to a political and social consciousness of the Mexican American.[28] Specific terms such as *Mexican American* or *Cuban American* are preferred by those who wish to acknowledge their cultural roots in a particular national heritage while simultaneously emphasizing their pride in being U.S. Americans.[29] Finally, *Latino* (or *Latina*) is a cultural and linguistic term that includes "all groups in the Americas that share the Spanish language, culture, and traditions."[30] As Earl Shorris notes, "language defines the group, provides it with history and home; language should also determine its name—Latino."[31] Because *Latino* and *Latina* suggest cultural distinctions, we will use them in this book.

Terms routinely used to describe members of other cultural groups include *Native Americans*, *Arab Americans*, *Asian Americans*, and *Pacific Islanders*. Each of these labels, as well as those previously described, obscures the rich variety of cultures that the single term represents. For instance, many tribal nations can be included under the term *Native American*, and members of those groups prefer a specific reference to their culture (e.g., Chippewa, Sioux, Navajo, Choctaw, Cherokee, and Inuit). Similarly, *Asian American* is a global term that can refer to Japanese Americans, Chinese Americans, Malaysian Americans, Korean Americans, and people from many other cultures that geographically originated in the part of the world loosely referred to as Asia. Even *European Americans* obscures differences among those whose

The United States is a nation of many immigrant groups. These immigrants, aboard ship in 1902, are headed for a new world and a new life. *(Photo by Williams H. Rau, 1902. From the collections of the Library of Congress.)*

heritage may be English, French, Italian, or German. Our use of these overly broad terms is not meant to deny the importance of cultural distinctions but to allow for an economy of words. We will use the broader, more inclusive, and less precise terms when making a generalization that describes a commonality among these cultures. When using examples that are limited to a particular culture, we will use the more specific nomenclature.

Notice that there are some inherent difficulties in our choices of cultural terms to refer to U.S. Americans. If precision were our only criterion, we would want to make many further distinctions. But we are also aware of the need for economy and the force of common usage. Although it is not our intent to advocate terms that ignore or harm particular cultural groups, we do prefer a vocabulary that is easily understood, commonly used, and positively regarded. Please remember, however, that the term preferred by specific individuals is an important reflection of the way they perceive themselves. Michael Hecht and Sidney Ribeau, for example, found differences in the expressed identities of individuals who defined themselves as "black" versus "black American."[32] Similarly, a "Chicana" defines herself differently than someone who labels herself a "Mexican American".

THE CHALLENGE OF LIVING IN AN INTERCULTURAL WORLD

As inhabitants of the twenty-first century, you will no longer have a choice about whether to live in a world of many cultures. The forces that bring people from other cultures into your life are dynamic, potent, and ever present. What does this great cultural mixing mean as you strive for success, satisfaction, well-being, and feelings of involvement and attachment to families, communities, organizations, and nations?

In each of the settings in which you conduct your lives—in work, school, the neighborhood, personal relationships, and the family—intercultural competence is crucial. Economic success increasingly depends on the ability to display competent communication behaviors with individuals from other cultures, even if the work is within the national boundaries of the United States. Corporations also bring people from one country to another, so within the work force of most nations there are representatives from cultures throughout the world. The citizenry itself includes many individuals who are strongly identified with a particular culture. Thus, it is no longer safe to assume that clients, customers, business partners, and co-workers will have similar cultural views about what is important and appropriate.

Diversity in languages and cultures has become a prominent influence within elementary schools, high schools, colleges, and universities. This mixture affects students' learning and interpersonal relationships. Teachers' interactions with students, parents' interactions with teachers, and students' interactions with other students are all mediated by the kinds of linguistic and cultural differences we describe in this book. Inevitably, cultural differences in communication affect the ability of everyone involved in the educational process to achieve their educational goals.

Personal satisfaction, too, will increasingly depend upon the ability to communicate competently with people from other cultures. Neighbors may speak different first languages, have different values, and celebrate different customs. As Dwight Conquergood says, "cities throughout the United States have become sites of extraordinary diversity."[33] Families are also becoming more culturally diverse, as marriages and adoptions contribute to the cultural mix. The challenge to those who live in the twenty-first century will be to understand and to appreciate cultural differences and to translate that understanding into competent interpersonal communication.[34]

There are some obvious consequences to living in an intercultural world. It will inevitably introduce doubt about others' expectations and will reduce the certainty that specific behaviors, routines, and rituals mean the same things to everyone. Renato Rosaldo, who believes that encounters with "difference" are now an inherent and inescapable part of modern urban life, provides a personal anecdote to illustrate alternative cultural responses to common, everyday experiences.

> I grew up speaking Spanish to my father and English to my mother. Consider the cultural pertinence of my father's response, during the late 1950s, to having taken our dog, Chico, to the veterinarian. Born and raised in Mexico, my father

U.S. Americans are as varied as the landscape. Here, a European American and a Filipino-American have a friendly conversation. *(Copyright © Myron W. Lustig & Jolene Koester.)*

arrived home with Chico in a mood midway between pain and amusement. Tears of laughter streamed down his cheeks until, finally, he mumbled something like, "What will these North Americans think of next?" He explained that when he entered the veterinarian's office a nurse in white had greeted him at the door, sat him down, pulled out a form, and asked, "What's the patient's name?" In my dad's view, no Mexican would ever come so close to confusing a dog with a person. To him, it was unthinkable that a clinic for dogs could ever resemble one for people with its nurses in white and its forms for the "patient."[35]

Cultural mixing implies that people will not always feel completely comfortable as they attempt to communicate in another language or as they try to talk with individuals who are not proficient in theirs. Their sense of "rights" and "wrongs" may be threatened when challenged by the actions of those with an alternative cultural framework. Many people will need to live in two or more cultures concurrently, shifting from one to another as they go from home to school, from work to play, and from the neighborhood to the shopping mall.

The tensions inherent in creating a successful intercultural community and nation are obvious. Examples abound that underscore how difficult it is for groups of culturally different individuals to live, work, and play together harmoniously. The consequences of failing to create a harmonious intercultural society are also obvious—human suffering, hatred passed on from one generation to another, disruptions in the economic life of a people, and unnecessary conflicts that sap people's creative talents and energies and that siphon off scarce resources from other important societal needs.

The joys and benefits of embracing an intercultural world are many as well. As the world is transformed into a place where cultural boundaries cease to be barriers and differences between people become reasons to celebrate and share rather than to fear and harm, you will have increased opportunities to understand, experience, and benefit from unfamiliar ways. You are a new kind of pilgrim, a pioneer on a new frontier.

SUMMARY

The chapter began with descriptions of the international and domestic imperatives for achieving intercultural communication competence. Throughout your lifetime, you will probably engage in many types of intercultural encounters.

The United States is an intercultural community, and four metaphors—melting pots, tributaries, tapestries, and garden salads—were introduced to describe its diversity. We suggested that the term *U.S. American* should be used to characterize someone from the United States, but noted that a variety of terms are used to refer to the nation's cultural groups. The goal is to find ways to refer to cultural groups that reflect their differences accurately while avoiding negative connotations and evaluations.

Living in an intercultural world provides numerous challenges and opportunities, as your success and well-being increasingly depend on your ability to behave competently in intercultural encounters. In chapter 2 we consider two concepts that are central to this book—communication and culture.

2

CHAPTER

Communication and Culture

This book is about interpersonal communication between people from different cultures. Our goal is to explain how you can achieve interpersonal competence in interactions that involve intercultural communication. This chapter provides a general analysis of the human communication process and its relationship to culture. These topics are of central importance to an understanding of intercultural communication, as they form the foundation for all of our subsequent ideas about the nature of intercultural transactions. Chapter 3 will continue the discussion by exploring the nature of both intercultural communication and intercultural competence.

COMMUNICATION

To understand intercultural communication events, you must study the more general processes involved in all human communication transactions. All communication events, including intercultural communication, are made up of a set of basic characteristics. Once these characteristics are known, they can be applied to intercultural interactions in order to analyze the unique ways in which intercultural communication differs from other forms of communication.

Defining Communication

The term *communication* has been used in many ways for varied, and often inconsistent, purposes.[1] Like all terms or ideas, we choose our specific definition because of its usefulness in explaining the thoughts and ideas we wish to convey. Consequently, our definition is not the "right" one, nor is it somehow "more correct" than the others. Indeed, as you might expect, our definition is actually very similar to many others with which you may be familiar. However, the definition we have selected is most useful for our purpose of helping you to achieve interpersonal competence when communicating in the intercultural setting.

We define *communication* as *a symbolic process in which people create shared meanings*. To understand what this definition means, we will explore its implications for the study of intercultural communication.

Characteristics of Communication

Three characteristics of our definition of communication require further elaboration. Our definition asserts that communication is symbolic, that it is a process, and that it involves shared meanings. Let's examine each of these characteristics more closely.

Communication Is Symbolic Symbols are central to the communication process because they represent the shared meanings that are communicated. A *symbol* is a word, action, or object that stands for or represents a unit of meaning. *Meaning*, in turn, is a perception, thought, or feeling that a person experiences and might want to communicate to others. These meaning-ful experiences could include sensations resulting from a room's temperature, thoughts about a teacher in a particular course, or feelings of happiness or anger because of what someone said. However, the private meanings within a person cannot be shared directly with others. They can only become shared and understood when they are interpreted as a message. A *message*, then, refers to the "package" of symbols used to create shared meanings. For example, the words in this book are symbols that, taken together, form the message that we, the authors, want to communicate to you.

People's behaviors are frequently interpreted symbolically, as an external representation of feelings, emotions, and internal states. To many people in the United States, for example, raising an arm with the hand extended and moving the hand and arm up and down symbolizes saying goodbye. Flags can symbolize a country, and most of the world's religions have symbols that are associated with their beliefs.

Messages do not have to be consciously or purposefully created with the specific intention of communicating a certain set of meanings for others to be able to make sense of the symbols forming the message. Rather, communication is always an interpretive process. Whenever people communicate, they must interpret the symbolic behaviors of others and assign significance to

CULTURE CONNECTIONS

If we are to achieve a richer culture, rich in contrasting values, we must recognize the whole gamut of human potentialities, and so weave a less arbitrary social fabric, one in which each diverse human gift will find a fitting place.

Source: Attributed to Margaret Mead.

some of those behaviors in order to create a meaningful account of the others' actions. This idea suggests that each person in a communication transaction may not necessarily interpret the messages in exactly the same way. Indeed, during episodes involving intercultural communication the likelihood is high that people will interpret the meaning of messages differently.

Communication Is a Process   People, relationships, activities, objects, and experiences can be described either in static terms or as part of a dynamic process. Viewing communication in static terms suggests that it is fixed and unchanging, whereas viewing it as a process implies things that are changing, moving, developing, and evolving. A process is a sequence of distinct but interrelated steps. To understand communication as a process, it is necessary to know how it can change over time. Like the old adage that "You can't stand in the same stream twice," communication events are unique, as seemingly identical experiences can take on vastly different meanings at different stages of the process.

Communication Involves Shared Meanings   The interpretive nature of communication suggests that correct meanings are not just "out there" to be discovered. Rather, meanings are created and shared by groups of people as they participate in the ordinary and everyday activities that form the context of common interpretations. Our focus, therefore, must be on the ways that people attempt to "make sense" of their common experiences in the world.

Interpersonal Communication

Interpersonal communication is a form of communication that involves a few individuals who are interacting directly with each other. We think it useful and practical to differentiate those relationships that involve a relatively small number of people—such as couples, families, friends, work groups, and even classroom groups—from those involving much larger numbers of people—such as public rallies or massive television audiences. Unlike other forms of communication, interpersonal communication involves person-to-

Verbal symbols are used in this Venezuelan message to express ideas and feelings. *(Copyright © Myron W. Lustig & Jolene Koester.)*

person interactions. Additionally, the perception that a social bond has developed between the interactants, however tenuous and temporary it may seem, is also much more likely.

Unlike public speaking or mass media communication events, in which messages are sent to large, undifferentiated, and heterogeneous audiences, interpersonal communication typically involves clearly identified participants who are able to select those with whom they interact. Additionally, when people interact directly with one other, they may use several sensory channels

CULTURE CONNECTIONS

Father, Mother, and Me,
　　Sister and Auntie say
All the people like us are We,
　　And every one else is They.
And They live over the sea,
　　While We live over the way,
But—would you believe it?—They look upon We
　　As only a sort of They!
All good people agree,
　　And all good people say,
All nice people, like Us, are We
　　And everyone else is They:
But if you cross over the sea,
　　Instead of over the way,
You may end by (think of it!) looking on We
　　As only a sort of They!

Source: Rudyard Kipling, "We and They," *Rudyard Kipling's Verse: Definitive Edition* (Garden City, NY: Doubleday, 1940) 768–769.

to convey information. Such details as looks, grunts, touches, postures, nods, smells, voice changes, and other specific behaviors are all available for observation and interpretation.

CULTURE

Definitions of *culture* are numerous. In 1952 Alfred L. Kroeber and Clyde Kluckhohn published a book with over 200 pages devoted to different definitions of the term.[2] Since then, many other scholars have offered additional definitions and approaches. Here we want to introduce four approaches that are relevant to your knowledge of culture and are important to the definition that we will use throughout this book.

Approaches to Defining Culture

The most common approach to defining culture is to enumerate or describe its components. E. B. Tylor, for example, a nineteenth-century anthropologist

These Costa Rican men engage in interpersonal communication—a form of communication that occurs in all cultures. *(Copyright © Myron W. Lustig & Jolene Koester.)*

who provided one of the earliest formal definitions of the term, describes culture as "that complex whole which includes knowledge, belief, art, morals, law, custom, and any other capabilities and habits acquired by man as a member of society."[3]

A second approach emphasizes the social heredity of a group of people, suggesting that the new members of a culture must be taught its fundamental ideas, practices, and experiences. The social heredity approach therefore asserts that culture is symbolically transmitted, often intergenerationally, from parents or other adults to children, who in turn grow up and teach their own children the culture's customs and expectations. This approach is important because it emphasizes that one does not become a member of a culture by birth but through a process of learning.

A third approach involves the beliefs, values, and norms that exist to guide people's behaviors in solving common problems. This approach, often called the perceptual or subjective culture approach, suggests that people behave as they do because of the perceptions they have about the world and their

CULTURE CONNECTIONS

Because my skin is black you will say I traveled Africa to find the roots of my race. I did not—unless that race is the human race, for except in the color of my skin, I am not African. If I didn't know it then, I know it now. I am a product of the culture that raised me. And yet Africa was suddenly like a magnet drawing me close, important in ways that I cannot explain, rising in my subconscious and inviting me. It was time I went . . .

Long before I ever went there Africa was alive in my imagination, crowding the dark corners of my dreams, stirring my fears. Now that I have been there, Africa lives in my memory like a gigantic vessel bearing all that I am and all that I will ever be, for Africa has opened my eyes and awakened my fears, brought them to life and kindled my compassion. . . .

I am not African, but somewhere deep in the hidden reaches of my being, Africa beats in my blood and shows itself in my hair, my skin, my eyes. Africa's rhythms are somehow my rhythms, and Africa speaks to me its languages of love and laughter.

I had some eerie feeling Africa could teach me about life and what it means to be human, deepen my appreciation for all that I am and all that I have, help me to find, perhaps, the face of God, perhaps even my own face, help me to step out of my cozy little world, out of myself so that I could see myself better and better define myself. Even if, as Thomas Wolfe suggested, you can't really go home again, perhaps it helps to know where home is, to know where you have come from.

Source: Eddy L. Harris, *Native Stranger* (New York: Simon & Schuster, 1992).

expectations about how they should behave in that world. Harry Triandis defines subjective culture as "a cultural group's characteristic way of perceiving the man-made part of its environment. The perception of rules and the group's norms, roles, and values are aspects of subjective culture."[4] This approach emphasizes that culture is a *shared* set of ideas and practices that exist in people's minds as a form of "mental software"[5] that governs people's behaviors. The consequences of a given subjective culture, then, can be seen in the repetitive patterns and regularities of people's behaviors.

A fourth approach, which emphasizes the interpretive or performance nature of culture, highlights how people express their culture in their everyday conversations and interactions. Often referred to as cultural communication, this approach views culture as emerging from the particular set of symbols and meanings that those within the culture attribute to behaviors. Donal Carbaugh defines culture from this view as "a system of expressive practices fraught with feeling, a system of symbols, premises, rules, forms, and the domains and dimensions of mutual meanings associated with these."[6] Thus, according to Carbaugh, culture refers to patterns of symbolic actions and meanings that are deeply felt, commonly understood, and widely accessible.[7] Cultural identities, which include these socially constructed and historically transmitted systems of symbols and meanings, are displayed in people's communication with others.[8]

Our concern in this book is with the link between culture and communication. Consequently, a definition of *culture* that lists its parts or components is not particularly helpful for understanding how it affects the communication process. Rather, our approach acknowledges that culture is learned, that culture is perceptual and guides behavior, and that culture is expressed as interpretations of shared symbols. These key elements will allow us to investigate how culture contributes to the symbolic process in which people create shared meanings.

Defining Culture for the Study of Communication

Our goal in presenting a particular definition of *culture* is to explain the important link between culture and communication. However, we emphasize that the way we define culture is not the "right" or "best" way. Rather, it is a definition that is useful for our purpose of helping you to understand the crucial link between culture and communication as you set out to improve your intercultural competence. We define *culture* as *a learned set of shared perceptions about beliefs, values, and norms, which affect the behaviors of a relatively large group of people.*

Culture Is Learned   Humans are not born with the genetic imprint of a particular culture. Instead, people learn about their culture through interactions with parents, other family members, friends, and even strangers who are part of the culture. In Chapter 4 we explain why some cultures are so different from others. For now, we want to describe the general process by which people learn their culture.

Culture is learned from the people you interact with as you are socialized. Watching how adults react and talk to new babies is an excellent way to see the actual symbolic transmission of culture among people. Two babies born at exactly the same time in two parts of the globe may be taught to respond to physical and social stimuli in very different ways. For example, some babies are taught to smile at strangers, whereas others are taught to smile only in very specific circumstances. In the United States, most children are asked from a very early age to make decisions about what they want to do and what they prefer; in many other cultures, a parent would never ask a child what he or she wants to do but would simply tell the child what to do.

Culture is also taught by the explanations people receive for the natural and human events around them. Parents tell children that a certain person is a good boy because   . The blank would be completed in contrasting ways by people from differing cultures. The people children interact with praise and encourage particular kinds of behaviors (such as crying or not crying, being quiet or being talkative). Certainly there are variations in what a child is

CULTURE CONNECTIONS

Joseph Campbell has said that the myths of every culture provide answers to four questions: (1) Who am I? (2) Who are we? (3) What is the nature of the world in which we live? and, (4) What is the nature of the answers to these questions?

taught from family to family in any given culture. However, our interest is not in these variations but in the similarities across most or all families that form the basis of a culture. Because our specific interest is in the relationship between culture and interpersonal communication, we focus on how cultures provide their members with a set of interpretations that they then use as filters to make sense of messages and experiences.

Culture Is a Set of Shared Perceptions   Shared perceptions establish the very important link between communication and culture. Cultures exist in the minds of people, not in external or tangible objects or behaviors. Integral to our discussion of communication is an emphasis on symbols as the means by which all communication takes place. The meanings of symbols exist in the minds of the individual communicators; when those symbolic ideas are shared with others, they form the basis for culture. Not all of an individual's symbolic ideas are necessarily shared with other people, and some symbols will be shared only with a few. A culture can form only if symbolic ideas are shared with a relatively large group of people.

Culture Involves Beliefs, Values, and Norms   The shared symbol systems that form the basis of culture represent ideas about beliefs, values, and norms. Because of their importance in understanding the ways in which cultures vary and their role in improving intercultural communication competence, the first section of Chapter 5 is devoted to their detailed explanation. For now, it is enough to know that beliefs refer to the basic understanding of a group of people about what the world is like or what is true or false. Values refer to what a group of people defines as good and bad or what it regards as important. Norms refer to rules for appropriate behavior, which provide the expectations people have of one another and of themselves.

Culture Affects Behavior   If culture was located solely in the minds of people, we could only speculate about what a culture is, since it is impossible for one person to see into the mind of another. However, these shared perceptions about beliefs, values, and norms affect the *behaviors* of large groups of people. In other words, the shared perceptions that characterize a culture give people guidelines about what things mean, what is important, and what should or should not be done. Thus, culture establishes predictability in human interac-

By reading and explaining to their children, parents help them to construct a common set of meanings. *(Copyright © Dorothi Littell Greco/The Image Works.)*

tions. Cultural differences are evident in the varying ways in which people conduct their everyday activities, as people "perform" their culture in their behavioral routines.

Within a given geographical area, people who interact with one another over time will form social bonds that help to stabilize their interactions and patterns of behavior. The stable patterns become the basis for making the predictions and forming expectations about others.

Culture Involves Large Groups of People   We differentiate between smaller groups of individuals, who may engage in interpersonal communication, from larger groups of people more traditionally associated with cultures. For example, if you work every day with the same group of people and you regularly see and talk to them, you would undoubtedly begin to develop shared perceptions and experiences that would affect the way you communicate. Although some people might want to use *culture* to refer to the bonds that develop among the people in a small group, we prefer to distinguish between the broad-based, culturally shared beliefs, values, and norms that people bring to their interactions and the unique expectations and experiences that arise as a result of particular interpersonal relationships that develop. Consequently, we will restrict the use of the term *culture* to much larger, societal levels of organization.

Culture is also often used to refer to other types of large groups of people. Mary Jane Collier and Milt Thomas, for example, assert that the term "can refer to ethnicity, gender, profession, or any other symbol system that is bounded and salient to individuals."[9] Our definition does not preclude the inclusion of groups such as women, the deaf, gays and lesbians, and others identified by Collier and Thomas. However, our emphasis is primarily on culture in its more traditional forms, which Collier and Thomas refer to as ethnicity.

Culture and Related Terms

Terms such as *nation, race,* and *ethnic group* are often used synonymously with the term *culture. Subculture* and *coculture* are other terms that are sometimes used in talking about groups of people. There are important distinctions, however, between these terms and the groups of people to which they might refer.

Culture and Nation   In our everyday language, people commonly treat *culture* and *nation* as equivalent terms. Although some nations are in fact predominantly inhabited by one cultural group, most nations contain multiple cultures within their boundaries. *Nation* is a political term referring to a government and a set of formal and legal mechanisms that have been established to regulate the political behavior of its people. These regulations often encompass such aspects of a people as how leaders are chosen, by what rules the leaders must govern, the laws of banking and currency, the means to establish military groups, and the rules by which a legal system is conducted. Foreign policies, for instance, are determined by a nation and not by a culture. The culture, or cultures, that exist within the boundaries of a nation-state certainly influence the regulations that a nation develops, but the term *culture* is not synonymous with *nation.*

The nation of Japan is often regarded as so homogeneous that the word *Japanese* is commonly used to refer both to the nation and to the culture. Though the Yamato Japanese culture overwhelmingly predominates within the nation of Japan, there are other cultures living there. These groups include the Ainu, an indigenous group with their own culture, religion, and language;

An African dance troupe displays the artistry of their culture in New York City. *(Copyright © Hazel Hankin and Stock, Boston, 1983.)*

other cultures that have lived in Japan for many generations and originate mainly from Okinawa, Korea, and China; and more recent immigrants also living there.[10] The United States is an excellent example of a nation that has several major cultural groups living within its geographical boundaries; European Americans, African Americans, Native Americans, Latinos, and various Asian American cultures are all represented in the United States. All the members of these different cultural groups are citizens of the nation of the United States.

Culture and Race   *Race* commonly refers to genetic or biologically based similarities among people, which are distinguishable and unique and function to mark or separate groups of people from one another. As we will discuss in Chapter 4, however, race is less a biological term than a political or social one. Though racial categories are inexact as a classification system, it is generally agreed that race is a more all-encompassing term than either *culture* or *nation*. Not all Caucasian people, for example, are part of the same culture or nation. Many western European countries principally include people from the Caucasian race. Similarly, among Caucasian people there are definite differences in culture. Consider the cultural differences among the primarily Caucasian countries of Great Britain, Norway, and Germany to understand the distinction between culture and race.

Sometimes race and culture do seem to work hand in hand to create visible and important distinctions among groups within a larger society; and

CULTURE CONNECTIONS

Chinese-Americans, when you try to understand what things in you are Chinese, how do you separate what is peculiar to childhood, to poverty, insanities, one family, your mother who marked your growing with stories, from what is Chinese? What is Chinese tradition and what is the movies?

Source: Maxine Hong Kingston, *The Woman Warrior: Memoirs of a Girlhood Among Ghosts* (New York: Vintage, 1989) 5–6.

sometimes race plays a part in establishing separate cultural groups. An excellent example of the interplay of culture and race is in the history of African American people in the United States. Although race may have been used initially to set African Americans apart from Caucasian U.S. Americans, African American culture provides a strong and unique source of identity to members of the black race in the United States. Scholars now acknowledge that African American culture, with its roots in traditional African cultures, is separate and unique and has developed its own set of cultural patterns. Although a person from Nigeria and an African American are both from the same race, they are from distinct cultures. Similarly, not all black U.S. Americans are part of the African American culture since many have a primary cultural identification with cultures in the Caribbean, South America, or Africa.

Race can, however, form the basis for prejudicial communication that can be a major obstacle to intercultural communication. Categorization of people by race in the United States, for example, has been the basis of systematic discrimination and oppression of people of color. We will explore the impact of racism more fully in Chapter 12.

Culture and Ethnicity *Ethnic group* is another term often used interchangeably with culture. *Ethnicity* is actually a term that is used to refer to a wide variety of groups who might share a language, historical origins, religion, identification with a common nation-state, or cultural system. The nature of the relationship of a group's ethnicity to its culture will vary greatly depending on a number of other important characteristics. For example, many people in the United States still maintain an allegiance to the ethnic group of their ancestors who emigrated from other nations and cultures. It is quite common for people to say they are German or Greek or Armenian when the ethnicity indicated by the label refers to ancestry and perhaps some customs and practices that originated with the named ethnic group. Realistically, many of these individuals now are typical members of the European American culture. In other cases, the identification of ethnicity may coincide more completely with culture. In the former Yugoslavia, for example, there are at least three major ethnic groups—Slovaks, Croatians, and Serbians—each with their own language and distinct culture, who were forced into one nation-state following World War II. It is also possible for members of an ethnic group to be part of many different cultures and/or nations. For instance, Jewish people share a common ethnic identification, even though they belong to widely varying cultures and are citizens of many different countries.

Culture, Subculture, and Coculture   *Subculture* is also a term sometimes used to refer to racial and ethnic minority groups that share both a common nation-state with other cultures and some aspects of the larger culture. Often, for example, African Americans, Arab Americans, Asian Americans, Native Americans, Latinos, and other groups are referred to as subcultures within the United States. The term, however, has connotations that we find problematic, because it suggests subordination to the larger European American culture. Similarly, the term *coculture* is occasionally employed in an effort to avoid the implication of a hierarchical relationship between the European American culture and these other important cultural groups that form the mosaic of the United States. In our shrinking and interdependent world, most cultures must coexist alongside other cultures. *Coculture* therefore strikes us as redundant, and we prefer to regard these groups of people as cultures in their own right.

SUMMARY

Our goal in this chapter has been to provide an understanding of the two key concepts underlying the study of intercultural competence—communication and culture. We began with a discussion of communication, which we defined as a symbolic process in which people create shared meanings. Next we discussed interpersonal communication as a form of communication involving a few individuals interacting directly with one another.

Finally, we considered the concept of culture. From the many available approaches to defining culture, we selected one that emphasizes the close relationship between culture and communication. We defined culture as a learned set of shared perceptions about beliefs, values, and norms, which affect the behaviors of a relatively large group of people. We emphasized that people are not born with a culture, but learn it through their interactions with others. Our definition located culture in the minds of people, adding that these shared ideas can be understood by their effects on behavior. We distinguished between culture and other groups to which people belong by suggesting that culture occurs only when beliefs, values, and norms affect large groups of people. We concluded the section by making some important distinctions between terms such as *culture, nation, race, ethnic group*, and *subculture*. In Chapter 3 we consider two additional concepts that are the focal points of this book—intercultural communication and intercultural competence.

3

CHAPTER

Intercultural Communication Competence

When does communication become intercultural communication? What distinguishes intercultural communication from communication that is not intercultural? What does it mean to be a competent intercultural communicator? In the previous chapter we defined the terms *communication* and *culture*. In this chapter we discuss competence and intercultural communication. Our purpose is to establish boundaries and a common understanding about these central ideas.

INTERCULTURAL COMMUNICATION

A simple way to define the term *intercultural communication* is to use the definition of *communication* that was provided in the previous chapter and insert the phrase "from different cultures." This addition would yield the following definition:

> Intercultural communication is a symbolic process in which people from different cultures create shared meanings.

This definition, although accurate, is difficult to apply. In the following examples we describe several situations and ask you to analyze them with this definition in mind. Our intention in the discussion that follows is to give you a more sophisticated understanding of the term *intercultural communication* by exploring more fully the meaning of the phrase "people from different cultures."

Examples of Intercultural Interactions

Read the description of each interaction and think carefully about the questions that follow. Decide whether you think the communication between the people involved is or is not intercultural. Our answers to these questions will be provided in the subsequent discussion.

Example 1

Dele is from Nigeria and Anibal is from Argentina. Both young men complete secondary education in their own countries and then come to the United States to study. They study at the same university, live in the same dormitory their first year on campus, and choose agriculture as their major. Eventually, they become roommates, participate in many of the same activities for international students, and have many classes together. After completing their bachelor's degrees, they enroll in the same graduate program. After four more years in the United States, each returns to his home country and takes a position in the country's Agricultural Ministry. In letters to each other, both comment on the difficulties they are experiencing in working with farmers from their own country.

Questions for Example 1

- When they first begin their studies in the United States, is the communication between Dele and Anibal intercultural communication?
- When they complete their studies in the United States, is the communication between Dele and Anibal intercultural communication?
- After they return to their home countries, is the communication between each man and the farmers with whom they work intercultural communication?

Example 2

Janet grows up in a small town of about 3,500 people in western Massachusetts. She is surrounded by her immediate family, many other relatives, and lots of friends. Her parents grew up in this same town, but Janet is determined to have experiences away from her family and away from the small portion of New England that has formed the boundaries of her existence. Despite parental concerns, Janet goes to one of California's major public universities, which is located in a large urban area, and she begins her life in the West. Janet is at first excited and thrilled to be living in California, but within a very short period of time, she begins to feel very isolated. She is assigned to live in a coeducational dormitory, and she finds it disconcerting to be meeting male students as she walks down the hallway in her bathrobe. Although her fellow students seem friendly, her overtures for coffee or movies or even studying together are usually met with a smile and a statement that "It would be great, but. . . ." The superficial friendliness of most of the people she meets starts to annoy her, and Janet becomes bad-tempered and irritable.

Questions for Example 2
- Is the culture of Massachusetts sufficiently different from that of California to characterize Janet's communication with her fellow students as intercultural?
- Would Janet have had the same kinds of feelings and reactions if she had moved into a coeducational dormitory at a university in urban Massachusetts?

Example 3
Even though Andy Wong's parents immigrated to the United States from Taiwan before he was born, they still speak Chinese at home and expect Andy and his brothers and sisters to behave like proper Chinese children. Because Andy is the eldest child, his parents have additional expectations for him. Andy loves his parents very much, but he finds their expectations difficult to fulfill. He thinks he speaks respectfully to his mother when he tells her that he is going out with his friends after dinner, but his parents tell him he is being disrespectful. The family reaches a major crisis when Andy announces that he is going to go to a college that has a good studio arts program, rather than pursue the solid science background his parents want him to have in preparation for medical school.

Question for Example 3
- Is Andy's communication with his parents intercultural, either because Andy is very U.S. American and his parents are Chinese or because parents and children have different cultures?

Example 4
Jane Martin works for a U.S. company that has a major branch in South Korea. Although Jane is fairly young, her boss has asked her to travel to Seoul to teach her Korean counterparts a new internal auditing system. Despite Jane's lack of linguistic skill in Korean (she speaks no Korean) and little experience in another country (she has spent a week in London and a week in Paris on holiday), she is confident that she will be successful in teaching the Korean employees the new system. She has won high praise for her training skills in the United States and the company promises to provide her with a good interpreter. "After all," Jane thinks, "we're all part of the same company—we do

the same kinds of work with the same kinds of corporate regulations and expectations. Besides, Koreans are probably familiar with U.S. Americans."

Questions for Example 4
- Is Jane's communication with South Koreans intercultural, or does working for the same corporation mean that Jane and her South Korean counterparts share a common culture?
- Is Jane's age a factor in communication with her Korean counterparts?
- Would you answer the previous questions any differently if Jane's company was sending her to the branch office in England rather than in South Korea?

Example 5
Angela enjoys watching soap operas on television. In fact, she's a real soap opera fanatic; she reads *Soap Opera Digest* for the summaries of the episodes, arranges her day to be able to watch her favorite shows, and uses her videocassette recorder to tape the ones she must miss. One afternoon, as Angela switches through the cable channels looking for her regular program, she stops at a channel with a program in Spanish that she immediately recognizes as a soap opera. Fascinated, Angela watches the entire program and believes that, despite having no knowledge of Spanish, she has followed the plot line accurately.

Questions for Example 5
- Do you accept Angela's assessment that she understood the Spanish soap opera because soap opera plots are all similar?
- Can intercultural communication take place even if those communicating do not share a common language?

Example 6
John has worked for the same company, based in Minneapolis, Minnesota, for the six years since his graduation from college. A recent promotion means that John has to move to his company's branch office in Milwaukee, Wisconsin. John faces difficulties almost immediately after beginning work in Milwaukee. His boss has a much different management style than the one with which John is familiar. His new job responsibilities require some knowledge and sophistication in areas in which John is not an expert. After several months on the job, John is feeling fairly beleaguered and is beginning to lose confidence in his abilities.

Question for Example 6
- Is John's communication with his boss intercultural communication?

Each of these examples represents a likely communication event in today's world. It is very probable that two people from different countries will

Intercultural interactions can be loud or soft and long or short and can occur among people of all ages. *(Copyright © Myron W. Lustig & Jolene Koester.)*

spend an extended period of time in a third country, as Dele and Anibal have. It is also very likely that these two people will, over time, form relationships that create a shared set of experiences. Moving from one part of a country to another is a commonplace occurrence, whether the goal is to attend a university, as Janet did, or to advance professionally, as John did. Immigration of people from one country to another also occurs frequently, producing communication problems typical of those experienced by U.S. born-and-raised Andy with his Chinese born-and-identified parents. The significance of the global marketplace means that work often takes people to countries around the world, as companies like Jane's become increasingly multinational. With the advent of modern communication technologies, many more people will be able to select television programs, films, music, radio shows, and computerized messages that are arranged in verbal and nonverbal codes different from their own. Angela's experience with the spanish soap opera will be repeatable almost everywhere. But are these examples, all of which involve communication, also examples of intercultural communication? Do any of them clearly *not* involve intercultural communication? In the next sections we attempt to provide answers to these questions.

Similarities and Differences Between Communicators

By applying the definition of intercultural communication given at the beginning of the chapter, it would be relatively simple to categorize each example. You would go through the examples and make a bipolar choice—either yes or no—based on whether the people in the examples were from different cultures. Thus, you would probably decide that the communication between Anibal and Dele was intercultural when they arrived in the United States. It would be much more difficult to judge their communication when they completed their studies. Perhaps you would decide that their communication with people from their own country after their return home was not intercultural, or perhaps you would say that it was. Similarly, you might be convinced that California is indeed a different culture from Massachusetts, or you might argue vehemently that it is not. Most likely you would decide that Jane's communication with her Korean counterparts was intercultural, even though they undoubtedly did share some common expectations about work performance because they were employed by the same company. Had her company decided to send Jane to England instead of Korea, her communication with her English co-workers would have been similarly intercultural. Yet you might feel a bit uncomfortable, as we are, with the idea of putting U.S.-Korean communication into the same category as U.S.-English communication.

The difficulties encountered in a simple yes-or-no decision lead us to suggest an alternative way of thinking about intercultural communication. What is missing is an answer to three questions that emerge from the preceding examples:

1. What differences among groups of people constitute cultural differences?
2. How extensive are those differences?
3. How does extended communication change the effects of cultural differences?

This last question suggests the possibility that initially one's interactions could be very intercultural, but subsequent communication events could make the relationship far less intercultural.

To demonstrate the importance of these questions, we would like you to take the examples presented earlier and arrange them in order from most intercultural to least intercultural.[1] Use a continuum like the one shown in Figure 3.1.

Most intercultural _____ **Least intercultural**

Figure 3.1. A continuum of interculturalness.

Thus, you will be identifying the degree of interculturalness in each inter-action and, in effect, you will be creating an "interculturalness" scale. It should even be possible to make distinctions among those communication situations that are placed in the middle, with some closer and some farther from the most intercultural end. When you place the examples on a contin-uum, they might look something like Figure 3.2.

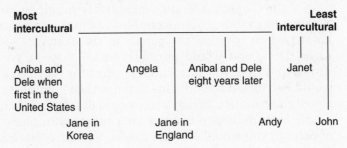

Figure 3.2. A continuum of interculturalness, with examples.

We suspect that the continuum you have created is very similar to ours. Where we might disagree is on how we ordered the examples placed near the middle.

The next important issue for understanding the definition of intercultural communication concerns the characteristics present in the encounters. What is it about the people, the communication, the situation, or some combina-tion of those factors that increases the likelihood that the communication be-comes intercultural?

What varies and changes across the examples is the degree of similarity or the amount of difference between the interactants. For instance, Anibal (from Argentina) and Dele (from Nigeria) are very different when they first come to study in the United States. Each speaks English, but as a second language to Spanish and Yoruba, respectively; their facility with English is initially weak, and they are uncomfortable with it. Additionally, their values, social customs, gestures, perceptions of attractiveness, and expectations about personal space and how friendships are established differ. Initially, Anibal and Dele are cul-turally very different, or heterogeneous, and their communication should cer-tainly be placed near the "Most intercultural" end of the continuum. How-ever, after eight years in the United States, having studied the same academic subjects, shared many of the same friends, and participated in many common experiences, their communication with each other does not have the same de-gree of interculturalness as it did initially. Certainly, each still retains part of his own cultural heritage and point of view, but the two men have also created an important set of common understandings between themselves that is not grounded in their respective cultural frameworks.

Janet, in contrast, was placed near the "Least intercultural" end of the continuum because of the degree of similarity, or homogeneity, she shares with Californians. They speak the same language, and their values, gestures,

Differences among people can make communication intercultural. *(Copyright © 1992 David H. Wells/The Image Works.)*

social perceptions, and expectations about relationships are all similar. Certainly, Californians use slang and jargon with which Janet is not familiar, but they speak, read, and study in English. And certainly, Californians, particularly these urban Californians, seem to place importance on different things than Janet does. She also thinks it unusual and a bit uncomfortable to be sharing a living space with men she does not even know. Nevertheless, the magnitude of these differences is relatively small.

There are learned differences among groups of people that are associated with their culture, such as cultural patterns, verbal and nonverbal codes, relationship rules and roles, and social perceptions. When such important differences are relatively large, they lead to dissimilar interpretations about the meanings of the messages that are created, and they therefore indicate that people are from different cultures. Thus,

> *People are from different cultures whenever the degree of difference between them is sufficiently large and important that it creates dissimilar interpretations and expectations about what are regarded as competent communication behaviors.*

Definition of Intercultural Communication

Previous definitions have described the central terms *communication* and *culture*. By combining the meanings of these terms with the ideas suggested

Intercultural communication occurs when there are significant differences among the communicators. What do you suppose are the consequences of these differences for the people shown here? *(Copyright © Beringer/Dratch/The Image Works.)*

in our discussion about the degrees of difference that can occur among people from dissimilar cultures, we offer the following definition of intercultural communication:

> *Intercultural communication is a symbolic process in which the degree of difference between people is large and important enough to create dissimilar interpretations and expectations about what are regarded as competent behaviors that should be used to create shared meanings.*

The degree to which individuals differ is the degree to which there is intercultureness in a given instance of communication. Situations in which the individuals are very different from one another are most intercultural, whereas those in which the individuals are very similar to one another are least intercultural.

INTERCULTURAL COMMUNICATION AND RELATED TERMS

The relationship between culture and communication is important to many disciplines. Consequently, many terms have been used to describe the various ways in which the study of culture and communication intersect: *cross-cultural communication, international communication, intracultural communi-*

cation, interethnic communication, and *interracial communication*. The differences among these terms can be confusing, so we would like to relate them to the focus of study in this book.[2]

Intercultural and Intracultural Communication

The term *intercultural*, used to describe the endpoints of the continuum, denotes the presence of at least two individuals who are culturally different from each other on such important attributes as their value orientations, preferred communication codes, role expectations, and perceived rules of social relationships. We would now like to relabel the "Least intercultural" end of the continuum, which is used to refer to communication between culturally similar individuals, as *intracultural*. John's communication with his new boss in Milwaukee is intracultural. Janet's communication with her fellow students in California is more intracultural than intercultural. Both *intercultural* and *intracultural* are comparative terms. That is, each refers to differences in the magnitude and importance of expectations that people have about what constitutes competent communication behaviors.

Interethnic and Interracial Communication

Just as *race* and *ethnic group* are terms commonly used to refer to cultures, *interethnic* and *interracial communication* are two labels commonly used as substitutes for *intercultural communication*. Usually, these terms are used to explain differences in communication between members of racial and ethnic groups who are all members of the same nation-state. For example, communication between African Americans and European Americans is often referred to as interracial communication. The large numbers of people of Latino origin who work and live with people of European ancestry produce communication characterized as interethnic. Sometimes the terms are also used to refer to communication between people from various ethnic or racial groups who are not part of the same nation but live in specific geographic areas. Although it may be useful in some circumstances to use the terms *interethnic* and *interracial*, we believe these types of communication are most usefully categorized as subsets of intercultural communication.

Both ethnicity and race contribute to the perceived effects of cultural differences on communication, which move that communication toward the "Most intercultural" end of the continuum. We will therefore rely on the broader term of *intercultural communication* when discussing, explaining, and offering suggestions for increasing your degree of competence in interactions that involve people from other races and ethnic groups. In Chapter 12, however, when considering particular obstacles to intercultural competence, we will give special attention to the painful and negative consequences of racism.

Cross-cultural and Intercultural Communication

Another distinction in cultural differences concerns cross-cultural and intercultural communication. The term *cross-cultural* is typically used to refer to the study of a particular idea or concept within many cultures. The goal of such investigations is to conduct a series of intracultural analyses in order to compare one culture to another on the attributes of interest. For example, someone interested in studying the marriage rituals in many cultures would be considered a cross-cultural researcher. Scholars who study self-disclosure patterns, child-rearing practices, or educational methods as they exist in many different cultures are doing cross-cultural research. Whereas intercultural communication involves interactions among people from different cultures, cross-cultural communication involves a comparison of interactions among people from the same culture to those from another culture. Cross-cultural comparisons are very useful for understanding cultural differences, and they are the basis for the information provided in Part Two. Our principle interest, however, is in using these cross-cultural comparisons to understand intercultural communication competence.

International and Intercultural Communication

International communication refers to interactions among people from different nations. As we suggested with the terms *interracial* and *interethnic communication*, we prefer *intercultural communication* to these narrower labels. Certainly, communication among people from different countries is likely to be intercultural communication, but that is not always true, as illustrated by the example of Anibal and Dele after eight years together in the United States. Also *international* limits our understanding of when and why intercultural communication might occur. It should be obvious from the discussion of interracial and interethnic communication that a person need not leave his or her own country to encounter intercultural communication.

COMPETENCE AND INTERCULTURAL COMMUNICATION

Competent interpersonal communication is a worthy and often elusive goal. Interpersonal competence in intercultural interactions is an even more difficult objective to achieve, because cultural differences create dissimilar meanings and expectations that require even greater levels of communication skill. We base our understanding of intercultural competence on the work of scholars who have studied communicative competence from a primarily intracultural perspective and on the conclusions of other scholars who have studied intercultural competence.

CULTURE CONNECTIONS

I fell in love with the minister's son the winter I turned 14. He was not Chinese, but as white as Mary in the manger. For Christmas I prayed for this blond-haired boy, Robert, and a slim new American nose.

When I found out that my parents had invited the minister's family over for Christmas Eve dinner, I cried. What would Robert think of our shabby *Chinese* Christmas? What would he think of our noisy *Chinese* relatives who lacked proper American manners? What terrible disappointment would he feel upon seeing not a roast turkey and sweet potatoes but *Chinese* food?

On Christmas Eve I saw that my mother had outdone herself in creating a strange menu. She was pulling black veins out of the backs of prawns. The kitchen was littered with appalling mounds of raw food: a slimy rock cod with bulging fish eyes that pleaded not to be thrown in a pan of hot oil. Tofu, which looked like stacked wedges of rubbery white sponges. A bowl soaking dried fungus back to life. A plate of squid, their backs crisscrossed with knife markings so they resembled bicycle tires.

And then they arrived—the minister's family and all my relatives in a clamor of doorbells and rumpled Christmas packages. Robert grunted hello, and I pretended he was not worthy of existence.

Dinner threw me deeper into despair. My relatives licked the ends of their chopsticks and reached across the table, dipping them into the dozen or so plates of food. Robert and his family waited patiently for platters to be passed to them. My relatives murmured with pleasure when my mother brought out the whole steamed fish. Robert grimaced. Then my father poked his chopsticks just below the fish eye and plucked out the soft meat. "Amy, your favorite," he said, offering me the tender fish cheek. I wanted to disappear.

At the end of the meal my father leaned back and belched loudly, thanking my mother for her fine cooking. "It's a polite Chinese custom to show you are satisfied," explained my father to our astonished guests. Robert was looking down at his plate with a reddened face. The minister managed to muster up a quiet burp. I was stunned into silence for the rest of the night.

After everyone had gone, my mother said to me, "You want to be the same as American girls on the outside." She handed me an early gift. It was a miniskirt in beige tweed. "But inside you must always be Chinese. You must be proud to be different. Your only shame is to have shame."

And even though I didn't agree with her then, I knew that she understood how much I had suffered during the evening's dinner. It wasn't until many years later— long after I had gotten over my crush on Robert—that I was able to appreciate fully her lesson and the true purpose behind our particular menu. For Christmas Eve that year, she had chosen all my favorite foods.

Source: Amy Tan, "Fish Cheeks."

CULTURE CONNECTIONS

I took a drink from every bottle held out to me. The man leaned over and slapped my knee—I was a good chap, I did not get drunk and fall on the floor. They laughed. I smiled to show I was cheerful and friendly, but I couldn't laugh because I didn't know what they were laughing at.

This, I thought, is what being a foreigner is really all about. It is not wandering through a strange country seeing unfamiliar people: it's when all the unfamiliar people stare at *you,* and find *you* strange: when you can't fit anonymously into a crowd: when your passing is an uncommon event. It's when you don't understand the joke, and the joke may very well be you.

Source: Liza Cody, Rift (New York: Scribner, 1988) 79.

The study of intercultural competence has been motivated primarily by practical concerns. Businesses, government agencies, and educational institutions want to select people for intercultural assignments who will be successful. Lack of intercultural competence means failed business ventures, government projects that have not achieved their objectives, and unsuccessful learning experiences for students.

Intracultural Communication Competence

Although there is still some disagreement among communication scholars about how best to conceptualize and measure communication competence, there is increasing agreement about certain of its fundamental characteristics.[3] In our discussion we draw heavily on the work of Brian Spitzberg and his colleagues. The following definition of communication competence illustrates the key components of their approach:

> Competent communication is interaction that is perceived as effective in fulfilling certain rewarding objectives in a way that is also appropriate to the context in which the interaction occurs.[4]

This definition provides guidance for understanding communicative and intercultural competence in several ways. A key word is *perceived* because it means that competence is best determined by the people who are interacting with each other. In other words, communicative competence is a social judgment about how well a person interacts with others. That competence involves a social perception suggests that it will always be specific to the context and interpersonal relationship within which it occurs. Therefore, whereas judgments of competence are influenced by an assessment of an individual's personal characteristics, they cannot be wholly determined by them, because competence involves an interaction between people.

Competent interpersonal communication results in behaviors that are regarded as *appropriate*. That is, the actions of the communicators fit the expectations and demands of the situation. Appropriate communication means that people use the symbols they are expected to use in a given context.

Competent interpersonal communication also results in behaviors that are *effective* in achieving desired personal outcomes. Satisfaction in a relationship or the accomplishment of a specific task-related goal is an example of an outcome people might want to achieve through their communication with others.

Thus, communication competence is a social judgment that people make about others. The judgment depends on the context, the relationship between the interactants, the goals or objectives that the interactants want to achieve, and the specific verbal and nonverbal messages that are used to accomplish those goals.

Approaches to the Study of Intercultural Competence

Four approaches have been used to investigate intercultural competence: the trait approach, the perceptual approach, the behavioral approach, and the culture-specific approach. Each of them adds to our understanding of intercultural competence.

The trait approach to intercultural competence attempts to identify the kinds of personality characteristics and individual traits that allow a person to avoid failure and achieve success in intercultural encounters. Those who have explored this approach have examined such characteristics as flexibility in thinking, "world-mindedness" (which is a positive attitude toward people of other cultures), psychological and social adjustment in one's own culture, and relativistic values (which means not being too rigid about the "correctness" of one's values). Researchers have occasionally succeeded in matching the characteristics of individuals to successful intercultural communication, but in many instances their efforts to do so have failed.[5] It is easy to understand why the trait approach has been so compelling. If the traits and attributes of people who are already competent intercultural communicators could be identified, those individuals could be selected as the intercultural representatives of businesses and governments. However, intercultural competence is far more complex than the simple absence or presence of particular personality and social

CULTURE CONNECTIONS

Meeting the world is not just a joyride and source of personal insight and enlightenment. As we reach out and acquaint ourselves with the world, we will not only think globally but, hopefully, feel globally as well. Thinking globally will instill in us the capacity for empathy—that honest concern for others that sees the connections between the yearning for freedom and equality in an East German in Leipzig, a South African in Johannesburg, and an African American in Atlanta; that sees the ties that bind a physician in a small African village, a nurse in the hills above Port-au-Prince, and a doctor in rural Mississippi. As it increasingly registers that we are all of the same human species, we will come to know that a homeless child in Palestine is no less deserving of our prayers and concern than a homeless child in Harlem.

Source: Johnetta B. Cole, *Conversations* (New York: Anchor Books-Doubleday, 1993).

characteristics. For example, a particular individual (whose personality attributes do not change from one encounter to the next) might behave very competently in some circumstances but not in others. Nevertheless, individual characteristics and attitudes must be taken into account when trying to understand intercultural competence.[5]

The perceptual approach to intercultural competence attempts to identify clusters of attitudes or perceptions that are related to intercultural competence: the ability to deal with psychological stress, to communicate effectively, and to establish interpersonal relationships.[6] The perceptual approach underscores the importance of the emotional or motivational dimension in the skillful enactment of competent behaviors.

The behavioral approach suggests that it is necessary to go beyond what people think they will do in intercultural interactions and observe what they actually do. Intercultural competence, from this perspective, is best studied by looking at specific communication behaviors during intercultural interactions.[7] Specific behaviors necessary for intercultural competence are described briefly in the last section of this chapter and discussed in greater detail in Chapter 13.

These approaches are all culture-general explanations because they assume that regardless of the cultures represented in an interaction, generic characteristics or skills associated with intercultural competence will apply. An alternative is to identify *culture-specific* perceptions and behaviors that are unique to particular interactants. One can then determine how well a particular person adapts her or his communication behaviors to the specific rules of interaction of a particular culture. Harry Triandis is among those who favor a culture-specific approach.[8] He has developed what he calls a "cultural as-similator," a series of incidents capturing important rules of interaction of specific cultures. When working with the assimilator, a person reads the description of an interpersonal incident and chooses the most appropriate response from among the alternatives provided. Triandis's approach emphasizes a person's knowledge of particular cultures and what behaviors are considered appropriate within them.

The four approaches to intercultural competence, taken together, suggest that intercultural communication is a complex phenomenon. More importantly, they also suggest that to achieve interpersonal competence in interactions with people from different cultures, a variety of personal and interpersonal components must be considered.

The Components of Intercultural Competence

Our central concern in this book is improving your intercultural competence, and the ideas presented here are the key to doing so. In the remaining chapters, we will return to the concepts that follow to suggest ways to improve your ability.

A word of caution is necessary before we begin, however. We cannot write a prescription guaranteed to assure competence in intercultural communication. The complexity of human communication in general, and intercultural communication in particular, denies the possibility of a quick fix. There is not necessarily only one way to be competent in your intercultural interactions. Even within the context of a specific person and specific setting, there may be several paths to competent interaction. The goal here is to understand the many ways that a person can behave in an interculturally competent manner.

The remaining portion of this chapter provides a description of the characteristics of people, what they bring to the intercultural communication situation, and the nature of the communication itself, all of which increase the possibility of competence in intercultural communication. Subsequent chapters build on this discussion by offering guidelines for achieving competence. The summary of previous research suggests that competent intercultural communication is contextual; it produces behaviors that are both appropriate and effective; and it requires sufficient knowledge, suitable motivations, and skilled actions. Let's examine each of these components.

Context   Intercultural competence is *contextual*. An impression or judgment that a person is interculturally competent is made with respect to both a specific relational context and a particular situational context. Competence is not independent of the relationships and situations within which communication occurs.

Thus, competence is not an individual attribute; rather, it is a characteristic of the association between individuals.[9] It is possible, therefore, for some-

The demonstration of intercultural communication competence depends on an awareness of the appropriate and effective behaviors in a particular context. The context of greeting someone requires a handshake for U.S. Americans and a bow for Japanese. *(Copyright © Michael Weisbrot/Stock, Boston.)*

one to be perceived as highly competent in one set of intercultural interactions and only moderately competent in another. For example, a Canadian woman living with a family in India might establish competent relationships with the female family members but be unable to relate well to the male members.

Judgments of intercultural competence also depend on cultural expectations about the permitted behaviors that characterize the settings or situations within which people communicate. The settings help to define and limit the range of behaviors that are regarded as acceptable. Consequently, the same set of behaviors may be perceived as very competent in one cultural setting and much less competent in another. As an obvious example that competence is situationally determined, consider what might happen when two people who come from very different cultural backgrounds are involved in a close business relationship. Whereas one person might want to use highly personalized nicknames and touching behaviors in public, the other person might regard such visible displays as unwarranted and therefore incompetent.

Many previous attempts to describe intercultural competence have erroneously focused on the traits or individual characteristics that make a person competent. Thus in the past, individuals have been selected for particular intercultural assignments based solely on such personality attributes as authoritarianism, empathy, self-esteem, and world-mindedness. Because intercultural competence is contextual, these trait approaches have been unsuccessful in identifying competent intercultural communicators. Although particular personality traits might allow a person to be more or less competent on particular occasions, there is no prescriptive set of characteristics that inevitably guarantees competence in all intercultural relationships and situations.

Appropriateness and Effectiveness   Both interpersonal competence and intercultural competence require behaviors that are appropriate and effective. By *appropriate* we mean those behaviors that are regarded as proper and suitable given the expectations generated by a given culture, the constraints of the specific situation, and the nature of the relationship between the interactants. By *effective* we mean those behaviors that lead to the achievement of desired outcomes. The following example illustrates this important distinction between appropriateness and effectiveness.

> Brian Holtz is a U.S. businessperson assigned by his company to manage its office in Thailand. Mr. Thani, a valued assistant manager in the Bangkok office, has recently been arriving late for work. Holtz has to decide what to do about this problem. After carefully thinking about his options, he decides there are four possible strategies:
>
> 1. Go privately to Mr. Thani, ask him why he has been arriving late, and tell him that he needs to come to work on time.
> 2. Ignore the problem.
> 3. Publicly reprimand Mr. Thani the next time he is late.
> 4. In a private discussion, suggest that he is seeking Mr. Thani's assistance in dealing with employees in the company who regularly arrive late for work, and solicit his suggestions about what should be done.

Holtz's first strategy would be effective, as it would probably accomplish his objective of getting Mr. Thani to arrive at work more promptly. However, given the expectations of the Thai culture, which are that one person never directly criticizes another, such behavior would be very inappropriate. Conversely, Holtz's second strategy would be appropriate but not effective, as there would probably be no change in Mr. Thani's behavior. The third option would be neither appropriate nor effective because public humiliation might force Mr. Thani, a valuable employee, to resign. The fourth option, which is the best choice, is both appropriate and effective. By using an indirect means

CULTURE CONNECTIONS

This summer I was one of 20 teens who spent five weeks at the University of Wisconsin at Superior studying acid rain with a National Science Foundation Young Scholars program. . . It was amazing, given the variety of backgrounds, to see the ignorance of some of the smartest young scholars on the subject of other religions.

On the first day, one girl mentioned that she had nine brothers and sisters. "Oh, are you Mormon?" asked another girl, who I knew was a Mormon herself. The first girl, shocked, replied, "No, I dress normal!" She thought Mormon was the same as Mennonite, and the only thing she knew about either religion was that Mennonites don't, in her opinion, "dress normal."

My friends, ever curious about [my] Judaism, asked me about everything from our basic theology to food preferences. . . .

Nobody was deliberately rude or anti-Semitic, but I got the feeling that I was representing the entire Jewish people through my actions. I realized that many of my friends would go back to their small towns thinking that all Jews liked Dairy Queen Blizzards and grilled cheese sandwiches. After all, that was true of all the Jews they knew (in most cases, me and the only other Jewish young scholar, period).

. . .

Ignorance was the problem I faced this summer. By itself, ignorance is not always a problem, but it leads to misunderstandings, prejudice and hatred. Many of today's problems involve hatred. If there weren't so much ignorance about other people's backgrounds, would people still hate each other as badly as they do now? Maybe so, but at least that hatred would be based on facts and not flawed beliefs.

Source: Chana Schoenberger, "Getting to Know About You and Me," *Newsweek,* September 20, 1993: 8.

to communicate his concerns, Mr. Thani will be able to "save face" while Holtz accomplishes his strategic goals.

Knowledge, Motivations, and Actions   Intercultural competence requires sufficient knowledge, suitable motivations, and skilled actions. Each of these components alone is insufficient to achieve intercultural competence.

Knowledge   Knowledge refers to the cognitive information you need to have about the people, the context, and the norms of appropriateness that operate in a specific culture. Without such knowledge, it is unlikely that you will interpret correctly the meanings of other people's messages, nor will you be able to select behaviors that are appropriate and that allow you to achieve

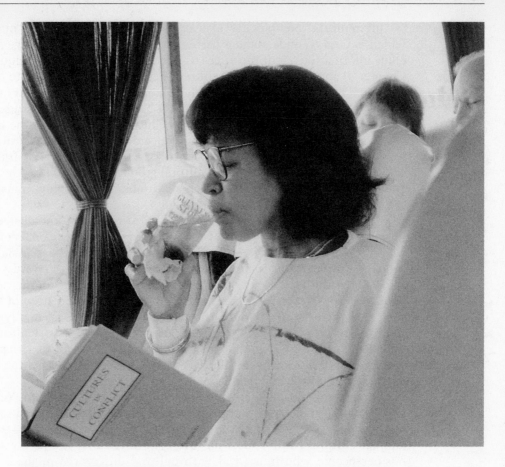

Learning about other cultures is a necessary prerequisite to achieving intercultural communication competence. *(Copyright © Myron W. Lustig & Jolene Koester.)*

your objectives. Consequently, you will not be able to determine what the appropriate and effective behaviors are in a particular context.

The kinds of knowledge that are important include culture-general and culture-specific information. The former provides insights into the intercultural communication process abstractly and can therefore be a very powerful tool in making sense of cultural practices, regardless of the cultures involved. For example, the knowledge that cultures differ widely in their preferred patterns (or rules) of interaction should help to sensitize you to the need to be aware of these important differences. This book is an excellent example of a source for culture-general knowledge. Knowledge about interpersonal communication and the many ways in which culture influences the communication process is very useful in understanding actual intercultural interactions.

Intercultural competence also depends on culture-specific information, which is used to understand a particular culture. Such knowledge should include information about the forces that maintain the culture's uniqueness (see Chapter 4) and facts about the cultural patterns that predominate (see Chapters 5 and 6). The type of intercultural encounter will also suggest other kinds of culture-specific information that might be useful. Exchange students might want to seek out information about the educational system in the host country. Businesspeople may need essential information about the cultural dynamics of doing business in a specific country or with people from their own country who are members of different cultural groups. Tourists would benefit from guidebooks that provide information about obtaining lodging, transportation, food, shopping, and entertainment.

An additional—and crucial—form of culture-specific knowledge involves information about the specific customs that govern interpersonal communication in the culture. For example, before traveling to Southeast Asia, it would be very useful to know that many Southeast Asian cultures regard a display of the soles of the feet as very offensive. This small bit of information can be filed away for later recall when travelers visit temples and attempt to remove their shoes. The imperative to learn about other cultures is equally strong for those cultures with which you interact on a daily basis. Culture-specific knowledge about the rules and customs of the multiple cultures that make up the cultural landscape of the United States is essential information if you are to be interculturally competent.

Often overlooked is knowledge of one's own cultural system. Yet the ability to attain intercultural competence may be very closely linked to this kind of knowledge. Knowledge about your own culture will help you to understand another culture. Fathi Yousef has even suggested that the best way to train businesspeople who must deal with cultural differences might be to teach them about the characteristics of their own culture rather than those of others.[10] The idea behind this admonition is that if people are able to understand how and why they interpret events and experiences, it is more likely that they would be able to select alternative interpretations and behaviors that are more appropriate and effective when interacting in another culture.

Motivations   Motivations include the overall set of emotional associations that people have as they anticipate and actually communicate interculturally. As with knowledge, different aspects of the emotional terrain contribute to the achievement of intercultural competence. Human emotional reactions include both feelings and intentions.

Feelings refer to the emotional or affective states that you experience when communicating with someone from a different culture. Feelings are not thoughts, though people often confuse the two; rather, feelings are your emotional and physiological reactions to thoughts and experiences. Feelings of happiness, sadness, eagerness, anger, tension, surprise, confusion, relaxation, and joy are among the many emotions that can accompany the intercultural communication experience. Feelings involve your general sensitivity to other cultures and your attitudes toward the specific culture and individuals with whom you must interact. How would you characterize your general motivation toward other cultures? Are you excited by the thought of talking with someone from a culture that is different from yours? Or are you anxious at the prospect? Do you think your culture is superior to other cultures? Are you even willing to entertain the idea that another culture's ways of doing various life activities might be as good as, or even better than, your culture's ways? Some people simply do not want to be confronted with things that differ from what they are used to. The different sights, sounds, and smells of another culture are often enough to send them running back to the safety of a hotel room. Eagerness and a willingness to experience some uncertainty is a necessary part of your motivation to achieve intercultural competence.

Intentions are what guide your choices in a particular intercultural interaction. Your intentions are the goals, plans, objectives, and desires that focus and direct your behavior. Intentions are often affected by the stereotypes you have of people from other cultures because stereotypes reduce the number of choices and interpretations you are willing to consider. For instance, if you begin an intercultural interaction having already formed a negative judgment of the other person's culture, it will be very difficult for you to develop accurate interpretations of the behaviors that you observe. Intentions toward the specific interaction partner also must be positive. If your intentions are positive, accurate, and reciprocated by the people with whom you are interacting, your intercultural competence will likely be enhanced.

Actions   Finally, actions refer to the actual performance of those behaviors that are regarded as appropriate and effective. Thus, you can have the necessary information, be motivated by the appropriate feelings and intentions, and still lack the behavioral skills necessary to achieve competence. For example, students from other cultures who enroll in basic public speaking classes often have an excellent understanding of the theory of speech construction. Additionally, they have a positive attitude toward learning U.S. speaking skills; they want to do well and are willing to work hard in preparation. Unfortunately, their speaking skills sometimes make it difficult for them to execute the delivery of a speech with the level of skill and precision that they would like.[11]

Jolene Koester and Margaret Olebe examine eight specific types of communication behaviors that are linked to judgments of intercultural communication competence.[12] These behaviors, which are important in all cultures, are described at the culture-general level. For example, actions that show respect for others and the ability to maintain conversations and manage communicative interactions are necessary in all cultures for someone to be judged as competent. However, the way each culture teaches its members to exhibit these actions is culture-specific. Even among the various cultural groups that live in the United States, the rules for taking turns in a conversation vary widely.

Table 3.1   BEHAVIORAL DIMENSIONS OF INTERCULTURAL COMPETENCE

Display of Respect	The ability to express respect and positive regard for another person
Interaction Posture	The ability to respond to others in descriptive, nonevaluative and nonjudgmental ways
Orientation to Knowledge	The terms people use to explain themselves and their world
Empathy	The capacity to behave as if you understand the world as others do
Task Role Behavior	Behaviors that involve the initiation of ideas related to group problem-solving activities
Relational Role Behavior	Behaviors associated with interpersonal harmony and mediation
Interaction Management	Skill in regulating conversations
Tolerance for Ambiguity	The ability to react to new and ambiguous situations with little visible discomfort

The eight types of communication behaviors are summarized in Table 3.1. We return to a more complete discussion of these behaviors in Chapter 13.

SUMMARY

This chapter has focused on competence and intercultural communication. The first section began with an analysis of intercultural communication and provided several examples. Next we explored issues related to the similarities and differences among communicators that produce intercultural communication. We suggested that intercultural communication is a symbolic process in which the degree of difference between people is large and important enough to create dissimilar interpretations and expectations about what are regarded as competent behaviors that should be used to create shared meanings.

The second section of the chapter differentiated between intercultural communication and related terms, including *intracultural*, *interethnic*, *interracial*, *cross-cultural*, and *international* communication.

The final section of the chapter focused on communication competence, which was described and followed by an examination of four approaches. Finally, three components of intercultural competence were discussed, including the interpersonal and situational contexts within which the communication occurs; the degree of appropriateness and effectiveness in the interaction; and the importance of knowledge, motivations, and actions.

4
CHAPTER

Why Cultures Differ

Cultures look, think, and communicate as they do because of the need to accommodate and adapt to the pressures and forces that influence the culture as a whole. Members of a culture seldom notice these forces because they usually exert a steady and continuous effect on everyone. Although for Isaac Newton a falling apple led to the discovery of the physical laws of thermodynamics, few people pay attention to the subtleties of commonplace events and circumstances. Instead, they remain oblivious to the powerful forces that create and maintain cultural differences. This tendency has led Gustav Ichheiser to declare that "nothing evades our attention as persistently as that which is taken for granted."[1]

In this chapter we ask you to explore with us the taken-for-granted forces that create and maintain cultural differences. Our goal is to explain *why* one culture differs from another. As you read, consider your own culture and compare it to one that is very different or foreign to you. Why are they different? Why aren't all cultures alike? Why do cultures develop certain characteristics? Why do cultures communicate as they do? Why are they changing?

First we'll discuss the forces that promote cultural differences, as well as their interrelationship. We then describe how understanding the ways that cultures change and adapt can improve your intercultural competence.

FORCES THAT CREATE CULTURAL DIFFERENCES

The forces that combine to create and sustain a culture are studied by scholars in many disciplines. Indeed, the ideas contained in this chapter are a sample of the many courses you would probably take as part of an undergraduate academic program, including anthropology, political science, economics, geography, biology, media effects, communication, sociology, and psychology. Our purpose in presenting these ideas to you is to allow you to understand both the complexity of the forces that produce cultural differences and the deeply embedded nature of culture for the individual. Our discussion will also demonstrate the influence of communication—how humans create shared meanings—on other aspects of a culture.

We have selected six forces that help to generate cultural differences, including a culture's history, ecology, technology, biology, institutional networks, and interpersonal communication patterns. Of course, this list is by no means exhaustive. Consider these forces as representing factors with the potential to influence the ways in which cultures develop and maintain their differences, yet change over time.

History

The unique experiences that have become part of a culture's collective wisdom constitute its *history*. Wars, inheritance rules, religious practices, economic consequences, prior events, legislative acts, and the allocation of power to specific individuals are all historical developments that contribute to cultural differences. As J. M. Roberts says of these powerful historical forces,

> The simple and obvious truth [is] that for most of human history most people's lives have been deeply and cruelly shaped by the fact that they have had little or no choice about the way in which they could provide themselves and their families with shelter and enough to eat. The possibility that things might be otherwise has only recently become a conceivable one to even a minority of the world's population and it became a reality for any substantial number of people only with changes in the economy of early modern Europe.[2]

As one of literally thousands of possible examples of the effects of historical forces on the development and maintenance of a culture, let us briefly consider a set of events that occurred in Europe during the late fourteenth century. The experience of bubonic plague, commonly known as the Black Death, was widely shared throughout most of Europe as well as in portions of Africa and Asia. It affected subsequent beliefs and behaviors for many generations.

In 1347, a trading ship traveling to Europe from the Black Sea carried an inadvertent cargo—a horrible disease known as the Black Death. It was spread rapidly by infected fleas carried by rats, and within two years it had traveled from the southern tip of Italy across the entire European continent, killing between one third and one half of the European population. There were recurring outbreaks about every decade until the early eighteenth century. Unlike famine, the Black Death attacked every level and social class. When the initial wave of the epidemic was over, the survivors began a reckless spending spree,

CULTURE CONNECTIONS

Racial, ethnic, and cultural differences among peoples play a major role in the events of our times, in countries around the world, and have played a major role in the long history of the human race. Both intergroup socioeconomic differences within a given country and large differences on a world stage between nations or whole civilizations reflect large cultural differences that have pervaded history. The history of cultural differences among peoples enables us to understand not only how particular peoples differ but also how cultural patterns in general affect the economic and social advancement of the human race.

A particular people usually has its own particular set of skills for dealing with the economic and social necessities of life—and also its own particular set of values as to what are the higher and lower purposes of life. These sets of skills and values typically follow them wherever they go. . . .

Cultures are not erased by crossing a political border or even an ocean, nor do they necessarily disappear in later generations which adopt the language, dress, and outward lifestyle of a country.

The cultural history of the human race is not simply the sum of the discrete histories of particular groups. Because groups interact in various ways—through trade, migration, or conquest, for example—the benefits of one group's cultural advantages spread to other groups. The most obvious way this happens is when products or services are interchanged. Sometimes the technology or the knowledge behind the technology also spreads. In addition, the interaction in itself tends to shatter cultural insularity, which can otherwise be stultifying.

Source: "The Role of Racial, Ethnic and Cultural Differences," *The Chronicle of Higher Learning,* August 10, 1994:B3.

fueled in large measure by the newly acquired wealth left by the dead and by a sense of anarchy. The diminished availability of workers meant that labor, now a scarce commodity, was in demand. Workers throughout Europe organized to bargain for economic and political parity, and revolts against religious and political institutions were commonplace over the next several centuries. Often, however, workers' demands for retribution were either unrealistic or unrelated to the actual causes of the unrest, and the targets of the revolts were frequently foreigners or other helpless victims who were used as scapegoats for political purposes.

Although the Black Death was not the only historical force behind European cultural change, and indeed is insufficient by itself as an explanation for the changes in modern Europe, it was certainly a crucial experience that was recounted across the generations and influenced the development of European cultures. For instance, though the Black Death can now be controlled by mod-

CULTURE CONNECTIONS

Consider the word hello. Iraqis who speak English use it when they mean goodbye. Or so it seems. "It was good to see you. Hello," they say. Or, perhaps, "You must leave. That's final. Hello." Foreign diplomats and journalists in Baghdad find this amusing. Perhaps, one suggests, it's not surprising Saddam hasn't gotten the message to pull out of Kuwait. We say goodbye, he says hello. Except—the Iraqis, in fact, are saying "ahlan wa-sahlan" in local dialect. It means welcome, whether you are coming or going. So American visitors blithely say goodbye, hear hello, and make jokes, while the Iraqis are saying welcome and wondering what the foreigners are sniggering about.

Differences in language, rhetoric, religion, logic, notions of truth and freedom, honor, trust, family, friendship, hospitality—all account for misunderstandings that persist between Arabs and the West. But they are not the core of the incomprehension. The essence can be summed up in a single word: history. It is an always present force in Arab life, and this is what so many Westerners find impossible to grasp. Americans, especially, have very little sense of their own past, and virtually no sense of the Middle East's. Given a problem to confront, an American typically will ask what comes next. An Arab will talk about what came before. "We don't dare to talk about the future, or even the present. Our refuge is the past," says Amin Mahmoud, a Palestinian history professor from Kuwait University who lost his savings and his home in the Iraqi invasion. "We always go back to the roots."

Source: Christopher Dickey, "Why We Can't Seem to Understand the Arabs," *Newsweek,* January 7, 1991: 26.

ern day antibiotics, a 1994 breakout of bubonic plague in India caused mass panic and widespread evacuations to other cities, thus inadvertently spreading the disease to uninfected areas before it was contained. One important consequence of the Black Death was the unchallenged expectation that all population increases were desirable, as new births would replace those who had died and would thereby lead to increased standards of living. This belief predominated for over 400 years, leading people to ignore the evidence that overcrowding in some cities was the cause of disease and famine. In 1798 Thomas Malthus challenged this belief, arguing that human populations might be limited by their available food supply.

Twentieth-century examples of the influence of historical events are also abundant. In the United States, for instance, consider the economic depression of 1929 and the fear of hyperinflation in 1979; the lessons learned in waging wars and making peace with Germany, Japan, Korea, Vietnam, Iraq, and

The Parthenon, at the Acropolis in Athens, Greece, has become a symbol of the important historical influence that the Greek culture has had on many other Western cultures. *Copyright © Myron W. Lustig & Jolene Koester.)*

Somalia; the bread lines and the gas lines; and the violent deaths of John F. Kennedy, Martin Luther King, Jr., John Lennon, and the astronauts aboard the Challenger. All of these events have had profound effects on the ways in which U.S. Americans view themselves and their country. You have undoubtedly heard parents or other elders describe historical events as significantly influencing them and the lives of everyone in their generation. Descriptions of these events are transmitted across generations and form the shared knowledge that guides a culture's collective actions. As David McCullough says of such events and experiences, "You have to know what people have been through to understand what people want and what they don't want. That's the nub of it. And what people have been through is what we call history."[3]

Ecology

The external environment in which the culture lives is the culture's ecology. It includes such physical forces as the overall climate, the changing weather patterns, the prevailing land and water formations, and the availability or un-availability of certain foods and other raw materials.

There is a considerable amount of evidence to demonstrate that ecological conditions affect a culture's formation and functioning in many important and often subtle ways. Often, the effects of the culture's ecology remain hidden to the members of a culture because the climate and environment are a pervasive and constant force. For example, the development and survival of cultures living in cold-weather climates demand an adaptation that often takes the form of an increased need for technology, industry, urbanization, tolerance for ambiguity, and social mobility.[4] In fact, many scholars have suggested that the large brains common to all humans developed as a result of the shrinking forest habitat that occurred during the Ice Age, around 2.5 million years ago.[5] Even basal metabolism, the bodily energy used in all human activities, has been found to be greatest among people who live in colder climates such as the arctic regions, and lowest among people living in the warm-weather tropics.[6]

Cultures that develop in warm climates are characterized by high levels of involvement and closer physical distances in communication. High-contact cultures tend to be located in such warm-weather climates as the Middle East, the Mediterranean region, Indonesia, and Latin America, whereas low-contact cultures are found in cooler climates such as Scandinavia, northern Europe, England, portions of North America, and Japan.[7]

In the United States, differences in climate are related to variations in self-perceptions and interaction patterns. Compared to residents in the warmer areas of the South, for instance, those living in the colder areas of the northern United States tend to be less verbally dramatic, less socially isolated, less authoritarian in their communication style, more tolerant of ambiguity, more likely to avoid touching others in social situations, and lower in feelings of self-importance or self-worth.[8] Surviving a harsh cold-weather climate apparently requires that people act in a more constrained and organized fashion, maintain flexibility to deal with an ambiguous and unpredictable environment, cooperate with others to stave off the wind and the weather, and recognize how puny humans are when compared to such powerful forces as ice storms and snow drifts.

Another important aspect of the ecological environment is the predominant geographical and geological features. For instance, an abundant water supply shapes the economy of a region and certainly influences the day-to-day lifestyles of people. If water is a scarce commodity, a culture must give a major portion of its efforts to locating and providing an item that is essential to human life. Energy expended to maintain a water supply is not available for other forms of accomplishment. Likewise, the shape and contour of the land, along with the strategic location of a culture in relation to other people and places, can alter the mobility, outlook, and frequency of contact with others. Natural resources such as coal, tin, wood, ivory, silver, gold, spices, precious stones, agricultural products, and domesticated animals all contribute to the ecological forces that help to create differences among cultures.

Snow, rain, and harsh weather require people to make adaptations to survive. The climate of a culture, along with other forces of cultural change, produces unique cultural characteristics. *(Photograph by Alex Webb. Copyright © Magnum Photos, Inc.)*

Think about the ecology in which you now live. Can you determine any specific effects that weather patterns such as temperature extremes, storminess, and humidity might have had on the way in which the members of your culture communicate? Do geographical formations such as mountains, plains, forests, lakes, and rivers influence certain characteristics of your culture? Are there cultural effects related to the availability of such natural resources as water, wood, and fertile topsoil? Though it may be impossible to determine all of the ways in which the ecology influences a culture, it is very useful to consider how ecological forces, along with the other forces for cultural change that are discussed in this chapter, can influence the way in which the culture adapts. As Marshall Singer has noted, "every group is confronted with environmental realities of one sort or another. Every group must deal with those realities in one way or another, or it will perish."[9]

As an example of a culture's inability to cope with changing climatic conditions, consider the collapse of "the cradle of civilization," which included some of the world's oldest cities in the fertile valleys of the Tigris and Euphrates rivers in what is now Syria and Iraq. Recent evidence suggests the downfall was triggered by an abrupt change in climate, which brought some 300 years of drought and dust storms to the region about 2200 B.C.[10] A comparable climatic change doomed the Vikings, who abandoned their last Greenland settlement during the late fifteenth century because the "Little Ice Age" that began in 1311 shortened the growing season on which their survival depended.

Technology

The inventions that a culture has created or borrowed are the culture's *technology*, including such inventions as tools, weapons, hydraulic techniques, navigational aids, paper clips, barbed wire, stirrups, and microchips. Changes in the available technology can radically alter the balance of forces that maintain a culture. For instance, while the Vikings were desperately overgrazing their lands in an unsuccessful attempt to survive the Little Ice Age, Greenland's natives, the Inuit, survived and even thrived because they had superior technology: the tools and knowledge for hunting ring seals during hard times.[11] Likewise, the invention of barbed wire allowed the U.S. American West to be fenced in, causing range wars and, ultimately, the end of free-roaming herds of cattle.[12] Similarly, stirrups permitted the Mongols to sweep across Asia, because they allowed riders to control their horses while fighting with their hands.

You have undoubtedly experienced the relationship of technology to culture. Can you remember when most U.S. American homes did not have a microwave oven? Two generations before microwave ovens became common, most homes also did not have refrigerators and freezers, relying instead on daily trips to the butcher and the baker, and on regular visits from the ice man and the milk man, to keep foods from spoiling. Think about how a family's food preparation has changed in the United States. Grocery stores now stock very different food products because of the prevalence of refrigerators and microwave ovens; entirely new industries have developed as well (as shown by the many freezer-to-microwave dishes).

An example of a technological change with even greater consequences is the microchip, which has led to the creation of computers, video games, hand-held calculators, and "smart" machines that are capable of adapting to changing circumstances. The corresponding revolution in the storage, processing, production, and transmission of printed words (such as this textbook) because of the computer has led to a society in which there is an abundance of information.

One special form of technology that has had a major influence on cultures around the world is the media. The media allow human beings to extend sen-

CULTURE CONNECTIONS

The first time I saw coconut-skating I was so sure it was a joke that I laughed out loud. The scowl that came back was enough to tell me that I had completely misunderstood the situation. In the Philippines a maid tends to be all business, especially when working for Americans.

But there she was, barefooted as usual, with half of a coconut shell under each broad foot, systematically skating around the room. So help me, *skating*.

If this performance wasn't for my amusement or hers (and her face said it wasn't), then she had gone out of her head. It wasn't the first time, nor the last, that my working hypothesis was that a certain local person was at least a part-time lunatic.

I backed out and strolled down the hall, trying to look cool and calm.

"Ismelda . . . Ismelda is skating in the living room," I said to Mary, who didn't even look up from the desk where she was typing.

"Yes, this is Thursday, isn't it.". . .

"She skates only on Thursdays? That's nice," I said as I beat an awkward retreat from Mary's little study room.

"Oh, you mean *why* is she skating—right?" Mary called after me.

"Yes, I guess that's the major question," I replied.

Mary, who had done part of her prefield orientation training in one of my workshops, decided to give me a dose of my own medicine: "Go out there and watch her skate; then come back and tell me what you see." And so I did.

Her typewriter clicked on, scarcely missing a beat, until I exclaimed from the living room hallway, "I've got it!"

"Well, good for you; you're never too old to learn." Mary's voice had just enough sarcasm in it to call me up short on how I must often sound to others. And while the typing went on I stood there admiring nature's own polish for hardwood floors, coconut oil, being applied by a very effective Southeast Asian method.

Source: Ted Ward, *Living Overseas* (The Free Press, 1984) 95–96.

sory capabilities to communicate across time and long distances with duplicate messages. Thus, media are any technologies that extend the ability to communicate beyond the limits of face-to-face encounters. Traditional media, such as books, newspapers, magazines, telegraph, telephone, photography, radio, phonograph, and television, have had a major influence in shaping cultures. The new media technologies, such as satellites, cassettes, videotape, videotext, teletext, cable television, videodisk, cellular phones, and the computer, further extend the capabilities of the traditional media.

Media are responsible for introducing ideas from one culture to another rapidly, in a matter of weeks or less. The latest designs from a Paris fashion show can be faxed to Hong Kong manufacturers within minutes of their dis-

Harnessing the energy of animals has been a major labor-saving technology. Using the bullock to grow rice is common in many parts of the world. *(Copyright © Myron W. Lustig & Jolene Koester.)*

play in France, and accurate copies of the clothing can be ready for sale in the United States within a very short time.

Especially relevant is the way in which media technologies influence people's perceptions about other cultures. How do "I Love Lucy" reruns, beamed by satellite to Jakarta, influence the way an Indonesian person tries to communicate with someone from the United States?[13] In what ways do U.S. action-adventure films, in which many of the characters commit acts of violence to resolve interpersonal disagreements, affect the expectations of people from Brazil when they visit the United States? To what extent do media programs accurately reflect a culture and its members? Media-generated stereotypes have important consequences for the processes and outcomes of intercultural communication.

Biology

The inherited characteristics cultural members share are the result of *biology*, as people with a common ancestry have similar genetic compositions. These hereditary differences often arise as an adaptation to environmental forces,

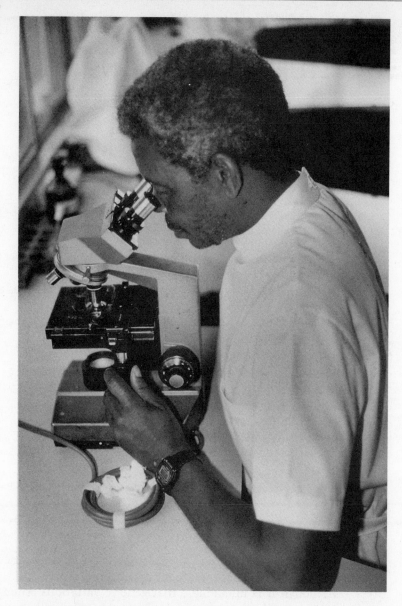

Technology allows people to change their knowledge about the world.
(Copyright © R. Lord/The Image Works.)

and they are evident in the biological attributes often referred to as "race." Depending on how finely you wish to make distinctions, there are anywhere from three to hundreds of human races. Biologists are quick to point out, however, that there is far more genetic diversity within each race than there is among races, as humans have had both the means and the motive to mate

CULTURE CONNECTIONS

What is it that makes me different?
My hair,
My clothes,
My almond-shaped eyes?
Or is it because I'm an Asian by descent.

I know, I was not born in America
But I accept America as my homeland. And all I ask is to be accepted for
who I am.

For so long I hated myself because I wasn't like the rest.
Tall with big eyes and pointy nose.
To top it off, I was not known by my true given name, but as a Chink.

What hurts is that I'm not a Chink, but a full blooded Vietnamese.

I didn't realize that what I am is a treasure,
Until three years ago when I learned I am special.

Now that my eyes are so opened
I will always walk with my head up high with dignity and pride
Because I am proud of who I am,
And that is Vietnamese.

Source: Bich-Ha Hoang, "Who Am I?" *Passages: An Anthology of the Southeast Asian Refugee Experience*, ed. Katsuyo K. Howard (Fresno, CA: California State University, Fresno, 1990) 137.

with others across the entire spectrum of human genetic differences. This makes race an arbitrary but sometimes useful term.[14]

Although it is undeniable that genetic variations among human cultures exist, it is equally clear that biology cannot explain all or even most of the differences among cultures. For example, the evidence from studies that have been conducted in the United States on differences in intelligence suggests that almost none of the variation in intelligence quotient (IQ) scores is related to genetic differences. Studies of interracial adoption, for instance, reveal that educational and economic advantages are the critical factors in determining children's IQ scores.[15] The data therefore suggest that although hereditary differences certainly exist, most of the distinctions among human groups result from cultural learning or environmental causes rather than from genetic or biological forces. As Michael Winkelman suggests, "biology provides the basis for acquiring capacities, while culture provides those specific skills as related to specific tasks and behaviors.[16]

Readily observable biological differences among groups of people have been amply documented, particularly for external features such as body shape, skin color, and other physical attributes. These visible differences among cultures are often used to define racial boundaries, though they can be affected by climate and other external constraints and are therefore not reliable measures of racial makeup. Better indicants of racial group distinctions, according to scientists who study their origins and changes, are the inherited single-gene characteristics such as differences in blood types, ear wax, and the prevalence of wisdom teeth. Type B blood, for instance, is common among Asian and African races, whereas Rh negative blood is relatively common among Europeans but rare among other races; Africans and Europeans have soft, sticky earwax, while Japanese and many American Indian groups have dry, crumbly earwax; and many Asians lack the third molars, or wisdom teeth, whereas about 15 percent of Europeans and almost all West Africans have them.[17] Of course, racial distinctions such as these are not what is intended by those who differentiate among individuals based on their physical characteristics.

A complicating factor in making racial distinctions is that virtually all human populations are of mixed racial origins. One controversial theory about human biological differences holds that all humans can trace their ancestry back to the genes of a single African woman, who lived between 166,000 and 249,000 years ago. An analysis of differences in the mitochondrial DNA of 189 people, 121 of whom were from Africa, was used to estimate the degree of relationship between people. Mitochondrial DNA, which are found in every living cell, are passed along substantially unchanged from a mother to her children.[18]

Because there are no "pure" races, membership in a particular racial category is less a matter of biology, genetics, and inherited characteristics than it is a matter of politics, social definitions, and personal preferences.[19] Experts have estimated, for instance, that about 25 percent of the genes of African Americans comes from white ancestors, and numerous African Americans have Native American ancestry as well. Conversely, up to 5 percent of the genes of European Americans comes from black ancestors.[20]

Unfortunately, most studies that claim to associate differences in people's biological race with innate IQ differences do not measure the degree to which genetic heritages come from particular racial stocks.[21] Instead, social definitions of race, which assess people's cultural rather than biological identities, are used by researchers to draw conclusions about innate biological differences. As culture is learned rather than inherited, any obtained differences in these studies are likely the result of lived experiences and intellectual opportunities, rather than inherited genetic differences.

However, the lack of a biological basis for racial distinctions does not mean that race is unimportant. Rather, race should be understood as a sociological term that refers to people who are believed by themselves or by others to constitute a group of people who share common physical attributes.

Racial differences are often used as the defining features to include some individuals in a particular group while excluding others. Interestingly, U.S. census data, and often social pressures, require individuals to include themselves in only one of the available racial categories, despite ample evidence that many people are of mixed race and have multiple ethnic identities. Thus a woman whose mother is a black Latino and whose father is a third-generation Korean American is often expected to disavow some parts of her heritage while identifying with other parts. Difficulties with the census classification system can be seen in the data on the Native American population, which seemingly quadrupled from 1960 to 1990. From 1980 to 1990 alone, the Native American population increased 118 percent in Alabama and 78 percent in New Jersey. As these increases are not related to "natural" causes such as fertility rates and immigration patterns, demographers have concluded that a newfound pride and an increasing sense of cultural awareness has led many people to so identify themselves on census forms.[22] Indeed, had the film "Dances with Wolves" been released before the census in April, 1990, rather than at the end of that year, the number of Native Americans would undoubtedly have been even higher.

Institutional Networks

Institutional networks are the formal organizations in societies that structure activities for large numbers of people. These include government, education, religion, work, professional associations, and even social organizations.

The importance of government as an organizing force is acknowledged by the emphasis placed in secondary schools on the different types of government systems around the globe. Because their form of government influences how people think about the world, this institutional network plays an important role in shaping culture.

The importance of institutional networks is also illustrated by the variability in the ways that people have developed to display spirituality, practice religion, and confront our common mortality. Indeed, religious practices are probably as old as humankind. Even 50,000 years ago, Neanderthal tribes in western Asia buried their dead with food, weapons, and fire charcoal, which were to be used in the next life.

Religion is an important institutional network that binds people to one another and helps to maintain cultural bonds. However, the manner in which various religions organize and connect people differs widely. In countries that practice Christianity or Judaism, people who are deeply involved in the practice of a religion usually belong to a church or synagogue. The congregation is the primary means of affiliation, and religious services are attended at the same place each time. As people become more involved in religious practices, they meet others and join organizations in the congregation, such as men's and women's clubs, Bible study, youth organizations, and Sunday school. Through

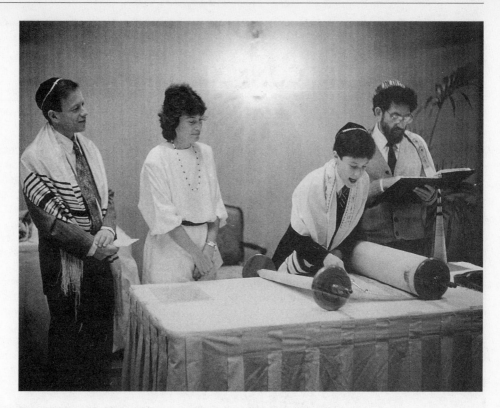

The practice of religion provides important institutional networks in most cultures. Here a young Jewish boy reads from the Torah at his Bar Mitzvah while his parents look on. *(Copyright © Emilio A. Mercado Photographers, The Picture Cube.)*

the institutional network of the church or synagogue, religious beliefs connect people to one another and reinforce the ideas that initially led them to join.

Religious organizations in non-Christian cultures are defined very differently, and the means by which they organize and connect people to one another are also very different. In India, for example, Hindu temples are seemingly everywhere. Some are very small and simple, whereas others are grand and elaborate. The idea of a stable congregation holding regularly scheduled services, as is done in the religious practices of Christianity and Judaism, is unknown. People may develop a level of comfort and affiliation with a particular temple, but they don't "join the congregation" and attend prayer meetings. They simply worship in whatever temple and at whatever time they deem appropriate.

Interpersonal Communication Patterns

The face-to-face verbal and nonverbal coding systems that cultures develop to convey meanings and intentions are called *interpersonal communication pat-*

CULTURE CONNECTIONS

Andrew Smookler, in describing what he calls "The Parable of the Tribes," provides the following story:

> Imagine a group of tribes living within reach of one another. If all choose the way of peace, then all may live in peace. But what if all but one choose peace, and that one is ambitious for expansion and conquest? What can happen to the others when confronted by an ambitious and potent neighbor? Perhaps one tribe is attacked and defeated, its people destroyed and its lands seized for the use of the victors. Another is defeated, but this one is not exterminated; rather, it is subjugated and transformed to serve the conqueror. A third seeking to avoid such disaster flees from the area into some inaccessible (and undesirable) place, and its former homeland becomes part of the growing empire of the power-seeking tribe. Let us suppose that others observing these developments decide to defend themselves in order to preserve themselves and their autonomy. But the irony is that successful defense against a power-maximizing aggressor requires a society to become more like the society that threatens it. Power can be stopped only by power, and if the threatening society has discovered ways to magnify its power through innovations in organization or technology (or whatever), the defensive society will have to transform itself into something more like its foe in order to resist the external force.
>
>   I have just outlined four possible outcomes for the threatened tribes: destruction, absorption and transformation, withdrawal, and imitation. *In every one of these outcomes the ways of power are spread throughout the system*. This is the parable of the tribes.

Smookler's point is this: *"No one is free to choose peace, but anyone can impose upon all the necessity for power."*

Source: A. B. Smookler, *The Parable of the Tribes: The Problem of Power in Social Evolution* (Boston: Houghton Mifflin, 1984) 21–22.

terns. These links include parents, siblings, peers, teachers, relatives, neighbors, employers, authority figures, and other social contacts.

Differences in interpersonal communication patterns both cause and result from cultural differences. Verbal communication systems, or languages, give each culture a common set of categories and distinctions with which to organize perceptions. These common categories are used to sort objects and ideas and to give meaning to shared experiences. Nonverbal communication systems provide information about the meanings associated with the use of space, time, touch, and gestures. They help to define the boundaries between members and nonmembers of a culture.

Interpersonal networks are often based on family relationships. Here one family travels together on a motorcycle. *(Copyright © Myron W. Lustig & Jolene Koester.)*

Interpersonal communication patterns are also important in maintaining the structure of a culture, because they are the means through which a culture transmits its beliefs and practices from one generation to another. The primary agents for conveying these basic tenets are usually parents, but the entire network of interpersonal relationships provides unrelenting messages about the preferred ways of thinking, feeling, perceiving, and acting in relation to problems with which the culture must cope. For instance, when a major storm causes death and the destruction of valuable property, the explanations given can shape the future of the culture. An explanation that says, "God is punishing the people because they have disobeyed" shapes a different perception of the relationship among humans, nature, and spirituality than an explanation that says, "Disasters such as this one happen because of cyclonic storms that are unrelated to human actions."

Cultures organize and assign a level of importance to their interpersonal communication patterns in various ways, which in turn influences other aspects of the culture. Ideas concerning such basic interpersonal relationships as *family* and *friend* often differ because of unique cultural expectations about the obligations and privileges that should be granted to a particular network of people. In the United States, for instance, college students consider it appropriate to live hundreds of miles from home if doing so will allow them to pursue the best education. Many Mexican college students, however, have refused similar educational opportunities because in Mexico one's family relationships are often more important than individual achievement. In the Republic of Korea, family members are so closely tied to one another in a hierarchy based on age and gender that the oldest male relative typically has the final say on such important matters as where to attend school, what profession to pursue, and whom to marry.

Because an understanding of cultural differences in interpersonal communication patterns is so crucial to becoming interculturally competent, it is a central feature of this book. Subsequent chapters will focus specifically on the importance of interpersonal communication patterns and will consider more general issues about the nature of interpersonal communication between cultures.

THE INTERRELATEDNESS OF CULTURAL FORCES

Although we have discussed the forces that influence the creation and development of cultural patterns as if each operated independently of all the others, we do wish to emphasize that they are all interrelated. Each force affects and is affected by all of the others. Each works in conjunction with the others by pushing and pulling on the members of a culture to create a vector of constraints that alters the cultural patterns.

Each culture is a bit like a rich and complex stew that has been cooked very slowly over a long period of time. Though all stews have certain commonalities, each starts from different varieties of the same ingredients, uses different spices, and is produced under different cooking conditions. Thus, even the same new ingredient, such as the introduction of a new variety of rice seed into different cultures, will produce different consequences or outcomes in each culture.

Changes in a culture's institutions or traditions cause its members to alter their behaviors in some way. These alterations, in turn, foster additional adjustments to the institutions or traditions in a continual process of adaptation and accommodation. Thus, nomadic herders change the land by plowing fields, and the plowed fields change the herders by making them remain in one place to farm. The ready availability of food allows towns and villages to become large cities, but cities require other technological improvements in roads and irrigation systems in order to sustain their increased size. Technological changes require corresponding institutional changes, as more complex social structures are needed to organize and coordinate joint activities.

An example of the interrelationship among these powerful forces is provided by Marshall Singer, who describes the effects of population, religion, resource availability, and life expectancy on the formation of certain cultural values and practices in Ireland and India during the late nineteenth century.[23] In Ireland, the population was large relative to the available food, and severe food shortages were common. Therefore, there was a pressing need to reduce the size of the population. Because the Irish were predominantly Catholic, artificial methods of birth control were unacceptable. Given the negative cultural value associated with birth control and the problems of overpopulation and lack of food, a cultural practice evolved that women did not marry before the age of about 30. The population was reduced, of course, by the delay in marriages. India, at about that same time, also had harsh economic conditions, but the average life expectancy was about 28 years, and nearly half of the children died before age 5. Given that reality, a cultural value evolved that the preferred age for an Indian woman to marry was around 12 or 13. That way, all childbearing years were available for procreation, thus increasing the chances for the survival of the culture.

Cultural adaptations and accommodations, however extreme, are rarely made consciously. Rather, cultures attempt to adjust to their unique configuration of forces by altering the shared and often unquestioned cultural assumptions that guide their thoughts and actions.

CULTURAL DIFFERENCES AND INTERCULTURAL COMPETENCE

In this chapter we have emphasized the forces that create differences among cultures because the changes and adaptations that occur as a consequence form the very basis for the special challenges involved in intercultural communication. Interestingly, amid all of these differences is a striking similarity among cultures in their response to other cultures. This directly influences the motivation and knowledge components of intercultural competence, thereby indirectly affecting the ability to act with appropriateness and effectiveness.

All cultures teach their members the "preferred" ways to respond to the world, which are often labeled as "natural" or "appropriate." Thus, people generally perceive their own experiences, which are shaped by their own cultural forces, as natural, human, and universal. Judgments about what is "right" or "natural" create emotional responses to cultural differences that interfere with our ability to understand the symbols used by other cultures. For example, European Americans think it is "human nature" to orient oneself to the future and to want to improve one's material status in life. Individuals whose cultures have been influenced by alternative forces, resulting in contrary views, are often judged negatively and treated with derision.

All cultures also train their members to use the categories of their own cultural experiences when judging the experiences of people from other cultures. Our culture tells us that the way we were taught to behave is "right" or "correct," and those who do things differently are wrong. This belief that the customs and practices of one's own culture are superior to those of other cultures is called *ethnocentrism*. Ethnocentrism is a learned belief in cultural superiority. When combined with the natural human tendency to prefer what is typically experienced, ethnocentrism produces emotional reactions to cultural differences that reduce people's willingness to understand disparate cultural messages. Because ethnocentrism is such an important belief and tends

CULTURE CONNECTIONS

"How do you live in America?" she asked, growing increasingly curious. When she heard about the long winter season with a snow ground cover that lasts for three to four months, she looked horrified and immediately tried to console me. Did I have to return to such a hardship? "Why not stay in Botswana," she suggested. She had, of course, imagined a one-room hut and lolwapa in the snow. I tried to mollify her concerns by drawing a picture of our house, with stairs, many rooms, a kitchen, a bath, and central heating. Even if houses provided necessary facilities and were big enough to walk around in, it would still be extremely difficult to remain confined for three months, she said. How did a person get food?

My Setswana vocabulary was not up to this conversation. Mrs. Kgosietsile interpreted as I gave an elaborate description of trucks unloading at grocery stores; sidewalks, streets, and snow plows; the family car with snow tires; down jackets and boots. From the look on her face, I might as well have described adaptations for living on the moon.

Determined to convince her that I actually enjoyed my life at home and failing adequate Setswana vocabulary, I sketched a picture of a mountainside with a pond at its base. I drew in all the winter sports I could think of—skiing, sledding, tobogganing, ice skating, snowshoeing, even a snow sculpture. She shook her head and only repeated that she would never want to put her toes down into the cold snow. But you would be wearing thick, warm boots, I reminded her.

"Why should my feet be weighted down? I like to feel the ground on the soles of my feet!" she insisted. "Where you live is a terrible place. I have an idea!" She brightened, "You bring over from your place that wheel you told me about—the one to make pots on—and then you must stay here with us. We will work together, and you will make pots when I am gone. We will add another hut for your family. Botswana is, after all, the best place to live!"

Source: Marianne Alverson, *Under African Sun* (Chicago: University of Chicago Press, 1987) 181–182.

to highlight and exaggerate cultural differences, we will discuss it more fully in Chapter 12. Now, however, we will provide some examples of ethnocentrism to illustrate its potential effects on the intercultural communication process.

As an interesting instance of ethnocentrism, consider beliefs about body odor. Most U.S. Americans spend large sums of money each year to rid themselves of natural body odor. They then replace their natural odors with artificial ones, as they apply deodorants, bath powders, shaving lotions, perfumes, hair sprays, shampoos, mousse, gels, toothpaste, mouthwash, and breath

Reactions to different foods often stimulate ethnocentric responses. Depending on your cultural background, your reaction to eating fish heads might be pleasure or disgust. *(Copyright © Myron W. Lustig & Jolene Koester.)*

mints. Many U.S. Americans probably believe that they do not have an odor—even after they have routinely applied most, if not all, of the artificial ones in the preceding list. Yet the same individuals will react negatively to culturally different others who do not remove natural body odors and who refuse to apply artificial ones.

Another example of ethnocentrism concerns the way in which cultures teach people to discharge mucus from the nose. Most U.S. Americans purchase boxes of tissues and strategically place them at various points in their homes, offices, and cars so that they will be available for use when blowing their noses. In countries where paper products are scarce and very expensive, people blow their noses onto the ground or the street. Pay attention to your reaction as you read this last statement. Most U.S. Americans, when learning about this behavior, react with a certain amount of disgust. But think about the U.S. practice of blowing one's nose into a tissue or handkerchief, which is then placed on the desk or into a pocket or purse. Now ask yourself which is really more disgusting—carrying around tissues with dried mucus in them or blowing the mucus onto the street? Described in this way, both practices have a certain element of repugnance, but because one's culture teaches that there is one preferred way, that custom is familiar and comfortable and the practices of other cultures are seen as wrong or distasteful.

To be a competent intercultural communicator, you must realize that you typically use the categories of your own culture to judge and interpret the behaviors of those who are culturally different from you. You must also be aware of your own emotional reactions to the sights, sounds, smells, and variations in message systems that you encounter when communicating with people from other cultures. The competent intercultural communicator does not necessarily suppress negative feelings, but acknowledges their existence and seeks to minimize their effect on her or his communication. If you are reacting strongly to some aspect of another culture, seek out an explanation in the forces that have shaped the culture.

Knowledge of the powerful forces that help to shape cultures—their history, ecology, biology, institutional networks, technology, and interpersonal communication patterns—is critical to your ability to escape the negative consequences of ethnocentrism. Without this culture-specific knowledge, it is very difficult to see specific aspects of a culture, which you might find troubling or simply puzzling, as part of the larger whole.

Competence in intercultural communication also demands an awareness of the different forces that sustain and maintain specific cultures. As a competent intercultural communicator, then, you should learn about the particular forces that shape the culture of those people with whom you will be communicating. By understanding something about these forces, you will understand others better and will be more likely to behave appropriately and effectively. Knowing that religious practices in India do not revolve around a formal place of worship, for instance, a visitor would not conclude that Indians are not religious because they do not worship at one temple. Information about the history of Canada's two language communities will allow the businessperson going to Quebec to recognize the importance of preparing documents in French rather than English. Similarly, knowledge of the importance of status differences among Latinos provides valuable information that could be used to show respect when interacting with members of that culture.

Certainly, then, part of your responsibility in preparing to be a competent intercultural communicator includes learning about the history, ecology, biology, institutional networks, technology, and interpersonal communication patterns of other cultures. Equally important, intercultural competence requires you to understand the forces that shape your own cultural heritage.

Knowing the interplay between the history of the United States, the ecology of a country with vast resources and a frontier mentality, and the prominent role given to technology as a solution to social problems, it is possible to comprehend the European American belief in progress and the possibility for success that is expected for each individual who simply works hard enough. By understanding these same dynamics for people from other cultures we may find that they have been shaped by very different forces of history, ecology, and technology, which have led to different views.

Differences among cultures produce motivations that inhibit people as they communicate interculturally. Ethnocentrism and a preference for one's own culture sustain emotional reactions that interfere with understanding.

SUMMARY

This chapter explained some of the reasons cultures differ. The shared experiences remembered by cultural members, or a culture's history, were considered first. In the United States, for instance, the lesson of the country's historical experiences affects U.S. Americans' views of their government's relationships with other countries. The ways in which a culture's unique ecology profoundly alters the collective actions of its people were illustrated. Next we discussed the biological or genetic forces affecting cultures. Genetic variations among people are only a small source of cultural differences. We also explained the role of the formal organizations of a culture, the institutional networks such as government, religion, work organizations, and other social organizations. These institutional networks organize groups of individuals and provide the regulations by which the culture functions as a collective. The undisputed effects of technology on a culture were explored next. Technological differences promote vast changes in the ways cultures choose to function. Finally, interpersonal communication patterns, the the means by which cultural patterns are transmitted from one generation to another, were considered. These interpersonal communication patterns include the links a culture emphasizes among parents, siblings, peers, teachers, relatives, neighbors, authority figures, and other social contacts. The reciprocal relationship between these forces of cultural change and accommodations were explored. The inevitability and constancy of change characterize all cultures.

Finally, the chapter focused on the consequences of cultural differences on the potential motivation of the intercultural communicator. The strong, necessary component of both culture-general and culture-specific knowledge in helping people respond to cultural differences was explained.

5
CHAPTER

Cultural Patterns and Communication: Foundations

If you have had even limited contact with people from other cultures, you know that they differ in both obvious and subtle ways. An obvious cultural difference is in the food people eat, such as the ubiquitous hamburger, the U.S. offering to the world's palate. We identify pasta with Italy, stuffed grape leaves with Greece and Turkey, sushi with Japan, curry with India and Southeast Asia, and kimchee with Korea.

Another obvious difference between cultures is the clothing people wear. Walk down the streets near United Nations Plaza in New York City or in diplomatic areas of Washington, D.C., and you will see men wearing colorful African dashikis, women in graceful and flowing Indian saris, and men from Middle Eastern cultures with long robes and headdresses.

Other cultural differences are more subtle and become apparent only after more extensive exposure. This chapter and the next are about those subtle, less visible differences that are taken for granted within a culture. In defining culture we called the effects of these subtle differences *shared perceptions*. Shared perceptions lead to actions that are regarded as appropriate and effective behaviors within a culture. They are therefore very important, and they result from the culture's collective assumptions about what the world is, shared judgments about what it should be, and widely held expectations about how people should behave. We are going to call these unseen but shared expectations *cultural patterns*. Cultural patterns cannot be seen, heard, tasted, or experienced because they exist only in the minds of people. Cultural patterns are made up of people's beliefs, values, and norms, and they provide a way of thinking about the world and orienting oneself to it. In other words, cultural patterns may be seen as mental programming that predisposes people to comprehend the world in a particular way.

It is extremely important that you understand differences in cultural patterns if you wish to develop competence in intercultural communication. Cultural patterns are the basis for interpreting the symbols used in communication. If the cultural patterns between people are sufficiently different, the symbols used in communicating will be interpreted differently and may be misunderstood—unless people are aware that no common set of behaviors is universally interpreted in the same way nor regarded with the same degree of favorability.

DEFINING CULTURAL PATTERNS

Shared beliefs, values, and norms that are stable over time and that lead to roughly similar behaviors across similar situations are known as *cultural patterns*. These cultural patterns affect perceptions of competence. Despite their importance in the development and maintenance of cultures, they can only be seen, heard, and experienced indirectly. However, the consequences of cultural patterns—shared interpretations that are evident in what people say and do—are readily observable. Cultural patterns are inside people, in their minds. They provide a way of thinking about the world, of orienting oneself to it. Therefore, cultural patterns are shared mental programs that govern specific behavior choices.

Cultural patterns provide the basic set of standards that guide thought and action. Some aspects of this mental programming are, of course, unique to each individual. Even within a culture, no two people are programmed identically, and these distinctive personality differences separate the members of a culture. In comparisons across cultures, some mental programs are essentially universal. A mother's concern for her newborn infant, for example, reflects a biological program that exists across all known cultures and is part of our common human experience.

In addition to those portions of our mental programs that are unique or universally held, there are those that are widely shared only by members of a particular group or culture. These collective programs can be understood only in the context of a particular culture, and they include such areas as the preferred degree of social equality, the importance of group harmony, the degree to which emotional displays are permitted, the value ascribed to assertiveness, and the like.

Cultural patterns are not so much consciously taught as unconsciously experienced as a byproduct of day-to-day activities. Most core assumptions are programmed at a very early age and are reinforced continuously. Saudi Arabians, for example, are taught to admire courage, patience, honor, and group har-

People from all cultures develop routines for child rearing and parenting. *(Copyright © Beryl Goldberg Photographer.)*

mony. European Americans are trained to admire achievement, practicality, material comfort, freedom, and individuality.

Because of their importance in shaping judgments about intercultural competence, we will discuss cultural patterns in great detail through several approaches. We emphasize both what is similar about all cultural patterns and

CULTURE CONNECTIONS

Convinced that the transition to a different language and culture is less complicated for a child, and also observing, with perhaps some degree of envy, the ease and spontaneity between the boys, I was not prepared for Keith's glum face upon his return. He ate his supper in silence, but just as I came to bid him good-night at his bedside, his eyes filled with tears. Bewildered, I cradled him, while he heaved with sobs and tried to get out the words.

"Moremi is . . . cruel . . . to the goats! He wouldn't let the limping goat stay in the kraal. He pushed it out. He made it go on. I tried to stop him. He laughed. He beat it. He kept the baby goat away from its *own* mother. It wanted to drink. He wouldn't let it. *Why* is he so mean? He never pets them."

As I was just about to launch into a soothing discourse on "let's try to understand Moremi," he interrupted.

"And the goats don't even have names, like in *Heidi!*"

The curtain lifted. *Heidi!* Yes, he had read it and loved it, and here was his chance to love and protect the goats! Amazed, I listened to him tell of the various goat families. He shared the minute details he had so keenly discovered. But before he fell back on his pillow to sleep, I tried to tell him just what I've been trying to tell myself these past days.

"Keith. We're in another place, another time. It is not like home where we have animals as pets to feed and cuddle, to take to the vet or enter in a show. It is not like Heidi's Alps where the goats' creamy milk keeps the children's cheeks rosy. I don't know *why* Moremi acts this way. Stay with him. Watch him. Try not to judge him. See if you can find out why. Maybe there *is* a reason that isn't cruel. And if you learn something new, tell me, because I would like to understand it with you."

He was asleep, and I continued to talk across the dark corner of the hut.

Source: Marianne Alverson, *Under African Sun* (Chicago: University of Chicago Press, 1987) 25–26.

what is different among them. We begin by describing the basic components of all cultural patterns: beliefs, values, and norms. We then turn to characteristics of cultural patterns. Chapter 6 presents three systematic approaches, or taxonomies, to describe the ways in which cultures differ.

COMPONENTS OF CULTURAL PATTERNS

In Chapter 2 we offered a definition of culture as a learned set of shared perceptions about beliefs, values, and norms. At that point, however, we left these three key terms undefined. We now explain in some detail the nature of beliefs, values, and norms, the components of cultural patterns.

Beliefs

A *belief* is an idea that people assume to be true about the world. Beliefs, therefore, are a set of learned interpretations that form the basis for cultural members to decide what is and what is not logical and correct.

Beliefs can range from ideas that are central to a person's sense of self to those that are more peripheral. Central beliefs include the culture's fundamental teachings about what reality is and expectations about how the world works. Less central, but also important, are beliefs based on or derived from the teachings of those regarded as authorities. Parents, teachers, and other important elders transmit the culture's assumptions about the nature of the physical and interpersonal world. Peripheral beliefs refer to matters of personal taste. They contribute to each person's unique configuration of ideas and expectations within the larger cultural matrix.[1]

Discussing culturally shared beliefs is difficult because people are usually not conscious of them. Culturally shared beliefs are so fundamental to assumptions about what the world is like and how the world operates that they are typically unnoticed. We hope you will come to realize through this discussion of cultural beliefs that much of what you consider to be reality may, in fact, not be reality to people from other cultures. What you consider to be the important "givens" about the world, such as the nature of people and their relationships with one another, are based on your culturally shared beliefs, which have been transmitted to and learned by you, and are not a description of some invariant, unchanging characteristic of the world.

A well-known example of a widely shared belief dates back to the time when Europeans believed that the earth was flat. That is, people "knew" that the earth was flat. Most people now "know" (believe) that the earth is basically round and would scoff at any suggestion that it is flat.

Another example of a belief for many European Americans is that in "reality" there is a separation between the physical and spiritual worlds. If a teacher one day started kicking the doorsill at the front of the room, the students might begin to worry about the teacher's mental health. The students would probably be unconcerned about the doorsill itself, nor would they be alarmed about the spirits who might reside there. Of course, you and they "know" that there are no spirits in doorsills. But people from Thailand and elsewhere "know" that spirits do indeed reside in inanimate objects such as doorsills, which is why doorsills should always be stepped over rather than on. In addition to their concern about the teacher, therefore, people from other cultures might conceivably worry about upsetting the spirits who dwell in the doorsill.

Members of the European American culture see humans as separate from nature. Based on this set of beliefs about the world, European Americans have set out to control nature. From the viewpoint of the typical European Ameri-

CULTURE CONNECTIONS

In the following excerpt about Native American people in the early part of this century, Nanapush, a 50-year-old man, along with a younger man, Eli, have been living in a cabin with very little food. Eli goes hunting for food, and Nanapush, while remaining physically behind, follows Eli by singing:

After six days I could not bear to hear any more from Eli. Each day of snow seemed endless, trapped with a sulking boy. Eli paced, muttered, slept, and also ate my cupboard completely bare, down to the last potato, and emptied the little bundle he brought, too, which would have lasted me the whole evil month. We went two days without anything but grease and crumbs of bread. On the seventh day I handed him his gun. He looked at it in surprise, but finally went north. I went out on my own, checking snares. I had caught some beardgrass, a clump of gray fur, a small carcass picked clean overnight by an owl, and a rabbit that was no good, full of worm. I went home and built the fire, drank some tea of dried nettles and considered that by the end of what looked to be a worse winter than I'd feared, I might be forced to boil my moccasins. That was one good thing at least. I hadn't taken to wearing tradestore boots of dyed leather. Those can kill you. After a while, I went and looked into the floursack, which I knew was already empty, and it was still empty. That's when I lay down.

In my fist I had a lump of charcoal, with which I blackened my face. I placed my otter bag upon my chest, my rattle near. I began to sing slowly, calling on my helpers, until the words came from my mouth but were not mine, until the rattle started, the song sang itself, and there, in the deep bright drifts, I saw the tracks of Eli's snowshoes clearly.

He was wandering, weak from his empty stomach, not thinking how the wind blew or calling on the clouds to cover the sky. He did not know what he hunted, what sign to look for or to follow. He let the snow dazzle him and almost dropped his gun. And then the song picked up and stopped him until he understood, from the deep snow and light hard crust, the high wind and rolling clouds, that everything around him was perfect for killing moose.

He had seen the tracks before, down near a frozen shallow slough. So he went there, knowing a moose is dull and has no imagination, although its hearing is particularly keen. He walked carefully around the rim of the depression. Now he was thinking. His vision had cleared and right away he saw the trail leading over the ice and back into the brush and overgrowth. Immediately, he stepped downwind and branched away, walked parallel and then looped back to find the animal's trail. He tracked like that, never right behind it, always careful of the wind, cautious on the harsh ground, gaining on his webbed shoes as the moose floundered and broke through the crust with every step until finally it came to a stand of young saplings, and fed.

Now the song gathered. I exerted myself. Eli's arms and legs were heavy, and without food he could not think. His mind was empty and I so feared that he would make a mistake. He knew that after the moose fed it would always turn downwind to rest. But the trees grew thicker, small and tightly clumped, and the shadows were a darker blue, lengthening.

Eli's coat, made by Margaret, was an old gray army blanket lined with the fur of rabbits. When he took it off and turned it inside out, so that only the soft pelts would brush the branches and not betray him as he neared, I was encouraged. He took his snowshoes off and left them in a tree. He stuffed his hat into his pocket, made his gun ready and then, pausing and sensitive for movement, for the rough shape, he slowly advanced.

Do not sour the meat, I reminded him now, *a strong heart moves slowly.* If he startled the moose so that adrenaline flowed into its blood, the meat would toughen, reveal the vinegar taste of fear.

Eli advanced with caution. The moose appeared. I hold it in my vision just as it was, then, a hulking male, brown and unsuspicious in the late ordinary light of an afternoon. The scrub it stood within was difficult and dense all around, and ready to deflect Eli's bullet.

But my song directed it to fly true.

The animal collapsed to its knees. Eli crashed from his hiding place, too soon, but the shot was good and the animal was dead. He used a tree limb to roll it on its back and then with his knife, cut the line down the middle. He was so cold he was almost in tears, and the warmth of the carcass dizzied him. To gain strength for the hard work ahead he carefully removed the liver, sliced off a bit. With a strip of cloth torn from the hem of his shirt, he wrapped that piece, sprinkled it with tobacco, and buried it under a handful of snow. Half of the rest, he ate. The other he saved for me.

He butchered carefully, but fast as possible, according to my instructions. One time in his youth, he had pierced the stomach of a deer with his knife, spreading its acids through the meat, and I'd hardly spoken to him all the rest of that day. He put his jacket right side out again, smeared it with tallow from a packet in his shirt, then quickly cut off warm slabs of meat and bound them to his body with sinew so that they would mold to fit him as they froze. He secured jagged ovals of haunch meat to his thighs, then fitted smaller rectangles down his legs, below the knees. He pressed to himself a new body, red and steaming, swung a roast to his back and knotted its ligaments around his chest. He bound a rack of ribs across his hat, jutting over his face, and tied them on beneath his chin. Last of all, he wrapped new muscles, wide and thick, around each forearm and past his elbows. What he could not pack, he covered with snow and branches, or hoisted laboriously into the boughs of an ash. He was too heavily laden to hide it all and the light was failing, so he fetched his snowshoes, then dragged the hide a distance away from the meat cache and left it for distraction. It was dusk then, and the walk was long.

There is a temptation, when it is terribly cold and the burden is heavy, to quicken pace to warm the blood. The body argues and steps fast, but the knowledge, informed by tales of hunters frozen with the flesh of their own bounty, resists. I know it well. Eli had become a thing of such cold by now, that, if he sweat, the films on his skin would freeze and draw from his blood all life, all warmth.

Without opening my eyes on the world around me, I took the drum from beneath my bed and beat out footsteps for Eli to hear and follow. Each time he speeded I slowed him. I strengthened the rhythm whenever he faltered beneath the weight he bore. In that way, he returned, and when I could hear the echo of his panting breath, I went outside to help him, still in my song.

Source: Louise Erdrich, *Tracks* (New York: Harper & Row, 1988) 101–104.

can, a person who believes, as the typical Indian woman does, that she "catches colds and fevers from evil spirits that lurk in trees"[2] would be seen as strange. European Americans "know" that people do not become ill from spirits that live in trees. Yet in the Indian culture, people "know" that human illness is caused by such spirits.

Values

Cultures differ not only in their beliefs but also in what they value. *Values* involve what a culture regards as good or bad, right or wrong, fair or unfair, just or unjust, beautiful or ugly, clean or dirty, valuable or worthless, appropriate or inappropriate, and kind or cruel. Because values are the *desired* characteristics or goals of a culture, a culture's values do not necessarily describe its *actual* behaviors and characteristics. However, values are often offered as the explanation for the way in which people communicate.

Many theorists provide insights into a culture's range of values. Milton Rokeach, for example, has written extensively about both beliefs and values. He suggests that there are two broad types of values—instrumental values and terminal values.[3] Instrumental values, which describe "good" ways of behaving or "ways to be," include such attributes as honesty, obedience, love, ambition, and independence. Terminal values refer to the end-states of existence that most of the members of a culture desire, or "things to have or achieve," and include such qualities as freedom, a comfortable life, wisdom, a world at peace, and true friendship.

From culture to culture, values differ in their valence and intensity. *Valence* refers whether the value is seen as positive or negative. *Intensity* indicates the strength or importance of the value, or the degree to which the culture identifies the value as significant. For example, in some U.S. American cultures, the value of respect for elders is negatively valenced and held with a modest degree of intensity. Many U.S. Americans value youth rather than old age. In Korea, Japan, and Mexico, however, respect for elders is a positively valenced value, and it is very intensely held. It would be possible after studying any particular culture to determine its most important values and each value's valence and intensity.

To channel the forces of nature, this farmer sprays chemical weed killer on the crop. *(Copyright © M Siluk/The Image Works.)*

Norms

The outward manifestations of beliefs and values are *norms*, socially shared expectations of appropriate behaviors. When a person's behaviors violate the culture's norms, social sanctions are usually imposed. Norms, like values, can vary within a culture in terms of their importance and intensity. Unlike values, however, norms can change over a period of time, whereas beliefs and values are much more enduring.

Norms exist for a wide variety of behaviors and include typical social routines. For example, the greeting behaviors of people within a culture are governed by norms. Similarly, good manners in a variety of situations are based on norms. Social routines exist to guide people's interactions at public functions and indicate how to engage in conversation, what to talk about, and how to disengage from the conversation. All these actions are based on norms for expected communication behaviors.

Norms are the surface characteristics that emerge from a culture's beliefs and values. Because norms are evident through behaviors, they can be readily observed. People are expected to behave according to their culture's norms, and they therefore come to see their own norms as the "right" way of commu-

CULTURE CONNECTIONS

The value systems of Australians and Americans combine competitive and coopera-tive strands, but in different ways. The Australian harmonizes them while the American sees them as mutually exclusive and is torn between them. Americans are always ready to put themselves in competition with the group or groups to which they belong; it is often "either the group or me." For the Australian it is "the group *and* me, with a great deal of personal privacy as well." Australians search for ways to collabo-rate with the competition while Americans seek ways to "beat" it. The American po-sition seems to be that too much cooperation weakens one's advantage. This may stem, in part, from the different ways such values are inculcated. For example, much is made of mandatory participation in team sports in Australian schools. Americans place more emphasis on the outstanding individual and early on learn "spectatorism," with its powerful identification with the few superior performers. Social welfare legis-lation is much more comprehensive and more readily accepted in Australia than in the United States. The degree to which social welfare is a continuing social, political, eco-nomic, and ideological battleground in the United States surprises Australians.

Source: George W. Renwick, *A Fair Go For All: Australian/American Interactions* (Yarmouth, ME: Intercultural Press, 1991) 18.

nicating. Norms, then, are linked to beliefs and values to form the patterns of a culture.

CHARACTERISTICS OF CULTURAL PATTERNS

In this section we describe a set of similarities underlying all cultural pat-terns. We first present ideas that draw heavily on the work of Kluckhohn and Strodtbeck and their theory of value orientations. Next we describe Stewart and Bennett's elaboration of those ideas.

Kluckhohn and Strodtbeck's Cultural Orientations

Florence Kluckhohn and Fred Strodtbeck wanted to make sense of the work of cultural anthropologists who for many years had described systematic varia-tions both between and within cultures. That is, cultures clearly differed from one another, but within every culture there were individuals who varied from

Prayer is an activity that reflects aspects of a person's culture. *(Copyright © Myron W. Lustig & Jolene Koester.)*

the cultural patterns most often associated with it.[4] To explain both these cultural-level and individual-level differences, Kluckhohn and Strodtbeck offered three conclusions that apply to all cultures:

1. People in all cultures face common human problems for which they must find solutions.
2. The range of alternative solutions to a culture's problems is limited.
3. Within a given culture, there will be preferred solutions, which most people within the culture will select, but there will also be people who will choose other solutions.

The first conclusion, that all cultures face similar problems, is not just about everyday concerns such as "Do I have enough money to get through the month?" or "Will my parent overcome a serious illness?" Rather, the problems involve relationships with others and with the world. Kluckhohn and Strodtbeck describe five problems or orientations that each culture must address:

1. What is the nature of human beings?
2. What is the relationship of humans to nature?
3. What is the orientation of humans to time?
4. What is the human orientation to activity?
5. What is the relationship of humans to each other?

Each culture, in its own unique way, must provide answers to these questions in order to develop a coherent and consistent interpretation of the world.

CULTURE CONNECTIONS

Spirit is an invisible force made visible in all life. In many African religions there is the belief that all things are inhabited by spirits which must be appeased and to which one can appeal. So, for example, when a master drummer prepares to carve a new drum, he approaches the selected tree and speaks to the spirit residing there. In his prayer he describes himself, his experience, and his expertise; then he explains his intent. He assures the spirit that he will remain grateful for the gift of the tree and that he will use the drum only for honorable purposes.

Source: Maya Angelou, *Wouldn't Take Nothing For My Journey Now* (New York: Random House, 1993) 33.

We will return to these questions, in modified form, in our discussion of Stewart and Bennett's ideas.

Kluckhohn and Strodtbeck's second conclusion is that a culture's possible responses to these universal human problems are limited, as cultures must select their solutions from a range of available alternatives. Thus, the culture's available alternatives to the problem "What is the nature of human beings?" can range from "Humans are evil" to "Humans are a mixture of good and evil" to "Humans are good." A culture's response to problems in the relationship of humans to nature can range from a belief that "People are subjugated by nature" to "People live in harmony with nature" to "People master nature." The culture's preferred time orientation can emphasize events and experiences from the past, the present, or the future. The culture's activity orientation can involve passive acceptance and a "being" orientation, a "being-in-becoming" (gradual transformation of the human) orientation or a more "doing," orientation. Finally, a culture's solution to how it should organize itself to deal with interpersonal relationships can vary along a continuum from "hierarchical social organization" to "group identification" to "individualism." Table 5.1 summarizes the Kluckhohn and Strodtbeck value orienta-

Table 5.1   KLUCKHOHN AND STRODTBECK'S VALUE ORIENTATIONS

Orientation	Postulated Range of Variations		
Human nature	Evil	Mixture of good and evil	Good
Man-nature	Subjugation to nature	Harmony with nature	Mastery over nature
Time	Past	Present	Future
Activity	Being	Being-in-becoming	Doing
Relational	Linearity	Collaterality	Individualism

CULTURE CONNECTIONS

In Nigeria, *Ibeji* figures [wooden statues] were carved at the birth of twins. In the event one of the infants died, it was feared the departed child would lure the twin's soul, so the soul of the deceased was given a home in the statue.

Inu-Hariko is a papier-mache dog that guards Japanese babies. And in India, when a child's first tooth appears, the tot is placed on a blanket. In one corner is a pile of coins. In the other, a book. If the child is drawn to the money, a future of wealth is forecast, but the child who heads toward the book is predicted to become a scholar.

Source: Chris Jenkins, "Cultures' Customs Complement Facts of Life" *San Diego Union,* Dec. 4, 1990, D1.

tion theory.

Kluckhohn and Strodtbeck's third conclusion is their answer to an apparent contradiction that scholars found when studying cultures. They argued that within any culture, a preferred set of solutions will be chosen by most people. However, not all people from a culture will make exactly the same set of choices, and in fact, some people from each culture will select other alternatives. For example, most people who are part of European American culture have a "doing" orientation, a veneration for the future, a belief in control over nature, a preference for individualism, and a belief that people are basically good and changeable. But clearly not everyone identified with the European American culture shares all of these beliefs.

Kluckhohn and Strodtbeck's ideas have been very influential among intercultural communication scholars, and they form the foundation for our understanding of cultural patterns. One very useful extension of Kluckhohn and Strodtbeck's ideas is provided by Stewart and Bennett. They explain in great detail the variations in beliefs, values, and norms that are typically associated with cultural patterns.

Stewart and Bennett's Cultural Orientations

Edward C. Stewart, and more recently Stewart along with Milton J. Bennett, compared the preferred cultural orientations of the typical middle-class European American with those of people from other cultures.[5] The ideas in this section are adapted from Stewart and Bennett's works, with modifications and refinements based on the thoughts of John Condon and Fathi Yousef.[6] Members of a culture generally have a preferred set of responses to the world. Imagine that for each experience, there is a range of possible responses from which a culture selects its preferred response. In this section we will describe these

CULTURE CONNECTIONS

Senegal lay before me, the beginning of the road into the heart of Africa. My mind looked only forward. . . .

The earth was not quite sand, separated from the desert by this river, but the dryness continued. The ground was not quite dirt, either, but fragile and brittle dust.

But the rains will one day come. When they do, the land will flower green and fertile. The earth will become mud and hold in place for a time. The world once again will seem abundant, but only for a time so short and so delicate that when the land dries again under the sun, the memories of bounty will be faint and the fertile time will seem as distant as a dream. . . .

I asked when the rainy season usually begins. The answers were vague, uncertain, as if to say: *We don't really remember. And what does it matter anyway?* "The rains will come when it's time for them to come," I was told. And the people will wait for them. If the rains don't come this year, they will come next year, or they will come the year after, or maybe the year after that. And the people will be here waiting.

Source: Eddy L. Harris, *Native Stranger* (New York: Simon & Schuster, 1992) 103.

alternative responses. In so doing, we will compare and contrast the cultural patterns of different cultural groups and suggest their implications for the process of interpersonal communication. Comparing the patterns of different cultures can sometimes be tricky because a feature of one culture, when compared to another culture, may appear very different than it would when compared to a third culture. Stewart and Bennett's ideas are especially useful because they describe a broad range of cultural patterns against which a particular culture can be understood.

The four major elements in Stewart and Bennett's description of cultural patterns address the manner in which a culture orients itself to activities, social relations, the self, and the world. As you read the descriptions in the sections that follow, try to recognize the preferred patterns of your culture. Also, focus on your own beliefs, values, and norms, as they may differ in certain respects from your culture's predominant pattern.

Activity Orientation   An activity orientation defines how the people of a culture view human actions and the expression of self through activities. This orientation provides answers to questions such as:

- Is it important to be engaged in activities in order to be a "good" member of one's culture?
- Can and should people change the circumstances of their lives?
- Is the desirable pace of life fast or slow?

- Is work very different from play?
- Which is more important, work or play?
- Is life a series of problems to be solved or simply a collection of events to be experienced?

To define their activity orientation, cultures usually choose a point on the being-becoming-doing continuum. "Being" is an activity orientation that values inaction and an acceptance of the status quo. African American and Greek cultures are usually regarded as "being" cultures. Another characterization of this orientation is a belief that all events are determined by fate and are therefore inevitable. Hindus from India often espouse this view.

A "becoming" orientation sees humans as evolving and changing; people with this orientation, including Native Americans and most South Americans, are predisposed to think of ways to change themselves as a means of changing the world.

"Doing" is the dominant characteristic of European Americans, who rarely question the assumption that it is important to get things done. Thus, European Americans ask, "What do you do?" when they first meet someone, a common greeting is "Hi! How are you doing?", and Monday morning conversations between co-workers often center on what each person "did" over the weekend. Similarly, young children are asked what they want to be when they grow up (though what is actually meant is "What do you want to do when you grow up?"), and cultural heroes are those who do things. The "doing" culture is often the striving culture, in which people seek to change and control what is happening to them. The common adage "Where there's a will there's a way" captures the essence of this cultural pattern. When faced with adversity, for example, European Americans encourage one another to fight on, to work hard, and not to give up.

A culture's activity orientation also suggests the pace of life. The fast, hectic pace of European Americans, governed by clocks, appointments, and schedules, has become so commonly accepted that it is almost a cliché. The pace of life in cultures such as India, Kenya, Argentina, and among African Americans is less hectic, more relaxed, and more comfortably paced. In African American culture, for example, orientations to time are driven less by a need to "get things done" and conform to external demands than by a sense of participation in events that create their own rhythm. As Jack Daniel and Geneva Smitherman suggest about time in African American culture,

> Being on time has to do with participating in the fulfillment of an activity that is vital to the sustenance of a basic rhythm, rather than with appearing on the scene at, say, "twelve o'clock sharp." The key is not to be "on time" but "in time."[7]

How a person measures success is also related to the activity orientation. In cultures with a "doing" orientation, activity is evaluated by scrutinizing a tangible product or by evaluating some observable action directed at others. In other words, activity should have a purpose or a goal. In the "being" and "becoming" cultures, activity is not necessarily connected to external products or actions; the contemplative monk or the great thinker is most valued. Thus the process of striving toward the goal is sometimes far more important than ac-

In Spain, friends regularly gather after work for en evening's conversation at a local café. The culture encourages people to value the time spent together. *(Copyright © Beryl Goldberg Photographer.)*

complishing it.

In "doing" cultures, work is seen as a separate activity from play and an end in itself. In the "being" and "becoming" cultures, work is a means to an end, and there is no clear-cut separation between work and play. For these individuals, social life spills over into their work life. When members of a "being" culture work in the environment of a "doing" culture, their behavior is often misinterpreted. A Latina employee described her conversation with a European American co-worker who expressed anger that she spent so much "work" time on the telephone with family and friends. For the Latina, it was important to keep in contact with her friends and family; for the European American, only work was done at work, and one's social and personal relationships were totally separated from the working environment. In a "doing" culture, employees who spend too much time chatting with their fellow employees may be reprimanded by a supervisor. In the "being" and "becoming" cultures, those in charge fully expect their employees to mix working and socializing. Along with the activity orientation of "doing" comes a problem-solution orientation. The preferred way of dealing with a difficulty is to see it as a challenge to be met or a problem to be solved. The world is viewed as something that ought to be changed in order to solve problems rather than as something that ought to be accepted as it is, with whatever characteristics it has.

In every culture, these preferences for particular orientations to activities shape the interpersonal communication patterns that will occur. In "doing" cultures, interpersonal communication is characterized by concerns about what people do and how they solve problems. There are expectations that peo-

Cultures with a "being" orientation value contemplative behaviors such as meditating. *(© Alan Carey, The Image Works)*

ple should be involved in activities, that work comes before play, and that people should sacrifice in other parts of their lives in order to meet their work responsibilities. In "being" cultures, interpersonal communication is characterized by being together rather than by accomplishing specific tasks, and there is generally greater balance between work and play. Table 5.2 summarizes the alternative cultural orientations to activities.

Social Relations Orientation   The social relations orientation describes how the people in a culture organize themselves and relate to one another. This orientation provides answers to questions such as:

- To what extent are some people in the culture considered better or superior to others?
- Can social superiority be obtained through birth, age, good deeds, or material achievement and success?
- Are formal, ritualized interaction sequences expected?

Table 5.2   ACTIVITY ORIENTATIONS

1. How do people define activity?

doing	becoming	being
striving		fatalistic
fast pace		slow pace
compulsive		easygoing

2. How do people evaluate activity?

techniques		goals
procedures		ideals

3. How do people regard and handle work?

an end in itself		a means to other ends
separate from play		integrated with play
a challenge		a burden
problem solving		coping with situations

- In what ways does the culture's language require people to make social distinctions?
- What responsibilities and obligations do people have to their extended families, their neighbors, their employers or employees, and others?

A social relations orientation can range from one that emphasizes differences and social hierarchy to one that strives for equality and the absence of hierarchy. Many European Americans, for example, emphasize equality and evenness in their interpersonal relationships, even though certain groups have been treated in discriminatory and unequal ways. Equality as a value and belief is frequently expressed and is called on to justify people's actions. The phrase "We are all human, aren't we?" captures the essence of this cultural tenet. From within this cultural framework, distinctions based on age, gender, role, or occupation are discouraged. Conversely, cultures such as Korean emphasize status differences between individuals. Mexican American culture, drawing on its cultural roots in traditional Mexican values, also celebrates status differences and formalizes different ways of communicating with people depending on who they are and what their social characteristics happen to be.

One noticeable difference in social relations orientations is in the degree of importance a culture places on formality. In cultures that emphasize formality, people address others by appropriate titles, and highly prescriptive rules govern the interaction. Conversely, in cultures that stress equality, people believe that human relationships develop best when those involved can be informal with one another. Students from other cultures who study in the United States are usually taken aback by the seeming informality that exists between teachers and students. Professors allow, even ask, students to call them by their first names, and students disagree with and challenge their teachers in front of the class. The quickness with which interpersonal relationships in the United States move to a first-name basis is mystifying to

CULTURE CONNECTIONS

I really enjoy that Americans are so informal. What I would get from a girl at home if I started to speak to her without being introduced! And everybody is very nice here. I cannot stop to read my map without one dozen people stopping to help me. At home it is even "impolite" to notice that another person has problems unless he asks for your help.

Source: Balasz Harrach, "The Telephone," *Minnesota Daily* (December 4, 1979): 81 (814). Harrach is a Hungarian exchange student.

those from cultures where the personal form of address is used only for selected, special individuals. Many U.S. Americans who share aspects of both European American culture and another culture also express difficulty with this aspect of cultural behavior.

In cultures such as Japan, Korea, and China, individuals identify with only a few distinct groups, and the ties that bind people to these groups are so strong that group membership may endure for a lifetime. Examples of these relationships include nuclear and extended families, friends, neighbors, work groups, and social organizations. In contrast, European Americans typically belong to many groups throughout their lifetimes, and although the groups may be very important for a period of time, they are easily discarded when they are no longer needed. That is, voluntary and informal groups are meant to be important for brief periods of time, often serving a transitory purpose. In addition, it is accepted and even expected that European Americans often change jobs and companies. "Best friends" may only be best friends for brief periods.

Another important way in which social relations orientations can vary is the way in which people define their social roles or their place in a culture. In some cultures, a person's place is determined by the family and the position into which a person is born. At the other extreme are cultures in which all people, regardless of family position, can achieve success and high status. Among African Americans and European Americans, for instance, there is a widespread belief that social and economic class should not predetermine a person's opportunities and choices. From the story of poor Abraham Lincoln, who went from a log cabin to the White House, to the Sylvester Stallone hero in the movie *Rocky*, who went from journeyman boxer to heavyweight champion of the world, there is a common belief that people should not be restricted by their birth.

Cultural patterns can also prescribe appropriate behaviors for men and women. In some cultures, very specific behaviors are expected; other cultures allow more ambiguity in the expected roles of women and men.

A culture's social relations orientation affects the style of interpersonal communication that is most preferred. Cultures may emphasize indirectness, obliqueness, and ambiguity, which is the typical pattern for Mexican Americans, or they may emphasize directness or confrontation, which is the typical European American pattern.

The European American preference for "putting your cards on the table" and "telling it like it is" presupposes a world in which it is desirable to be explicit, direct, and specific about personal reactions and ideas, even at the expense of social discomfort on the part of the person with whom one is interacting. For European Americans, good interpersonal communication skills include stating directly one's personal needs and reactions to the behaviors of others. Thus, if European Americans hear that others have complained about them, they would probably ask, "Why didn't they tell me directly if they have a problem with something that I have done?"

Contrast this approach to that of Asian cultures such as Japan, Korea, Thailand, and China, where saving face and maintaining interpersonal harmony are so highly valued that it would be catastrophic to confront another person directly and verbally express anger. The same values are also usually preferred in many Asian American cultures. Yet a Filipino American man describes being very discouraged and upset when, on a visit to the Philippines, he would ask people to meet him and, although it seemed to him that they had agreed verbally, subsequently they did not appear. As he says of the experience, "They would never say no; rather they would say yes or I'll try." Unfortunately, he felt as if he had been "stood up" several times, until someone explained to him that Filipinos think it is rude to turn down an invitation directly.

The tendency to be verbally explicit in face-to- face interactions is related to a preference for direct interaction rather than interaction through intermediaries. Among European Americans there is a belief that ideally people should depend only on themselves to accomplish what needs to be done. Therefore, the notion of using intermediaries to accomplish either personal or professional business goals is not widely accepted.

Although African Americans prefer indirectness and ambiguity in conversations with fellow cultural members, they do not choose to use intermediaries in these conversations. In many cultures, however, the use of intermediaries is the preferred method of conducting business or passing on information.[8] Marriages are arranged, business deals are made, homes are purchased, and other major negotiations are all conducted through third parties. These third parties soften and interpret the messages of both sides, thereby shielding the parties from direct, and therefore risky and potentially embarrassing, transactions with each other. Similarly, among many cultures from southern Africa, such as Swaziland, there is a distinct preference for the use of intermediaries to deal with negotiations and conflict situations. Consider the experience of the director of an English program in Tunisia, a culture that depends on intermediaries. One of the Tunisian teachers had been consistently late to his morning classes. Rather than calling the teacher in and directly ex-

Table 5.3   SOCIAL RELATIONS ORIENTATIONS

1. How do people relate to others?
   as equals ————————————————————————————————————hierarchical
   informal ————————————————————————————————————formal
   member of many groups ————————————————————member of few groups
   weak group identification————————————————strong group identification
2. How are roles defined and allocated?
   achieved————————————————————————————————————ascribed
   gender roles similar————————————————————gender roles distinct
3. How do people communicate with others?
   directly ————————————————————————————————————indirectly
   no intermediaries ————————————————————————intermediaries
4. What is the basis of social reciprocity?
   independence _____interdependence _____dependence
   autonomy————————————————————————————————————obligation

plaining the problem, the director asked the teacher's friend about the teacher's health and happiness. The director indicated that the teacher's late arrival for class may have been a sign that something was wrong. The friend then simply indirectly conveyed the director's concern to the late teacher, who was late no more.

A culture's social relations orientation also affects the sense of social reciprocity, that is, the underlying sense of obligation and responsibility between people. Some cultures prefer independence and a minimum number of obligations and responsibilities; alternatively, other cultures accept obligations and encourage dependence. The nature of the dependence is often related to the types of status and the degree of formality that exists between the individuals. Cultures that depend on hierarchy and formality to guide their social interactions are also likely to have both a formal means for fulfilling social obligations and clearly defined norms for expressing them. Table 5.3 summarizes the alternative cultural orientations to social relations.

Self-Orientation   Self-orientation describes how people's identities are formed, whether the culture views the self as changeable, what motivates individual actions, and the kinds of people who are valued and respected. A culture's self-orientation provides answers to questions such as:

- Do people believe they have their own unique identities that separate them from others?
- Does the self reside in the individual or in the groups to which the individual belongs?
- What responsibilities does the individual have to others?
- What motivates people to behave as they do?
- Is it possible to respect a person who is judged "bad" in one part of life but is successful in another part of life?

For most European Americans, the emphasis on the individual self is so strong and so pervasive that it is almost impossible for them to comprehend a

CULTURE CONNECTIONS

Southeast Asian refugees come from societies where modesty is praised, where a man who is truly good will never say he is good. But they now live in a society where the most successful group often is the one that stands up and states its case the loudest.

"Public relations is a new term for us. Americans are masters of the art," one leader said, asking to remain anonymous for fear of sounding brash. Unlike Americans, he said, "I don't like to see my name in the paper. I am reluctant to do interviews, unless it is my duty."

Even something as simple and essential as venturing downtown to discuss issues with City Council members remains a foreign journey, leaders admit. Until that happens there will likely not be a Southeast Asian leader known to the general public, much less a council member or county supervisor.

Source: Tony Bizjak and Jeannie Wong, "New Life, Old Ways," *Sacramento Bee,* May 26, 1991: A15.

different point of view. Thus, many European Americans believe that the self is located solely within the individual and the individual is definitely separate from others. From a very young age, children are encouraged to make their own decisions. Alternatively, cultures may define who people are only through their associations with others because individuals' self-definitions may not be separate from that of the larger group. Consequently, there is a heightened sense of interdependence, and what happens to the group (family, work group, or social group) happens to the person. For example, Mary Jane Collier, Sidney Ribeau, and Michael Hecht found that Mexican Americans "place a great deal of emphasis on affiliation and relational solidarity."[9] The sense of being bonded or connected to others is very important to members of this cultural group. Vietnamese Americans have a similarly strong affiliation with their families.

The significance to intercultural communication of a culture's preferences for defining the self is evident in the statement of a Latina student describing her friendship with a second-generation Italian American woman, whose family has also maintained "traditional values."

> I think we are able to communicate so well because our cultural backgrounds are very similar. I have always been family-oriented and so has she. This not only allowed us to get along, but it allowed us to bring our families into our friendship. [For instance] a rule that the two of us had to live by up to this point has been that no matter how old we may get, as long as we are living at home we must ask our parents for permission to go out.

The preeminent status of the individual and the individual's right to speak freely are central characteristics of the European American cultural pattern. *(Copyright © Myron W. Lustig and Jolene Koester)*

Related to self-orientation is the culture's view of whether people are changeable. Naturally, if a culture believes that people can change, it is likely to expect that human beings will strive to be "better," as the culture defines and describes what "better" means.

The source of motivation for human behavior is also part of a culture's self-orientation. Among African Americans and European Americans, individuals are motivated to achieve external success in the form of possessions, positions, and power. Self-orientation combines with the "doing" orientation to create a set of beliefs and values that place individuals in total control of their own fate. Individuals must set their own goals and identify the means necessary to achieve them. Consequently, failure is viewed as a lack of willpower and a disinclination to give the fullest individual effort. In this cultural framework, individuals regard it as necessary to rely on themselves rather than on others.

Another distinguishing feature of the cultural definition of self is whether the culture emphasizes duties, rights, or some combination of the two. One culture that induces its members to act because it is their duty to do so is Japan. In contrast, for European Americans, the concept of duties to others is not a powerful motivator.

An additional part of self-orientation is the set of characteristics of those individuals who are valued and cherished. Cultures vary in their allegiance to the old or to the young, for example. Many cultures venerate their elders and view them as a source of wisdom and valuable life experience. Individuals in these cultures base decisions on the preferences and desires of their elders. Many Asian and Asian American cultures illustrate this preference. The value on youth typifies the European American culture, in which innovation and new ideas, rather than the wisdom of the past, are regarded as important. European Americans venerate the upstart, the innovator, and the person who tries something new. Table 5.4 summarizes the alternative cultural orientations to the self.

World Orientation Cultural patterns also tell people how to locate themselves in relation to the spiritual world, nature, and other living things. A world orientation provides answers to questions such as:

- Are human beings intrinsically good or evil?
- Are humans different from other animals and plants?
- Are people in control of, subjugated by, or living in harmony with the forces of nature?
- Do spirits of the dead inhabit and affect the human world?
- How should time be valued and understood?

In the African and African American worldview, human beings live in an interactive state with the natural and spiritual world. Daniel and Smitherman describe a fundamental tenet of the traditional African worldview as that of "a dynamic, hierarchical unity between God, man, and nature, with God serving

Table 5.4 SELF ORIENTATIONS

1. How should people form their identities?
   by themselves ——————————————————————with others
2. How changeable is the self?
   changeable ——————————————————unchangeable
   self-realization stressed _____self-realization not stressed
3. What is the source of motivation for the self?
   reliance on self ——————————————————reliance on others
   rights ——————————————————————duties
4. What kind of person is valued and respected?
   young ——————————————————————aged
   vigorous ——————————————————————wise
   innovative ——————————————————prominent
   material attributes ——————————————spiritual attributes

CULTURE CONNECTIONS

There's something deeply satisfying about being on your own reservation, something more than nationalism, more than security. It's a feeling of survival, of being a link in an improbable continuity. It's a responsibility fulfilled, an important promise kept, a preference for what seems less than what the outside world offers but in fact is more than imagined. Those fond of make-believe noble savages are devoted to the notion that there is a mystical quality at the root of the relationship between Indians and the land, but they misunderstand. Land is the opposite of magic: it's real, solid, firm. Land is legacy, it enables and supports life, it's both a source and a destination. Land is rocks, hidden roots, dirt, and buried bones, very personal and simultaneously communal. And if it's not yours by right of blood and memory, you always enter for the first time as a trespasser.

Source: Michael Dorris, *The Broken Cord* (New York: Harper Perennial, 1989) 53.

as the head of the hierarchy."[10] In this view of the relationship between the spiritual and material world, humans are an integral part of nature. Thus, in the African and African American world view, "One becomes a 'living witness' when he aligns himself with the forces of nature and instead of being a proselytized 'true believer' strives to live in harmony with the universe."[11] Native American groups, as well, clearly have a view of humans as living in harmony with nature.[12] Latino culture places a great value on spirituality but views humans as being subjugated to nature, with little power to control circumstances that influence their lives.[13]

Most European Americans view humans as separate and distinct from nature and other forms of life. Because of the supremacy of the individual and the presumed uniqueness of each person, most European Americans regard nature as something to be manipulated and controlled in order to make human life better. Excellent examples of this cultural belief can be found in news reports whenever a natural disaster occurs in the United States. For instance, when a large earthquake hit the Los Angeles area in January, 1994, and many people were killed when an apartment building and freeways collapsed, political leaders from California were outraged that the state's buildings and bridges could be unsafe. The assumption in these pronouncements was that the consequences of natural forces such as earthquakes could have been prevented simply by using better technology and by reinforcing the structures to withstand the forces of nature.

This position is also associated with a belief that disease, poverty, and adversity can be overcome in order to achieve health and wealth. In this cultural framework the "natural" part of the human experience—illness, loss, even

In the Vietnamese culture, a memorial service is performed for the dead one year from the time of death to release the spirits. *(Jerry Berndt, © Stock, Boston, Inc. 1991. All rights reserved.)*

death—can be overcome, or at least postponed, by selecting the right courses of action and having the right kinds of attitudes.

The spiritual and physical worlds can be viewed as distinct or as one. Among European Americans there is generally a clear understanding that the physical world, of which humans are a part, is separate from the spiritual world. If people believe in a spiritual world, it exists apart from the everyday places where people live, work, and play. Individuals who say they are psychic or who are mind readers are viewed with suspicion and curiosity. Those who have seen ghosts are questioned in an effort to find a more "logical" and "rational" explanation. In other cultural frameworks, however, it is "logical" and "rational" for spirits to live in both animate and inanimate objects.[14]

The final aspect of a culture's world orientation concerns how people conceptualize time. Some cultures choose to describe the past as most important, others emphasize the present, and still others emphasize the future. Native Americans and Latinos are present-oriented. European Americans, of course, are future-oriented. Alternatives in cultural orientations to the world are sum-

CULTURE CONNECTIONS

The interpretation of historical data from a strictly Eurocentric perspective can lead to serious intercultural conflict, based on wrong premises.

Let me give an example of how cultural misunderstandings can be propagated on the basis of different views. In the nineteenth century, Cecil John Rhodes sought to gain control of a large territory of southern Africa, controlled by the Ndebele King Lobengula, and sent emissaries to the powerful king in an effort to secure his consent. After many days of discussion with Lobengula, the white emissaries returned to Rhodes with the signature of Lobengula on a piece of paper. They told Rhodes that the king had given Rhodes all of his territory. Rhodes sent a column of soldiers into the area with the instructions to shoot any black on sight. Thus began the country of Rhodesia.

Rhodes may have believed that King Lobengula gave him title to the land, but Lobengula never believed that he had. Two cultural views of the world clashed, and the Europeans automatically assumed the correctness of their view. An Afrocentric analysis points out that Lobengula could never have sold or given the land away, since it did not belong to him but to the ancestors and the community. He could grant Rhodes permission to hunt, to farm, and even to build a house, but not to own land. Only in this manner could the king follow the discourse of his ancestors. It took nearly one hundred years, two revolts, and a seven-year war to correct the situation. A rigid Eurocentrism made Rhodes believe that Lobengula had signed his country over to him.

Similarly, I am certain that the Indians did not believe they had sold Manhattan Island for twenty-three dollars worth of trinkets, no matter what the Dutch thought. Native Americans revered the land in much the same way as Africans. No king or clan leader could sell what did not belong to him. On the basis of European contractual custom, the Dutch may have actually thought they were purchasing the island from the Indians; but this was obviously a view based on their own commercial traditions.

Ascertaining the view of the other is important in understanding human phenomena. African responses and actions, however, have too often been examined from Eurocentric perspectives.

Source: Molefi K. Asante, *The Afrocentric Idea* (Philadelphia: Temple University Press, 1987) 10.

marized in Table 5.5.

A culture's underlying patterns, according to Stewart and Bennett, consist of orientations to activity, social relations, the self, and the world. The interdependence among these aspects of culture are obvious from the preceding discussion. Stewart and Bennett's taxonomy provides a way to understand, rather than to judge, different cultural predispositions, and it demonstrates

Table 5.5   WORLD ORIENTATIONS

1. What is the nature of humans in relation to the world?

separate from nature————————————————————integral part of nature

humans modify nature ————————————————humans adapt to nature

health natural ————————————————————disease natural

wealth expected ————————————————————poverty expected

2. What is the world like?

spiritual-physical dichotomy ————————————spiritual-physical unity

empirically understood ————————————————magically understood

technically controlled ————————————————spiritually controlled

3. How do people define and value time?

future ————————————————present ————————————————past

scarce resource ————————————————————unlimited

precisely measurable ————————————————undifferentiated

linear ————————————————————————cyclical

that there are different ways of defining the "real," "good," and "correct" ways to behave.

CULTURAL PATTERNS AND INTERCULTURAL COMPETENCE

There is a strong relationship between the foundations of cultural patterns and intercultural competence. Remember that intercultural competence depends on knowledge, motivation, and actions, which occur in specific contexts with messages that are both appropriate and effective.

The patterns of a culture create the filter through which all verbal and nonverbal symbols are interpreted. Because all cultures have distinct beliefs, values, and norms, symbols do not have universal interpretations, nor will the interpretations have the same degree of favorability. Judgments of competence are strongly influenced by the underlying patterns of a person's cultural background. In every intercultural interaction, a cultural pattern that is different from one's own may be used to interpret one's messages. Every intercultural interaction, then, can be viewed as a puzzle or a mystery that needs to be solved.

How individuals define the relational context is always related to the mental programming that cultures provide. One person's definition of the relationship (e.g., friend) may not match that of the person with whom he or she interacts (e.g., fellow student), causing radically different expectations and interpretations of behaviors.

In solving the intercultural puzzle, it is critical to remember another valuable insight from Kluckhohn and Strodtbeck's foundational work. Although a culture (the collectivity of people) will make preferred choices about beliefs, values, and norms, not all cultural members will necessarily share all of those preferred choices, nor will they share them with the same degree of intensity.

A Dolharubang, a stone sculpture positioned outside of the town gates in ancient Korea, was believed to prevent all evil spirits from entering. The Dolharubang symbolizes a cultural belief about the relationship between the spiritual and the physical worlds. *(Copyright © Myron W. Lustig & Jolene Koester.)*

The immediate consequence of this conclusion for the development of intercultural competence is that every person represents the cultural group with which he or she identifies, but to a greater or lesser degree. A cultural pattern may be the preferred choice of most cultural members, but what can be accurately described for the culture in general cannot necessarily be assumed to be true for a specific individual. In simple terms, this principle translates into an important guideline for the development of intercultural competence: Even though you may have culture-specific information, you can never assume that

CULTURE CONNECTIONS

When I took Noah to visit a sick Maasai boy, it was the first time he had been to a hospital. What immediately impressed him was that most of the doctors wore eyeglasses. He assumed that the eyeglasses imbued their wearers with magical abilities to diagnose and cure diseases. Another time, he asked me to help him fill out a school form. It asked the color of his eyes. Did they mean the brown part, the white part, or the black ring? he asked. He had written down all three.

Source: Cheryl Bernstein, *Maasai Days* (New York: Anchor Books, 1989) 48.

every person from that culture matches the profile of the typical cultural member.

Because cultural patterns describe what people perceive as their reality, what they view as desirable, and how they should behave, there are repercussions for the motivational component of intercultural competence. Recall that communicators' feelings in intercultural interactions affect their ability to be open to alternative interpretations. Yet if cultural patterns predispose people to a particular definition of what is real, good, and right, reactions to others as unreal, bad, or wrong may create psychological distance between interactants. When confronting a set of beliefs, values, and norms that are inconsistent with their own, many people will negatively evaluate them. Strong emotional reactions are often predictable; after all, these variations from other cultures challenge the basic view people have of their world. Nevertheless, other cultures' ways of believing and their preferred values are not crazy or wrong, just different.

Cultural patterns form the basis for what is considered to be communicatively appropriate and effective. Examples that illustrate how beliefs, values, and norms set the boundaries of appropriateness and effectiveness include such instances as speaking your mind, in contrast to being quiet; defending yourself against a criticism, in contrast to accepting it; confronting another person about a problem rather than indirectly letting her or him know of the concern; and emphasizing the differences in status in relationships, in contrast to emphasizing commonality. Simply knowing what is appropriate and what has worked to accomplish your personal objectives in your own culture may not, and in all likelihood will not, have similar results when you interact with culturally different others. Intercultural competence usually requires alternative choices for actions. Consequently, we recommend that before acting, you should contemplate, draw on your culture-specific knowledge, and make behavioral choices that are appropriate for interacting with members of the other culture.

The patterns of a culture shape, but do not determine, the mental programming of its people. Because cultural patterns define how a person sees and defines reality, they are a powerful emotional force in competent intercultural interaction.

SUMMARY

This chapter began the discussion about cultural patterns, which are invisible differences that characterize cultures. Beliefs, values, and norms are the ingredients of cultural patterns. Beliefs are ideas that people assume to be true about the world. Values are the desired characteristics of a culture. Norms, the final component of cultural patterns, are socially shared expectations of appropriate behaviors.

Cultural patterns are shared among a group of people, and they form the foundation for maintenance of cultures. They are stable over relatively long periods of time, and they lead most members of a culture to behave in roughly similar ways when they encounter similar situations.

Florence Kluckhohn and Fred Strodtbeck's theory of value orientations suggests that each culture addresses common human issues with a preferred set of choices. However, not all people in the culture make exactly the same choices.

Edward Stewart and Milton Bennett focus on the way cultures orient themselves to activities, socia.l relations, the self, and the world. The activity orientation defines how people express themselves through activities and locate themselves on the being-becoming-doing continuum. The social relations orientation describes the preferred forms of interpersonal relationships within a culture. The self-orientation indicates the culture's conception of how people understand who they are in relation to others. The world orientation locates a culture in the physical and spiritual worlds.

6
CHAPTER

Cultural Patterns and Communication: Taxonomies

- TAXONOMIES OF CULTURAL PATTERNS
  Hall's High- and Low-Context Cultural Patterns
  Hofstede's Cultural Patterns
  Bond's Confucian Cultural Patterns

- CULTURAL TAXONOMIES AND
  INTERCULTURAL COMPETENCE

- SUMMARY

In the previous chapter, we provided an overview of the patterns that underlie all cultures. We described the nature of cultural patterns and the importance of beliefs, values, and norms in helping cultures to cope with problems. We now focus on specific conceptual taxonomies that are useful for understanding cultural differences.

We have chosen three different but related taxonomies to describe variations in cultural patterns. The first was developed by Edward Hall, who noted that cultures differ in the extent to which their primary message patterns are high context or low context. The second describes the ideas of Geert Hofstede, who identifies four dimensions along which cultures vary and provides a statistical profile of how and to what degree cultures actually differ from one another. The third describes the work of Michael Bond and his colleagues, who focus on an Asian perspective in their description of Confucian cultural values.

TAXONOMIES OF CULTURAL PATTERNS

As you read the descriptions of cultural patterns by Hall, Hofstede, and Bond, we caution you to remember three points. First, there is nothing sacred about these approaches and the internal categories they employ. Each approach takes the whole of cultural patterns (beliefs, values, and norms) and divides them in different ways.

Second, the parts of each of the systems are interrelated. We begin the description of each system at an arbitrarily chosen point, presupposing other parts of the system that have not yet been described. Cultural patterns are understandable not in isolation but as a unique whole.

Finally, individual members of a culture may vary greatly from the pattern that is typical of that culture. Therefore, as you study these approaches to cultural patterns, we encourage you to make some judgments about how your own culture fits into the pattern. Then, as you place it within the pattern, also try to discern how you, as an individual, fit into the patterns described. Similarly, as you learn about other cultural patterns, please remember that a specific person may or may not be a typical representative of that culture. As you study your own cultural patterns and those of other cultures, you improve the knowledge component of intercultural competence.

Hall's High- and Low-Context Cultural Patterns

Edward T. Hall, whose writings about the relationship between culture and communication are well-known, organizes cultures by the amount of information implied by the setting or context of the communication itself, regardless of the specific words that are spoken.[1] Hall argues that every human being is faced with so many perceptual stimuli—sights, sounds, smells, tastes, and bodily sensations—that it is impossible to pay attention to them all. Therefore, one of the functions of culture is to provide a screen between the person and all of those stimuli to indicate what perceptions to notice and how to interpret them. Hall's approach is compatible with the other approaches discussed in this chapter. Where it differs is the importance it places on the role of context.

According to Hall, cultures differ on a continuum that ranges from high to low context. High-context (HC) cultures prefer to use high-context messages in which most of the meaning is either implied by the physical setting or is presumed to be part of the individual's internalized beliefs, values, and norms; very little is provided in the coded, explicit, transmitted part of the message. Examples of high-context cultures include Japanese, African American, Mexican, and Latino cultures. Low-context (LC) cultures prefer to use low-context messages, in which the majority of the information is vested in the explicit code. Low-context cultures include German, Swedish, European American, and English cultures.

A simple example of high-context communication is interactions that take place in a long-term relationship between two people, who are often able to interpret even the slightest gesture or the briefest comment. The message does not need to be stated explicitly because it is carried in the shared understandings about the relationship.

A simple example of low-context communication is now experienced by more and more people as they interact with computers. For computers to "understand" a message, every statement must be very precise. Many computers will not accept or respond to instructions that do not have every space, period,

CULTURE CONNECTIONS

During the period of June 1–7, 1989 (the Tienanmen Square shooting occurred on June 3) there was much confusion regarding who was in control of the Chinese government and what their position would be toward political and economic reform in China. There were rumors that Chinese leader Deng Xiaopeng was dead and civil war was imminent. American politicians frequently made direct statements in support of the pro-democracy movement and called for the Chinese government to allow reform. . . .The Chinese government released no statements to clarify the situation. However, when Chinese Premier Li Peng (a conservative hard-liner) appeared on Chinese national television wearing a "Chairman Mao uniform" instead of the more common western business suit, viewers could easily interpret the government's position. The context (what he was wearing) spoke far louder than what he was doing (performing ceremonial protocol). The "Chairman Mao uniform" was popular during the conservative reign of Chairman Mao Tse Tung. The fact Premier Li Peng appeared on Chinese national television wearing such clothing indicated he was in charge and that he was a conservative leader. Nothing needed to be stated. In a low context culture such as the United States, we would expect our leader to state his or her position rather than to have to interpret intentions based on clothing.

Source: Jeannette Kenner Muir, *C-Span in the Communication Classroom* (Annandale, VA: Speech Communication Assoc., 1992) 98–99.

letter, and number in precisely the right location. The message must be overt and very explicit.

Hall's description of high- and low-context cultures is based on the idea that some cultures have a preponderance of messages that are high context, others have messages that are mostly low context, and some cultures have a mixture of both. Hall also describes other characteristics of high- and low-context cultures, which reveal the beliefs, values, and norms of the cultural system. These characteristics include the use of covert or overt messages, the importance of ingroups and outgroups, and the culture's orientation to time.

Use of Covert and Overt Messages   In a high-context culture such as Japan, meanings are internalized and there is a large emphasis on nonverbal codes. Hall describes messages in high-context cultures as almost preprogrammed, in which very little of the interpretation of the message is left to chance because people already know that in the context of the current situation, the communicative behaviors will have a specific and particular message. In low-context cultures, people look for the meaning of others' behaviors in the messages that

The Japanese tea ceremony is a perfect example of a high-context event in a high-context culture. The ceremony is a highly scripted and ritualized experience that is almost incomprehensible to those who have not been trained to understand the meanings in even the most subtle behaviors. Yet the meanings are unambiguous to those who have studied the ceremony. *(Photo by Martin Keene. © Topham-PA/The Image Works.)*

are plainly and explicitly coded. The details of the message are expressed precisely and specifically in the words that people use as they try to communicate with others.

Another way to think about the difference between high- and low-context cultures is to imagine something with which you are very familiar, such as repairing a car, cooking, sewing, or playing a particular sport. When you talk about that activity with someone else who is very familiar with it, you will probably be less explicit and instead use a more succinct set of verbal and nonverbal messages. You will talk in a verbal shorthand that does not require you to be specific and precise about every aspect of the ideas that you are expressing, because the others will know what you mean without their specific presentation. However, if you talk to someone who does not know very much about the activity, you will have to explain more, be more precise and specific, and provide more background information.

In a high context culture, much more is taken for granted and assumed to be shared, and consequently the overwhelming preponderance of messages are coded in such a way that they do not need to be explicitly and verbally transmitted. Instead, the demands of the situation and the shared meanings among the interactants mean that the preferred interpretation of the messages is already known.

The difference between high-context and low-context cultural styles is illustrated in a dialogue between a European American (low-context culture) and Malaysian (high-context culture); the Malaysian's message is revealed only by implication. Both people in the dialogue teach at a community college in the United States, and the Malaysian's objective in this conversation is to have the European American drive him off campus for lunch because he does not have a car.

> MALAYSIAN: Can I ask you a question?
> EUROPEAN AMERICAN: Yes, of course.
> MALAYSIAN: Do you know what time it is?
> EUROPEAN AMERICAN: Yes, it's two o'clock.
> MALAYSIAN: Might you have a little soup left in the pot?
> EUROPEAN AMERICAN: What? I don't understand.
> MALAYSIAN: (becoming more explicit since the colleague is not getting the point): I will be on campus teaching until nine o'clock tonight, a very long day for any person, let alone a hungry one!
> EUROPEAN AMERICAN: (finally getting the point): Would you like me to drive you to a restaurant off campus so you can have lunch?
> MALAYSIAN: What a very good idea you have!

Reactions in high-context cultures are likely to be reserved, whereas reactions in low-context cultures are frequently very explicit and readily observable. It is easy to understand why this is so. In high-context cultures, an important purpose in communicating is to promote and sustain harmony among the interactants. Unconstrained reactions could threaten the face or social esteem of others. In low-context cultures, however, an important purpose in communicating is to convey exact meaning. Explicit messages help to achieve this goal. If messages need to be explicit, so will people's reactions. Even when the message is understood, a person cannot assume that the meanings are clear in the absence of verbal messages coded specifically to provide feedback.

Importance of Ingroups and Outgroups   In high-context cultures, it is very easy to determine who is a member of the group and who is not. Because so much of the meaning of messages is embedded in the rules and rituals of situations, it is easy to tell who is acting according to those norms. As there are fixed and specific expectations for behaviors, deviations are easy to detect.

Another distinction concerns the emphasis placed on the individual in contrast to the group as a source of self-identity. In a high-context culture, the commitment between people is very strong and deep, and responsibility to

Table 6.1   CHARACTERISTICS OF LOW- AND HIGH-CONTEXT CULTURES

High-context cultures	Low-context cultures
Covert and implicit	Overt and explicit
Messages internalized	Messages plainly coded
Much nonverbal coding	Details verbalized
Reactions reserved	Reactions on the surface
Distinct ingroups & outgroups	Flexible ingroups & outgroups
Strong interpersonal bonds	Fragile interpersonal bonds
Commitment high	Commitment low
Time open and flexible	Time highly organized

others takes precedence over responsibility to oneself. Loyalties to families and the members of one's social and work groups are long-lasting and unchanging. This degree of loyalty differs from that found in a low-context culture, in which the bonds between people are very fragile and the extent of involvement and commitment to long-term relationships is lower.

Orientation to Time   The final distinguishable characteristic of high- and low-context cultures is their orientation to time. In the former, time is viewed as more open, less structured, more responsive to the immediate needs of people, and less subject to external goals and constraints. In low-context cultures, time is highly organized, in part because of the additional energy required to understand the messages of others. Low-context cultures are almost forced to pay more attention to time in order to complete the work of living with others.

As Table 6.1 indicates, Edward Hall's placement of cultures onto a continuum that is anchored by preferences for high-context messages and low-context messages offers a way to understand other variations in cultural patterns. A high-context culture chooses to use covert and implicit messages that rely heavily on nonverbal code systems. In a high-context culture, the group is very important, as are traditions, and members of the ingroup are easily recognized. Time is less structured and more responsive to people's needs. Low-context cultures are characterized by the opposite attributes: Messages are explicit and dependent on verbal codes, group memberships change rapidly, innovation is valued, and time is highly structured.

Hofstede's Cultural Patterns

Geert Hofstede's impressive studies of cultural differences in work-related value orientations offer another approach to understanding the range of cultural differences.[2] Hofstede's approach is based on the assertion that people carry mental programs that are developed during childhood and are reinforced by their culture. These mental programs contain the ideas of a culture and are expressed through its dominant values. To identify the principal values of different cultures, Hofstede surveyed over 100,000 employees of IBM, a large multinational business organization with branches in 72 countries. The fol-

CULTURE CONNECTIONS

Notice how Ann Landers, in devaluing obligations to elders and one's family, provides a typical U.S. American response to an interpersonal communication dilemma.

DEAR ANN: I come from a very large, middle-class, Asian family. We emigrated from Vietnam 10 years ago.

As a result of that unforgettable war, the desperation for freedom, being a refugee living in a foreign country with a different culture (Canada) and facing an uncertain future, I am mature beyond my years—yet I am treated like a child.

All my life I have been an obedient, dutiful daughter. Being the youngest girl in the family has its benefits, but there are also many drawbacks.

To explain: I am a straight-A student, but I am not allowed to have any dates even though I am now 22. I cannot go anywhere without my mother's permission. I must finish college, have a job, build a career and be what my family expects me to be. Ann, I feel like a prisoner.

Being raised in an Asian family will always assure obedient and dutiful children. My mother is very strict and domineering. I was trained to be an achiever. I am not permitted to have any close friends, male or female. Consequently, I have become a loner.

You'd be amazed how many Asian children are in this same position. Please don't suggest family counseling because that is definitely out of the question. Thank you for being a true friend in whom I can confide. Sign me . . .

OPPRESSED, REPRESSED
AND DEPRESSED IN
VANCOUVER, B.C.

DEAR VANCOUVER: With all due respect to your cultural heritage, a woman of 22 should be free to have friends, both male and female, so that she can develop culturally and emotionally as well as intellectually.

I urge you to discuss this problem with a professor at your school. Your mother's life has been a very hard one and she deserves respect, but you are entitled to a life of your own and I urge you to assert yourself.

Source: Ann Landers, *Los Angeles Times*, January 2, 1991, E6.

lowing descriptions are based on the information obtained in 50 countries and 3 regions with sample sizes large enough to permit valid inferences.[3]

Through theoretical reasoning and statistical analyses, Hofstede identified four dimensions along which dominant patterns of a culture can be ordered: power distance, uncertainty avoidance, individualism-collectivism, and masculinity-femininity. Recent evidence suggests that Hofstede's dimensions are applicable not only to work-related values but also to cultural values generally.[4]

As you consider Hofstedes dimensions, keep several cautions in mind: First, most of his data were collected from males in one large multinational corporation. Therefore, the respondents may represent a unique point of view based on gender, level of education, and other demographic and economic factors. Second, the 50 countries and 3 regions in Hofstede's study underrepresent some parts of the world, such as the countries that had been part of the Soviet Bloc, Arab countries, and countries from Africa other than South Africa. Since these countries represent large and important cultures, Hofstede's empirical identification of four dimensions of cultural values must not be taken as definitive. Finally, Hofstede collected his data over 20 years ago, and economic and political conditions that affect cultural patterns have changed dramatically in some of the countries. Nevertheless, his work represents the best available attempt to measure empirically the nature and strength of value differences among cultures.

Power Distance   One of the basic concerns in all cultures, and a problem for which they all must find a solution, is the issue of human inequality. Contrary to the claim in the U.S. Declaration of Independence that "all men are created equal," all people in a culture do not have equal levels of status or social power. Depending on the culture, some people might be regarded as superior to others because of their wealth, age, gender, education, physical strength, birth order, personal achievements, family background, occupation, or a wide variety of other characteristics.

Cultures also differ in the extent to which they view such status inequalities as good or bad, right or wrong, just or unjust, and fair or unfair. That is, all cultures have particular value orientations about the appropriateness or importance of status differences and social hierarchies. Hofstede refers to these variations as the *power distance* dimension, which reflects the degree to which the culture believes that institutional and organizational power should be distributed unequally and the decisions of the power holders should be challenged or accepted.

CULTURE CONNECTIONS

Gian Singh John, a recognized authority on Sikh culture, boiled it down to this: "The family is everything, the first priority to a Sikh. With us, it is not 'I,' it is 'we.' "

Source: "Sikh Culture Has Melded Smoothly in Yuba-Sutter," *Sacramento Bee,* February 17, 1991, B4.

Hofstede has created a power distance index (PDI) to assess a culture's relative location on the power distance dimension. At one extreme are such cultures as Austria, Denmark, Israel, and New Zealand. These cultures, all of which have relatively low PDIs and prefer small power distances as a cultural value, believe in the importance of minimizing social or class inequalities, questioning or challenging authority figures, reducing hierarchical organizational structures, and using power only for legitimate purposes. Conversely, cultures in the Arab countries, Guatemala, Malaysia, and the Philippines all have relatively high PDIs and prefer large power distances. They believe that each person has a rightful and protected place in the social order, that the actions of authorities should not be challenged or questioned, that hierarchy and inequality are appropriate and beneficial, and that those with social status have a right to use their power for whatever purposes and in whatever ways they deem desirable. Table 6.2 provides a numerical rating of the 50 countries and 3 regions on the power distance dimension.

Predictors of Power Distance   What can account for the differences in a culture's preferred level of power distance? Surprisingly, Hofstede suggests that three factors—climate, population size, and wealth—are strongly implicated.

Climate, as measured by geographical latitude, is by far the single best predictor of a culture's power distance. Cultures that live in high-latitude climates far from the equator, and therefore have moderate to cold climates, tend to have low PDI scores. Cultures that live in low-latitude climates near the equator, and therefore have tropical or subtropical climates, tend to have high PDI scores. Hofstede speculates that the relationship between climate and power distance occurs because of the extent to which a culture's climate requires the culture to invent technological solutions to the weather problems that threaten its very survival.

In colder and more extreme climates, human survival requires more protection against the hardships of nature. Consequently, survival and population growth can occur only if the culture can develop solutions that counteract the extreme forces of nature. The need for solutions to its climatic problems predisposes the culture to seek less traditional and more innovative answers to its common problems, which leads in turn to a greater need for modernization, mass literacy, independent thinking, decentralization of political power, technological innovations, and a general questioning of authority. Conversely, survival in warmer climates is far less dependent on intervention with nature. The need for technological solutions to problems is low, more traditional approaches to obstacles are preferred, formal mass education is not required for survival, and independent thinking is not as necessary. People are therefore more likely to learn from their elders, and consequently there is less questioning of authority in general.

Population size is another predictor of power distance. Generally speaking, the larger the culture, the greater the power distance is likely to be. As the

Table 6.2   RATINGS OF FIFTY COUNTRIES AND THREE REGIONS ON HOFSTEDE'S POWER DISTANCE DIMENSION

	Power Distance*		Power Distance*
Malaysia	218	South Korea	15
Guatemala	177	Iran	5
Panama	177	Taiwan	5
Philippines	172	Spain	1
Mexico	112	Pakistan	−8
Venezuela	112	Japan	−13
Arab Countries	107	Italy	−32
Ecuador	98	Argentina	−36
Indonesia	98	South Africa	−36
India	93	Jamaica	−55
West Africa	93	U.S.A	−78
Yugoslavia	89	Canada	−83
Singapore	79	Netherlands	−87
Brazil	56	Australia	−96
France	52	Costa Rica	−101
Hong Kong	52	Germany	−101
Colombia	47	Great Britain	−101
Salvador	42	Switzerland	−106
Turkey	42	Finland	−110
Belgium	38	Norway	−120
East Africa	33	Sweden	−120
Peru	33	Ireland	−133
Thailand	33	New Zealand	−161
Chile	29	Denmark	−180
Portugal	29	Israel	−203
Uruguay	19	Austria	−212
Greece	15		

*A large positive score means the country prefers a large power distance; a large negative score means the country prefers a small power distance. The average score is zero. Ratings are in standardized scores, with the decimal point omitted.

Source: Adapted from Geert Hofstede, *Cultures and Organizations: Software of the Mind* (London: McGraw-Hill, 1991) 26.

size of any social group increases, it must inevitably develop additional rules and formal procedures for coping with the increased complexities that arise. Additionally, large social groups will require more centralized concentrations of political power to function effectively. Consequently, for cultures with large populations to function effectively, they must adopt a political hierarchy that is more distant, more impersonal, and less accessible than that needed by

An accepted principle of many cultures requires people to show respect and acknowledge social differences. Bowing, and the depth of the bow, gives a clear indicator of the relative social status of these two men. The one bowing more deeply is subordinate to the other. *(Photograph by Marc Riboud. © Magnum Photos, Inc.)*

cultures with small populations. The need to concentrate political power in the hands of a few select people will help to create and reinforce a cultural norm that social hierarchy is desirable and that authorities should not be questioned or challenged.

Hofstede's third predictor of power distance is wealth. However, Hofstede suggests that it is the distribution of wealth, rather than the sheer amount of wealth, that best predicts power distance. His analyses reveal that the more unequally wealth is distributed within a culture, the greater the culture's power distance. More evenly distributed wealth is related to cultures that value education, technology, and a decentralization of political power. These attributes lead to an increased tendency to question authority and to value a small power distance. Conversely, an unequal distribution of wealth is related to a centralized political system, a decreased tendency to question the actions of authorities, and a large power distance.

Consequences of Power Distance   The consequences of the degree of power distance that a culture prefers are evident in family customs, the relationships between students and teachers, organizational practices, and in other areas of social life. Even the language systems in high-PDI cultures emphasize distinctions based on a social hierarchy.

Children raised in high-PDI cultures are expected to obey their parents without challenging or questioning them, while children raised in low-PDI cultures put less value on obedience and are taught to seek reasons or justifications for their parents' actions. Even the language of high-PDI cultures is more sensitive to hierarchical distinctions; the Chinese and Korean languages, for instance, have separate terms for older brother, oldest brother, younger sister, youngest sister, and so on.

Students in high-PDI cultures are expected to comply with the wishes and requests of their teachers, and conformity is regarded very favorably. As a consequence, the curriculum in high-PDI cultures is likely to involve a great deal of rote learning, and students are discouraged from asking questions because questions might pose a threat to the teacher's authority. In low-PDI cultures, students regard their independence as very important, and they are less likely to conform to the expectations of teachers or other authorities. The educational system itself reinforces the low-PDI values by teaching students to ask questions, to solve problems creatively and uniquely, and to challenge the evidence leading to conclusions.

In the business world, managers in high-PDI cultures are likely to prefer an autocratic or directive decision-making style, whereas subordinates in these cultures expect and want to be closely supervised. Alternatively, managers in low-PDI cultures prefer a consultative or participative decision-making style, and their subordinates expect a great deal of autonomy and independence as they do their work.

European Americans tend to have a relatively low power distance, though it is by no means exceptionally low. However, when European Americans communicate with people from cultures that value a relatively large power distance, problems related to differences in expectations are likely. For example, European American exchange students in a South American or Asian culture sometimes have difficulty adapting to a world in which people are expected to do as they are told without questioning the reasons for the requests. Conversely, exchange students visiting the United States from high-PDI cultures sometimes feel uneasy because they expect their teachers to direct and supervise their work closely, but they may have also been taught that it would be rude and impolite to ask for the kinds of information that might allow them to be more successful.

Uncertainty Avoidance   A second concern of all cultures is how they will adapt to changes and cope with uncertainties. The future will always be un-

CULTURE CONNECTIONS

My job was managing the household. I told Joseph I didn't want any servants,. . . Joseph wasn't listening.

"We can't afford servants," I protested. . . .

"You'll like Kamau," he said. "He is a good man."

"It's not a question of liking," I said. "I don't want a cook. It's ridiculous for the two of us to have a cook and a yard man."

"A man in my position must have servants. It's expected. In America, I kept silent and learned your ways. Now you must learn."

"But servants, Joseph? It's so un-American."

He laughed and took my hand. "Kamau is of my age group—we were initiated together. We will help him. It is not a matter of choice." As it turned out, many things were not a matter of choice—my husband's monthly salary contributed to the school fees of several brothers or cousins and our garden was freely harvested by his family.

Source: Geraldine Kennedy, *From the Center of the Earth* (Clove Park Press, 1991) 15.

known in some respects. This unpredictability and the resultant anxiety that inevitably occurs are basic in human experience.

Cultures differ in the extent to which they prefer and can tolerate ambiguity, and therefore in the means they select for coping with change. Thus, all cultures differ in their perceived need to be changeable and adaptable. Hofstede refers to these variations as the *uncertainty avoidance* dimension, the extent to which the culture feels threatened by ambiguous, uncertain situations and tries to avoid them by establishing more structure.

Hofstede has created an uncertainty avoidance index (UAI) to assess a culture's relative location along the uncertainty avoidance dimension. At one extreme are cultures such as Denmark, Jamaica, Ireland, and Singapore, all of which have relatively low UAIs. These cultures therefore have a high tolerance for uncertainty and ambiguity; they believe in minimizing the number of rules and rituals that govern social conduct and human behavior, in accepting and encouraging dissent among cultural members, in tolerating people who behave in ways that are considered socially deviant, and in taking risks and trying new things. Conversely, Greece, Guatemala, Portugal, and Uruguay all have relatively high UAIs and prefer to avoid uncertainty as a cultural value. These cultures desire or even demand consensus about societal goals, and they do not tolerate dissent or allow deviation in the behaviors of cultural members. They try to ensure certainty and security through an extensive set of rules and regulations. Table 6.3 provides a numerical rating of the 50 countries and 3 regions on the uncertainty avoidance dimension.

Table 6.3   RATINGS OF FIFTY COUNTRIES AND THREE REGIONS ON HOFSTEDE'S UNCERTAINTY AVOIDANCE DIMENSION

	Uncertainty Avoidance*		Uncertainty Avoidance*
Greece	193	Ecuador	6
Portugal	160	Germany	−2
Guatemala	148	Thailand	−6
Uruguay	143	Iran	−27
Belgium	119	Finland	−27
Salvador	119	Switzerland	−31
Japan	110	West Africa	−48
Yugoslavia	94	Netherlands	−52
Peru	89	East Africa	−56
France	85	Australia	−60
Chile	85	Norway	−64
Spain	85	South Africa	−68
CostaRica	85	New Zealand	−68
Panama	85	Indonesia	−72
Argentina	85	Canada	−72
Turkey	81	U.S.A.	−81
South Korea	81	Philippines	−89
Mexico	69	India	−106
Israel	65	Malaysia	−122
Colombia	60	Great Britain	−126
Venezuela	44	Ireland	−126
Brazil	44	Hong Kong	−157
Italy	40	Sweden	−151
Pakistan	19	Denmark	−176
Austria	19	Jamaica	−218
Taiwan	15	Singapore	−239
Arab Countries	11		

*A large positive score means the country prefers to avoid uncertainty; a large negative score means the country does not prefer to avoid uncertainty. The average score is zero. Ratings are in standardized scores, with the decimal point omitted.

Source: Adapted from Geert Hofstede, *Cultures and Organizations: Software of the Mind* (London: McGraw-Hill, 1991) 113.

Predictors of Uncertainty Avoidance   Unlike the power distance dimension, there are no straightforward explanations to account for the differences in a culture's preferred level of uncertainty avoidance. In general, high-UAI cultures tend to be those that are beginning to modernize and are therefore characterized by a high rate of change. Historically, these cultures tend to have an extensive system of legislative rules and laws with which to resolve disputes, and they often embrace religions such as Catholicism and Islam, which stress absolute certainties. Conversely, low-UAI cultures tend to be advanced in their level of modernization and are therefore more stable and predictable in their rate of change. These cultures are likely to have far fewer rules and laws that govern social conduct, preferring instead to resolve disputes by negotiation or conflict. They are also more likely to adopt religions such as Buddhism and Unitarianism, which emphasize relativity.

Consequences of Uncertainty Avoidance   Cultures must cope with the need to create a world that is more certain and predictable, and they do so by inventing rules and rituals to constrain human behaviors. Because members of high-UAI cultures tend to be worried about the future, they have high levels of anxiety and are highly resistant to change. They regard the uncertainties of life as a continuous threat that must be overcome. Consequently, high-UAI cultures develop many rules to control social behaviors, and they often adopt elaborate rituals and religious practices that have a precise form or sequence.

Members of low-UAI cultures tend to live day to day, and they are more willing to accept change and take risks. Conflict and competition are natural, dissent is acceptable, deviance is not threatening, and individual achievement is regarded as beneficial. Consequently, low-UAI cultures need few rules to control social behaviors, and they are unlikely to adopt religious rituals that require precise patterns of enactment.

Differences in level of uncertainty avoidance can result in unexpected problems in intercultural communication. For instance, European Americans tend to have a moderately low level of uncertainty avoidance. When these U.S. Americans communicate with someone from a high-UAI culture such as Japan or France, they are likely to be seen as too nonconforming and unconventional, and they may view their Japanese or French counterparts as rigid and overly controlled. Conversely, when these U.S. Americans communicate with someone from an extremely low-UAI country such as Ireland or Sweden, they are likely to be viewed as too structured and uncompromising, whereas they may perceive their Irish or Swedish counterparts as too willing to accept dissent.

Individualism-Collectivism   A third concern of all cultures involves people's relationships to the larger social groups of which they are a part. People must live and interact together for the culture to survive. In doing so, they must develop a way of relating that strikes a balance between showing concern for themselves and concern for others.

Cultures differ in the extent to which individual autonomy is regarded favorably or unfavorably. Thus, cultures vary in their tendency to encourage people to be unique and independent or conforming and interdependent. Hofstede refers to these variations as the *individualism-collectivism* dimension, the degree to which a culture relies on and has allegiance to the self or the group.

Hofstede has created an individualism index (IDV) to assess a culture's relative location on the individualism-collectivism dimension. At one extreme are Australia, Belgium, the Netherlands, and the United States. Such cultures, all of which have relatively high IDVs and therefore are highly individualistic, believe that people are only supposed to take care of themselves, and perhaps

CULTURE CONNECTIONS

At the center of the old Sioux society was the tiyospaye, the extended family group, the basic hunting band, which included grandparents, uncles, aunts, in-laws, and cousins. The tiyospaye was like a warm womb cradling all within it. Kids were never alone, always fussed over by not one but several mothers, watched and taught by several fathers. The real father, as a matter of fact, selected a second father, some well-thought-of relative with special skills as a hunter or medicine man, to help him bring up a boy, and such a person was called "Father" too. And the same was true for the girls. Grandparents in our tribe always held a special place for caring for the little ones, because they had more time to devote to them, when the father was out hunting, taking the mother with him to help with the skinning and butchering.

Source: Mary Crow Dog, *Lakota Woman* (New York: Harper Perennial, 1991).

their immediate families. In individualist cultures, the autonomy of the individual is paramount. Key words used to invoke this cultural pattern include *independence, privacy, self,* and the all-important *I.* Decisions are based on what is good for the individual, not the group, because the person is the primary source of motivation. Similarly, a judgment about what is right or wrong can be made only from the point of view of each individual.

Such cultures as Guatemala, Indonesia, Pakistan, and West Africa all have relatively low IDVs and prefer a collectivist orientation as a cultural value. These cultures require an absolute loyalty to the group, though the relevant group might be as varied as the nuclear family, the extended family, a caste or jati (a subgrouping of a caste), or even the organization for which a person works. In collectivist cultures, decisions that juxtapose the benefits to the individual and the benefits to the group are always based on what is best for the group, and the groups to which a person belongs are the most important social units. In turn, the group is expected to look out for and take care of its individual members. Consequently, collectivist cultures believe in obligations to the group, dependence of the individual on organizations and institutions, a "we" consciousness, and an emphasis on belonging. For example, Hui-Ching Chang and G. Richard Holt emphasize that the Chinese cultural pattern of relationships is built on an other-oriented perspective. Interpersonal bonding, from this point of view, is not due solely to "honest communication" but also has its basis in obligations and expectations that are already established and ongoing.[5] Table 6.4 provides a numerical rating of the 50 countries and three regions on the individualism-collectivism dimension.

Predictors of Individualism-Collectivism   There is a strong relationship between a culture's location on the power distance dimension and its location

Table 6.4   RATINGS OF FIFTY COUNTRIES AND THREE REGIONS ON HOFSTEDE'S INDIVIDUALISM-COLLECTIVISM DIMENSION

	Individualism*		Individualism*
U.S.A.	190	Turkey	−24
Australia	186	Uruguay	−28
Great Britain	182	Greece	−32
Canada	147	Philippines	−44
Netherlands	147	Mexico	−52
New Zealand	143	East Africa	−64
Italy	131	Yugoslavia	−64
Belgium	127	Portugal	−64
Denmark	123	Malaysia	−68
Sweden	111	Hong Kong	−72
France	111	Chile	−80
Ireland	107	West Africa	−92
Norway	103	Singapore	−92
Switzerland	99	Thailand	−92
Germany	95	Salvador	−96
South Africa	87	South Korea	−100
Finland	79	Taiwan	−103
Austria	47	Peru	−107
Israel	43	Costa Rica	−111
Spain	32	Pakistan	−115
India	20	Indonesia	−115
Japan	12	Colombia	−119
Argentina	12	Venezuela	−123
Iran	−8	Panama	−127
Jamaica	−16	Ecuador	−139
Brazil	−20	Guatemala	−147
Arab Countries	−20		

*A large positive score means the country prefers individualism; a large negative score means the country prefers collectivism. The average score is zero. Ratings are in standardized scores, with the decimal point omitted.

Source: Adapted from Geert Hofstede, *Cultures and Organizations: Software of the Mind* (London: McGraw-Hill, 1991) 53.

on the individualism-collectivism dimension. High-PDI cultures tend to be collectivistic, whereas low-PDI cultures tend to be individualistic. Consequently, there are some similarities to the power distance dimension in predicting a culture's level of individualism-collectivism.

The best predictor of individualism-collectivism is economic development; wealthy cultures tend to be individualistic, whereas poor cultures tend to be collectivistic. Though it is impossible to determine whether increased economic development leads to increased levels of individualism or vice

The cultural pattern in Thailand is collectivist, and university students proudly wear uniforms to their classes. *(Copyright © Myron W. Lustig & Jolene Koester.)*

versa, there is strong evidence to suggest that cultures become more individualistic as they become more economically advanced.

Another predictor is climate. Cultures in colder climates tend to be individualistic, whereas cultures in warmer climates tend to be collectivistic. As we suggested in the discussion of power distance, colder climates are likely to foster and support individual initiative and innovative solutions to problems, whereas warmer climates make individual achievements far less necessary.

Consequences of Individualism-Collectivism   Huge cultural differences can be explained by differences on the individualism-collectivism dimension. We have already noted that collectivistic cultures tend to be group-oriented. A related characteristic is that they typically impose a very large psychological distance between those who are members of their group (the ingroup) and those who are not (the outgroup). Ingroup members are required to have unquestioning loyalty, whereas outgroup members are regarded as almost inconsequential. Conversely, members of individualistic cultures do not perceive a large chasm between ingroup and outgroup members; ingroup members are not as close, but outgroup members are not as distant. Scholars such as Harry Triandis believe that the individualism-collectivism dimension is by far the most important attribute that distinguishes one culture from another.[6]

Individualist cultures train their members to speak out as a means of resolving difficulties. In classrooms, students from individualistic cultures are likely to ask questions of the teacher; students from collectivistic cultures are not. Similarly, people from individualistic cultures are more likely than those from collectivistic cultures to use confrontational strategies when dealing with interpersonal problems; those with a collectivistic orientation are likely to use avoidance, third-party intermediaries, or other face-saving techniques. Indeed, a common maxim among European Americans, who are highly individualistic, is that "the squeaky wheel gets the grease" (suggesting that one should make noises in order to be rewarded); the corresponding maxim among the Japanese, who are somewhat collectivistic, is "the nail that sticks up gets pounded" (so one should always try to blend in).

Masculinity-Femininity   The final issue that concerns all cultures, and for which they must all find solutions, pertains to the extent to which they prefer achievement and assertiveness or nurturance and social support. Hofstede refers to these variations as the *masculinity-femininity* dimension, though an alternative label is achievement-nurturance. This dimension indicates the degree to which a culture values such behaviors as assertiveness and the acquisition of wealth or caring for others and the quality of life.

Hofstede has created a masculinity index (MAS) to assess a culture's relative location along the masculinity-femininity dimension. At one extreme are such cultures as Austria, Italy, Japan, and Mexico. These cultures, all of which have a relatively high MAS, believe in achievement and ambition, in judging people on the basis of their performance, and in the right to display the material goods that have been acquired. The people in high-MAS cultures also believe in ostentatious manliness and very specific behaviors and products are associated with appropriate male behavior.

Low-MAS cultures, such as Chile, Portugal, Sweden, and Thailand, believe less in external achievements and shows of manliness and more in the importance of life choices that improve intrinsic aspects of the quality of life, such as service to others and sympathy for the unfortunate. People in these feminine cultures are also likely to prefer equality between the sexes, less prescriptive role behaviors associated with each gender, and an acceptance of nurturing roles for both women and men. Table 6.5 provides a numerical rating of the 50 countries and 3 regions on the masculinity-femininity dimension.

Predictors of Masculinity-Femininity   The best predictor of masculinity-femininity is climate. Masculine cultures tend to live in warmer climates near the equator, and feminine cultures typically reside in colder climates away from the equator. As he suggested in the argument relating climate to power distance, Hofstede speculates that colder climates require more technology for the culture to survive, which in turn imposes a need for education and equality. Hofstede extends this argument to include equality between the

Table 6.5 RATINGS OF FIFTY COUNTRIES AND THREE REGIONS ON HOFSTEDE'S MASCULINITY-FEMININITY DIMENSION

	Masculinity*		Masculinity*
Japan	255	Brazil	1
Austria	167	Singapore	-4
Venezuela	134	Israel	-10
Italy	117	Indonesia	-15
Switzerland	117	West Africa	-15
Mexico	112	Turkey	-21
Ireland	106	Taiwan	-21
Jamaica	106	Panama	-26
Great Britain	95	Iran	-32
Germany	95	France	-32
Philippines	84	Spain	-37
Colombia	84	Peru	-43
South Africa	79	East Africa	-48
Ecuador	79	Salvador	-54
U.S.A.	73	South Korea	-59
Australia	68	Uruguay	-65
New Zealand	51	Guatemala	-81
Greece	46	Thailand	-98
Hong Kong	46	Portugal	-114
Argentina	40	Chile	-125
India	40	Finland	-153
Belgium	29	Yugoslavia	-153
Arab Countries	23	Denmark	-180
Canada	18	Netherlands	-191
Malaysia	7	Norway	-224
Pakistan	7	Sweden	-241

A large positive score means the country prefers masculinity; a large negative score means the country prefers femininity. The average score is zero. Ratings are in standardized scores, with the decimal point omitted.

Source: Adapted from Geert Hofstede, *Cultures and Organizations: Software of the Mind* (London: McGraw-Hill, 1991) 84.

sexes because cold-weather climates impose a need for both men and women to master a set of complex skills that make sexual inequality less functional and therefore less likely.

Consequences of Masculinity-Femininity Members of highly masculine cultures believe that men should be assertive and women should be nurturant. Sex roles are clearly differentiated, and sexual inequality is regarded as beneficial. The reverse is true for members of highly feminine cultures: Men are far less interested in achievement, sex roles are far more fluid, and equality between the sexes is the norm.

Teachers in masculine cultures praise their best students because academic performance is rewarded highly. Similarly, male students in these high-MAS cultures strive to be competitive, visible, successful, and vocationally-oriented. In feminine cultures, teachers rarely praise individual achievements and academic performance because social accommodation is more highly regarded. Male students try to cooperate with one another and develop a sense of solidarity; they try to behave modestly and properly; they select subjects because they are intrinsically interesting rather than vocationally rewarding; and friendliness is much more important than brilliance.

Each of Hofstede's four dimensions provides insights into the influence of culture on the communication process. Cultures with similar configurations on the four dimensions would be likely to have similar communication patterns, and cultures that are very different from one another would probably behave dissimilarly. Table 6.6 groups the countries on the basis of their similarities.

Bond's Confucian Cultural Patterns

Michael H. Bond, a Canadian who has lived in Asia for the past 25 years, believes that the previously described taxonomies have a Western bias, as they were developed by scholars from Europe or the United States who necessarily brought to their work an implicit set of assumptions and categories about the types of cultural values they would likely find. To overcome this possible limitation, Bond assembled a large team of researchers from Hong Kong and Taiwan to develop and administer a Chinese Value Survey to university students in 23 countries around the world.[7]

Four dimensions of cultural patterns were found: integration, human-heartedness, moral discipline, and Confucian work dynamism. The first three correspond to dimensions of cultural patterns previously described by Hofstede.

The *integration* dimension refers broadly to a sense of social stability. Those high on this dimension value behaviors that display tolerance, noncompetitiveness, interpersonal harmony, and group solidarity. The integration dimension is closely related to Hofstede's individualism-collectivism dimension.

The *human-heartedness* dimension refers to a sense of gentleness and compassion. Those high on this dimension value expressions of patience, courtesy, and kindness toward others. The human-heartedness dimension is similar to Hofstede's masculinity-femininity dimension.

The *moral discipline* dimension refers to a sense of restraint and moderation in one's daily activities. Those high on this dimension prefer to follow the middle way, regard personal desires as a negative attribute, and attempt to keep themselves disinterested and pure in their activities and relationships. The moral discipline dimension is similar to Hofstede's dimension of power distance.

Table 6.6   GROUPINGS ON HOFSTEDE'S FOUR DIMENSIONS

Type of Culture	Characteristics	Countries or Regions
More Developed Latin	Medium to High PDI High UAI Medium to High IDV Medium MAS	Argentina, Belgium, Brazil, Italy, France, Spain
Less Developed Latin	Medium to High PDI High UAI Low IDV Low to High MAS	Chile, Columbia, Peru, Costa Rica, Ecuador, Guatemala, Mexico, Panama, Portugal, Salvador, Uruguay, Venezuela
Caribbean	Low PDI Low to Medium UAI Medium IDV High MAS	Jamaica
More Developed Asian	Medium PDI High UAI Medium IDV High MAS	Japan
Less Developed Asian	Medium to High PDI Low to Medium UAI Low IDV Medium MAS	Hong Kong, India, Indonesia, Malaysia, Pakistan, Philippines, Singapore, South Korea, Taiwan, Thailand
African	Medium to High PDI Low UAI Low IDV Medium to Low MAS	East Africa, West Africa
Near Eastern	Medium to High PDI Medium to High UAI Low IDV Medium MAS	Arab Countries, Greece, Iran, Turkey, Yugoslavia
Germanic	Low PDI Medium to High UAI Medium to High IDV Medium to High MAS	Austria, Germany, Israel, Switzerland
Anglo	Low PDI Low UAI High IDV High MAS	Australia, Canada, Great Britain, Ireland, New Zealand, South Africa, U.S.A.
Nordic	Low PDI Low to Medium UAI High IDV Low MAS	Denmark, Finland, Netherlands, Norway, Sweden

Source: Based on data reported in: Geert Hofstede, *Cultures and Organizations: Software of the Mind* (London: McGraw-Hill, 1991) 26, 53, 84, 113.

These children in Shanghai, China exemplify many of the values in Confucianism—group solidarity, courtesy, and hard work. *(© Alice Grossman Photographer, The Picture Cube.)*

The *Confucian work dynamism* dimension refers to a person's orientation toward life and work. Those at one extreme on this dimension admire persistence, thriftiness, a sense of shame, and status differences within interpersonal relationships; Hofstede suggests that these attributes all characterize people who have a long-term orientation toward life. Those at the other extreme on this dimension have a deep appreciation for tradition, personal steadiness and stability, maintaining the "face" of self and others, balance or reciprocity when greeting others, giving and receiving favors, and giving gifts, all of which reflect a short-term orientation toward changing events.[8] According to Bond, both ends of the continuum describe patterns that are consistent with the teachings of Confucius but are unrelated to Hofstede's cultural dimensions. Table 6.7 provides a numerical rating of 23 countries on the Confucian values dimension. Because Confucian cultural patterns are substantially different from those described in previous taxonomies, we will examine them in greater detail.[9]

Table 6.7 RATINGS OF TWENTY-THREE COUNTRIES ON BOND'S CONFUCIAN VALUES DIMENSION

	Confucian Value*
China	252
Hong Kong	175
Taiwan	143
Japan	119
South Korea	101
Brazil	66
India	52
Thailand	34
Singapore	6
Netherlands	−8
Bangladesh	−22
Sweden	−47
Poland	−50
Germany	−54
Australia	−54
New Zealand	−57
U.S.A.	−61
Great Britain	−75
Zimbabwe	−75
Canada	−82
Philippines	−96
Nigeria	−106
Pakistan	−163

*A large positive score means the country prefers the Confucian value of a long-term orientation; a large negative score means the country does not prefer the Confucian value of a long-term orientation and therefore prefers a short-term orientation. The average score is zero. Ratings are in standardized scores, with the decimal point omitted.

Source: Geert Hofstede, *Cultures and Organizations: Software of the Mind* (London: McGraw- Hill, 1991) 166.

Confucian Values Kong Fu Ze, who was renamed Confucius by Jesuit missionaries, was a Chinese civil servant of humble origins who lived about 2500 years ago. An intellectual like the Greek philosopher Socrates (who lived 80 years later), Confucius was known for his wit and great wisdom. He was regularly surrounded by many followers, who recorded his teachings and who provide us with what we now know of his ideas.

Confucianism is not a religion but a set of practical principles and ethical rules for daily life. Derived of what Confucius understood as the lessons of Chinese history, these ideas have long held a central place not only in China but also in Japan, Korea, and elsewhere in Asia. Key principles of Confucian teaching include the following:

CULTURE CONNECTIONS

She wasn't considering what a big risk I took to help her. She knew that if her mother found out about this, I would be in more trouble than she. Peanut was younger than I was, so I was responsible for her behavior. And I was scared of what Old Aunt and New Aunt would do.

Of course, you probably don't understand this kind of thinking, how I could be in trouble for Peanut, why I was scared. In China back then, you were always responsible to somebody else. It's not like here in the United States—freedom, independence, individual thinking, do what you want, disobey your mother. No such thing. Nobody ever said to me, "Be good, little girl, and I will give you a piece of candy." You did not get a reward for being good, that was expected. But if you were bad—your family could do anything to you, no reason needed.

Source: Amy Tan, *The Kitchen God's Wife* (New York:Ivy Books, 1991) 161–162.

1. *Social order and stability are based upon unequal relationships between people.* The five basic human relationships, and the essential social virtues that correspond to each role, include: leader and follower (justice and loyalty), father and son (love and closeness), husband and wife (initiative and obedience), older brother and younger brother (friendliness and reverence), and friends (mutual faithfulness). Each of these relationships, including those among friends (who differ, however slightly, in age and in other indicants of status), presumes the existence and legitimacy of a social hierarchy and the reciprocal, complementary obligations that each position in the hierarchy requires: the higher-status person in each pair must provide protection and consideration, while the lower-status person owes respect and obedience. Additionally, there are different norms for the degree and form of the respect or obedience that is shown, depending on whether the relationship is close or distant.

2. *The family is the prototype for all social relationships.* Like the outwardly-expanding rings resulting from a pebble tossed into a lake, the virtues learned within family relationships form the central core that specifies how to interact with others in the widening circle of social relationships. Similarly, the roles regulating family relationships can be extended to include the whole town, organization, or country. As Hui-Ching Chang and G. Richard Holt explain,

Since the family serves as the basis of the society, one relates to the outside world in the same way one relates to the family members. Even if there is no blood connection or marriage relation, Chinese are still able to follow the rules of ordering between interactants. The common rule, based on the Confucian teachings is: if the other is older than twice one's age, one must treat him like a father; if the other is older within ten years, one must treat him like one's elder brother; if the other is not older than five years, one can walk with him a minor distance to show respect. In other words, regardless of who one interacts with, one must follow the rules for ordering.[10]

Thus, a person is not an isolated individual concerned with personal gain and voluntary group membership; rather, like a proper family member, a person has obligations to seek the common good for the benefit of others, to "behave like your actions reflect on all Chinese."[11] As June Ock Yum suggests, this mutual interdependence "requires that one be affiliated with relatively small and tightly knit groups of people and have a relatively long identification with those groups."[12] From childhood onward, therefore, people are taught to make a sharp distinction between ingroup and outgroup members. Similarly, children are trained to act with restraint, to overcome their individuality, and to maintain the appearance of group harmony; a person's thoughts, however, remain free.

Harmony is sustained through the maintenance of "face," or people's sense of dignity, self-respect, and prestige. Indeed, the English word "face" is derived from the Chinese term, and losing one's social dignity is indeed akin to losing one's eyes, ears, nose, and mouth. Social relations, according to Confucius, should be conducted so that everyone's face is maintained. Thus, intermediaries are used to initiate social contacts and avoid conflicts, indirect language is used to avoid embarrassing confrontations, and formality is used to maintain a heightened sense of politeness that preserves face.

3. *Proper social behavior consists of not treating others as you would not like to be treated yourself.* This negatively phrased Golden Rule, which emphasizes benevolence toward others, does not extend as far as the Christian injunction to "Love thy enemy"; rather, Confucian teachings invoke this rule only in the context of a reciprocal relationship, where there are shared expectations about social obligations and responsibilities. This principle also refers to the kinds of people with whom others should associate; those who are upright, devoted, and learned are most desirable, while those who are fawning, flattering, and too eloquent should be avoided. Lest it seem that the burden for change and adaptation falls solely on the others with whom a person interacts, Confucius taught that a person must first learn to be sensitive to and sympathetic of others' feelings before she or he can expect to achieve harmonious relationships. Thus, a person should first examine her- or himself when problems in communication and interpersonal relationships arise. Ideally, people should learn to harmonize not only with others but with the universe as well.

4. *People should be skilled, educated, hard-working, thrifty, modest, patient, and persevering.* Teaching and learning is highly valued,

This admonition, in many languages, provides a warning to travelers in Thailand about proper behavior toward others. *(Copyright © Myron W. Lustig & Jolene Koester.)*

moderation in all things is preferred, conspicuous consumption is frowned on, losing one's temper is unacceptable, and persistence in solving difficult problems is widely valued. Because human nature is assumed to be inherently good, it is the responsibility of each individual to train his or her moral character in these standards of behavior. The goal of such practices is to help promote a world at peace, where no one needs to govern or be governed.

Comparing Bond to Hofstede   Hofstede recently concluded that three of his original four dimensions describe cultural expectations for particular social behaviors: power distance refers to relationships with people higher or lower in rank, individualism-collectivism to expected behaviors toward the group, and masculinity-femininity to the expectations surrounding gender differences.[13] As we suggested in Chapter 5, each of these dimensions of cultural patterns represents a universal social choice that must be made by all cultures and that is learned from the family and throughout the social institutions of a

CULTURE CONNECTIONS

I wanted my children to have the best combination: American circumstances and Chinese character. How could I know that these two things do not mix?

Source: Amy Tan, *The Joy Luck Club* (New York: Ivy Books, 1989).

culture: power distance is taught by the degree to which children are encouraged to have their own desires and motivations, individualism-collectivism by the degree of solidarity and expected unity in the family, and masculinity-femininity by the role models presented to children. It is not coincidental, therefore, that these three cultural patterns appear in surveys conducted from both a European and an Asian perspective.

Hofstede's fourth dimension, uncertainty avoidance, refers not to social behaviors but to people's search for truth. This dimension was found only when investigated by researchers with a European perspective, as the search for the one essential truth seems not to be as important in China and other Asian cultures as it is in western Europe. Conversely, Bond's fourth dimension, Confucian dynamism, refers to people's search for virtue. It was found only when investigated by researchers with an Asian perspective. The discrepancy in findings between the Asian and the European perspectives, Hofstede and Bond conclude, provides

> a powerful illustration of how fundamental a phenomenon culture really is. It not only affects our daily practices (the way we live, the way we are brought up, the way we manage, the way we are managed); it also affects the theories we are able to develop to explain our practices. Culture's grip on us is complete.[14]

CULTURAL TAXONOMIES AND INTERCULTURAL COMPETENCE

The major lesson in this chapter is that cultures vary systematically in their choices about solutions to basic human problems. The taxonomies presented offer lenses through which cultural variations can be understood and appreciated, rather than negatively evaluated and disregarded. The categories in these taxonomies can help you to describe the fundamental aspects of cultures. As frames of reference, they provide mechanisms to understand all intercultural communication events. In any intercultural encounter, people may be communicating from very different perceptions of what "reality" is, what is "good," and what is "correct" behavior. The competent intercultural communicator must recognize that cultural variations in addressing basic human is-

CULTURE CONNECTIONS

According to legend . . . all Japanese nationals are genealogically related to the emperor at some distant point.

That understanding of Japan was never more evident . . . than during the prolonged final illness and death of Emperor Hirohito in 1989. Over the three months that the emperor lay dying, the Japanese practiced a "self restraint" *(jishuku)* that included restrictions on loud music, neon advertisements, drinking parties, foreign travel, and highly visible festivities of any kind. The *jishuku* continued into the period of mourning after Hirohito's death. No explicit rules of conduct were ever published, because everyone seemed to know intuitively what was allowed.

Source: Ellen K. Coughlin, Review of *Off Center: Power and Culture Relations Between Japan and the United States* by Masao Miyoshi, *Chronicle of Higher Education,* November 27, 1991, A12.

sues such as social relations, emphasis on self or group, and preferences for verbal or nonverbal code usage will *always* be a factor in intercultural communication.

The taxonomies presented allow you to use culture-specific knowledge to improve intercultural competence. First, begin by seeking out information about the cultural patterns of those individuals with whom you engage in intercultural communication. To assist your understanding of the culture, select one of the taxonomies presented and seek information that allows you to create a profile of the culture's preferred choices. Libraries are a natural starting place for this kind of knowledge. So, too, are representatives of the culture. Engage them in conversation as you try to understand their culture. Most people welcome questions from a genuinely curious person. Be systematic in your search for information by using the categories thoroughly. Think about the interrelatedness of the various aspects of the culture's patterns.

Second, study the patterns of your own culture. Because you take your beliefs, values, and norms for granted, stepping outside of your cultural patterns by researching them is very useful. You might want to describe the preferences of your own culture by using one of the taxonomies.

The third step requires only a willingness to reflect on your personal preferences. Do your beliefs, values, and norms match those of the typical person in your culture? How do your choices coincide with and differ from the general cultural description?

Finally, mentally consider your own preferences by juxtaposing them with the description of the typical person from another culture. Note the similarities and differences in beliefs, values, and norms. Can you predict where misinterpretations may occur because of contrasting assumptions about what is important and good? For example, the European American who shares the culture's preference for directness would inevitably encounter difficulties in communication with a typical member of the Japanese culture or a typical Latino cultural member. Similarly, knowing that you value informality, and usually act accordingly, can help you to monitor your expressions when communicating with someone from a culture that prefers formality. The European American's concept of time as linear often causes problems in communication with people from other cultures. Interpretations of behavior as "late," "inattentive," or "disrespectful," rather than just "different," can produce alternative ways of viewing the ticking of the clock.

SUMMARY

This chapter discusses three important taxonomies that can be used to describe cultural variations. Edward Hall placed cultures on a continuum from high context to low context. High-context cultures prefer messages in which most of the meaning is either implied by the physical setting or is presumed to be part of the individual's internalized beliefs, values, and norms; low-context cultures prefer messages in which the information is contained within the explicit code.

Geert Hofstede identified four dimensions along which dominant patterns of a culture can be ordered: power distance, uncertainty avoidance, individualism-collectivism, and masculinity-femininity. The power distance dimension assesses the degree to which the culture believes that institutional power should be distributed equally or unequally. The uncertainty avoidance dimension describes the extent to which cultures prefer and can tolerate ambiguity and change. The individualism-collectivism dimension describes the degree to which a culture relies on and has allegiance to the self or the group. The masculinity-femininity dimension indicates the degree to which a culture values assertiveness and the acquisition of wealth or caring for others and the quality of life.

Michael Bond and his colleagues also identified four dimensions along which cultural patterns can be ordered: integration, human-heartedness, moral discipline, and Confucian work dynamism. The integration dimension refers to a culture's social stability and is similar to Hofstede's individualism-collectivism dimension. The human-heartedness dimension refers to a preference for gentleness and compassion and is similar to Hofstede's masculinity-femininity dimension. The moral discipline dimension refers to a sense of restraint and moderation and is similar to Hofstede's dimension of power distance. The Confucian work dynamism dimension refers to a long-term orientation toward life and work.

The taxonomies presented in this chapter offer alternative lenses through which cultures can be understood and appreciated. Taken together, they provide multiple frames of reference that can be used to understand intercultural communication.

PART **THREE**

Coding Intercultural Communication

7
CHAPTER

Verbal Intercultural Communication

In this chapter we consider the effects of language systems on people's ability to communicate interculturally. In so doing we explore the accuracy of a statement by the world-famous linguistic philosopher Ludwig Wittgenstein, who asserted that "the limits of my language are the limits of my world."

THE POWER OF LANGUAGE IN INTERCULTURAL COMMUNICATION

Consider the following examples, each of which illustrates the pivotal role language in human interaction:

A U.S. business executive is selected by her company for an important assignment in Belgium, not only because she has been very successful but also because she speaks French. She prepares her materials and presentation and sets off for Belgium with high expectations for landing a new contract for her firm. Once in Belgium, she learns that although the individuals in the Belgium company certainly speak French, and there are even individuals who speak German or English, their first language and the preferred language for conducting their business is Flemish. Both the U.S. business executive and her company failed to consider that Belgium is a multicultural and multilingual country populated by Walloons who speak French and Flemings who speak Flemish.

Vijay is a student from India who has just arrived in the United States to attend graduate school at a major university. Vijay began to learn English in primary school, and since his field of study is engineering, even his classes in the program leading to his Bachelor's degree were conducted in English. Vijay considers himself to be proficient in the English language. Nevertheless, during his first week on campus he is bewildered by the language of those around him. People seem to talk so fast that Vijay has difficulty differentiating one word from another. Even when he recognizes the words, he cannot quite understand what people mean by them. His dormitory roommate seemed to say, "I'll catch you later" when he left the room. The secretary in the departmental office tried to explain to him about his teaching assistantship and the students assigned to the classes he was helping to instruct. Her references to students who would attempt to "crash" the course were very puzzling to him. His new faculty advisor, sensing Vijay's anxiety about all of these new situations, told him to "hang loose" and "go with the flow." When Vijay inquired of another teaching assistant about the meaning of these words, the teaching assistant's only reaction was to shake his head and say, "Your advisor's from another time zone!" Needless to say, Vijay's bewilderment continued.

Language—whether it is English, French, Swahili, Flemish, Hindi, or one of the world's other numerous languages—is a taken-for-granted aspect of people's lives. Language is learned without conscious awareness. Children are capable of using their language competently before the age of formal schooling. Even during their school years, they learn the rules and words of the language and do not attend to how the language influences the way they think and perceive the world. It is usually only when people speak their language to those who do not understand it or when they struggle to become competent in another language that they recognize language's central role in the ability to function, to accomplish tasks, and most important, to interact with others. It is only when the use of language no longer connects people to others or when individuals are denied the use of their language that they recognize its importance.

CULTURE CONNECTIONS

Say "language" and you are saying pride, identity, roots, communication, and all the things that stir the heart. As President Mario Soares of Portugal put it: "My country is my language."

Source: David Lawday, " 'Unity' Spells Trouble," *Atlantic Monthly*, April 1990: 30.

There is a set of circumstances involving communication with people from other cultural backgrounds in which awareness of language becomes paramount. Intercultural communication usually means interaction between people who speak different languages. Even when the individuals seem to be speaking the same language—a person from Spain interacting with someone from Venezuela, a French Canadian conversing with a French-speaking citizen of Belgium, or a British person visiting the United States—the differences in the specific dialects of the language and the different cultural practices that govern language use can mystify those involved and they can realistically be portrayed as two people who speak different languages.

In this chapter we explore the nature of language and how verbal codes affect communication between people of different cultural backgrounds. Because this book is written in English and initially intended for publication and distribution in the United States, many of the examples and comparisons refer to characteristics of the English language as it is used in the United States. We begin with a discussion of the characteristics and rule systems that create verbal codes and the process of interpretation from one verbal code to another. We then turn to a discussion of the all-important topic of the relationship among language, culture, thought, and intercultural communication. As we consider this issue, we explore the Sapir-Whorf hypothesis of linguistic relativity and assess the scholarly evidence that has been amassed both in support of the hypothesis and in opposition to it. We also consider the importance of language in the identity of ethnic and cultural groups. The chapter concludes with a consideration of verbal codes and intercultural competence.

DEFINITION OF VERBAL CODES

Discussions about the uniqueness of human beings usually center on our capability to manipulate and understand symbols that allow interaction with others. In a discussion of the importance of language, Charles F. Hockett noted that language allows people to understand messages about many different topics from literally thousands of people. Language allows us to talk with others, to understand or disagree with them, to make plans, to remember the past, to imagine future events, and to describe and evaluate objects and experiences that exist in some other location. Hockett also pointed out that language is taught to individuals by others and thus is transmitted from generation to generation in much the same way as culture. In other words, language is learned.[1]

Popular references to language often include not only spoken and written language but also "body language." However, we prefer to study the latter under the more encompassing description of nonverbal codes in Chapter 8. Here we will concentrate on understanding the relationship of spoken and written language, or verbal codes, to intercultural communication competence.

Can you guess what the yellow vehicle identified in Malay as "Bas Sekolah" is used for? *(Copyright © Myron W. Lustig & Jolene Koester.)*

The Features of Language

Verbal means "word." Therefore, a *verbal code* is *a set of rules about the use of words in the creation of messages*. Words can obviously be either spoken or written. Verbal codes, then, include both oral (spoken) language and nonoral (written) language.

Children first learn the oral form of a language. Parents do not expect two-year-olds to read the words on the pages of books. Instead, as parents speak aloud to a child, they identify or name objects in order to teach the child the relationship between the language and the objects or ideas the language represents. In contrast, learning a second language as an adolescent or adult often proceeds more formally, with a combination of oral and nonoral approaches. Students in a foreign language class are usually required to buy a textbook that contains written forms of the language, which then guide students in understanding both the oral and the written use of the language.

The concept of a written language is familiar to all students enrolled in U.S. college and university classes, as they all require at least reasonable proficiency in the nonoral form of the English language. Fewer and fewer languages exist only in oral form. When anthropologists and linguists discover a culture that has a unique oral language, they usually attempt to develop a written form of it in order to preserve it. Indeed, many Hmong who immigrated to the United States from their hill tribes in Southeast Asia have had to learn not only the new language of English but also, in many instances, the basic fact that verbal codes can be expressed in written form. Imagine the enormous task it must be not only to learn a second language but also first to understand that language can be written.

Our concern in this chapter is principally with the spoken verbal codes that are used in face-to-face intercultural communication. Nevertheless, because the written language also influences the way the language is used orally, written verbal codes play a supporting role in our discussion, and some of our examples and illustrations draw on written expressions of verbal codes in intercultural communication.

An essential ingredient of both verbal and nonverbal codes is symbols. As you recall from Chapter 2, symbols are words, actions, or objects that stand for or represent a unit of meaning. The relationship between symbols and what they stand for is often highly arbitrary, particularly for verbal symbols.

Another critical ingredient of verbal codes is the system of rules that governs the composition and ordering of the symbols. Everyone has had to learn the rules of a language—how to spell, correct grammar, and vocabulary—and to gain enough mastery of the language to tell jokes, to poke fun, and to be sarcastic. Even more than differences in the symbols themselves, it is the variations in rules for ordering and using symbols that produce the different languages people use.

Rule Systems in Verbal Codes

Five different but interrelated sets of rules combine to create a verbal code, or language. These parts or components of language are called phonology, morphology, semantics, syntactics, and pragmatics.

Phonology   When you listen to someone who speaks a language other than your own, you will often hear different (some might even say "strange") sounds. The basic sound units of a language are called *phonemes*, and the rules for combining phonemes constitute the *phonology* of a language. Examples of phonemes in English include the sounds you make when speaking, such as [k], [t], or [a].

The phonological rules of a language tell speakers which sounds to use and how to order them. For instance, the word *cat* has three phonemes: a hard [k] sound, the short [a] vowel, and the [t] sound. These same three sounds, or phonemes, can be rearranged to form other combinations: *act*, *tack*, or even *tka*. Of course, as someone who speaks and writes English, your knowledge of the rules for creating appropriate combinations of phonemes undoubtedly suggests to you that *tka* is improper. Interestingly, you know that *tka* is incorrect even though you probably cannot describe the rules that make it so.[2]

Languages have different numbers of phonemes. English, for example, depends on about 45 phonemes. The number of phonemes in other languages range from as few as 15 to as many as 85.[3]

Mastery of another language requires practice in reproducing its sounds accurately. Sometimes it is difficult to hear the distinctions in the sounds

Each language is a composite of rules that identify the appropriate sounds, their correct order, and their corresponding meanings. As this Thai menu shows, learning a new language sometimes requires a completely new alphabet. *(Copyright © Myron W. Lustig & Jolene Koester.)*

made by those proficient in the language. Even when the differences can be heard, the mouths and tongues of those learning another language are sometimes unable to produce these sounds. In intercultural communication, imperfect rendering of the phonology of a language—in other words, not speaking the sounds as native speakers do—can make it difficult to be understood accurately. Accents of second-language speakers, which we discuss in more detail later in this chapter, can provoke negative reactions in native speakers.

Morphology Phonemes combine to form *morphemes*, which are the smallest units of meaning in a language. The 45 English phonemes can be used to generate more than 50 million morphemes! For instance, the word *comfort*, whose meaning refers to a state of ease and contentment, contains one morpheme. But the word *comforted* contains two morphemes: *comfort* and *-ed*. The latter is a suffix that means that the comforting action or activity happened in the past. Indeed, though all words contain at least one morpheme, some words (such as *uncomfortable*, which has three morphemes) can contain

CULTURE CONNECTIONS

The multilingual Dutch are worried that the expansion of the European Union (EU) could sound the death knell for their mother tongue.

No longer content to sit back and watch while English, French, and German conquer the Netherlands, they have gone on the offensive to fight for the rights of their native language.

Part of the problem is the Dutch ability to master foreign languages and their constant exposure to them.

Films and television programs from abroad are usually shown in their original languages. Foreign books and newspapers are widely read in a country where all children start to learn English at the age of 10.

Source: "Polyglot Dutch Worry That European Unity Will Doom Language," *The Christian Science Monitor,* January 26, 1994.

two or more. Note that morphemes refer only to meaning units. Though the word *comfort* contains smaller words such as *or* or *fort*, these other words are coincidental to the basic meaning of *comfort*.

Semantics   As noted above, morphemes—either singly or in combination—are used to form words. The study of the meaning of words is called *semantics*. The most convenient and thorough source of information about the semantics of a language is the dictionary, which defines what a word means in a particular language. A more formal way of describing the study of semantics is to say that it is the study of the relationship between words and what they stand for or represent. You can see the semantics of a language in action when a baby is being taught to name the parts of the body. Someone skilled in the language points to and touches the baby's nose and simultaneously vocalizes the word *nose*. Essentially, the baby is being taught the vocabulary of a language. Competent communication in any language requires knowledge of the words needed to express ideas. You have probably experienced the frustration of trying to describe an event but not being able to think of words that accurately convey the intended meaning. Part of what we are trying to accomplish with this book is to give you a vocabulary that can be used to understand and explain the nature of intercultural communication competence.

Communicating interculturally necessitates learning a new set of semantic rules. The baby that grows up where people speak Swahili does not learn to say *nose* when the protruding portion of the face is touched; instead, he or she is taught to say *pua*. For an English speaker to talk with a Swahili speaker about his or her nose, at least one of them must learn the word for nose in the other's language. When learning a second language, much time is devoted to learning the appropriate associations between the words and the specific objects, events, or feelings that the language system assigns to them. Even those whose intercultural communication occurs with people who speak the "same" language must learn at least some new vocabulary. The U.S. American visiting Great Britain will confront new meanings for words. *Boot* refers to the storage place in a car, or what the U.S.-English-speaking person would call the *trunk*. *Chips* to the British is *French fries* to the U.S. American. A Band-Aid in the United States is called a *plug* in Great Britain. As Winston Churchill so wryly suggested, the two countries are indeed "divided by a common language."

The discussion of semantics is incomplete without noting one other important distinction: the difference between the denotative and connotative meanings of words. *Denotative meanings* are the public, objective, and legal meanings of a word. Denotative meanings are those found in the dictionary or law books. In contrast, *connotative meanings* are personal, emotionally charged, private, and specific to a particular person.

As an illustration, consider a common classroom event known as a *test*. When used by a college professor who is speaking to a group of undergraduate students, *test* is a relatively easy word to define denotatively. It is a formal examination that is used to assess a person's degree of knowledge or skill. But the connotative meanings of *test* probably vary greatly from student to student; some react to the idea with panic, and others are blasé and casual. Whereas denotative meanings tell us, in an abstract sense, what the words mean objectively, our interest in intercultural communication suggests that an understanding of the connotative meanings—the feelings and thoughts evoked in others as a result of the words used in the conversation—is critical to achieving intercultural competence.

As an example of the importance of connotative meanings, consider the experience reported by a Nigerian student who was attending a university in the United States. When working with a fellow male student who was African American, the Nigerian called to him by saying, "Hey, boy, come over here." To the Nigerian student, the term *boy* connotes a friendly and familiar relationship, is a common form of address in Nigeria, and is often used to convey a perception of a strong interpersonal bond. To the African American student, however, the term *boy* evokes images of racism, oppression, and an attempt to place him in an inferior social status. Fortunately, the two students were friends and were able to talk to each other to clarify how they each interpreted the Nigerian student's semantic choices; further misunderstandings were avoided. Often, however, such opportunities for clarification do not occur.

Another example is seen in a casual conversation of a U.S. American student and an Arab student. The former had heard a radio news story about the intelligence of pigs and was recounting the story as "fact" when the Arab student forcefully declared, "Pigs are dirty animals, and they are very dumb." The U.S. American student describes her reaction: "In my ignorance, I argued with him by telling him that it was true and had been scientifically proven." It was only later that she learned that as part of the religious beliefs of devout Muslims, pigs are believed to be unclean. Learning the connotative meanings of language is essential in achieving competence in another culture's verbal code.

Syntactics   The fourth component of language is *syntactics*, the relationship of words to one another. When children are first learning how to combine words into phrases, they are being introduced to the syntactics of their language. Each language stipulates the correct way to arrange words. In English it is not acceptable to create a sentence such as the following: "On by the book desk door is the the." It is incorrect to place the preposition *by* immediately following the preposition *on*. Instead, each preposition must have an object, which results in phrases such as "on the desk" and "by the door." Similarly, articles such as *the* in a sentence are not to be presented one right after the other. Instead, the article is placed near the noun, which produces a sentence that includes "the book," "the door," and "the desk." The syntactics of English grammar suggest that the words in the preceding nonsense sentence might be rearranged to form the grammatically correct sentence "The book is on the desk by the door." The order of the words helps establish the meaning of the utterance.

Each language has a set of rules that govern the sequence of the words. To learn another language you must learn those rules. The sentence "John has, to the store to buy some eggs, gone" is an incorrect example of English syntax but an accurate representation of German syntax.

Pragmatics   The final component of all verbal codes is *pragmatics*, the effect of language on human perceptions and behaviors. The study of pragmatics focuses on how language is actually used. A pragmatic analysis of language goes beyond phonology, morphology, semantics, and syntactics. Instead, it considers how users of a particular language are able to understand the meanings of specific utterances in particular contexts. By learning the pragmatics of language use, you understand how to participate in a conversation and you know how to sequence the sentences you speak as part of a conversation. For example, when you are eating a meal with a group of people and somebody says, "Is there any salt?", you know that you should give the person the salt shaker rather than simply answer "yes."

To illustrate how the pragmatics of language use can affect intercultural communication, imagine yourself as a dinner guest in a Pakistani household. You have just eaten a delicious meal. You are relatively full but not so full that it would be impossible for you to eat more if it was considered socially appropriate to do so. Consider the following dialogue:

> HOSTESS: I see that your plate is empty. Would you like some more curry?
>
> YOU: No, thank you. It was delicious, but I'm quite full.
>
> HOSTESS: Please, you must have some more to eat.
>
> YOU: No, no thank you. I've really had enough. It was just great, but I can't eat another bite.
>
> HOSTESS: Are you sure that you won't have any more? You really seemed to enjoy the brinjals.

What is your next response? What is the socially appropriate answer? Is the hostess pressing you to have another helping because in her culture your reply is not interpreted as a true negative response until you have given it at least three times? Or is it considered socially inappropriate for a dinner guest not to accept a second helping of food? Even if you knew Urdu, the language spoken in Pakistan, you would have to understand the pragmatics of language use in order to respond appropriately.

The rules governing the pragmatics of a language are firmly embedded in the larger rules of the culture and are intimately associated with the cultural patterns discussed in Chapters 5 and 6. For example, cultures vary in the degree to which they encourage people to ask direct questions and to make direct statements. Imagine a student from the United States who speaks some Japanese and who subsequently goes to Japan as an exchange student. The U.S. American's culturally learned tendency is to deal with problems directly, and he may therefore confront his Japanese roommate about the latter's habits in order to "clear the air" and establish an "open" relationship. Given the Japanese cultural preference for indirectness and face-saving behaviors, the U.S. American student's skill in Japanese does not extend to the pragmatics of language use. As Wen-Shu Lee suggests, these differences in the pragmatic rule systems of languages also make it very difficult to tell a joke—or even to understand a joke—in a second language.[4] Humor requires a subtle knowledge of both the expected meanings of the words (semantics) and their intended effects (pragmatics).

Interpretation and Intercultural Communication

Translation can be defined as the use of verbal signs to understand the verbal signs of another language.[5] Translation usually refers to the transfer of written verbal codes between languages. *Interpretation* refers to the oral process of moving from one code to another. When heads of state meet, they are accompanied by an interpreter. The translator, in contrast to the interpreter, usually has more time to consider how she or he wants to phrase a particular passage in a text. Interpreters must make virtually immediate decisions about which words or phrases would best represent the meanings of the speaker.

The Role of Interpretation in Today's World   Issues surrounding the interpretation of verbal codes from one language to another are becoming more and more important for all of us. Such issues include whether the words or the ideas of the original should be conveyed, whether the translation should reflect the style of the original or that of the translator, and whether an interpreter should correct cultural mistakes.

In today's global marketplace, health-care workers, teachers, government workers, and businesspeople of all types find that they are increasingly required to use professional interpreters to communicate verbally with their clients and thus fulfill their professional obligations.[6] Similarly, instructions for assembling consumer products that are sold in the United States but manufactured in another country often demonstrate the difficulty in moving from

This store announces its services in multiple languages. *(Gabor Demjen Photographer, Stock, Boston.)*

one language to another. Even though the words on the printed instruction sheet are in English, the instructions may not be correct or accurately interpreted.

Issues in interpretation, then, are very important. People involved in intercultural transactions must often depend on the services of multilingual individuals who can help to bridge the intercultural communication gap.

Types of Equivalence   If the goal in interpreting from one language to another is to represent the source language as closely as possible, a simpler way of describing the goal is with the term *equivalence*. Those concerned about developing a science of translation have described a number of different types of equivalence. *Dynamic equivalence* has been offered as one goal of good translation and interpretation.[7] Five kinds of equivalence must be considered in moving from one language to another; vocabulary, idiomatic, grammatical-syntactical, experiential, and conceptual equivalence.[8]

Vocabulary Equivalence   To establish vocabulary equivalence, the interpreter seeks a word in the target language that has the same meaning in the source language. This is sometimes very difficult to do. Perhaps the words

CULTURE CONNECTIONS

In Phoenix, Spanish-speakers who don't declare plants, fruits and vegetables when trying to clear U.S. Customs wind up dead. At least that's what a new bilingual sign said.

Sky Harbor International Airport posted bilingual signs this week in preparation for two airlines' flights to Mexico. But they were riddled with incorrect words, misspellings and mixed tenses and sexes.

One sign warned travelers who don't declare all plants, fruits, vegetables and meats: "Violadores Seran Finados." Officials meant that violators would be fined, but the sign really said: "Violators Will Be Deceased."

Worse, "violadores" is commonly used to refer to rapists in some parts of Mexico, said Eva Ramirez, a Spanish language teaching associate at Arizona State University.

One sign omitted a tilde—the squiggly mark over an "n" in Spanish—in the word "año," thus changing its meaning from "year" to "anus." The sign dealt with the state's drinking age of 21.

The signs were gone Friday, a day after Mayor Paul Johnson, who had asked for the bilingual signs, ordered them removed.

"The airport hired a poor translator," City Manager Frank Fairbanks said. "We certainly regret it. We apologize to anybody we may have offended."

He said airport workers would try to fix the signs with the help of a station manager from Aeromexico.

Source: "Airport's Message Lost in Translation," *Sacramento Bee,* May 30, 1992, 15.

spoken in the source language have no direct equivalents in the target language. For instance, in Igbo, a language spoken in Nigeria, there is no word for *window*. The word in Igbo that is used to represent a window, *mpio*, actually means "opening." Likewise, there is no word for *efficiency* in the Russian language, and the English phrase "A house is not a home" has no genuine vocabulary equivalent in Spanish. Alternatively, there may be several words in the target language that have similar meanings to the word in the source language, so the interpreter must select the word that best fits the intended ideas. An interpreter will sometimes use a combination of words in the target language to approximate the original word, or the interpreter may offer several different words to help the listener understand the meaning of the original message.

Idiomatic Equivalence An idiom is an expression that has a meaning contrary to the usual meaning of the words. Phrases such as "Eat your heart out," "It's raining cats and dogs," and "Eat humble pie" are all examples of id-

Could you order from this menu in Prague? *(Copyright © Myron W. Lustig & Jolene Koester.)*

ioms. Idioms are so much a part of language that people are rarely aware of using them. Think of the literal meaning of the following idiom: "I was so upset I could have died." Or consider the plight of a Malaysian student who described his befuddlement when his fellow students in the United States initiated conversations by asking, "What's up?" His instinctive reaction was to look up, but after doing so several times he realized that the question was an opening to conversation rather than a literal reference to something happening above him. Another example is the request a supervisor in a university media center made to a student assistant from India, who tended to take conversations and instructions literally. The supervisor instructed the assistant to "put this videotape on the television." The supervisor was later surprised to learn that the videotape was literally placed on top of the television, instead of being played for the class. The challenge for interpreters is to understand the intended meanings of idiomatic expressions and to translate them into the other language.

Grammatical-Syntactical Equivalence   The discussion later in this chapter about some of the variations among grammars highlights the problems in establishing equivalence in grammatical or syntactical rule systems. Quite simply, some languages make grammatical distinctions that others do not. For instance, when translating from the Hopi language into English, the interpreter has to make adjustments for the lack of verb tenses in Hopi because tense is a necessary characteristic of every English utterance.

Experiential Equivalence   Differing life experiences are another hurdle the interpreter must overcome. The words presented must have some mean-

CULTURE CONNECTIONS

While others worry about the pollution of their language by foreign words, English always has room for more. For example, "detente" and "elite" come from French, "sauna" from Finnish and "tomato" from Nahuatl.

Here are 10 words and phrases that have no equivalent in English, and are selected from the book, "They Have a Word For It," by Howard Rheingold.

1. **Cavioli riscaldati** (Italian)—The attempt to revive a dead love affair. Literally, "reheated cabbage," usually unworkable and messy.
2. **Dohada** (Sanskrit)—Unorthodox cravings of pregnant women.
3. **Drachenfutter** (German)—A gift brought home from a husband to his wife after he has stayed out late. Literally, "dragon fodder."
4. **Esprit de L'escalier** (French)—The brilliantly witty response to a public insult that comes into your mind only after you have left the party. Literally "the spirit of the staircase."
5. **Kyoikumama** (Japanese)—A mother who pushes her children into academic achievement. A derogatory term which literally means "education mama."
6. **Nakhes** (Yiddish)—A mixture of pleasure and pride, particularly the kind that a parent gets from a child.
7. **Ondinnonk** (Iroquoian)—The soul's innermost benevolent desires or the angelic parts of human nature.
8. **Razbliuto** (Russian)—The feeling a man has for someone he once loved but now does not.
9. **Schaddenfreude** (German)—The joy that one feels as a result of someone else's misfortune. Like seeing a rival slip on a banana peel.
10. **Tartle** (Scottish)—To hesitate in recognizing a person or thing, as happens when you are reintroduced to someone whose name you cannot recall.

Source: Howard Rheingold, They Have a Word for It.

ing within the experiential framework of the person to whom the message is directed. If people have never seen a television, for instance, a translation of the phrase "I am going to stay home tonight and watch television" would have virtually no meaning to them. Similarly, though clocks are a common device for telling time and they govern the behaviors of most U.S. Americans, many people live in cultures in which there are no clocks and no words for this concept. Some Hmong people, upon moving to the United States, initially had difficulty with the everyday experience of telling time with a clock.

Conceptual Equivalence Conceptual equivalence takes us back to the discussion in Chapters 5 and 6 about cultural patterns being part of a person's definition of reality. Conversation with people with radically different cultural patterns requires making sense of the variety of concepts that each culture defines as real and good.

LANGUAGE, THOUGHT, CULTURE, AND INTERCULTURAL COMMUNICATION

Every language has its own unique features and ways of allowing those who speak it to identify specific objects and experiences. These linguistic features, which distinguish each language from all others, affect how the speakers of the language perceive and experience the world. To understand the effects of language on intercultural communication, questions such as the following must be explored:

- How do initial experiences with language shape or influence the way in which a person thinks?
- Do the categories of a language—its words, grammar, and usage—influence how people think and behave?

More specifically, consider the following question:

- Does a person who learns to speak and write Arabic, when growing up in Saudi Arabia, "see" and "experience" the world differently than does a person who grows up speaking and writing Tagalog in the Philippines?

Although many scholars have advanced ideas and theories about the relationships among language, thought, culture, and intercultural communication, the names most often associated with these issues are Benjamin Lee Whorf and Edward Sapir. Their theory is called linguistic relativity.

The Sapir-Whorf Hypothesis of Linguistic Relativity

Until the early part of the twentieth century, in Western Europe and the United States language was generally assumed to be a neutral medium that did not influence the way people experienced the world.[9] During that time, the answer to the preceding question would have been that regardless of whether people grew up learning and speaking Arabic or Tagalog, they would experience the world similarly. The varying qualities of language would not have been expected to affect the people who spoke those languages. Language, from this point of view, was merely a vehicle by which ideas were presented rather than a shaper of the very substance of those ideas.

In 1921 anthropologist Edward Sapir began to articulate an alternative view of language, asserting that language influenced or even determined the ways in which people thought. Sapir's student, Benjamin Whorf, continued to present and develop Sapir's ideas into the 1950s. Together, their ideas became

This young Indian girl is studying Urdu, the language of Indian Muslims. The Sapir-Whorf hypothesis underscores the relationship between her language and her experiences in the world. *(Cary Wolinsky. Copyright © by Stock, Boston, Inc., 1986. All rights reserved.)*

subsumed under several labels, including the theory of linguistic determinism, the theory of linguistic relativity, the Sapir-Whorf hypothesis, and the Whorfian hypothesis. The following quotation from Sapir is typical of their statements:

> Human beings do not live in the objective world alone, nor alone in the world of social activity as ordinarily understood, but are very much at the mercy of the particular language which has become the medium of expression for their society. It is quite an illusion to imagine that one adjusts to reality essentially without the use of language and that language is merely an incidental means of solv-

CULTURE CONNECTIONS

The elevator descended crankily, as if it too wanted to be finished for the day. Rita still calls it a lift, Gillian remembered idly. She still calls gas petrol after seven years here. I wonder if I'd still say elevator if I lived in England . . . . I know I'd say washcloth—I can't imagine saying faceflannel. My language has become a mongrel breed of English anyhow; I don't speak pure American any more, but I don't speak British English, or true Canadian. I scramble them all. I say 'sneakers' and pronounce 'missile' as if it were a prayer book, and prehistoric American slang like 'nifty' and 'baloney' pops out of my mouth, but I use bloody as an intensifier, call university forms bumf, and think Rankin fancies himself. I used to say 'apartment,' but now I sometimes say 'flat' and sometimes 'suite,' the way they do here. When I sleep late, I sleep in. It's a good thing there aren't three sides of the road to drive on.

Source: Nora Kelley, *My Sister's Keeper* (New York: St. Martin's Press, 1992) 33–34.

ing specific problems of communication or reflection. The fact of the matter is that the "real world" is to a large extent unconsciously built up on the language habits of the group. . . . We see and hear and otherwise experience very largely as we do because the language habits of our community predispose certain choices of interpretation.[10]

Our discussion of the Sapir-Whorf hypothesis is not intended to provide a precise rendering as articulated by Sapir and Whorf, which is virtually impossible to do. During the three decades in which they formally presented their ideas to the scholarly community, their views shifted somewhat and their writings include both "firmer" or more deterministic views of the relationship between language and thought and "softer" views that describe language as merely influencing or shaping thought.

In the "firm" or deterministic version of the hypothesis, language functions like a prison—once people learn a language, they are irrevocably affected by its particulars. Furthermore, it is never possible to translate effectively and successfully between languages, which makes competent intercultural communication an elusive goal.

The "softer" position is a less causal view of the nature of the language-thought relationship. In this version, language shapes how people think and experience their world, but this influence is not unceasing. Instead, it is possible for people from different initial language systems to learn words and categories sufficiently similar to their own so that communication can be accurate.

If substantial evidence had been found to support the firmer version of the Sapir-Whorf hypothesis, it would represent a dismal prognosis for competent

CULTURE CONNECTIONS

In the Hopi language there are no words for war or aggression.

Source: Thom Akeman, "Hopis, Who Have No Word for War, Finally Wage One," *Sacramento Bee*, June 10, 1990.

intercultural communication. Because so few people grow up bilingually, it would be impossible to transcend the boundaries of our linguistic experiences. Fortunately, the weight of the scholarly evidence, which we summarize in the following section, debunks the notion that people's first language traps them inescapably in a particular pattern of thinking. Instead, evidence suggests that language plays a powerful role in *shaping* how people think and experience the world. Although the shaping properties of language are significant, linguistic equivalences can be established between people from different language systems.[11]

Sapir and Whorf's major contribution to the study of intercultural communication is that they called attention to the integral relationship among thought, culture, and language. In the following section, we discuss some of the differences in the vocabulary and grammar of languages and consider the extent to which these differences can be used as evidence to support the two positions of the Sapir-Whorf hypothesis. As you consider the following ideas, examine the properties of the languages you know. Are there specialized vocabularies or grammatical characteristics that shape how you think and experience the world as you use these languages?

Variations in Vocabulary   The best-known example of vocabulary differences associated with the Sapir-Whorf hypothesis is the large number of words for snow in the Eskimo language. (The language is variously called Inuktitut in Canada, Inupit in Alaska, and Kalaallisut in Greenland.) Depending on whom you ask, there are from 7 to 50 different words for snow in the Inuktitut language.[12] For example, there are words that differentiate falling snow, (*gana*) and fully fallen snow (*akilukak*). The English language has fewer words for snow and no terms for many of the distinctions made by Eskimos. The issue raised by the Sapir-Whorf hypothesis is whether the person who grows up speaking Inuktitut actually perceives snow differently than does someone who grew up in Southern California and may only know snow by second-hand descriptions. More important, could the Southern Californian who lives with the Inupit in Alaska learn to differentiate all of the variations of snow and to use the specific Eskimo words appropriately? The firmer version of the Sapir-Whorf hypothesis suggests that linguistic differences are accompanied by perceptual differences, so that the English speaker looks at snow differently than does the Eskimo speaker.

There are numerous other examples of languages that have highly specialized vocabularies for particular features of the environment. For instance, in the South Sea islands, there are numerous words for coconut, which not only refer to the object of a coconut but also indicate how the coconut is being used or to a specific part of the coconut.[13] Similarly, in classical Arabic over 6,000 words are used to refer to a camel.[14]

Another variation in vocabulary concerns the terms a language uses to identify and divide colors in the spectrum. For example, the Kamayura Indians of Brazil have a single word that refers to the colors that English speakers would call blue and green. The best translation of the word the Kamayuras use is "parakeet colored."[15] The Dani of West New Guinea divide all colors into only two words, that are roughly equivalent in English to "dark" and "light."[16] The important issue, however, is whether speakers of these languages are able to distinguish among the different colors when they see them or can experience only the colors suggested by the words available for them to use. Do the Kamayura Indians actually see blue and green as the same color simply because they use the same word to identify both? Or does their language simply identify colors differently than does English?

Do you think that you could learn to distinguish all of the variations of the object "snow" that are important to the Eskimos? Could you be taught to see all of the important characteristics of a camel or a coconut? Such questions are very important in accepting or rejecting the ideas presented in the firm and soft versions of the Sapir-Whorf hypothesis.

Researchers looking at the vocabulary variations in the color spectrum have generally found that although a language may restrict how a color can be labeled verbally, people can still see and differentiate among particular colors. In other words, the Kamayura Indians can, in fact, see both blue and green, even though they use the same linguistic referent for both colors.[17] The deterministic version of the Sapir-Whorf hypothesis, then, is not supported by the evidence on color perception and vocabulary.

What about all those variations for snow, camels, or coconuts? Are they evidence to support the strong version of the Sapir-Whorf hypothesis? A starting point for addressing this issue is to consider how English speakers use other words along with essentially the one word English has for "particles of water vapor that when frozen in the upper air fall to earth as soft, white, crystalline flakes." English speakers are able to describe verbally many variations of snow simply by adding modifiers to the root word. People who live in areas with a lot of snow are quite familiar with *dry snow*, *heavy snow*, *slush*, or *dirty snow*. Skiers have a rich vocabulary to describe variations in snow on the slopes. It is possible, therefore, for a person who has facility in one language to approximate the categories of another language. The deterministic position of Sapir-Whorf, then, is difficult to support. Even Sapir and Whorf's own work can be used to argue against the deterministic interpretation of

CULTURE CONNECTIONS

The in-law situation was overwhelming for me, an only child. There is no Kikuyu word for uncle or aunt so Joseph had six fathers and the mamas were even more numerous—small, wiry women who smelled like butter when they hugged me.

Source: Kathleen Coskran, "Facing Mount Kenya," *From the Center of the Earth*, ed. Geraldine Kennedy (Santa Monica, CA: Clover Park Press, 1991) 16.

their position because in presenting all of the Eskimo words for snow, Whorf provided their approximate English equivalences.

A better explanation for linguistic differences is that variations in the complexity and richness of a language's vocabulary reflect what is important to the people who speak that language. To an Eskimo, differentiating among varieties of snow is much more critical to survival and adaptation than it is to the Southern Californian, who may never see snow. Conversely, Southern Californians have numerous words to refer to four-wheeled motorized vehicles, which are very important objects in their environment. However, we are certain that differences in the words and concepts of a language do affect the ease with which a person can change from one language to another because there is a dynamic interrelationship among language, thought, and culture.

Variations in Linguistic Grammars   A rich illustration of the reciprocal relationship among language, thought, and culture can be found in the grammatical rules of different languages. In the following discussion, you will once again see how the patterns of a culture's beliefs, values, and norms, as discussed in Chapters 5 and 6, permeate all aspects of the culture. Because language shapes how its users organize the world, the patterns of a culture will be reflected in its language and vice versa.

Cultural Conceptions of Time   Whorf himself provided detailed descriptions of the Hopi language that illustrate how the grammar of a language is related to the perceptions of its users. Hopi do not linguistically refer to time as a fixed point or place but rather as a movement in the stream of life. The English language, in contrast, refers to time as a specific point that exists on a linear plane divided into past, present, and future. Hopi time is more like an ongoing process; the here and now (the present) will never actually arrive, but it will always be approaching. The Hopi language also has no tenses, so the people do not place events into the neat categories of past, present, and future that native speakers of English have come to expect. As Stephen Littlejohn has suggested, the consequences of these linguistic differences is that

Hopi and SAE [Standard Average European] cultures will think about, perceive, and behave toward time differently. For example, the Hopi tend to engage in lengthy preparing activities. Experiences (getting prepared) tend to accumulate as time gets later. The emphasis is on the accumulated experience during the course of time, not on time as a point or location. In SAE cultures, with their spatial treatment of time, experiences are not accumulated in the same sense. Elaborate and lengthy preparations are not often found. The custom in SAE cultures is to record events (space-time analogy) such that what happened in the past is objectified in space (recorded).[18]

Because a culture's linguistic grammar shapes its experiences, the speakers of Hopi and English will experience time differently and each may find it difficult to understand the view of time held by the other. Judgments about what is "natural" or "right" or "common sense" will obviously vary and will be reinforced by the linguistic habits of each group.

Showing Respect and Social Hierarchy   Languages allow, and to a certain extent force, speakers to display respect for others. For instance, it is much easier to show respect in Spanish than it is in English. Consider the following sentences:

¿Sabe Usted dónde está la profesora?
Know you where is the professor?

¿Sabes dónde está la profesora?
Know you where is the professor?

These distinctly different Spanish sentences are identical when translated into English. The sentences in Spanish reflect the differences in the level of respect that must be shown between the person speaking and the person being addressed. The pronoun *Usted* is used in the first example to mark the speaker's question as particularly formal or polite. The *s* in *Sabes* in the second example marks the relationship between the speaker and the person being addressed as familiar or informal. In the actual practice of Spanish, a younger person would not use the informal grammatical construction to address an older person, just as an older person would not use the formal *Usted* with a person who was much younger.

This example illustrates once again that the grammar of a language can at least encourage its users to construct their interactions with others in particular ways. When a language directs a speaker to make distinctions among the people with whom the speaker interacts, in this instance by showing linguistically a greater respect for some and not others, the language helps to remind its users of social distinctions and the behaviors that are appropriate to them. Thus, language professors who teach Spanish to English-speaking students often note that the English speaker is not respectful.

The degree to which a language demands specific words and grammatical structures to show the nature of the relationship between the communicators suggests how much a culture values differences between people. In the frameworks of the ideas presented in Chapters 5 and 6, Spanish culture would be more likely to value a hierarchical social organization and a large power distance. Chinese, Japanese, and Korean languages also reflect the relative social status between the addressor and addressee. In Hindi, Korean, and other languages, there are specific words for older brother, older sister, younger brother, and younger sister, which remind all siblings of their relative order in the family and the norms or expectations appropriate to specific familial roles. Languages with grammatical and semantic features that make the speakers decide whether to show respect and social status to others are constant reminders of those characteristics of social interaction. In contrast, a language with few terms to show status and respect tends to minimize those status distinctions in the minds of the language's users.

Pronouns and Cultural Characteristics   English is the only language that capitalizes the pronoun *I* in writing. English does not, however, capitalize the written form of the pronoun *you*. Is there a relationship between the individualism that characterizes most of the English-speaking countries and this feature of the English language? In contrast, consider that there are more than 12 words for *I* in Vietnamese, in Chinese more than 10, and over 100 in Japanese.[19] Does a language that demands a speaker to differentiate the self (the "I") from other features of the context (for example, other people or the type of event) shape the way speakers of that language think about themselves? If "I" exist, but "I" am able to identify myself linguistically only through reference to someone else, will "I" not have a different sense of myself than the English-speaking people who see themselves as entities existing apart from all others?[20]

As an example of the extreme contrasts that exist in the use and meanings of pronouns, consider the experiences of Michael Dorris, who lived in Tyonek, Alaska, an Athabaskan-speaking Native American community:

> Much of my time was spent in the study of the local language, linguistically related to Navajo and Apache but distinctly adapted to the subarctic environment. One of its most difficult features for an outsider to grasp was the practice of almost always speaking and thinking in a collective plural voice. The word for people, "dene," was used as a kind of "we"—the subject for virtually every predicate requiring a personal pronoun—and therefore any act became, at least in conception, a group experience.[21]

Imagine having been trained in the language that Dorris describes. Would speaking such a language result in people who think about themselves as part of a group rather than as individuals?[22] Alternatively, if you are from a culture that values individualism, would you have difficulty communicating in a language that requires you always to say *we* instead of *I*? If your cultural background is more group-oriented, would it be relatively easy for you to speak in a language that places you as part of a group?

Linguistic Relativity and Intercultural Communication   The semantic and syntactic features of language are powerful shapers of the way people experience the physical and social world. Sapir and Whorf's assertions that language *determines* our reality have proven to be false. Language does not determine our ability to sense the physical world, nor does the language first learned create modes of thinking from which there is no escape. However, language shapes and influences our thoughts and behaviors. The vocabulary of a language reflects what you need to know to cope with the environment and the patterns of your culture. The semantics and syntactics of language gently nudge you to notice particular kinds of things in your world and to label them in particular ways. All of these components of language create habitual response patterns to the people, events, and messages that surround you. Your language intermingles with other aspects of your culture to reinforce the cultural patterns you are taught.

The influence of a particular language is something you can escape; it is possible to translate to or interact in a second language. But as the categories for coding or sorting the world are provided primarily by your language, you are predisposed to perceive the world in a particular way, and the reality you create is different from those who use other languages with other categories.

When the categories of languages are vastly different, people will have trouble communicating with one another. Differences in language affect what is relatively easy to say and what seems virtually impossible to say. As Wilma M. Roger has suggested, "Language and the cultural values, reactions, and expectations of speakers of that language are subtly melded."[23]

We offer one final caution. For purposes of discussion we have artificially separated vocabulary and grammar, as if language is simply an adding together of these two elements. In use, language is a dynamic and interrelated system that has a powerful effect on people's thoughts and actions. The living, breathing qualities of language as spoken and used, with all the attendant feelings, emotions, and experiences, are difficult to convey adequately in an introductory discussion such as this one.

Language and Intercultural Communication

The earlier sections of this chapter may have given the impression that language is stable and used consistently by all who speak it. However, even in a country that has predominantly only one language, there are great variations in the way the language is spoken (accents) and there are wide deviations in how words are used and what they mean. Among U.S. Americans who speak English, it is quite common to hear many different accents. It is also quite common to hear words, phrases, and colloquial expressions that are common to only one region of the country. Think of the many voices associated with the speaking of English in the United States. Do you have an auditory image of the way someone sounds who grew up in New York City? How about someone who grew up in Georgia? Wisconsin? Oregon? The regional variations in the ways English is spoken reflect differences in accents and dialects.

Increasingly, U.S. Americans speak many first languages other than English. As noted in Chapter 1, multiple language systems are represented in U.S. schools. Employers in businesses must now be conscious of the different languages of their workers. In addition, specialized linguistic structures develop for other functions within the context of a larger language. Because language differences are powerful factors that influence the relationships between ethnic and cultural groups who live next to and with each other in communities

CULTURE CONNECTIONS

Jim says his English was not quite perfect when he came to America. One day on a San Diego freeway he saw one lane up a ramp was long. But a lane marked "Car Pool" was free.

"I wasn't sure what 'Car Pool' meant. Pool? Car? Ah, yes, a lane for cars that wanted a car wash. But it seemed an easy way to get onto the freeway so I used it," says Jim. A Highway Patrol officer saw him.

"I explained to the officer that 'Car Pool' means car wash. Yes?"

"No," said the officer. "That's all right," I said, "I really don't want my car washed. "How did you get your driver's license," asked the officer. "With an interpreter," I said.

"The officer said, 'Welcome to America,' and gave me a ticket," Jim says.

Dennis, who with his wife Georgia, operates Madison Avenue's Georgia's Greek Cuisine, came to America intending at first just to visit. Then he met Georgia. But, in coming, he, like Jim, was not perfect in English.

When his airliner from Athens landed, a customs inspector examined Dennis' customs form.

Inspector: "How old are you, sir?"

Dennis: "I'm very well, thank you, sir."

Source: R. H. Growald, "Funny Things Happen on the Way to Becoming Greek-Americans," *San Diego Union-Tribune,* October 5, 1991, B3.

and countries, we will examine the variations among languages of groups of people who essentially share a common political union.[24] We begin by considering the role of language in maintaining the identity of a cultural group and in the relationship between cultural groups who share a common social system. We then talk about nonstandard versions of a language, including accents, dialects, and argot, and we explore their effects on communication with others.

Language, Ethnic Group Identity, and Dominance   Each person commonly identifies with many different social groups. For example, you probably think of yourself as part of a certain age grouping, as male or female, as married or unmarried, and as a college student or someone who is simply interested in learning about intercultural communication. You may also think of yourself as African American, German American, Vietnamese American, Latino, Navajo, or one of the many other cultural groups comprising the population of the United States. You may also identify with a culture from outside of the United States.

In many world countries, the "mixing" of people across linguistic and cultural boundaries has resulted in public signs providing information in multiple languages. *(Copyright © Granitsas/The Image Works.)*

Henri Tajfel argues that humans categorize themselves and others into different groups to simplify their understanding of people. When you think of someone as part of a particular social group, you associate that person with the values of that group.[25] In this section we are particularly concerned with the ways in which language is used to identify people in a group, either by group members themselves or by outsiders from other groups. Some of the questions we are concerned with include the following: How important is language to the members of a culture? What is the role of language in the maintenance of a culture? Why do some languages survive over time while others do not? What role does language play in the relationship of one culture to another?

The importance that cultures attribute to language has been well established.[26] In fact, some would argue that the very heart of a culture is its language and that a culture dies if its language dies.[27] However, it is difficult to determine the exact degree of importance that language has for someone who identifies with a particular group because there are so many factors that affect the strength of that identification. For example, people are more likely to have a strong sense of ethnic and linguistic identity if their language is acknowledged in some way by members of other important cultural groups. In several states within the United States, for example, there have been heated legal battles to allow election ballots to be printed in languages other than English. Those advocating this option are actually fighting to gain official status and support for their languages.

A language will remain vital and strong if groups of people who live near one another use the language regularly. The sheer number of people who identify with a particular language and their distribution within a particular country or region have a definite effect on the vigor of the language. For people who are rarely able to speak the language of their culture, the centrality of the language and the cultural or ethnic identity that goes with it are certainly diminished. Their inability to use the language results in lost opportunities to express their identification with the culture that it symbolizes.

The extent to which a culture maintains a powerful sense of identification with a particular language is called *perceived ethnolinguistic vitality*, which refers to "the individual's subjective perception of the status, demographic characteristics, and institutional support of the language community."[28] Very high levels of perceived ethnolinguistic vitality mean that members of a culture will be unwilling to assimilate their linguistic behavior with other cultures that surround them.[29] Howard Giles, one of the foremost researchers in how languages are used in multilingual societies, concludes that there are likely to be intense pressures on cultural members to adopt the language of the larger social group and to discontinue the use of their own language when

1. the members of a culture lack a strong political, social, and economic status;
2. there are few members of the culture compared to the number of people in other groups in the community; and
3. institutional support to maintain their unique cultural heritage is weak.[30]

When multiple languages are spoken within one political boundary, there are inevitably political and social consequences. In the United States, for example, English has maintained itself as the primary language over a long period of time. Immigrants to the United States have historically been required to learn English in order to participate in the wider political and commercial aspects of the society. Schools offered classes only in English, television and radio programs were almost exclusively in English, and the work of government and business also required English. The English-only requirement has not been imposed without social consequences, however. In Micronesia, for example, where there are nine major languages and many dialects, people are demonstrably apprehensive about communicating with others when they must use English instead of their primary language.[31]

In recent years in the United States, there has been a change in the English-only pattern. Now in many areas of the country there are large numbers of people for whom English is not the primary language. As a consequence, teaching staffs are multilingual; government offices provide services to non-English speakers; and cable television has an extensive array of entertainment and news programming in Spanish, Chinese, Japanese, Arabic, and so on.

In some countries formal political agreements acknowledge the role of multiple languages in the government and educational systems. Canada has two official languages: English and French. Belgium uses three: French, German, and Flemish. In Singapore, English, Mandarin, Malay, and Tamil are all official languages, and India has over a dozen.

When India was established in 1948, one of the major problems concerned a national language. Although Hindi was the language spoken by the largest number of people, the overwhelming majority of the people did not speak it. India's solution to this problem was to identify 16 national languages, thus formalizing in the constitution the right for government, schools, and commerce to operate in any of them. Even that solution has not quelled the fears of non-Hindi speakers that Hindi will predominate. In the mid-1950s there was political agitation to redraw the internal state boundaries based on the languages spoken in particular regions. Even now, major political upheavals periodically occur in India over language issues.

Because language is such an integral part of most people's identities, a great deal of emotion is attached to political choices about language preferences. However, what is most central to intercultural competence is the way in which linguistic identification influences the interaction that occurs between members of different cultural groups. In interpersonal communication, language is used to discern ingroup and outgroup members. That is, language provides an obvious and highly accurate cue about whether people share each other's cultural background. If others speak as you do, you are likely to assume that they are similar to you in other important ways.

People also make a positive or negative evaluation about the language that others use. Generally speaking, there is a pecking order among languages that is usually buttressed and supported by the prevailing political order. As Ellen Bouchard Ryan, Howard Giles, and Richard J. Sebastian suggest,

> In every society the differential power of particular social groups is reflected in language variation and in attitudes toward those variations. Typically, the dominant group promotes its patterns of language use as dialect or accents by minority group members reduce their opportunities for success in the society as a whole. Minority group members are often faced with difficult decisions regarding whether to gain social mobility by adopting the language patterns of the dominant group or to maintain their group identity by retaining their native speech style.[32]

In the United States, there has been a clear preference for English over the multiple other languages that people speak, and those who speak English are evaluated according to their various accents and dialects. African Americans, for instance, have often been judged negatively for their use of Black Standard English, which has grammatical forms that differ from those used in Standard American English.[33] In the next section, we discuss the consequences of these evaluations and the effects of alternative forms of language use on intercultural communication competence.

Alternative Versions of a Language   No language is spoken precisely the same way by all who use it. The sounds made by a person from England when speaking English differ from the speech of English-speaking U.S. Americans. Even among those who share a similar language and reside in the same country, there are important variations in the way the language is spoken. These differences in language use include the way the words are pronounced, the meanings of particular words or phrases, and the patterns for arranging the words (grammar). Terms often associated with these alternative forms of a language include *dialect*, *accent*, *argot* (pronounced "are go"), and *jargon*.

Dialects and Accents   Dialects are versions of a language with distinctive vocabulary, grammar, and pronunciation that are spoken by particular groups of people or within particular regions. Dialects can play an important role in intercultural communication because they often trigger a judgment and evaluation of the speaker. Dialects are measured against a "standard" spoken version of the language. The term *standard* does not describe inherent or naturally occurring characteristics but, rather, historical circumstances. For example, among many U.S. Americans, Standard American English is often the preferred dialect and conveys power and dominance. But as John R. Edwards has suggested, "As a dialect, there is nothing intrinsic, either linguistically or esthetically, which gives Standard English special status."[34] However, other dialects of English are frequently accorded less status and are often considered inappropriate or unacceptable in education, business, and government. Speakers of Black Standard English, for example, are sometimes unfairly assumed to be less reliable, less intelligent, and of lower status than those who speak Standard American English.[35]

Accents, or distinguishable marks of pronunciation, are closely related to dialects. Research studies repeatedly demonstrate that speakers' accents are used as a cue to form impressions of them.[36] Those of you who speak English with an accent or in a nonstandard version may have experienced the negative reactions of others, and you know the harmful effects such judgments can have on intercultural communication. Studies repeatedly find that accented speech and dialects provoke stereotyped reactions in listeners, so that the speakers are usually perceived as having less status, prestige, and overall competence. Interestingly, these negative perceptions and stereotyped responses sometimes occur even when the listeners themselves use a nonstandard dialect.[37]

If you are a speaker of Standard American English, you speak English with an "acceptable" accent. Can you recall conversations with others whose dialect and accent did not match yours? In those conversations, did you make negative assessments of their character, intelligence, or goodwill? Such a response is fairly common. Negative judgments that are made about others sim-

CULTURE CONNECTIONS

For a people who are neither Spanish nor live in a country in which Spanish is the first language; for a people who live in a country in which English is the reigning tongue but who are not Anglo; for a people who cannot entirely identify with either standard (formal, Castillian) Spanish nor standard English, what recourse is left to them but to create their own language? A language which they can connect their identity to, one capable of communicating the realities and values true to themselves—a language with terms that are neither *español ni inglés,* but both. We speak a patois, a forked tongue, a variation of two languages.

Chicano Spanish sprang out of the Chicanos' need to identify ourselves as a distinct people. We needed a language with which we could communicate with ourselves, a secret language.

Source: Gloria Anzaldúa, *Borderlands/La Frontera: The New Mestiza* (San Francisco: Spinsters/Aunt Lute, 1987).

ply on the basis of how they speak are obviously a formidable barrier to competence in intercultural communication. For example, an Iranian American woman describes the frustration and anger experienced by her father, a physician, and her mother, a nurse, when they attempted to communicate with others by telephone. Though both of her parents had immigrated to the United States many years before, they spoke English with a heavy accent. These educated people were consistently responded to as if they lacked intelligence simply because of their accent. Out of sheer frustration they usually had their daughter, who spoke English with a U.S. accent, conduct whatever business needed to be accomplished on the telephone.

Jargon and Argot Both jargon and argot are specialized forms of vocabulary. *Jargon* refers to a set of words or terms that are shared by those with a common profession or experience. For example, students at a particular college or university share a jargon related to general education requirements, registration techniques, add or drop procedures, activity fees, and so on. Members of a particular profession depend on a unique set of meanings for words that are understood only by other members of that profession. The shorthand code used by law-enforcement officers, lawyers, those in the medical profession, and even professors at colleges and universities are all instances of jargon.

Argot refers to a specialized language that is used by a large group within a culture to define the boundaries of their group from others who are in a more powerful position in society. As you might expect, argot is an important feature in the study of intercultural communication. Unlike jargon, argot is typically used to keep those who are not part of the group from understanding what members say to one another. The specialized language is used to keep those from the outside, usually seen as hostile, at bay.

Code switching   Because of the many languages spoken in the United States, you will likely have many opportunities to hear and perhaps to participate in a form of language use called code switching. Code switching refers to the selection of the language to be used in a particular interaction by individuals who can speak multiple languages. The decision to use one language over another is often related to the setting in which the interaction occurs—a social, public, and formal setting versus a personal, private, and informal one. In his poignant exploration about speaking Spanish in an English-speaking world, Richard Rodriguez describes his attachment to the language associated with this latter setting.

> When I was a boy, things were different. The accent of *los gringos* was never pleasing nor was it hard to hear. Crowds at safeway or at bus stops would be noisy with sound. And I would be forced to edge away from the chirping chatter above me. . . .
>
> But then there was Spanish. *Español*: my family's language. *Español*: the language that seemed to me to be a private language. I'd hear strangers on the radio and in the Mexican Catholic church across town speaking in Spanish, but I couldn't really believe that Spanish was a public language, like English. Spanish speakers, rather, seemed related to me, for I sensed that we shared—through our language—the experience of feeling apart from *los gringos*.... Spanish seemed to me the language of home. . . .
>
> A family member would say something to me and I would feel myself specially recognized. My parents would say something to me and I would feel embraced by the sounds of their words. Those sounds said: *I am speaking with ease in Spanish. I am addressing you in words I never use with* los gringos. *I recognize you as someone special, close, like no one outside. You belong with us. In the family.*[38]

A person's conversational partner is another important factor in code-switching decisions. Many African Americans, for instance, switch their linguistic codes based on the culture and gender of their conversational partners.[39]

The topic of conversation is another important influence on the choice of a linguistic code. One study found that Moroccans, for instance, would typically use French when discussing scientific or technological topics and Arabic when discussing cultural or religious ones. Interestingly, people's attitudes toward a particular topic were found to be consistent with the underlying beliefs, values, and norms of the culture whose language they choose to speak.[40]

VERBAL CODES AND INTERCULTURAL COMPETENCE

The link between knowledge of other verbal codes and intercultural competence is obvious. To speak another language proficiently requires an enormous amount of effort, energy, and time. The opportunity to study another language

CULTURE CONNECTIONS

It is one of the remarkable aspects of language that we can appear to take on different personalities simply by making different sounds than the ones to which we are accustomed. For those who are truly bilingual this seems so obvious as to hardly bear mentioning: they flit easily between tongues—an English set of vowels and mannerisms flows into Urdu patterns and intotations with scarcely a ripple—though they will talk casually about "my Pakistani self" and "my English persona." But for those of us who came late to another language, it is always something of an odd experience to see and feel it happen, the moment when you notice another personality overtaking your familiar one, the moment when you become "Italian" or "Japanese." It's the moment when you stop worrying about grammar and accent, and allow the other language to possess you, to pass through you, to transform you.

When I speak Spanish, the language that I know best besides English, I find my facial muscles set in a different pattern, and new, yet familiar gestures taking over my hands. I find myself shrugging and tossing my head back, pulling down the corners of my mouth and lifting my eyebrows. I touch people all the time and don't mind that they stand so close to me and blow cigarette smoke into my face. I speak more rapidly and fluidly and I use expressions that have no counterpart in English, expressions that for all my experience as a translator, I simply can't turn into exact equivalents. To speak another language is to lead a parallel life; the better you speak any language, the more fully you live in another culture.

Source: Barbara Wilson, *Trouble in Transylvania: A Cassandra Reilly Mystery* (Seattle: Seal Press, 1993) 159–160.

in your college curriculum is a choice we highly recommend to prepare you for the multicultural and multilingual world of the twenty-first century. Those world citizens with facility in a second or third language will be needed in every facet of society.

Many English speakers have a false sense of security because English is studied and spoken by so many people around the world. There is an arrogance in this position that should be obvious because it places all of the responsibility for learning another language on the non-English speaker. Furthermore, even if two people from different cultures are using the verbal code system of one of the interactants, significant influences on their communication arise from their initial languages.

The multicultural nature of the United States and the interdependence of world cultures means that multiple cultures and multiple languages will be a standard feature of people's lives. Despite our strong recommendation that you learn and be tolerant of other languages, it is virtually impossible for anyone to be proficient in all of the verbal codes that might be encountered in intercultural communication. However, there are important ways to improve competence in adjusting to differences in verbal codes when communicating interculturally.

First, the study of at least one other language is extraordinarily useful in understanding the role of differences in verbal codes in intercultural communication. Genuine fluency in a second language demonstrates experientially all of the ways in which language embodies another culture. It also reveals the ways in which languages vary and how the nuances of language use influence the meanings of symbols. Even if you never become genuinely proficient in it, the study of another language teaches much about the culture of those who use it and the categories of experience the language can create. Furthermore, such study demonstrates, better than words written on a page or spoken in a lecture, the difficulty in gaining proficiency in another language and may lead to an appreciation of those who are struggling to communicate in second or third languages.

Short of becoming proficient in another language, learning about its grammatical features can help you understand the messages of the other person. Study the connections between the features of a verbal code and the cultural patterns of those who use it. Even if you are going to communicate with people from another culture in your own first language, there is much that you can learn about the other person's language and the corresponding cultural patterns that can help you to behave appropriately and effectively.

Knowledge of another language is one component of the link between competence and verbal codes. Motivation, in the form of your emotional reactions and your intentions toward the culturally different others with whom you are communicating, is another critical component. Trying to get along in another language can be an exhilarating and very positive experience, but it can also be fatiguing and frustrating. The attempt to speak and understand a new verbal code requires energy and perseverance. Most second language learners, when immersed in its cultural setting, report a substantial toll on their energy.

Functioning in a culture that speaks a language different from your own can be equally tiring and exasperating. Making yourself understood, getting around, obtaining food, and making purchases all require a great deal of effort. Recognizing the possibility of irritability and fatigue when functioning in an unfamiliar linguistic environment is an important prerequisite to intercultural competence. Without such knowledge, the communicator may well blame his or her personal feelings of discomfort on the cultures that are being experienced.

The motivation dimension also concerns your reactions to those who are attempting to speak your language. In the United States, for example, those who speak English often lack sympathy for and patience with those who do not. If English is your first language, notice those learning it and provide whatever help you can. Respond patiently. If you do not understand, ask questions

The multicultural nature of many business, government, and social exchanges requires more and more linguistic expertise from world citizens. *(© David Strickler/The Image Works.)*

and clarify. Try making your verbal point in alternative ways by using different sets of words with approximately equivalent meanings. Speak slowly, but do not yell. Lack of skill in a new language is not caused by a hearing impairment. Be aware of the jargon in your speech and provide a definition of it. Above all, to the best of your ability, withhold judgments and negative evaluations; instead, show respect for the enormous difficulties associated with learning a new language.

An additional emotional factor to monitor in promoting intercultural competence is your reaction to nonstandard versions of a language. The negative evaluations that nonstandard speech often triggers are a serious impediment to competence.

Competence in intercultural communication can be assisted by behaviors that indicate interest in the other person's verbal code. Even if you have never studied the language of those with whom you regularly interact, do attempt to learn and use appropriate words and phrases. Get a phrase book and a dictionary to learn standard comments or queries. Learn how to greet people and to acknowledge thanks. At the same time, recognize your own limitations and depend on a skilled interpreter when needed.

Intercultural competence requires knowledge, motivation, and actions that recognize the critical role of verbal codes in human interaction. Though learning another language is a very important goal, it is inevitable that you will need to communicate with others with whom you do not share a common verbal code.

SUMMARY

In this chapter we have explored the vital role of verbal codes in intercultural communication. The features of language and the five rule systems were discussed. Phonology, the rules for creating the sounds of language, and morphology, the rules for creating the meaning units in a language, were described briefly. The study of the meaning of words (semantics), the rules for ordering the words (syntactics), and the effects of language on human perceptions and behaviors (pragmatics) were also described. We then described the difficulties in establishing equivalence in the process of interpretation from one language to another.

The important relationships among language, thought, culture, and behavior were explored. The Sapir-Whorf hypothesis of linguistic relativity, which concerns the effects of language on people's thoughts and perceptions, was discussed. We noted that the firmer version of the hypothesis portrays language as the determiner of thought and the softer version portrays language as a shaper of thought; variations in words and grammatical structures from one language to another provide important evidence in the debate on the Sapir-Whorf hypothesis; and that each language, with its own unique features, serves as a shaper rather than determiner of human thought, culture, and behavior.

Finally, variations in language use within a nation were considered. Language plays a central role in establishing and maintaining the identity of a particular culture. Language variations also foster a political hierarchy among cultures within a nation; nonstandard versions of a language, including accents, dialects, jargon, and argot, are often regarded less favorably than the standard version. The concept of code switching, and some factors that affect the selection of one language over another, were also discussed. The chapter concluded with a discussion of intercultural competence and verbal communication.

8

CHAPTER

Nonverbal Intercultural Communication

Learning to communicate as a native member of a culture involves knowing far more than the culture's verbal code. Vocabulary and grammar, the words of a language combined with the rules to string those words together in meaningful units, are actually only a small portion of the message that people exchange when they communicate. In this chapter we explain the types of messages that, taken together, constitute the nonverbal communication system.

DEFINITION OF NONVERBAL CODES

The importance of nonverbal codes in communication has been well established. Nonverbal communication is a multichanneled process that is usually performed spontaneously; it typically involves a subtle set of nonlinguistic behaviors that are often enacted subconciously.[1] Nonverbal behaviors can become part of the communication process when someone intentionally tries to

187

convey a message or when someone attributes meaning to the nonverbal behavior of another, whether or not the person intended to communicate a particular meaning.

An important caution related to the distinction between verbal and nonverbal communication must be made as you learn about nonverbal code systems. Though we describe the communication of verbal and nonverbal messages in separate chapters for explanatory convenience, it would be a mistake to assume that they are actually separate and independent communication systems.[2] In fact, they are inseparably linked together to form the code systems through which the members of a culture convey their beliefs, values, thoughts, feelings, and intentions to one another. As Sheila Ramsey suggests,

> Verbal and nonverbal behaviors are inextricably intertwined; speaking of one without the other is, as Birdwhistell says, like trying to study "noncardiac physiology." Whether in opposition or complementary to each other, both modes work to create the meaning of an interpersonal event. According to culturally prescribed codes, we use eye movement and contact to manage conversations and to regulate interactions; we follow rigid rules governing intra- and interpersonal touch, our bodies synchronously join in the rhythm of others in a group, and gestures modulate our speech. We must internalize all of this in order to become and remain fully functioning and socially appropriate members of any culture.[3]

Thus our distinction between verbal and nonverbal messages is a convenient, but perhaps misleading, way to sensitize you to the communication exchanges within and between cultures.

Characteristics of Nonverbal Codes

Unlike verbal communication systems, there are no dictionaries or formal sets of rules to provide a systematic list of the meanings of a culture's nonverbal code systems. The meanings of nonverbal messages are usually less precise than are those of verbal codes. It is difficult, for example, to define precisely the meaning of a raised eyebrow in a particular culture.

Nonverbal communication messages function as a "silent language" and impart their meanings in subtle and covert ways.[4] People process nonverbal messages, both the sending and receiving of them, with less awareness than they process verbal messages. Contributing to the silent character of nonverbal messages is the fact that most of them are continuous and natural, and they tend to blur into one another. For example, raising your hand to wave goodbye is a gesture made up of multiple muscular movements, yet it is interpreted as one continuous movement.

Skill in the use of nonverbal message systems has only recently begun to receive formal attention in the educational process, a reflection of the out-of-awareness character of nonverbal codes.

Relationship of Nonverbal to Verbal Communication

The relationship of nonverbal communication systems to the verbal message system can take a variety of forms. Nonverbal messages can be used to accent, complement, contradict, regulate, or substitute for the verbal message.

Nonverbal messages are often used to *accent* the verbal message by emphasizing a particular word or phrase, in much the same way as *italics* add emphasis to written messages. For instance, the sentence "He did it" takes on somewhat different meanings, depending on whether the subject (*He* did it), the verb (He *did* it), or the object of the verb (He did *it*) is emphasized.

Nonverbal messages that function to clarify, elaborate, explain, reinforce, and repeat the meaning of verbal messages *complement* the verbal message. Many U.S. Americans shake their heads up and down while saying yes to reinforce the verbal affirmation. Similarly, smiling while talking to someone helps to convey a generally pleasant tone and encourages a positive interpretation of the verbal message. Pointing forcefully at someone while saying "*He* did it!" helps to elaborate and underscore the verbal message.

Nonverbal messages can also *contradict* the verbal message. These contradictions could occur purposefully, as when you say yes while indicating no with a wink or a gesture; or they may be out of your conscious awareness, as when you say, "I'm not upset," while your facial expression and tone of voice indicate just the opposite. Contradictions between the verbal and nonverbal channels often indicate that something is amiss. Though the contradictory cues might indicate an attempt at deception, a less evaluative interpretation might simply be that the verbal message is not all that the person could convey. In intercultural communication, these apparent incongruities, when they occur, might serve as a cue that something is wrong.

When nonverbal messages help to maintain the back-and-forth sequencing of conversations, they function to *regulate* the interaction. Conversations are highly structured, with people typically taking turns at talking in a

CULTURE CONNECTIONS

When Dith Pran was asked what he would reply if asked if Khmers care less about the death of their loved ones than other people do, he said, "The only difference, maybe, is that with Cambodians, the grief leaves the face quickly, but it goes inside and stays there for a long time."

Source: Paul Opstad, "Some Considerations in Counseling Cambodians," *Intercultural News Network*, 1(4) (July/August, 1990): 2.

smooth and highly organized sequence. Speakers use nonverbal means to convey that they want the other person to talk or that they do not wish to be interrupted, just as listeners indicate when they wish to talk and when they prefer to continue listening. Looking behaviors, vocal inflections, gestures, and general cues of readiness or relaxation all help to signal a person's conversational intentions.

Finally, nonverbal messages that are used in place of the verbal ones function as a *substitute* for the verbal channel. They are used when the verbal channel is blocked or when people choose not to use it. Head nods, hand gestures, facial displays, body movements, and various forms of physical contact are often used as a substitute for the verbal message.

The specific nonverbal messages used to accent, complement, contradict, regulate, or substitute for the verbal messages will vary from culture to culture. In intercultural communication, difficulties in achieving competence in another verbal code are compounded by variations in the nonverbal codes that accompany the spoken word.

CULTURAL UNIVERSALS IN NONVERBAL COMMUNICATION

Charles Darwin believed that certain nonverbal displays were universal.[5] The shoulder shrug, for example, is used to convey such messages as "I can't do it," "I can't stop it from happening," "It wasn't my fault," "Be patient," and "I do not intend to resist." Michael Argyle has listed a number of characteristics of nonverbal communication that are universal across all cultures: (1) the same body parts are used for nonverbal expressions; (2) nonverbal channels are used to convey similar information, emotions, values, norms, and self-disclosing messages; (3) nonverbal messages accompany verbal communication and are used in art and ritual; (4) the motives for using the nonverbal channel, such as when speech is impossible, are similar across cultures; and (5) nonverbal messages are used to coordinate and control a range of contexts and relationships that are similar across cultures.[6]

Paul Ekman's research on facial expressions demonstrates the universality of many nonverbal emotional displays.[7] Ekman discovered three separate sets of facial muscles that operate independently and can be manipulated to form a variety of emotional expressions. These muscle sets include the forehead and brow; the eyes, eyelids, and base of the nose; and the cheeks, mouth, chin, and rest of the nose. The muscles in each of these facial regions are combined in a variety of unique patterns to display emotional states. For example, fear is indicated by a furrowed brow, raised eyebrows, wide-open eyes, creased or pinched base of the nose, taut cheeks, partially open mouth, and upturned upper lip. Because the ability to produce such emotional displays is consistent across cultures, there is probably a biological or genetic basis that allows these behaviors to be produced in all humans in a particular way.

Another universal aspect of nonverbal communication is the need to be territorial. Robert Ardrey, an ethologist, has concluded that territoriality is an innate, evolutionary characteristic that occurs in both animals and humans.[8] Humans from all cultures mark and claim certain spaces as their own.

Although some aspects of nonverbal code systems are universal, it is also clear that cultures choose to express emotions and territoriality in differing ways. These variations are of particular interest in intercultural communication.

CULTURAL VARIATIONS IN NONVERBAL COMMUNICATION

Most forms of nonverbal communication can be interpreted only within the framework of the culture in which they occur. Cultures vary in their nonverbal behaviors in three ways. First, cultures differ in the specific *repertoire* of behaviors that are enacted. Movements, body positions, postures, vocal intonations, gestures, spatial requirements, and even dances and ritualized actions are specific to a particular culture.

Second, all cultures have *display rules* that govern when and under what circumstances various nonverbal expressions are required, preferred, permitted, or prohibited. Thus, children learn both how to communicate nonverbally and the appropriate display rules that govern their nonverbal expressions. Display rules indicate such things as how far apart people should stand while talking, whom to touch and where, the speed and timing of movements and gestures, when to look directly at others in a conversation and when to look away, whether loud talking and expansive gestures or quietness and controlled movements should be used, when to smile and when to frown, and the overall pacing of communication.

The norms for display rules vary greatly across cultures. For instance, Judith N. Martin, Mitchell R. Hammer, and Lisa Bradford found that Latinos and European Americans differ in their judgments about the importance of displaying behaviors that signal approachability (smiling, laughing, and pleasant facial expressions) and poise (nice appearance, appropriate conversational distance, and appropriate posture) in conversations. The differences are related to whether the interaction is viewed as primarily task-oriented or socially-oriented, and whether the conversational partner is from their own or from another cultural group. Specifically, approachability and poise behaviors are most important for Latinos when working with other Latinos and when socializing with people from other cultures. In contrast, European Americans think it most important to display these behaviors only when socializing with another European American.[9]

Such differences in display rules can cause discomfort and misinterpretations. For instance, a Mexican American female visited her relatives in Mexico. Upon her arrival, she reports,

> All of the relatives came to greet me and everyone shook my hand, hugged me, and kissed me on the cheek. I didn't find this very odd at first, because even though I had never seen some of these relatives, we were family and being affectionate doesn't bother me. The difference occurred when I would go out with my

CULTURE CONNECTIONS

A gesture might have no meaning in one culture but shared significance in another. In Mexico, lifting the left arm vertically and simultaneously hitting the bottom of the elbow with the palm of the other hand delivers a message about which there is no ambiguity. The gesture suggests that someone should have an incestuous relationship with this mother. A person might use this same gesture, almost unconsciously, when he swats the backside of his arm to get rid of a bothersome insect.

cousins and their friends. When Maria would drop off Monica and me, they would kiss each other on the cheek. When a friend would come to the house, the greeting would always be a kiss on the cheek. It didn't matter if it was in public or private. It was as natural to them as shaking hands or hugging.

Display rules also indicate the intensity of the behavioral display that is acceptable. In showing grief or intense sadness, for instance, people from southern Mediterranean cultures may tend to exaggerate or amplify their displays, European Americans may try to remain calm and somewhat neutral, the British may understate their emotional displays by showing only a little of their inner feelings, and the Japanese and Thai may attempt to mask their sorrow completely by covering it with smiling and laughter.[10]

Third, cultures vary in the *interpretations* or meanings that are attributed to particular nonverbal behaviors. Three possible interpretations could be imposed on a given instance of nonverbal behavior: It is random, it is idiosyncratic, or it is shared.[11] An interpretation that the behavior is random means that it has no particular meaning to anyone. An idiosyncratic interpretation suggests that the behaviors are unique to special individuals or relationships, and they therefore have particular meanings only to these people. For example, family members often recognize that certain unique behaviors of a person signify a specific emotional state. Thus, a family member who tugs on her ear may indicate, to other family members, that she is about to explode in anger. The third interpretation is that the behaviors have shared meaning and significance, as when a group of people jointly attribute the same meaning to a particular nonverbal act.

However, cultures differ in what they regard as random, idiosyncratic, and shared. Thus, behaviors that are regarded as random in one culture may have shared significance in another. For example, John Condon and Fathi Yousef describe an incident in which a British professor in Cairo inadvertently showed the soles of his shoes to his class while leaning back in his chair; the Egyptian students were very insulted.[12] The professor's random behavior of leaning back and allowing the soles of his shoes to be seen was a nonverbal behavior with the shared meaning of insult in Egyptian culture. Such differ-

CULTURE CONNECTIONS

In Bulgaria, the gestures for yes and no are the opposite of the U.S. American gestures. To indicate yes Bulgarians will shake their head from side to side. No is indicated by an upward tilting of the head, followed by a slight downward movement.

The gesture of an outstretched arm with pointed thumb has a shared meaning in the United States of a request for a ride. In other cultures—Italy, for example—the shared meaning of this gesture is negative and derogatory. *Alan Carey/© The Image Works.)*

ences in how cultures define *random* can lead to problems in intercultural communication; if one culture defines a particular behavior as random, that behavior will probably be ignored when someone from a different culture uses it to communicate something.

Even nonverbal behaviors that have shared significance in each of two cultures may mean something very different to their members. As Ray Birdwhistell suggests, "A smile in one society portrays friendliness, in another embarrassment, and in still another may contain a warning that unless tension is reduced, hostility and attack will follow."[13] Aaron Wolfgang noted similar differences in interpretations when he compared Jamaican and Canadian reactions to such commonplace behaviors as clapping the hands for attention:

> In Barbados, a waiter in the dining room attempting to get the attention of some Canadian diners to show them to their table by clapping, shrugged his shoulders when they would not respond. In the English-Canadian culture clapping the hands would be considered inappropriate, or for that matter almost any expressive or gestural movement for attention would be frowned upon.[14]

Nonverbal repertoires, their corresponding display rules, and their preferred interpretations are not taught verbally. Rather, they are learned directly through observation and personal experience in a culture. Because they are frequently acquired outside of conscious awareness, they are rarely questioned or challenged by their users and are often noticed only when they are violated. In intercultural communication, therefore, misunderstandings often occur in the interpretations of nonverbal behaviors because different display rules create very different meanings about the appropriateness and effectiveness of particular interaction sequences. Consider, for instance, the following example:

> An American college student, while having a dinner party with a group of foreigners, learns that her favorite cousin has just died. She bites her lip, pulls herself up, and politely excuses herself from the group. The interpretation given to this behavior will vary with the culture of the observer. The Italian student thinks, "How insincere; she doesn't even cry." The Russian student thinks, "How unfriendly; she didn't care enough to share her grief with her friends." The fellow American student thinks, "How brave; she wanted to bear her burden by herself."[15]

As you can see, cultural variations in nonverbal communication alter the behaviors that are displayed, the meanings that are imposed on those behaviors, and the interpretations of the messages.

NONVERBAL MESSAGES IN INTERCULTURAL COMMUNICATION

Messages are transmitted between people over some sort of channel. Unlike written or spoken words, however, nonverbal communication is *multichanneled*. Thus, several types of nonverbal messages can be generated by a single

These Chinese Malaysian school kids illustrate several kinds of nonverbal messages. Notice the meaning you attribute to their dress, facial expression, body posture, gestures, and the distance they are sitting from each other. *(Copyright © Myron W. Lustig & Jolene Koester.)*

speaker at a given instant. When we "read" or observe the nonverbal behaviors of others, we might notice where they look, how they move, how they orient themselves in space and time, what they wear, and the characteristics of their voice. All of these nonverbal codes use particular channels or means of communicating messages, which are interpreted in a similar fashion by members of a given culture. We will discuss six types of nonverbal codes to demonstrate their importance in understanding how members of a culture attempt to understand, organize, and interpret the behaviors of others. We will consider body movements, space, touch, time, voice, and other nonverbal code systems.

Body Movements

The study of body movements, or body language, is known as *kinesics*. Kinesic behaviors include gestures, head movements, facial expressions, eye behaviors, and other physical displays that can be used to communicate. Of

These Argentinean men are greeting one another with an Abrazzo welcome, a common behavior in which the left hand is used to grip the other person's arm during a handshake. The Abrazzo displays warmth and a close, personal relationship. *(© Owen Franken, Stock, Boston, Inc., 1988. All rights reserved.)*

course, like all other forms of communication, no single type of behavior exists in isolation. Specific body movements can be understood only by taking the person's total behavior into account.

Paul Ekman and Wallace Friesen have suggested that there are five categories of kinesic behaviors: emblems, illustrators, affect displays, regulators, and adaptors.[16] We will consider each type of kinesic behavior in turn.

Emblems   Emblems are nonverbal behaviors that have a direct verbal counterpart. Emblems that are familiar to most U.S. Americans include such gestures as the two-fingered peace symbol and arm waving to indicate hello or goodbye.

Emblems are typically used as a substitute for the verbal channel, either by choice or when the verbal channel is blocked for some reason. Underwater divers, for example, have a rich vocabulary of kinesic behaviors that are used to communicate with their fellow divers. Similarly, a baseball coach uses kinesic signals to indicate a particular pitch or type of play, which is usually conveyed by an elaborate pattern of hand motions that involve touching the cap, chest, wrist, and other areas in a pattern known to the players.

Emblems, like all verbal languages, are symbols that have been arbitrarily selected by the members of a culture to convey their intended meanings. For example, there is nothing peacelike in the peace symbol, which is a nonverbal emblem that can be displayed by extending the index and middle fingers upward from a clenched fist. Indeed, in other cultures the peace symbol has other meanings; Winston Churchill used the same symbol to indicate victory, and to many people in South American countries it is regarded as an obscene gesture. The meanings of emblems are learned within a culture and, like verbal codes, are used consciously by the culture's members when they wish to convey specific ideas to others. Because emblems have to be learned to be understood, they are culture-specific.

Emblems can be a great source of misunderstanding in intercultural communication because the shared meanings for an emblem in one culture may be different in another. In Turkey, for instance, to say no nonverbally,

> Nod your head up and back, raising your eyebrows at the same time. Or just raise your eyebrows; that's "no.". . .
>
> By contrast, wagging your head from side to side doesn't mean "no" in Turkish; it means "I don't understand." So if a Turk asks you, "Are you looking for the bus to Ankara?" and you shake your head, he'll assume you don't understand English, and will probably ask you the same question again, this time in German.[17]

Illustrators   Illustrators are nonverbal behaviors that are directly tied to, or accompany, the verbal message. They are used to emphasize, explain, and support a word or phrase. They literally illustrate and provide a visual representation of the verbal message. In saying "The huge mountain," for example, you may simultaneously lift your arms and move them in a large half-circle. Similarly, you may point your index finger to emphasize an important idea or use hand motions to convey directions to a particular address. Unlike emblems, however, none of these gestures has meaning in itself. Rather, the meaning depends on the verbal message it underscores.

Illustrators are less arbitrary than emblems, which makes them more likely to be universally understood. But differences in both the rules for displaying illustrators and in the interpretations of them can be sources of intercultural misunderstanding. In Asian cultures, for example, calling for a person or a taxi while waving an index finger is very inappropriate, akin to calling a dog. Instead, the whole right hand is used, palm down, with the fingers together in a scooping motion toward the body. Similarly, punching the fist into the open palm as a display of strength may be misinterpreted as an obscene

A flat-footed squat is a comfortable, relaxing position in many cultures. This body posture is learned from childhood. If you are from a culture in which this behavior is not common, you might want to try it for a while. Without regular use, the leg muscles will not stretch enough to feel restful. (Copyright © Myron W. Lustig & Jolene Koester.)

gesture whose meaning is similar to a Westerner's use of the middle finger extended from a closed fist.

Affect Displays   Affect displays are facial and body movements that show feelings and emotions. Expressions of happiness or surprise, for instance, are displayed by the face and convey a person's inner feelings. Though affect displays are shown primarily through the face, postures and other body displays can also convey an emotional state.

Many affect displays may be universally recognized. The research of Paul Ekman and his colleagues indicates that regardless of culture, the primary

CULTURE CONNECTIONS

Mainland professors don't always understand that a Hawaiian student's reluctance to participate in class discussions, or the student's avoidance of eye contact (to show respect for an elder), does not signal lack of interest.

Source: Joyce Mercer, "Native Hawaiians Push to Extend and Deepen University's Diversity," *Chronicle of Higher Education,* August 3, 1994, A28.

emotional states include happiness, sadness, anger, fear, surprise, disgust, contempt, and interest.[18] In addition to these *primary affect displays*, there are about 30 *affect blends*, combinations of the primary emotions. While recent evidence supports Ekman's view,[19] James A. Russell argues that more information is needed to prove that there are indeed universal interpretations of emotional displays. He suggests that the categories for interpreting affect displays may actually vary somewhat across cultures.[20]

Affect displays may be unconscious and unintentional, such as a startled look of surprise, a blush of embarrassment, or dilated pupils due to pleasure or interest. Or affect displays may be conscious and intentional, as when we purposely smile and look at another person to convey warmth and affection. Cultural norms often govern both the kind and amount of affect displays shown. The Chinese, for instance, typically have lower frequency, intensity, and duration of affect displays than their European counterparts.[21]

Regulators   Regulators are nonverbal behaviors that help to synchronize the back-and-forth nature of conversations. This class of kinesic behaviors helps to control the flow and sequencing of communication and may include head nods, eye contact, postural shifts, back-channel signals (such as "Uh huhm" or "Mmm-mmm"), and other turn-taking cues.

Regulators are used by speakers to indicate whether others should take a turn and by listeners to indicate whether they wish to speak or would prefer to continue listening. They also convey information about the preferred speed or pacing of conversations and the degree to which the other person is understood and believed.

Regardless of culture, taking turns is required in all conversations. Thus, for interpersonal communication to occur, talk sequences must be highly coordinated. Regulators are those subtle cues that allow people to maintain this high degree of coordination.

Regulators are culture-specific. For instance, people from high-context cultures such as Korea and Japan are especially concerned with meanings conveyed by the eyes. In an interesting study comparing the looking behaviors of

African Americans and European Americans in a conversation, Marianne LaFrance and Clara Mayo found that there were many differences in the interpretations of turn-taking cues. European Americans tend to look directly into the eyes of the other person when they are the listeners, whereas African Americans prefer to look away. Unfortunately, to African Americans such behaviors by European Americans may be regarded as invasive or confrontational when interest and involvement is intended. Conversely, the behaviors of African Americans could be regarded by the European Americans as a sign of indifference or inattention when respect is intended. LaFrance and Mayo also found that when African American speakers pause while simultaneously looking directly at their European American listeners, the listeners often interpret this as a signal to speak, only to find that the African American person is also speaking.[22]

Adaptors   Adaptors are personal body movements that occur as a reaction to an individual's physical or psychological state. Scratching an itch, fidgeting, tapping a pencil, and smoothing one's hair are all behaviors that fulfill some individualized need.

Adaptors are usually performed unintentionally, without conscious awareness. They seem to be more frequent under conditions of stress, impatience, enthusiasm, or nervousness, and they are often interpreted by others as a sign of discomfort, uneasiness, irritation, or other negative feelings.

Space

The use of space functions as an important communication system in all cultures. Cultures are organized in some spatial pattern, and that pattern can reveal the character of the people in that culture. Two important features of the way cultures use the space around them are the different needs for personal space and the messages that are used to indicate territoriality.

Cultural Differences in the Use of Personal Space   Wherever you go, whatever you do, you are surrounded at all moments by a personal space "bubble." Edward Hall, who coined the term *proxemics* to refer to the study of how people differ in their use of personal space, has suggested that people interact within four spatial zones or distance ranges: intimate, personal, social, and public.[23] These proxemic zones are characterized by differences in the ways that people relate to one another and in the behaviors that typify the communication that will probably occur in them. Table 8.1, which is based on Hall's observations of U.S. Americans, displays the differences from zone to zone in the types and intensity of sensory information that is received by those who are involved in a communication experience.

Personal space distances are culture-specific. People from colder climates, for instance, typically use large physical distances when they communicate, whereas those from warm-weather climates prefer close distances. The personal space bubbles for northern Europeans are therefore large, and people expect others to keep their distance. The personal space bubbles for Europeans get smaller and smaller, however, as one travels south toward the Mediter-

Table 8.1 ZONES OF SPATIAL DIFFERENCE

Spatial Distance Zone	Spatial Distance (in feet)	Usage	Other Characteristics
Intimate	0–1$\frac{1}{2}$	Loving; comforting; protecting; fighting	Minimal conversation; smell and feel of other; eye contact unlikely
Personal	1$\frac{1}{2}$–4	Conversations with intimates, friends, and acquaintances;	Touch possible; much visual detail
Social	4–12	Impersonal and social gatherings	More formal tone; some visual detail lost; eye contact likely
Public	12–up	Lectures; concerts; plays; speeches; ceremonies; protection	Subtle details lost; only obvious attributes noticed

ranean. Indeed, the distance that is regarded as intimate in Germany, Scandi-navia, and England overlaps with what is regarded as a normal conversational distance in France and the Mediterranean countries of Italy, Greece, and Spain. Consequently, northern Europeans think their southern counterparts get "too close for comfort," whereas the southern Europeans regard their northern neighbors as "too distant and aloof."

The habitual use of the culturally proper spacing distance is accompanied by a predictable level and kind of sensory information. For example, if the standard cultural spacing distance in a personal conversation with an acquain-tance is about 3 feet, people will become accustomed to the sights, sounds, and smells of others that are usually acquired at that distance. For someone who is accustomed to a larger spacing distance, at 3 feet the voices will sound too loud, it might be possible to smell the other person's breath, the other per-son will seem too close and perhaps out of the "normal" focal range, and the habitual ways of holding the body may no longer work. Then, the culturally learned cues that are so helpful within one's culture can become a hindrance. One European American student, for instance, in commenting on a party that was attended by many Italians and Spaniards, exclaimed, "They would stand close enough that I could almost feel the air coming from their mouths." Sim-ilar reactions to intercultural encounters are very common. As Edward and Mildred Hall have suggested,

> Since most people don't think about personal distance as something that is cul-turally patterned, foreign spatial cues are almost inevitably misinterpreted. This can lead to bad feelings which are then projected onto the people from the other culture in a most personal way. When a foreigner appears aggressive and pushy, or remote and cold, it may mean only that her or his personal distance is differ-ent from yours.[24]

Cultures differ in the use of space and touching. These Russian men are greeting each other after church services. *(© John Nordell/The Picture Cube)*

Cultural Differences in Territoriality   Do you have a favorite chair or classroom seat that you think "belongs" to you? Or do you have a room, or perhaps just a portion of a room, that you consider to be off limits to others? The need to protect and defend a particular spatial area is known as *territoriality*, a set of behaviors that people display to show that they "own" or have the right to control the use of a particular geographic area.

People mark their territories in a variety of ways. It can be done formally using actual barriers such as fences and signs that say "No Trespassing" or

"Keep Off the Grass." Territories can also be marked informally by nonverbal markers such as clothing, books and other personal items that indicate a person's intent to control or occupy a given area.

Cultural differences in territoriality can be exhibited in three ways. First, cultures can differ in the general degree of territoriality that its members tend to exhibit. Some cultures are far more territorial than others. For instance, as Hall and Hall point out in their comparison of Germans and French,

> People like the Germans are highly territorial; they barricade themselves behind heavy doors and soundproof walls to try to seal themselves from others in order to concentrate on their work. The French have a close personal distance and are not as territorial. They are tied to people and thrive on constant interaction and high-information flow to provide them the context they need.[25]

Second, cultures can differ in the range of possible places or spaces about which they are territorial. A comparison of European Americans with Germans, for example, reveals that both groups are highly territorial. Both have a strong tendency to establish areas that they consider to be their own. In Germany, however, this feeling of territoriality extends to "all possessions, including the automobile. If a German's car is touched, it is as though the individual himself has been touched."[26]

Finally, cultures can differ in the typical reactions exhibited in response to invasions or contaminations of their territory. Members of some cultures prefer to react by withdrawing or avoiding confrontations whenever possible. Others respond by insulating themselves from the possibility of territorial invasion, using barriers or other boundary markers. Still others react forcefully and vigorously in an attempt to defend their "turf" and their honor.

Touch

Touch is probably the most basic component of human communication. It is experienced long before we are able to see and speak, and it is a fundamental part of the human experience.

The Meanings of Touch   Stanley E. Jones and A. Elaine Yarbrough have identified five meanings of touch that are important in understanding the nature

CULTURE CONNECTIONS

The word "testimony" originally referred to the custom whereby two men would hold each other's testicles in a gesture of trust and friendship. The word evolved to mean evidence in support of facts or assertions; the gesture evolved into the modern-day handshake.

of intercultural communication.[27] Touch is often used to indicate *affect*, the expression of positive and negative feelings and emotions. Protection, reassurance, support, hatred, dislike, and disapproval are all conveyed through touch; hugging, stroking, kissing, slapping, hitting, and kicking are all ways in which these messages can be conveyed. Touch is also used as a sign of *playfulness*. Whether affectionately or aggressively, touch can be used to signal that the other's behavior should not be taken seriously. Touch is frequently used as a means of *control*. "Stay here," "move over," and similar messages are communicated through touch. Touching for control may also indicate social dominance. High-status individuals in most Western countries, for instance, are more likely to touch than to be touched, whereas low-status individuals are likely to receive touching behaviors from their superiors.[28] Touching for ritual purposes occurs mainly on occasions involving introductions or departures. Shaking hands, clasping shoulders, hugging, and kissing the cheeks or lips are all forms of greeting rituals. Touching is also used in *task-related* activities. These touches may be as casual as a brief contact of hands when passing an object, or they may be as formal and prolonged as a physician taking a pulse at the wrist or neck.

Cultural Differences in Touch   Cultures differ in the overall amount of touching they prefer. High-contact cultures such as those in the Middle East, Latin America, and southern Europe touch each other in social conversations much more than do people from noncontact cultures such as Asia and northern Europe. These cultural differences can lead to difficulties in intercultural communication. Germans, Scandinavians, and Japanese, for example, may be perceived as cold and aloof by Brazilians and Italians, who in turn may be regarded as aggressive, pushy, and overly familiar by northern Europeans. As Edward and Mildred Hall have noted, "In northern Europe one does not touch others. Even the brushing of the overcoat sleeve used to elicit an apology."[29] A comparable difference was observed by Dean Barnlund, who found that U.S. American students reported being touched twice as much as did Japanese students.[30]

Cultures also differ in where people can be touched. In Thailand and Malaysia, for instance, the head should not be touched because it is considered to be sacred and the locus of a person's spiritual and intellectual powers. In the United States, the head is far more likely to be touched.[31]

Cultures vary in their expectations about who touches whom. In Japan, for instance, there are deeply held feelings against the touch of a stranger. These expectations are culture-specific, and even cultures that live near one another can have very different norms. Among the Chinese, for instance, shaking hands among people of the opposite sex is perfectly acceptable; among many Malay, it is not. Indeed, for those who practice the Muslim religion, casual touching between members of the opposite sex is strictly forbidden. Both men and women have to cleanse themselves ritually before praying if they happen to make physical contact with someone of the opposite sex. Holding hands, for example, or walking with an arm across someone's shoulder or around the waist, or even grabbing an elbow to help another across the street, are all considered socially inappropriate behaviors between men and women. In some places there are even legal restrictions against public displays of hugging and kissing, even among married couples. However, this social taboo refers only to opposite-sex touching; it is perfectly acceptable for women to hold hands or for men to walk arm in arm. Many European Americans, of course, have the opposite reaction; they react negatively to same-sex touching (particularly among men) but usually do not mind opposite-sex touching.

Finally, cultures differ in the settings or occasions in which touch is acceptable. Business meetings, street conversations, and household settings all evoke different norms for what is considered appropriate. Cultures make distinctions between those settings that they regard as public and those considered private. Although some cultures regard touching between men and women as perfectly acceptable in public conversations, others think that such activities should occur only in the privacy of the home; to them, touch is a highly personal and sensitive activity that should not occur where others might see it.

Time

The study of how people use, structure, interpret, and understand the passage of time is called *chronemics*. We consider chronemics from two perspectives: time orientations and time systems.

Time Orientations   Time orientation refers to the value or importance the members of a culture place on the passage of time. In Chapter 2 we indicated that communication is a process, which means that people's behaviors must be understood as part of an ongoing stream of events that changes over a period of time. Chapters 5 and 6 suggested that members of a culture share a similar worldview about the nature of time. We also indicated that different cultures can have very different conceptions about the appropriate ways to comprehend events and experiences. Specifically, some cultures are predominantly past-oriented, others are present-oriented, and still others prefer a future-oriented worldview. As we briefly review these cultural orientations about time, take note of the amazing degree of interrelationship—in this case the link between a culture's nonverbal code system and its cultural patterns—that characterizes the various aspects of a culture.

Past-oriented cultures regard previous experiences and events as most important. These cultures place a primary emphasis on tradition and the wisdom passed down from older generations. Consequently, they show a great deal of deference and respect for parents and other elders, who are the links to these past sources of knowledge. Events are circular, as important patterns perpetually reoccur in the present; therefore, tried-and-true methods for overcoming obstacles and dealing with problems can be applied to current difficulties. Many aspects of the British, Chinese, and Native American experiences, for instance, can be understood only by reference to their reverence for traditions, past family experiences, or tribal customs. An example of a past-oriented culture is the Samburu, a nomadic tribe from northern Kenya who revere their elders.

> The elders are an invaluable source of essential knowledge, and in an environment that by its very nature allows only a narrow margin for error, the oldest survivors must possess the most valuable knowledge of all. The elders know their environment intimately—every lie and twist of it. The land, the water, the vegetation; trees, shrubs, herbs—nutritious, medicinal, poisonous. They know each cow, and have a host of specific names for the distinctive shape and skin patterns of each animal in just the same way that Europeans distinguish within the general term flower, or tree.[32]

Present-oriented cultures regard current experiences as most important. These cultures place a major emphasis on spontaneity and immediacy and on experiencing each moment as fully as possible. Consequently, people do not participate in particular events or experiences because of some potential future gain; rather, they participate because of the immediate pleasure the activity provides. Present-oriented cultures typically believe that unseen and even unknown outside forces, such as fate or luck, control their lives. Cultures such as those in the Philippines and many Central and South American countries are usually present-oriented, and they have found ways to encourage a rich appreciation for the simple pleasures that arise in daily activities.

Future-oriented cultures believe that tomorrow—or some other moment in the future—is most important. Current activities are not accomplished and appreciated for their own sake but for the potential future benefits that might be obtained. For example, you go to school, study for your examinations, work hard, and delay or deny present rewards for the potential future gain that a rewarding career might provide. People from future-oriented cultures, which include many European Americans, believe that their fate is at least partially in their own hands and that they can control the consequences of their actions.

Time Systems   Time systems are the implicit cultural rules that are used to arrange sets of experiences in some meaningful way. There are three types of time systems: technical, formal, and informal.

Technical time systems are the precise, scientific measurements of time that are calculated in units such as light years or atomic pulses. Technical time is not used by the typical member of a culture because it is most applicable to specialized settings such as the research laboratory. Consequently, it is of little relevance to the common experiences that members of a culture share.

Formal time systems refer to the ways in which the members of a culture describe and comprehend units of time. Time units can vary greatly from culture to culture. Among many Native American cultures, for instance, time is segmented by the phases of the moon, the changing seasons, the rise and fall of the tides, or the movements of the sun. Similarly, when a Peruvian woman was asked for the distance to certain Inca ruins, she indicated their location by

CULTURE CONNECTIONS

I accepted an appointment as visiting professor of psychology at the federal university in Niteroi, Brazil, a midsized city across the bay from Rio de Janeiro. As I left home for my first day of class, I asked someone the time. It was 9:05 a.m., which allowed me time to relax and look around the campus before my 10 o'clock lecture. After what I judged to be half an hour, I glanced at a clock I was passing. It said 10:20! In panic, I broke for the classroom, followed by gentle calls of "Hola, professor" and "Tudo bem, professor?" from unhurried students, many of whom, I later realized, were my own. I arrived breathless to find an empty room.

Frantically, I asked a passerby the time. "Nine forty-five" was the answer. No, that couldn't be. I asked someone else. "Nine fifty-five." Another said: "Exactly 9:43." The clock in a nearby office read 3:15. I had learned my first lesson about Brazilians: Their timepieces are consistently inaccurate. And nobody minds.

My class was scheduled from 10 until noon. Many students came late, some very late. Several arrived after 10:30. A few showed up closer to 11. Two came after that. All of the latecomers wore the relaxed smiles that I came, later, to enjoy. Each one said hello, and although a few apologized briefly, none seemed terribly concerned about lateness. They assumed that I understood.

The idea of Brazilians arriving late was not a great shock. . . . The real surprise came at noon that first day, when the end of class arrived.

Back home in California, I never need to look at a clock to know when the class hour is ending. The shuffling of books is accompanied by strained expressions . . .

When noon arrived in my first Brazilian class, only a few students left immediately. Others slowly drifted out during the next 15 minutes, and some continued asking me questions long after that.

Source: Robert Levine & Ellen Wolff, "Social Time: The Heartbeat of Culture," *Psychology Today* (Sussex Publishers, 1985).

referring nonverbally to a position in the sky that represented the distance the sun would travel toward the horizon before the journey would be complete.[33] Among European Americans, the passage of time is segmented into seconds, minutes, hours, days, weeks, months, and years.

Time's passage may likewise be indicated by reference to significant events such as the birth of a royal son or an important victory in battle. Time intervals for particular events or activities may also be based on significant external events such as the length of a day or the phases of the moon. Alternatively, time intervals may be more arbitrary, as in the length of a soccer game or the number of days in a week. These ways of representing the passage of time, however arbitrary, are the culture's formal time system. Sequences such

The domination of one's daily life by the ubiquitous calendar is a characteristic of monochronic cultures. *(Bob Daemmrich. Copyright © by Stock, Boston, Inc., 1988. All rights reserved.) S. Stone/ The Picture Cube.*

as the months in the year are formally named and are explicitly taught to children and newcomers as an important part of the acculturation process.

The formal time system includes agreements among the members of a culture on such important issues as the extent to which time is regarded as valuable and tangible. European Americans, of course, typically regard time as a valuable, tangible commodity that is used or consumed to a greater or lesser degree.

Informal time systems refer to the assumptions cultures make about how time should be used or experienced. How long should you wait for someone who will be ready soon, in a minute, in a while, or shortly? When is the proper time to arrive for a 9:00 A.M. appointment or an 8:00 P.M. party? As a dinner guest, how long after your arrival would you expect the meal to be served? How long should you stay after the meal has been concluded? Cultures have unstated expectations about the timing and duration of such events. Although these expectations differ, depending on such factors as the occasion and the relative importance of those being met or visited, they are widely held and consistently imposed as the proper or appropriate way to conduct oneself as a competent member of the culture. In this regard, Edward Hall has reported,

> The time that it takes to reach an agreement or for someone to make up his mind operates within culturally defined limits. In the U.S. one has about four minutes in the business world to sell an idea. In Japan the well-known process of "nemawashi"—consensus building, without which nothing can happen—can take weeks or months. None of this four-minute sell.[34]

Perhaps the most important aspect of the culture's informal time system is the degree to which it is monochronic or polychronic.[35] A *monochronic* time system means that things should be done one at a time, and time is segmented into precise, small units. In a monochronic time system, time is viewed as a commodity; it is scheduled, managed, and arranged. European Americans, like members of other monochronic cultures, are very time-driven. The ubiquitous calendar or scheduler that many European Americans carry, which tells them when, where, and with whom to engage in activities, is an apt symbol of a monochronic culture. An event is regarded as separate and distinct from all others and should receive the exclusive focus of attention it deserves. These events also have limits or boundaries, so that there is an expected beginning and ending point that has been scheduled in advance. Thus European Americans

> find it disconcerting to enter an office overseas with an appointment only to discover that other matters require the attention of the man we are to meet. Our ideal is to center the attention first on one thing and then move on to something else.[36]

A *polychronic* time system means that several things are being done at the same time. In Spain and among many Spanish-speaking cultures in Central and South America, for instance, relationships are far more important than schedules. Appointments will be quickly broken, schedules readily set aside, and deadlines unmet without guilt or apology when friends or family members require attention. Those who use polychronic time systems often schedule multiple appointments simultaneously, so keeping "on schedule" is an impossibility that was never really a goal. European Americans, of course, are upset when they are kept waiting for a scheduled appointment, particularly when they discover that they are the third of three appointments that have been scheduled at exactly the same hour.

Cultural Differences in Perceptions and Use of Time   Cultures differ in their time orientations and in the time systems they use to give order to experiences. Misunderstandings can occur between people who have different time orientations. For instance, someone from a present-oriented culture might view people from past-oriented cultures as too tied to tradition and people from future-oriented cultures as passionless slaves to efficiency and materialism. Alternatively, someone from a future-oriented culture might view those from present-oriented cultures as self-centered, hedonistic, inefficient, and foolish.[37] This natural tendency to view one's own practices as superior to all others is a common source of problems in intercultural communication.

Cultures also differ in the formal and informal time systems they use to determine how long an event should take, and even how long "long" is. Misinterpretations often occur when individuals from monochronic and polychronic cultures attempt to interact. Each usually views the other's responses to time "commitments" as disrespectful and unfriendly.

Voice

Earlier in this chapter we stated that nonverbal messages are often used to accent or underscore the verbal message by adding emphasis to particular words or phrases. Indeed, the many qualities of the voice itself, in addition to the actual meaning of the words, form the *vocalic* nonverbal communication system. Vocalics also include many nonspeech sounds such as belching, laughing, and crying and vocal "filler" sounds such as *uh*, *er*, *um*, and *Uh-huh*.

Vocal vs. Verbal Communication   Vocalic qualities include pitch (high to low), rate of talking (fast to slow), conversational rhythm (smooth to staccato), and volume (loud to soft). Because spoken (i.e., verbal) language always has some vocal elements, it is difficult to separate the meaning conveyed by the language from that conveyed by the vocalic components. However, if you can imagine that these words you are now reading are a transcript of a lecture we have given, you will be able to understand clearly the distinctions we are describing. Although our words—the language spoken—are here on the printed page, the vocalics are not. Are we speaking rapidly or slowly? How does our inflection change to emphasize a point or to signal a question? Are we yelling, whispering, drawling, or speaking with an accent? Do our voices indicate that we are tense, relaxed, strained, calm, bored, or excited? The answers to these types of questions are conveyed by the speaker's voice.

Cultural Differences in Vocal Communication   There are vast cultural differences in vocalic behaviors. For example, unlike English, many Asian languages are tonal. The same Chinese words when said with a different vocalic tone or pitch can have vastly different meanings. Mà, for example, could mean "mother," "a pileup," "horse," or "scold," depending on the tone used in its expression.

In addition to differences in tone or pitch, there are large cultural differences in the loudness and frequency of speaking. Latinos, for instance, perceive themselves as talking more loudly and more frequently than European Americans.[38]

The emotional meanings conveyed by the voice are usually taken for granted by native language users, but they can be the cause of considerable problems when they fail to conform to preconceived expectations. For instance, when a Saudi Arabian man is speaking in English, he will usually transfer his native intonation patterns without necessarily being aware that he has done so. In Arabic, the intonation pattern is such that many of the individual words in the sentence are stressed. Although a flat intonation pattern is used in declarative sentences, the intonation pattern for exclamatory sentences is much stronger and more emotional than that in English. The higher pitch of Arabic speakers also conveys a more emotional tone than that of English speakers. Consequently, differences in vocal characteristics may result in unwarranted negative impressions. The U.S. American may incorrectly perceive that the Saudi Arabian is excited or angry when in fact he is not. Questions by the Saudi that merely seek information may sound accusing. The monotonous tone of declarative sentences may be perceived as demonstrating apathy or a lack of interest. Vocal stress and intonation differences may be perceived as aggressive or abrasive when only polite conversation is intended. Conversely, the Saudi Arabian may incorrectly interpret certain behaviors of

CULTURE CONNECTIONS

Smelling another person's cheeks as a form of greeting is also used by the Arabs. To the Arab, to be able to smell a friend is reassuring. Smelling is a way of being involved with another, and to deny a friend his breath would be to act ashamed. In some rural Middle Eastern areas, when Arab intermediaries call to inspect a prospective bride or a relative, they sometimes ask to smell her. Their purpose is not to make sure that she is freshly scrubbed; apparently what they look for is any lingering odor of anger or discontent.

Source: A. J. Almany and A. J. Alwan, *Communicating with the Arabs* (Prospect Heights, IL: Waveland Press, 1982) 17.

the U.S. American speaker as an expression of calmness and pleasantness when anger or annoyance is being conveyed. Similarly, a statement that seems to be a firm assertion to the U.S. American speaker may sound weak and doubtful to the Saudi Arabian.[39]

Other Nonverbal Code Systems

Many other nonverbal code systems are relevant to an understanding of intercultural communication because virtually everything we say, do, create, and wear can communicate messages about ourselves and our culture. These other codes include the chemical, dermal, physical, and artifactual systems that create a multichanneled set of nonverbal messages.

Chemical Code System   The interpretations made from chemically based body functions form the chemical code system. Chemical codes include natural body odor, tears, sweat, gas, household smells, and similar phenomena. People have distinct chemical code systems that are affected by their way of living, food preferences, habits, and environment. These differences are often used to make judgments or interpretations about members of a culture. For instance, most meat-eating Westerners have a distinct body odor that may be unpleasant to cultures that do not consume red meat. Similarly, many hotels in Malaysia have posted signs that say "No Durians" to discourage their guests from bringing in the pungent, sweet-tasting fruit that many consider to be a delicacy. Among many Arabic-speaking cultures, attempts to mask body odors with perfumes is considered an insult; this chemical information is so favorably regarded that close spatial distances in conversations are used to obtain it.

Dermal Code System   The short-term changes in skin texture or sensitivity that result from physical or psychological reactions to the environment form the dermal code system. Dermal codes include blushing, blanching, goose flesh, and related experiences. Particularly in high-context cultures, subtle changes in skin tonalities may be carefully observed to obtain the information needed to act appropriately.

Physical Code System   The relatively unchanging aspects of the body form the physical code system: weight, body shape, facial features, skin color, eye color, hair, characteristics that denote age and gender, and similar features. Indeed, the cultural standards for beauty vary greatly, as can expectations about how people should look.

Artifactual Code System   The creations that people make, use, or wear are the artifactual code system. These aspects of material culture include the tools, clothing, buildings, furnishings, jewelry, lighting, and color schemes that are common to the members of a culture. Clothing styles, cosmetics, and body ornamentations, for instance, are used to fulfill the culture's needs for modesty, self-expression, or privacy. Differences in privacy needs, in particular, are often indicated by such features as closed doors in the United States, sound-proofed doors in Germany, tree-lined barriers at property lines in England, or paper-thin walls in Japan.

SYNCHRONY OF NONVERBAL COMMUNICATION CODES

Cultures train their members to synchronize the various nonverbal behaviors to form a response pattern that typifies the expected behaviors in that culture. Subtle variations in the response patterns are clearly noticed, even when they differ by only a few thousandths of a second. William Condon, who describes himself as "a white, middle-class male," suggests that interactional synchrony is learned from birth and occurs within a fraction of a second. Condon compares the differences in the speech and gestures of African Americans and European Americans:

> If I say the word "because" both my hands may extend exactly together. In Black behavior, however, the right hand may begin to extend with the "be" portion slightly ahead of the left hand and the left hand will extend rapidly across the "cause" portion. This creates the syncopation, mentioned before, which can appear anywhere in the body. A person moves in the rhythm and timing of his or her culture, and this rhythm is in the whole body. . . . It may be that those having different cultural rhythms are unable to really "synch-in" fully with each other. ... I think that infants from the first moments of life and even in the womb are getting the rhythm and structure and style of sound, the rhythms of their culture, so that they imprint to them and the rhythms become part of their very being.[40]

Behavioral synchrony in the use of nonverbal codes can be found in virtually all cultures. Not only must an individual's many behaviors be coordinated appropriately, they must also mesh properly with the words and move-

CULTURE CONNECTIONS

Elizabeth Ebenego walked in my front door. She'd dropped in because she saw my lamp on so late and wondered why. Cameroonians are curious people. She stopped short at the sight of Gary. He stood up to shake her hand. She glanced at me and a warm pleased look suffused her face before she modestly lowered her head scarf over her brow. . . .

I said, "This is Gary Bartlett—Elizabeth Ebenego. Gary's here from St. Bonaventure's in Kumba."

"Pleased to make your acquaintance."

Gary said, "Same here." He smiled and looked into her eyes. Elizabeth reached up and lowered her scarf a little more. Cameroonian women become embarrassed when men look into their eyes. Cameroonian men don't do that to women. It's an offensive gesture. But women are fairly used to white men doing that to them.

Source: Mary Ann Tirone-Smith, "Gary and the Pigs," *From the Center of the Earth*, ed. Geraldine Kennedy (Santa Monica, CA: Clover Park Press, 1991) 172.

ments of the other interactants. Coordination in Japanese bowing behaviors, for example, requires an adaptation to the status relationships of the participants; the inferior must begin the bow, and the superior decides when the bow is complete. If the participants are of equal status, they must begin and end their bows simultaneously. This is not as easy as it seems, for as one Japanese man relates,

> Perfect synchrony is absolutely essential to bowing. Whenever an American tries to bow to me, I often feel extremely awkward and uncomfortable because I simply cannot synchronize bowing with him or her. . . . bowing occurs in a flash of a second, before you have time to think. And both parties must know precisely when to start bowing, how deep, how long to stay in the bowed position, and when to bring their heads up.[41]

Similar degrees of coordination and synchrony can be found in everyday activities. A sensitivity to these different nonverbal codes can help you to become more interculturally competent.

NONVERBAL COMMUNICATION AND INTERCULTURAL COMPETENCE

The rules and norms that govern most nonverbal communication behaviors are both culture-specific and outside of conscious awareness. That is, although members of a culture know and follow their culture's expectations, they probably learned the norms for proper nonverbal expressiveness very early in childhood and these norms may never have been articulated verbally.[42] Sometimes, therefore, the only way you will know that a cultural norm exists is when you break it!

An important consequence of this out-of-awareness aspect is that members of a culture use their norms to determine appropriate nonverbal behaviors and then make negative judgments about others' feelings, motives, intentions, and even their attractiveness if these norms are violated.[43] Often the violations will be inaccurately attributed to aspects of personality, attitudes, or intelligence rather than to a mismatch between learned nonverbal codes. U.S. Americans, for instance, highly value positive nonverbal displays and typically regard someone who smiles as more intelligent than someone who does not; the Japanese, however, whose cultural norms value constraint in nonverbal expressiveness, do not equate expressiveness with intelligence.[44] The very nature of nonverbal behaviors makes inaccurate judgments difficult to recognize and correct.

The following suggestions will help you use your knowledge of nonverbal communication to improve your intercultural competence. These suggestions are designed to help you notice, interpret, and use nonverbal communication behaviors to function more appropriately and more effectively in intercultural encounters.

Researchers have been known to take weeks or even months to analyze the delicate interaction rhythms involved in a single conversation. Of course, most people do not have the luxury of a month to analyze someone's comments before responding. However, the knowledge that the patterns of behavior will probably be very complex will help sensitize you to them and may encourage you to notice more details.

No set of behaviors is universally correct, so the "right" behaviors can never be described in a catalog or list. Rather, the proper behaviors are those that are appropriate and effective in the context of the culture, setting, and occasion. What is right in one set of circumstances may be totally wrong in another. Although it is useful to gather culture-specific information about appropriate nonverbal behaviors, even this knowledge should be approached as relative because prescriptions of "right" behavior rarely identify all of the situational characteristics that cultural natives "know."

By monitoring your emotional reactions to differences in nonverbal behaviors, you can be alert to the interpretations you are making and, therefore, to the possibility of alternative meanings. Strong visceral responses to differences in smell, body movement, and personal spacing are quite common in intercultural communication. Knowledge that these might occur, followed by care in the interpretation of meanings, is critical.

Skillful interpretation includes observation of general tendencies. Focus on what members of the other culture prefer and the ways in which they typically behave. How, when, and with whom do they gesture, move, look, and touch? How are time and space used to define and maintain social relationships? It is much harder to pay attention to these general tendencies than you might think because in all likelihood you have not had much practice in consciously looking for patterns in the commonplace, taken-for-granted activities through which cultural effects are displayed. Nevertheless, it is possible, with practice, to improve your observation skills.

Even after making observations, be tentative in your interpretations and generalizations. You could be wrong. You will be far more successful in making sense of others' behaviors if you avoid the premature closure that comes with assuming you know for certain what something means. Think of your explanations as tentative working hypotheses rather than as unchanging facts.

Next, look for exceptions to your generalizations. These exceptions are very important because they help you to recognize that no one individual, regardless of the thoroughness and accuracy with which you have come to understand a culture, will exactly fit the useful generalizations you have formed. The exceptions that you note can help you to limit the scope of your generalizations and to recognize the boundaries beyond which your judgments may simply not apply. Maybe your interpretations apply only to men or students or government officials or potential customers. Maybe your evaluations of the way time and space are structured apply only to business settings or among those whose status is equal or with particular people like yourself. Though it is necessary to make useful generalizations to get along in another culture, it is equally necessary to recognize the limits of these generalizations.

Finally, practice to improve your ability in observing, evaluating, and behaving in appropriate and effective ways. Practice will increase your skill in recognizing that there are specific patterns to another's behavior, then in correctly interpreting their meanings and likely consequences, and finally in selecting a response that is both appropriate and effective. Like all skills, your level of intercultural competence can improve with practice. Of course, the most appropriate form of practice is one that closely approximates the situations in which you will have to use the skills you are trying to acquire. Therefore we encourage you to seek out and willingly engage in intercultural communication experiences.

SUMMARY

Although there is some evidence that certain nonverbal communication tendencies are common to all humans, cultures vary greatly in the repertoire of behaviors and circumstances in which nonverbal exchanges occur. A smile, a head nod, and eye contact may all have different meanings in different cultures.

This chapter considered the important nonverbal code systems used to supplement, reinforce, or substitute for the verbal code systems. Nonverbal code systems are the silent language of communication. They are less precise and less consciously used and interpreted than verbal code systems, but they can have powerful effects on perceptions of and interpretations about others. The nonverbal code systems relating to body movements, space, touch, time, voice, and other nonverbal code systems were each described. Finally, the interrelationship of these nonverbal code systems with one another and with the verbal code system was explored.

The Effects of Code Usage in Intercultural Communication

Practical, everyday communication experiences—greeting a friend, buying something from a shopkeeper, asking directions, or describing a common experience—require messages to be organized in a meaningful way. Cultures differ, however, in the patterns that are preferred for organizing ideas and communicating them to others. These differences affect what people regard as logical, rational, and a basis for sound reasoning and conclusions.

This chapter focuses on the consequences for intercultural communication of differences in the way cultures use verbal and nonverbal communication. Do people in particular cultures have distinctive preferences for what, where, when, and with whom to speak? Are there differences in what are regarded as the ideal ways to organize ideas and present them to others? What constitutes appropriate forms of reasoning, evidence, and proof in a discussion or argument? Is proof accomplished with a statistic, an experience, an expert's testimony, or a link between some aspect of the problem and the emotions of the listener? What is considered "rational" and "logical"? In short, how do conversations differ because of the differences in culture, language, and nonverbal codes?

Intercultural communication competence requires more than just an accurate translation of the verbal and nonverbal codes that others use. The "logic" of how those codes are organized and used must also be understood.

The chapter begins by considering alternative cultural preferences for the organization of messages. Cultural variations in persuasive communication are considered next. Finally, differences in the structure of conversations are presented as another way in which code systems influence intercultural communication.

PREFERENCES IN THE ORGANIZATION OF VERBAL CODES

Cultures have distinct preferences for organizing ideas and presenting them in written discourse and in the organizational structures that characterize public speaking. Consider what you have been taught in English composition courses as the "correct" way to structure an essay, or remember the organizational patterns used to structure the content of a speech. The premise underlying this discussion is that cultures have preferred ways for people to organize and convey thoughts and feelings. These preferences influence the ways people communicate and the choices that are made to arrange ideas in a specific pattern.

The effects of code usage on organizing ideas is visible to teachers of English as a second language (ESL). Even after nonnative English speakers have learned to master the vocabulary and grammar of the English language, they are unlikely to write an essay in what is considered "correct" English form. In fact, because of the particular style for the organization and presentation of ideas, ESL teachers can often identify the native language of a writer even when the essay is written in English. Robert Kaplan, one of the most influential investigators of cultural and linguistic differences in organizational patterns, refers to speaking and writing correctly as learning the "logic" of the language.[1]

In this chapter, we first describe the organizational features of the English language as it is used in the United States. We then explore the organizational features associated with other languages used in particular cultures. We conclude with a discussion of the effects of these varying organizational preferences on intercultural communication.

Organizational Preferences in the Use of U.S. English

For most cultures, the correct use of language is most easily observed as the language is formally taught in the school system. English is a standard feature of the U.S. high school curriculum, and English composition is a requirement for virtually all U.S. college students. The development of oral communication skills, which usually includes training in public speaking, is also a common requirement for many college students. In both written and oral communication courses, users of U.S. English explicitly learn rules that govern how ideas are to be presented. Indeed, the features that characterize a well-organized essay in

U.S. English are very similar to the features of a well-organized public speech.

The structure of a good essay or speech in U.S. English requires the development of a specific theme. A thesis statement, which is the central organizing idea of the speech or essay, is the foundation on which speakers or writers develop their speech or essay. Ideally, thesis statements are clear and specific; speakers and writers must present their ideas in a straightforward and unambiguous manner. In many instances, the student of U.S. English is taught to provide the thesis statement in the opening paragraph of the essay or in the introduction to the speech.

The paragraph is the fundamental organizational unit of written English. As a standard textbook for college writing courses indicates,

> A paragraph is a unit of thought composed of sentences, [which are themselves] smaller units of thoughts, relating to a single topic. . . . The main idea of the paragraph often appears in a topic sentence, usually located at or near the beginning of the paragraph.[2]

There are other rules that guide how paragraphs are combined into an essay or main points into a speech. Generally, correct organization means that writers or speakers in U.S. English clearly state their thesis at the beginning and provide the audience with an overview of their main points.

As the key to good organization, students are taught to outline the main points of the essay or speech by subordinating supporting ideas to the main ideas. In fact, most teachers give students explicit instructions to help them learn to organize properly.

In U.S. English there is also a preferred way to develop the main points. If a speaker is talking about scuba diving, with main points on equipment and safety tips, he or she is expected to develop the point on equipment by talking only about equipment. Safety tips should not be mentioned in the midst of the discussion about equipment. If the speaker gave examples related to safety tips in the middle of the discussion on equipment, listeners (or readers) trained in the preferences embedded in U.S. English would become confused and would think the speaker was disorganized. A teacher would probably comment on the organizational deficiencies and might lower the student's grade because the speech does not match the expected form of a well-organized speech.

The organizational pattern preferred in the formal use of U.S. English can best be described as linear. This pattern can be visualized as a series of steps or progressions that move in a straight line toward a particular goal or idea. Thus, the preferred organizational pattern forms a series of "bridges," wherein each idea is linked to the next.

Organizational Preferences in Other Languages and Cultures

Some years ago Robert Kaplan systematically began to study the preferred organizational patterns of nonnative speakers of English. In an article that is usually credited with launching a specialization called contrastive rhetoric, Kaplan characterized the preferences for the organization of paragraphs among

CULTURE CONNECTIONS

A word of warning is very much in order here, however. Unconsciously, most Americans tend to judge the intelligence and reliability of Japanese by the fluency of their English—and that's a fundamental error. A Japanese may discuss a deal with a potential U.S. partner in flawless American English and even in purely American terms of reference. But unless he has a death wish, when he discusses that same deal with his Japanese colleagues, he's going to do so in Japanese terms of reference. So if the American really wants the deal to go through, he had better take the trouble to find out how his proposal can be tailored to Japanese patterns of thought and behavior. In short, language skills alone are simply not enough to bridge the cultural gap.

Source: Robert C. Christopher, *The Japanese Mind* (New York: Fawcett Columbine, 1983) 99–100.

people from different language and cultural groups.[3]

Satoshi Ishii elaborates on Kaplan's depiction of organizational preferences when he describes the preferred structure of a paragraph in Japanese as a "gyre."[4] Ishii characterizes a gyre as an approach to an idea by "indirection" and explains the Japanese paragraph as a series of "stepping stones" that depend on indirection and implication, rather than on explicit links, to connect ideas and provide a main point. The rules for language use in Japan demand that the speaker not tell the listener the specific point being conveyed; to do so is considered rude and inappropriate. Rather, the Japanese delicately circle a topic in order to imply its domain. The U.S. English concepts of thesis statements and paragraph topic sentences have no real equivalent in Japanese.

Imagine the consequences of an intercultural interaction between a Japanese person and a U.S. American. What might happen if one of them is able to speak in the other's language and is sufficiently skilled to convey meaning linguistically but is not adept at the logic of the language? The Japanese person is likely to think that the U.S. American is rude and aggressive. Conversely, the U.S. American is likely to think that the Japanese person is confusing and imprecise. Both people in this intercultural interaction are likely to feel dissatisfied, confused, and uncomfortable.

The circularity in the structure of the Japanese paragraph also characterizes the writing of those whose first language is Hindi, one of India's national languages. Yamuna Kachru indicates that a Hindi paragraph does not develop just one unified thought or idea.[5] Rather, the preferred style allows the writer to digress and to include material related to many ideas. When using English, speakers of Hindi exhibit characteristics of the Hindi organizational style in their English paragraphs.

How do you think U.S. teachers of English would grade an assignment that was written in English by a native Hindi speaker? We can easily imagine the comments about the lack of organization and the poor development of the ideas. Kachru, in fact, concludes that Indian writing and speaking conventions show a marked preference for nonlinearity and are therefore perceived, from a Western perspective, as illogical.

Speakers of Indian English like to provide many minor contextual points of a story before advancing the thesis, whereas speakers of British English tend first to provide the thesis of the story and then give the relevant information.[6] Chinese discourse styles are similar to those of Indian English. Rather than relying on a preview statement to orient the listener to the discourse's overall direction, Chinese relies heavily on contextual cues. Chinese speech also tends to use single words such as *because*, *as*, and *so* to replace whole clause connectives, such as "in view of the fact that" "to begin with," or "in conclusion," that are commonly used in English.[7] In Arabic, writing is structured using repetition, parallelism, and coordination between sentences.[8]

Another difference in organizational structure concerns languages that are speaker-responsible and those that are listener-responsible. In English, which is a speaker-responsible language, the speaker provides the structure and therefore much of the specific meaning of the statement.[9] As the speaker tells the listener exactly what is going to be talked about and what the speaker wants the listener to know, prior knowledge of the speaker's intent is not necessary. In Japanese, which is a listener-responsible language, speakers need only indicate indirectly what they are discussing and what they want the listener to know when the conversation is over. The listener is forced to construct the meaning, and usually does so, based on shared knowledge between the speaker and the listener.

CULTURE CONNECTIONS

The Albanian way of expressing ideas is markedly circuitous. But for someone who has spent years learning that direct declarative sentences are the key to communication, I have to admire the poetry that creeps in with the ramble.

The basic words and the simple conversations are the most delightful. A conversation about buying bread raises voices. At first, I feared an argument was ensuing and I couldn't imagine what about. Now I know to sit back and enjoy the emotion, the vocal dance.

Source: Christina Nifong, "Tending a Blaze of Beautiful Words," *The Christian Science Monitor*, December 9, 1993, 20.

In sum, cultural patterns interact with code systems to create expectations about what is considered the proper or logical way to organize the presentation of ideas. What is considered the right way to organize ideas within one culture may be regarded as illogical, disorganized, unclear, and perhaps even rude, discourteous, and ineffective in another. In intercultural communication, people make judgments about the clarity and logic of others' thoughts, and their assumptions about what is rational or logical may vary greatly and may lead to misunderstandings.

CULTURAL VARIATIONS IN PERSUASION

Persuasion, or the use of symbols to influence others, is most often identified with formal, public settings, such as when a candidate for political office tries to win votes through speeches and advertisements. Persuasion, however, also occurs in everyday interactions between people.

Persuasion in Intercultural Encounters

Attempts to influence others to accept an idea or to engage in some behavior are a common feature of everyday conversation. For example, you might have tried to convince your employer to give you a day off from work. Or perhaps you negotiated with a salesperson on the price of a new television. Or maybe you tried to convince your teacher that the due date for your term paper should be delayed a week. All of these events involve persuasion.

In today's multicultural world, any of the preceding examples could involve culturally heterogeneous representatives. An Asian student may need to ask a European American teacher for an extension on an assignment. An African American who supervises employees from a variety of cultural groups may need to convince them to implement a change in office procedures. The Latino businessperson may want to sell his company's new information system to a Brazilian manager of a company in Argentina. The tourist in Nigeria may want hotel room service in the middle of the night. All of these communicative situations require knowledge and skill in using the appropriate means of persuasion; whereas members of some cultures genuinely enjoy the persuasive or argumentative encounter, many others shun such confrontations.[10]

The effective use of verbal and nonverbal codes in persuasion varies greatly from culture to culture. For instance, there are differences in what cultures consider to be acceptable evidence, who is regarded as an authority, how evidence is used to create persuasive arguments, and what ideas are reasonable. These preferred ways to convince others are called the culture's *persuasive style*. When people from diverse cultures communicate, the differences in their persuasive styles are often very evident.

The word *logical* is often used to describe the preferred persuasive style of a culture. Logic and rationality seem to be invoked as though there were some

CULTURE CONNECTIONS

"The American style of learning is to ask questions, discuss the theory and then go do it and ask more questions," he said. "The Japanese style is to observe the master, not ask questions and then get your hands dirty at the very beginning. If you ask questions, it can suggest that the master didn't do his job properly. The different styles can cause problems."

Source: *Sacramento Bee,* June 2, 1991, A18.

firm "truth" somewhere that simply has to be discovered and used in order to be convincing. We are suggesting, however, that "because logic has cultural aspects, an understanding of social life requires an understanding of how people think in their own cultural context."[11] In other words, what is regarded as logical and rational varies from culture to culture. The phrase that best sums up these variations is *ethno-logics* or *alternative logics.*

Cultural Differences in Argumentation

There are several approaches to the topic of persuasion. The approach we prefer was first described by philosopher Stephen Toulmin.[12] We have chosen this approach because it is the most culturally neutral; it is relatively easy to understand how each of the elements that Toulmin describes can be radically changed by a shift in cultural perspective. This approach can also be used to demonstrate how cultural backgrounds influence what people regard as reasonable, logical, and therefore persuasive. In fact, Toulmin himself claims that what people call rationality varies from culture to culture and from time to time:

> Within different cultures and epochs, reasoning may operate according to different methods and principles, so that different milieus represent (so to say) the parallel "jurisdictions" of rationality.[13]

Toulmin says that when people are actually using arguments to convince others, they depend on three key elements: evidence, warrants, and claims or conclusions. People select evidence from many choices. The evidence is then linked to some conclusion or "claim" that they want the other person to accept. The link between the evidence and the claim is based on what Toulmin calls a warrant. You might think of the warrant as a value assumption—which may not even be verbally stated in the presentation of the argument—that describes the world as it is or as it should be. Each of these terms is explained in greater detail in the following sections.

Evidence   Evidence is what a persuader offers to those she or he is trying to persuade. We have available to us in any given persuasive situation a myriad of sensory information or ideas. For example, suppose that students are trying to persuade a teacher to give an extension on a paper's due date. There have probably been numerous events that students could select as evidence. Maybe many students had been ill for a day, or perhaps the teacher had been sick. Or perhaps during one critical lecture, the noise of construction workers just outside the classroom made it difficult to pay attention to the discussion. Any of these events might be used as evidence to support the claim that the paper's due date ought to be postponed. An idea or experience does not become evidence, however, until it is selected for use in the persuasive interaction. What we choose from among all of the available cues is highly influenced by our culture.

There are no universally accepted standards about what constitutes evidence. Among many devout Muslims and Christians, for instance, parables or stories—particularly from the Koran or Bible—are a powerful form of evidence. The story is offered, and the lesson from the story is assumed to be conclusive. In other cultures, the story itself must be scrutinized to determine how illustrative it is compared to other possible cases.

The European American culture prefers physical evidence and eyewitness testimony, and members of that culture see "facts" as the supreme kind of evidence. Popular mysteries on television or in best-selling books weave their tales by giving clues through the appearance of physical evidence or facts—a button that is torn off a sleeve, a record of calls made from one person's telephone to another, or a bankbook that shows regular deposits or withdrawals. From all of these pieces of evidence, human behavior and motivation are regarded as apparent. In certain portions of Chinese culture, however, physical evidence is discounted because no connection is seen between those pieces of the physical world and human actions. People from cultures that view the physical world as indicative of human motivation have difficulty understanding this Buddhist point of view.

The use of testimony in the persuasive process also varies greatly from one culture to another. In certain African cultures, the words of a witness would be discounted or even totally disregarded because the people believe that if you speak up about seeing something, you must have a particular agenda in mind; in other words, no one is regarded as objective. The U.S. legal system, however, depends on the testimony of others; witnesses to traffic accidents, for example, are called to give testimony concerning the behavior of the drivers involved in the accident.

Warrants   A warrant is the link between the evidence and the claim. The warrant can be thought of as a linking assumption that makes it possible to move mentally from the evidence to the claim. Sometimes the warrant is not explicitly stated. In some of the preceding examples you should be able to identify the warrant easily. For instance, if the telephone bill of a suspect in a murder trial lists a call to the home of the person who was murdered, the warrant, or the assumption, is that the suspect had some kind of deliberate con-

CULTURE CONNECTIONS

Written contracts, *keiyaka,* are not as common in Japan as they are in the West, and even those contracts in Japan that are concluded in writing are not expected to be any more binding because of it. In the West agreements are to be based on and justified by principles, which written contracts attempt to specify and make binding. In Japan agreements, written or not, are based on "agreement," and both parties understand that conditions can change, that shifts might need to occur. So they accommodate themselves for this possibility ahead of time, by investing no great faith in a mere piece of paper.

To the Japanese a *relationship* is what holds agreements together. To the Westerners, *justice* is what binds agreements.

Source: William Bohnaker, *The Hollow Doll* (New York: Ballantine Books, 1990) 92.

Rules of acceptable evidence, the testimony of witnesses, and other procedural characteristics of legal systems provide excellent examples of cultural variations in argumentation. The couple in this photograph are seeking a divorce in the People's Republic of China. (*Marc Riboud, Magnum.*)

nection with the deceased. In the U.S. American legal system, this warrant would help the prosecutor to claim that the suspect had a motive for the murder.

Perhaps the best way to think about warrants is to refer to the discussion of cultural patterns in Chapters 5 and 6. These cultural patterns are the underlying assumptions that we use to connect evidence with conclusions or claims. Michael Cole and Sylvia Scribner offer the following illustration of cultural differences in warrants:

> In central Liberia, as well as many other parts of Africa, it is believed that certain men (variously called *zos*, *shamen*, and *witchdoctors*) can control lightning and direct it to hit anyone or anything they choose. As evidence of such powers, a college student from this region offered the following story: In his town, there was an occasion upon which someone stole meat from the cooking pot of the lightning *zo*. Angered, the *zo* announced that if the meat was not returned immediately, he would direct lightning to hit the guilty person on the following Saturday. On the appointed day, the meat had not been returned and the people all took to their houses in fear; a storm blew up, and when it was over the people found a dead dog, apparently killed by lightning. The student, and all the townspeople, took the dog's death as *prima facie* evidence of the power of the *zo*.[14]

In Liberia, the cultural assumption, operating as the underlying warrant in this argument, is that the material (human) world interacts with the natural or spiritual world. It is this warrant that allowed the townspeople to accept the dog's death as evidence.

Claims or Conclusions   The claim, or conclusion, of your persuasive appeal is what you want the other person to accept, believe, or do when your argument to them is completed. It is the idea you are seeking to justify in the minds of the person you are trying to persuade. In some cases your conclusion might also mean that the person to whom you are appealing will behave in a particular way. When you are attempting to persuade someone, you may present a series of arguments in which you establish several claims or conclusions.

Cultural Differences in Styles of Persuasion

As we have suggested, in any culture there are preferred choices for the types of evidence that people will accept. In addition, warrants—the underlying cultural patterns that function as assumptions in persuasion—also vary among cultures. There are cultural differences in the ways people prefer to arrange their evidence, warrants, and claims; this is the culture's "persuasive style."[15]

John Condon says that many U.S. Americans have difficulty with the persuasive style of someone from Mexico because Mexicans are more emotional and dramatic and have less concern about the accuracy of details. When a U.S. American visiting Mexico asks a shopkeeper a question, the shopkeeper's goal is to keep the visitor happy; thus an answer is provided even if it is not accurate.[16] Similarly, Lubman describes a fundamental difference between U.S.

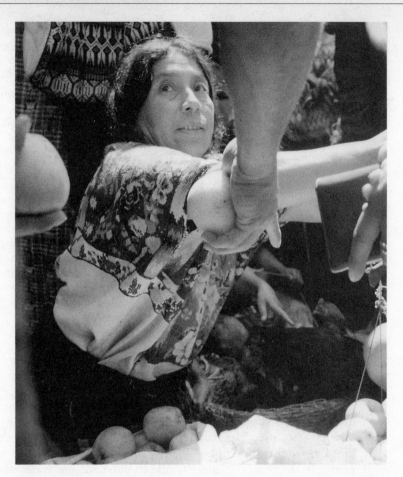

People the world over depend on persuasion to transform interested customers into purchasing customers. Here a Guatemalan Indian woman uses her sales pitch to influence a shopper. *(Copyright © Myron W. Lustig & Jolene Koester.)*

Americans and Chinese in a persuasive encounter. The U.S. Americans use alternative ways of saying the same thing, and they display changes in their positions during the course of a discussion. The Chinese, on the other hand, simply restate their position repeatedly; they would never publicly change their position without private consultation among themselves.[17]

We would like to elaborate on the idea of persuasive style because, like many of the other characteristics of a culture, it is an important cultural attribute that is taken for granted within a culture but affects communication between cultures. As we have cautioned elsewhere, not every person in a culture will select the culture's preferred style. Rather, we are describing a cultural tendency, a choice or preference that most people in the culture will select most of the time.

CULTURE CONNECTIONS

When taking a taxi in Saudi Arabia, one should not say, "Take me to the airport." Instead suggest that a ride to the airport might be pleasant. The driver knows you are going to the airport, but it irritates him to be ordered when a suggestion will do.

Barbara Johnstone describes three general strategies of persuasion that can form a culture's preferred style: the quasilogical, presentational, and analogical.[18] Each of these styles depends on different kinds of evidence, organizational patterns, warrants, and claims. As you read the descriptions of these styles, try to imagine what a persuasive encounter would be like and what might happen if others preferred a different persuasive style.

Quasilogical Style   The preferred style for members of many Western cultures is one Johnstone calls quasilogical. In this style, the preference is to use statistics and testimony from expert, objective witnesses as evidence. The evidence is then connected to the claim in a way that resembles formal logic. In formal logic, once the listener accepts or believes the individual pieces of evidence, the conclusions follow "logically" and must also be accepted. In the quasilogical style, the speaker or persuader will connect the evidence to the claims by using such words as *thus*, *hence*, and *therefore*. The form or arrangement of the ideas is very important.

The underlying assumption of this style is that if the idea is "true," it simply needs to be presented in a logical way so that its truthfulness becomes apparent to the listener. Those who prefer the quasilogical style assume that it is possible to discover what is true or false and right or wrong about a particular experience. In other words, they believe that events can be objectively established and verified.

Presentational Style   The presentational style emphasizes and appeals to the emotional aspects of persuasion. In this style, it is understood that people, rather than the idea itself, are what make an idea persuasive. That is, ideas themselves are not inherently persuasive; what makes them compelling is how they are presented to others. Thus, an immutable truth does not exist, and there are no clear rights or wrongs to be discovered.

In this style, the persuader uses language to create an emotional response. The rhythmic qualities of words and the ability of words to move the hearer visually and auditorily are fundamental to this style of persuasion. You have probably read poetry or literature that stimulated a strong emotional reaction. Those who use a presentational style persuade in the same way. By the use of words, the ideas of the speaker become so vivid and real that the persuasive idea almost becomes embedded in the consciousness of the listener. The language of this style of persuasion is filled with sensory words that induce the listener to *look*, *see*, *hear*, *feel*, and ultimately *believe*.

Analogical Style   The analogical style seeks to establish an idea (a claim) and to persuade the listener by providing an analogy, a story, or a parable in which there is either an implicit or explicit lesson to be learned. The storybook pattern that begins "Once upon a time" is one example of this style. An assumption underlying the analogical style is that the collective experience of groups of people—the culture—is persuasive, rather than the ideas themselves or the characteristics of a dynamic individual. Historical precedent takes on great importance because what convinces is a persuader's ability to choose the right historical story to demonstrate the point. In the analogical style, skill in persuasion is associated with the discovery and narration of the appropriate story—a story that captures the essence of what the persuader wants the listeners to know.

Persuasive encounters involving people with different stylistic preferences may result in neither person being persuaded by the other. To a person with a cultural preference for a quasilogical style, the presentational style will appear emotional and intuitive, and the analogical style will appear irrelevant. To those using the presentational style, the quasilogical style will appear dull, insignificant, and unrelated to the real issues. To those using the analogical style, the quasilogical style will seem blunt and unappealing.

A study of cultural differences among European American, Latino, and Bahamian speakers lends support to the importance of adapting one's persuasive approach to the particular cultural context.[19] An interesting example of the clash in preferences for persuasive styles is found in Jesse Jackson's speech given to the 1988 Democratic Presidential Nominating Convention, where Jackson was running for that nomination. Jackson's speaking style was misinterpreted by many in the media, who were primarily European Americans, because they did not understand that his presentational speaking style followed the oral tradition of African American speakers. Jackson was accused of factual exaggeration, lying, and being overly dramatic and emotional. Yet his speaking style was grounded in a rich rhetorical tradition in which "argument" and "reasoning" are presented as part of a performance, with dramatic emphases to make the ideas clear and vivid.[20]

CULTURAL VARIATIONS IN THE STRUCTURE OF CONVERSATIONS

All conversations differ on a number of important dimensions: the length; the nature of the relationship between the conversants; the kinds of topics discussed; the way information is presented; how signals are given to indicate interest and involvement; and even whether conversation is regarded as a useful, important, and necessary means of communicating. In this section, we explore some of the differences in the way cultures shape the use of codes to

CULTURE CONNECTIONS

Asking directions often leads to irritation. . . .

In Japan, Latin America, the Mediterranean countries, and many others, a tourist who is lost must make a conscious effort to avoid being misdirected. This is done by never signaling the kind of answer you would like to hear. Say "Could you direct me to the post office?" but never say "The post office is straight ahead, isn't it?"

The second question invites a yes or no answer, and since it is rude to say no, you will be told yes, even though you are walking directly away from the place you want to be.

Source: Paul S. Pierre, "Being Offensive Without Trying Is Easy Overseas," *Sacramento Bee*, April 9, 1989, E1 and E4.

create conversations. Our usual caution applies: When cultural tendencies are described, remember that not all members of the culture will necessarily reflect these characteristics.

Value of Talk and Silence

The importance given to words varies greatly from one culture to the next. Among African Americans and European Americans, for example, words are considered very important. In informal conversations between friends, individuals often "give my word" to assure the truth of their statement. In the legal setting, people swear that their words constitute "the truth, the whole truth, and nothing but the truth." Legal obligations are contracted with formal documents to which people affix their signatures—another set of words. The spoken word is seen as a reflection of a person's inner thoughts. Even the theories of communication that are presented in most books about communication—including this one—are highly influenced by underlying assumptions that give words the ability to represent thoughts. In this characteristically Western approach to communication, people need words to communicate accurately and completely with one another.

Other cultures are far more hesitant about the value of words. Asian cultures such as Japan, Korea, and China, and southern African cultures such as Swaziland, Zambia, and Lesotho, have quite a different evaluation of words and talking.

D. Lawrence Kincaid says that "the Eastern perspective places more emphasis than the Western on the meaning of silence and on saying nothing or as little as is necessary."[21] Because of a combination of historical and cultural

CULTURE CONNECTIONS

Arreola's circuitous response to Haydon's question had been an artful demonstration of Mexican dissimulation, a national attribute that Haydon found alternately maddening and beguiling. It was the Mexican way to avoid directness. To be too definite was to run great risk; one might offend, or one might commit oneself to an irrevocable path that one might later regret. It was best to be oblique, to leave room for other options, for an unforeseen change of heart or mind. Better to couch one's ideas in flowery language, in ambiguities which later could be interpreted in a variety of ways. Better to be cautious.

Source: David L. Lindsay, *In the Lake of the Moon* (New York: Bantam Books, 1988) 176.

forces, spoken words in Japan, Korea, and China are viewed with some suspicion and disregard. Akira Tsujimura considers one of the major characteristics of Japanese communication to be "communication without the use of language."[22] Donald Klopf elaborates:

> The desire not to speak is the most significant aspect or feature of Japanese language life. The Japanese hate to hear someone make excuses for his or her mistakes or failures. They do not like long and complicated explanations. Consequently, the less talkative person is preferred and is more popular than the talkative one, other conditions being equal. If one has to say something normally, it is said in as few words as possible.[23]

In Korea, the strong religious and cultural influence of Confucian values has devalued oral communication and made written communication highly regarded. June-Ock Yum, in an interesting exploration of the relationship between Korean philosophy and communication, says, "Where the written communication was dominant, spoken words were underrated as being apt to run on and on, to be mean and low. To read was the profession of scholars, to speak the act of menials."[24] Buddhism, also a major influence on Korean thought, teaches, "True Communication is believed to occur only when one speaks without the mouth and when one hears without the ears."[25]

In Swaziland people are similarly suspicious of those who talk excessively. As Peter Nwosu has observed,

> The Swazis are quick to attribute motives when a person during negotiations is very pushy, engages in too much self-praise, or acts like he or she knows everything. "People who talk a lot are not welcome; be calm, but not too calm that they suspect you are up to some mischief," remarks an official of the Swazi

Embassy in Washington, D.C. Indeed, there is such a thin line between talkativeness and calmness that it is difficult for a foreigner to understand when one is being "too talkative" or "too calm."[26]

People from Finland are also less willing than European Americans to talk, even among close friends.[27]

The consequences of these differences in preferences for talking is illustrated by a Japanese American student and an African American student who became roommates. Over a period of a few weeks, the African American student sought social interaction and conversation with his Japanese American roommate, who seemed to become less and less willing to converse. The African American student interpreted this reticence as an indication of dislike and disinterest rather than as an indication of cultural differences in conversational preferences. Finally, he decided to move to a different room, because he felt too uncomfortable with the silence to remain.

There are also different cultural preferences for silence and the place of silence in conversations. Keith Basso describes a number of interpersonal communication experiences in which members of the Apache tribe prefer silence, whereas non-Native Americans might prefer to talk a lot: meetings between strangers, the initial stages of a courtship, an individual returning home to relatives and friends after a long absence, a person verbally expressing anger, someone being sad, and during a curing ceremony.[28] Basso gives this assessment of the value placed on introductions:

> The Western Apache do not feel compelled to "introduce" persons who are unknown to each other. Eventually, it is assumed, strangers will begin to speak. However, this is a decision that is properly left to the individuals involved, and no attempt is made to hasten it. Outside help in the form of introductions or other verbal routines is viewed as presumptuous and unnecessary.
>
> Strangers who are quick to launch into conversations are frequently eyed with undisguised suspicion. A typical reaction to such individuals is that they "want something," that is, their willingness to violate convention is attributed to some urgent need which is likely to result in requests for money, labor, or transportation.[29]

In sum, the fundamental value and role of talk as a tool for conversation varies from culture to culture.

Rules for Conversations

Cultures provide an implicit set of rules to govern interaction. Verbal and nonverbal codes come with a set of cultural prescriptions that determine how they should be used. In this section we explore some of the ways in which conversational structures can vary from one culture to another. Communication scholars using an ethnographic perspective have been at the forefront of these investigations, and we draw heavily on their efforts.[30] In Chapter 11 we

CULTURE CONNECTIONS

For a person from the Vietnamese culture, it is not typical to display emotions or tensions externally through gestures or facial expressions. If a boss becomes angry with an employee, the boss will respond by leaving the work area for a brief period of time. If a husband becomes angry with his wife, his likely response is to leave silently and stay with friends for a couple of days. Teachers, when they become angry with students, are very quiet. The influence of Confucianism is offered as explanation for this lack of the display of tension or emotion, because Confucianism suggests following a path of moderation, avoiding exaggeration, and cultivating equanimity. Westerners often mistake the lack of visible emotional expressiveness as impassiveness, placidity, or even hypocrisy.

also consider some aspects of conversational structures that are particularly relevant to the development of intercultural relationships.

Some of the ways in which conversational rules can vary are illustrated in the following questions:

- How do you know when it is your turn to talk in a conversation?
- When you talk to a person you have never met before, how do you know what topics are acceptable for you to discuss?
- In a conversation, must your comments be directly related to those that come before?
- When you are upset about a grade, how do you determine the approach to take in a conversation with the teacher, or even *if* you should have a conversation with the teacher?
- When you approach your employer to ask for a raise, how do you decide what to say?
- If you want someone to do something for you, do you ask for it directly or do you mention it to others and hope that they will tell the first person what it is that you want?
- If you decide to ask for something directly, do you go straight to the point and say, "This is what I need from you," or do you hint at what you want and expect the other person to understand?
- When you speak, do you use grand language filled with images, metaphors, and stories or do you simply and succinctly present the relevant information?

Cultural preferences would produce many different answers to these questions. For example, European Americans signal a desire to speak in a conversation by leaning forward a small degree, slightly opening their mouth, and es-

Like all exchanges, this conversation among Argentinean women is governed by a complex set of rules about who talks to whom, for how long, and on what topics. Yet the conversational participants are unlikely to be consciously aware of these rules until someone breaks them. *(Copyright © Michael Dwyer, Stock, Boston, Inc., 1994. All rights reserved.)*

tablishing eye contact. In another culture, those same sets of symbols could be totally disregarded because they have no meaning, or they could mean something totally different (for example, respectful listening). Acceptable topics of conversations for two U.S. American students meeting in a class might include their majors, current interests, and where they work. Those same topics in some other cultures might be regarded as too personal for casual conversations, but discussions about religious beliefs and family history might seem perfectly acceptable. Though European Americans expect comments in a conversation to be related to previous ones, Japanese express their views without necessarily responding to what the other has said.[31]

William Gudykunst and Stella Ting-Toomey describe cultural variations in conversational style along four dimensions: direct-indirect, elaborate-succinct, personal-contextual, and instrumental-affective.[32] Cultures that prefer a direct style, such as European Americans, use verbal messages that are explicit in revealing the speaker's true intentions and desires. In contrast, those that prefer indirection will veil the speaker's true wants and needs with ambiguous statements. African American, Japanese, and Korean cultures, for example, prefer the indirect style.

CULTURE CONNECTIONS

The black [American] culture is characterized by an oral tradition. Knowledge, attitudes, ideas, notions are traditionally transmitted orally, not through the written word. It is not unusual, then, that the natural leader among black people would be one with exceptional oratorical skills. He must be able to talk, to speak—to preach. In the black religious tradition, the successful black preacher is an expert orator. His role involves more, however. His relationship with his parishioners is reciprocal; he talks to them, and they talk back to him. That is expected. In many church circles this talk-back during a sermon is a firm measure of the preacher's effectiveness.

Source: Charles V. Hamilton, *The Black Preacher in America* (New York: William Morrow, 1972) 42, quoted in Molefi Kete Asante, *The Afrocentric Idea* (Philadelphia: Temple University Press, 1987) 47.

Cultural conversational styles also differ on a dimension of elaborate to succinct. The elaborate style, which is found in most Arab and Latino cultures, results in the frequent use of metaphors, proverbs, and other figurative language. The expressiveness of this style contrasts with the succinct style, in which people give precisely the amount of information necessary. In the succinct style, there is a preference for understatement and long pauses, as in Japanese American and Chinese American cultures.

In cultures that prefer a personal style, in contrast to those that prefer a contextual style, there is an emphasis on conversations in which the individual, as a unique human being, is the center of action. This style is also characterized by more informality and less status-oriented talk. In the contextual style, the emphasis is on the social roles that people have in relationships with others. Japanese, Chinese, and Indian cultures all emphasize the social role or the interpersonal community in which a particular person is embedded. The style is very formal and heightens awareness of status differences by accentuating them.

In the instrumental style, communication is goal-oriented and depends on explicit verbal messages. Affective styles are more emotional and require a sensitivity to the underlying meanings in both the verbal and nonverbal code systems. Thomas Kochman has articulated some of the differences in conversational styles between European Americans and African Americans:

The differing potencies of black and white public presentations are a regular cause of communicative conflict. Black presentations are emotionally intense, dynamic, and demonstrative; white presentations are more modest and emotionally restrained.[33]

CULTURE CONNECTIONS

What's confusing to English speakers about Athabaskans

They do not speak

They keep silent

They avoid situations of talking

They only want to talk to close acquaintances

They play down their own abilities

They act as if they expect things to be given to them

They deny planning

They avoid direct questions

They never start a conversation

They talk off the topic

They never say anything about themselves

They are slow to take a turn in talking

They ask questions in unusual places

They talk with a flat tone of voice

They are too indirect, inexplicit

They don't make sense

They just leave without saying anything

What's confusing to Athabaskans about English speakers

They talk too much

They always talk first

They talk to strangers or people they don't know

They think they can predict the future

They brag about themselves

They don't help people even when they can

They always talk about what is going to happen later

They ask too many questions

They always interrupt

They only talk about what they are interested in

They don't give others a chance to talk

They are always getting excited when they talk

They aren't careful when they talk about things or people

Source: Ronald Scollon and Suzanne Wong-Scollon, "Athabaskan-English Interethnic Communication," *Cultural Communication and Intercultural Contact*, Donal Carbaugh (Hillsdale, NJ: Lawrence Erlbaum, 1990) 284.

Melanie Booth-Butterfield and Felecia Jordan similarly found that African American females were more expressive, more involved with one another, more animated, and more at ease than were their European American counterparts, who appeared more formal and restrained.[34] Because of these differences in conversational style, an African American and a European American may judge each other negatively.

Ronald Scollon and Suzanne Wong-Scollon, who have studied the Athabaskan, a cultural group of native peoples in Alaska and northern Canada, describe similar problems in intercultural communication:

> When an Athabaskan and a speaker of English talk to each other, it is very likely that the English speaker will speak first. . . . The Athabaskan will feel it is important to know the relationship between the two speakers before speaking. The English speaker will feel talking is the best way to establish a relationship. While the Athabaskan is waiting to see what will happen between them, the English speaker will begin speaking, usually asking questions in fact, to find out what will happen. Only where there is a longstanding relationship and a deep understanding between the two speakers is it likely that the Athabaskan will initiate the conversation.[35]

Regulating conversations is also problematic for the English speaker and Athabaskans because the latter use a longer pause—about a half second longer—between turns. The effects of this slightly longer pause would be comical if the consequences for intercultural communication were not so serious.

> When an English speaker pauses, he waits for the regular length of time (around one second or less), that is, *his* regular length of time, and if the Athabaskan does not say anything, the English speaker feels he is free to go on and say anything else he likes. At the same time the Athabaskan has been waiting his regular length of time before coming in. He does not want to interrupt the English speaker. This length of time we think is around one and one-half seconds. It is just enough longer that by the time the Athabaskan is ready to speak the English speaker is already speaking again. So the Athabaskan waits again for the next pause. Again, the English speaker begins just enough before the Athabaskan was going to speak. The net result is that the Athabaskan can never get a word in edgewise (an apt metaphor in this case), while the English speaker goes on and on.[36]

These very real differences in the nature of conversations play a critical role in intercultural communication. The ultimate result is often a negative judgment of other people rather than a recognition that the variability in cultural preferences is creating the difficulties.

EFFECTS OF CODE USAGE ON INTERCULTURAL COMPETENCE

Developing competence in the practical, everyday use of verbal and nonverbal codes is undoubtedly a major challenge for the intercultural communicator. But simply knowing the syntactic rules of other code systems is not sufficient to be able to use those code systems well.

The most important knowledge you can take away from this chapter is the realization that people from other cultures may organize their ideas, persuade others, and structure their conversations in a manner that differs from yours. You should attempt, to the greatest extent possible, to understand your own preferences for using verbal and nonverbal codes to accomplish practical goals. If you can, mentally set aside your beliefs and the accompanying evaluative labels. Instead, recognize that your belief system and the verbal and nonverbal symbols that are used to represent it were taught to you by your culture and constitute only one among many ways of understanding the world and accomplishing one's personal objectives.

Look for the differences in the ways that people from other cultures choose to accomplish their interpersonal objectives. Look for alternative logics. Approach the unfamiliar as a puzzle to be solved rather than as something to be feared or dismissed as illogical, irrational, or wrong. Much can be learned about the effects of code usage by observing others. If your approach is not successful, notice how members of the culture accomplish their objectives.

SUMMARY

The chapter described the effects on intercultural communication of cultural differences in the way verbal and nonverbal codes are used. These differences affect how people attempt to understand messages, organize ideas, persuade others, and engage in discussions and conversations.

We began with a discussion of differences in cultural preferences for organizing and arranging messages, and we contrasted the organizational preferences of U.S. English, which are typically linear, with those of other languages and cultures.

Cultural variations in persuasion and argumentation were considered next. We emphasized that appropriate forms of evidence, reasoning, and rationality are all culturally based and can affect intercultural communication. Indeed, there are major differences in persuasive styles that are taken for granted within a culture but that affect the communication between cultures.

Cultural variations also exist in the structure of conversations. The importance given to talk and silence, the social rules and interaction styles that are used in conversations, and even the cues used to regulate the back-and-forth sequencing of conversations can all create problems for intercultural communicators.

Differences in the way people prefer to communicate can affect the ability to behave appropriately and effectively in intercultural encounters. These cultural preferences typically operate outside of awareness and may lead to judgments that others are "wrong" or "incorrect" when they are merely different.

10
CHAPTER

Intercultural Competence in Interpersonal Relationships

All relationships imply connections. When you are in an interpersonal relationship you are connected—in a very important sense, you are bound together—with another person in some substantial way. Of course, the nature of these ties is rarely physical. Rather, in interpersonal relationships you are connected to others by virtue of your shared experiences, interpretations, perceptions, and goals.

CULTURAL VARIATIONS IN INTERPERSONAL RELATIONSHIPS

In Chapter 2 we indicated that communication is interpersonal as long as it involves a small number of participants who can interact directly with one another and who therefore have the ability to adapt their messages specifically for one another. Of course, different patterns of interpersonal communication are likely to occur with different types of interpersonal relationships. We believe it is useful to characterize the various types of interpersonal relationships by the kinds of social connections the participants share.

CULTURE CONNECTIONS

I remember asking a twenty-year-old student in economics at Delhi University . . . if she loved the childhood friend her parents had decided she should marry. "That's a very difficult question," she answered. "I don't know. This whole concept of love is very alien to us. We're more practical. I don't see stars, I don't hear little bells. But he's a very nice guy, and I think I'm going to enjoy spending my life with him. Is that love?" She shrugged.

Source: Elisabeth Bumiller, *May You Be the Mother of a Hundred Sons* (New York: Fawcett Columbine, 1990) 8.

Types of Interpersonal Relationships

Some interpersonal connections occur because of blood or marriage. Others exist because of overlapping or interdependent objectives and goals. Still others bind people together because of common experiences that help to create a perception of "we-ness." However, all interpersonal relationships have as their common characteristic a strong connection among the individuals.

The number of interpersonal relationships that you have throughout your life is probably very large. Some of these relationships are complex and involved, whereas others are simple and casual; some are brief and spontaneous, while others may last a lifetime. Some of these relationships, we hope, have involved people from different cultures.

Interpersonal relationships between people from different cultures can be difficult to understand and describe because of the contrasts in culturally based expectations about the nature of interpersonal communication. However, regardless of the cultures involved or the circumstances surrounding the relationship's formation, there is always some sort of bond or social connection that links or ties the people to one another. The participants may be strangers, acquaintances, friends, romantic partners, or family or kinship members. Each relationship carries with it certain expectations for appropriate behaviors that are anchored within specific cultures. People in an intercultural relationship, then, may define their experiences very differently and may have dissimilar expectations; for example, a stranger to someone from one culture may be called a friend by someone from another culture.

Strangers You will undoubtedly talk to many thousands of people in your lifetime, and most of them will be strangers to you. But what exactly is a stranger? Certainly, a stranger is someone whom you do not know and who is

CULTURE CONNECTIONS

When one American passes another on the street, in the middle of the day and in a neighborhood not known to be dangerous, there is a good chance, if one exchanges glances with the other, that he or she will smile or nod, or even say hello to the stranger, without it going any further. This often surprises French visitors in the United States. As a respectable, gray-haired man said to me, "If I were younger, I would think all these pretty girls were giving me the eye. . . . They seem like such flirts when they smile at you like that. . . . If this were France. . . ." This same sudden and fleeting rapport among strangers can be established just as well through conversation in the United States, here again without consequence. It can even last a long time, as at American dinners and parties, at which one meets "very nice" people, with whom one has long conversations, and whom one will never see again (which French people find deeply disturbing).

Source: Raymonde Carroll, *Cultural Misunderstandings: The French–American Experience* (Chicago: The University of Chicago Press, 1987) 30.

therefore unfamiliar to you. But is someone always a stranger the first time you meet? How about the second time, or the third? What about the people you talked with several times, although the conversation was restricted to the task of seating you in a restaurant or pricing your groceries so names were never actually exchanged? Are these people strangers to you? Your answers to these questions, like so many of the ideas described in this book, depend on what you have been taught by your culture.

In the United States, for instance, the social walls that are erected between strangers may not be as thick and impenetrable as they are in some collectivistic cultures. European Americans, who are often fiercely individualistic as a cultural group, may not have developed the strong in-group bonds that would promote separation from outsiders. Among the Greeks, however, who hold collectivistic values, the word for "non-Greek" translates as "stranger."

Even in the United States, the distinction between stranger and non-stranger is an important one; young children are often taught to be afraid of people they do not know. Compare, however, a U.S. American's reaction toward a stranger to that of a Korean in a similar situation. In Korea, which is a family-dominated collectivist culture, a stranger is anyone to whom you have not been formally introduced. Strangers in Korea are "nonpersons" to whom the rules of politeness and social etiquette simply do not apply. Thus, Koreans may jostle you on the street without apologizing or, perhaps, even noticing. However, once you have been introduced to a Korean, or the Korean antici-

CULTURE CONNECTIONS

A friendly American is not necessarily an American friend. Though an American may be willing to have long, intimate conversations with a stranger, that doesn't mean a dinner invitation is forthcoming.

Source: Sophia Dembling, "Culture Shock: The American Way Can Be Odd to Outsiders," *Sacramento Bee,* October 6, 1991: T8.

pates in other ways that he or she may have an ongoing interpersonal relationship with you, elaborate politeness rituals are required.

Acquaintances   An acquaintance is someone you know, but only casually. Therefore, interactions tend to be on a superficial level. The social bonds that link acquaintances are very slight. Acquaintances will typically engage in social politeness rituals, such as greeting one another when first meeting or exchanging small talk on topics generally viewed as more impersonal such as the weather, hobbies, fashions, and sports. But acquaintances do not typically confide in one another about personal problems or discuss private concerns. Of course, the topics appropriate for small talk, which do not include personal and private issues, will differ from one culture to another. Among European Americans, it is perfectly appropriate to ask a male acquaintance about his wife; in the United Arab Emirates, it would be a major breach of social etiquette to do so. In New Zealand, it is appropriate to talk about national and international politics; in Pakistan, these and similar topics should be avoided. In Austria, discussions about money and religion are typically sidestepped; elsewhere, acquaintances may well be asked "personal" questions about their income and family background.

Friends   As with many of the other terms that describe interpersonal relationships, *friend* is a common expression that refers to many different types of relationships. "Good friends," "close friends," and "just friends" are all commonly used expressions among U.S. Americans. Generally speaking, a friend is someone you know well, someone you like, and someone with whom you feel a close personal bond. A friendship usually includes higher levels of intimacy, self-disclosure, involvement, and intensity than does acquaintanceship. In many ways, friends can be thought of as close acquaintances.

Unlike kinships, friendships are voluntary, even though many friendships start because the participants have been thrust together in some way. Because they are voluntary, friendships usually occur between people who see themselves as similar in some important ways and who belong to the same social class.

CULTURE CONNECTIONS

I grew up for a good portion of my life in the United States. In the course of living here, I've made many American friends. My relationships with them are very close, in that I even confide in them, but somehow I feel something is missing. There seems to exist a barrier against how close we can really be. I guess this is especially notice-able to me because of the fact that my early childhood was spent in a culture that put a great deal of value on friendship.

Source: Mee Her, "Friends in Bed" in *Passages: An Anthology of the Southeast Asian Refugee Experience* compiled by Katsuyo K. Howard, Southeast Asian Student Services, Cal. State Univ.-Fresno, 1990.

European American friendships tend to be very compartmentalized be-cause they are based on a shared activity, event, or experience. The European American can study with one friend, play racquetball with another, and go to the movies with a third. As suggested in Chapter 5, this pattern occurs be-cause European Americans typically classify people according to what they do or have achieved rather than who they are. Relations among European Ameri-cans are therefore fragmented, and they view themselves and others as a com-posite of distinct interests. Conversely, the Thai are likely to react more to the other person as a whole and will avoid forming friendships with those whose values and behaviors are in some way deemed undesirable.[1] Unlike friendships in the United States, in Thailand a friend is accepted completely or not at all; a person cannot disapprove of some aspect of another's political beliefs or personal life and still consider her or him to be a friend.

John Condon has noted that the language people use to describe their in-terpersonal relationships often reflects the underlying cultural values about their meaning and importance. Thus, Condon says, friendships among Euro-pean Americans are expressed by terms such as *friends*, *allies*, and *neighbors*, all of which reflect an individualistic cultural value. However, among African Americans and some Southern whites, closeness between friends is expressed by such terms as *brother*, *sister*, or *cousin*, suggesting a collectivist cultural value. Mexican terms for relationships, like the cultural values they represent, are similar to those of African Americans. Thus when European Americans and Mexicans speak of close friendships, the former will probably use a word such as *partner*, which suggests a voluntary association, whereas Mexicans may use a word such as *brother* or *sister*, which suggests a lasting bond that is beyond the control of any one person.[2]

As interpersonal relationships move from initial acquaintance to close friendship, five types of changes in perceptions and behaviors will probably occur. First, friends interact more frequently; they talk to each other more often, for longer periods of time, and in more varied settings than acquaintances do. Second, the increased frequency of interactions means that friends will have more knowledge about and shared experiences with each other than will acquaintances, and this unique common ground will probably develop into a private communication code to refer to ideas, objects, and experiences that are exclusive to the relationship. Third, the increased knowledge of the other person's motives and typical behaviors means that there is an increased ability to predict a friend's reactions to common situations. The powerful need to reduce uncertainty in the initial stages of relationships, which we discuss in greater detail later in this chapter, suggests that acquaintanceships are unlikely to progress to friendships without the ability to predict the others' intentions and expectations. Fourth, the sense of "we-ness" increases among friends. Friends often feel that their increased investment of time and emotional commitment to the relationship creates a sense of interdependence, so that individual goals and interests are affected by and linked to each person's satisfaction with the relationship. Finally, close friendships are characterized by a heightened sense of caring, commitment, trust, and emotional attachment to the other person, so that the people in a friendship view it as something special and unique.[3]

Intercultural friendships can vary in a variety of ways: whom a person selects as a friend, how long a friendship lasts, the prerogatives and responsibilities of being a friend, the number of friends that a person prefers to have, and even how long a relationship must develop before it becomes a friendship. African American friends, for instance, expect to be able to confront and criticize one another, sometimes in a loud and argumentative manner.[4] Latinos, Asian Americans, and African Americans feel that it takes them, on the average, about a year for an acquaintanceship to develop into a close friendship, whereas European Americans feel that it takes only a few months.[5] For intercultural friendships to be successful, therefore, they may require an informal agreement between the friends about each of these aspects for the people involved to have shared expectations about appropriate behaviors.

Romantic Partners   The diversity of cultural norms that govern romantic relationships is an excellent example of the wide range of cultural expectations. Consider, for instance, the enormous differences in cultural beliefs, values, and norms about love, romance, dating, and marriage.

Among European Americans, dating usually occurs for romance and companionship. A dating relationship is not viewed as a serious commitment that will necessarily, or even probably, lead to an engagement. If they choose to do so, couples will marry because of love and affection for each other. Although family members may be consulted before a final decision is made, the choice to marry is made almost exclusively by the couples themselves.

In Argentina and Spain, dating is taken more seriously. Indeed, dating the same person more than twice may mean that the relationship will lead to an engagement and, ultimately, marriage. Yet engagements in these Spanish-speaking cultures typically last a long time and may extend over a period of

In every culture, expectations about the behaviors of friends are controlled by a set of rules or expectations about social episodes. *(Copyright © Frank Siteman/The Picture Cube.)*

years, as couples work, save money, and prepare themselves financially for marriage.

In Indonesia, the opportunities for men and women to be together, particularly in unchaperoned settings, are much more restricted. In India, casual dating relationships and similar opportunities for romantic expression among unmarried individuals are still quite rare; marriages are likely to be arranged by parents, usually with the consent of the couple. This pattern of familial involvement can also be found in Arabic-speaking cultures, where marriage imposes great obligations and responsibilities on the families of the couple. In Algeria, for instance, a marriage is seen as an important link between families, not individuals. Consequently, the selection of a spouse may require the approval of the entire extended family. Moreover, in both India and Algeria, romantic love is believed to be something that develops after marriage, not before. Even in Colombia, where because of changes in customs and cultural practices arranged marriages are no longer fashionable, the decision to get married requires family approval. Yet research by Ge Gao on the nature of romantic relationships within the United States and China found a great deal of similarity in the communication between romantic partners.[6]

In intercultural communication, contrasting sets of rules may cause difficulties in managing the friendship appropriately and effectively. *(Copyright Owen Franken © Stock, Boston, Inc.) W. Hill/ The Image Works.*

Family   Family or kinship relationships are also characterized by large cultural variations. Particularly important to the development of intercultural relationships are these factors: how the family is defined, or who is considered to be a member of the family; the formality of roles and behavioral expectations for particular family members; and the importance of the family in social relationships and personal decisions.

Among European Americans, and even among members of most European cultures, family life is primarily confined to interactions among the mother, father, and children. Households usually include just these family members, though the extended family unit also includes grandparents, aunts, uncles,

CULTURE CONNECTIONS

By itself or taken together, none of these—not the food, not the language, not the psycho-sexual politics—defines a marriage, or even an interracial relationship. At the core, in the heart of lightness—the cynical among you should avert your eyes—there is love. We use however we differ and whatever we have in common to help us discover who we are, who we think we are, who we think we ought to be, and why. Because, for reasons more elemental than food or language or politics, the white woman who is my wife and I have found, in each other, a home.

Source: Jose Arcellana, "Special Relations," *Filipinas*, February 1993: 35.

and cousins. Though the amount and quality of interaction among extended family members will vary greatly from family to family, members of the extended family rarely live together in the same household or take an active part in the day-to-day lives of the nuclear family members.

Family relationships in other cultures can be quite different. Among Latinos, for instance, the extended family is very important.[7] Similarly, in India the extended family dominates; grandparents, aunts, uncles, and many other relatives may live together in one household. Families in India include people who would be called second or third cousins in the European American family, and the unmarried siblings of those who have become family members through marriage may also be included in the household. These "family members" would rarely be defined as such in the typical European American family. Among Native Americans family refers to all members of the clan.[8] No particular pattern of family relationships can be said to typify the world's cultures. Many Arab families, for instance, include multiple generations of the male line. Often three generations—grandparents, married sons and their wives, and unmarried children—will live together under one roof. Among certain cultural groups in Ghana, however, just the opposite pattern can be found; families have a matrilineal organization, and the family inheritance is passed down through the wife's family rather than the husband's.

Expected role behaviors and responsibilities also vary among cultures. In Argentina, family roles are very clearly defined by social custom; the wife is expected to raise the children, manage the household, and show deference to the husband. In India, the oldest male son has specific family and religious obligations that are not requirements for other sons in the same family. Languages sometimes reflect these specialized roles. In China, for example,

> A sister-in-law is called by various names, depending on whether she is the older brother's wife, the younger brother's wife, or the wife's sister. Aunts, uncles, and cousins are named in the same way. Thus, a father's sister is "ku," a mother's sister is "yi," an uncle's wife is "shen," and so on.[9]

These members of a Malay family represent three generations under one roof. Extended families such as these are common in many parts of the world. *(Copyright © Myron W. Lustig & Jolene Koester.)*

Families also differ in their influence over a person's social networks and decision making. In some cultures, the family is the primary means through which a person's social life is maintained. In others, such as among European Americans, families are almost peripheral to the social networks that are established. In the more collectivist cultures such as Japan, Korea, and China, families play a pivotal role in making decisions for children, including the choice of university, profession, and even marital partner. In contrast, in individualistic cultures, where children are taught from their earliest years to make their own decisions, a characteristic of "good parenting" is to allow children to "learn for themselves" the consequences of their own actions.

The increasing number of people creating intercultural families, in which husband and wife represent different cultural backgrounds, poses new challenges for family communication. Often, the children in these families are raised in an intercultural household that is characterized by some blending of the original cultures. Differences in the expectations of appropriate social roles—of wife and husband, son and daughter, older and younger child, or husband's parents and wife's parents—require a knowledge of and sensitivity to the varying influences of culture on family communication.

Dimensions of Interpersonal Relationships

People throughout the world use three primary dimensions to interpret interpersonal communication messages: control, affiliation, and activation.

Control   Control involves status or social dominance. We have control to the extent that we have the power and prestige to influence the events around us. Depending on the culture, control can be communicated by a variety of behaviors including touching, looking, talking, and the use of space. Supervisors, for instance, are more likely to touch their subordinates than vice versa. In many cultures, excessive looking behaviors are viewed as attempts to "stare down" the other person and are usually seen as an effort to exert interactional control. Similarly, high-power individuals seek and are usually given more personal space and a larger territory to control than their low-power counterparts. Of course, many of these same behaviors, when used in a different context, could also indicate other aspects of the interpersonal relationship. Excessive eye contact, for example, might not be an indication of power; it may merely mean that the two individuals are deeply in love. Usually, however, there are other situational cues that can be used to help interpret the behaviors correctly.

Control is often conveyed by the specific names or titles used to address another person. Do you address physicians, teachers, and friends by their first names, or do you say *Doctor, Professor,* or *Mr.* or *Ms.?* In Malaysia and many other places, personal names are rarely used among adults because such use might imply that the other person has little social status. Instead,

> a shortened form or a pet name is often used if a kin term is not appropriate. This is to avoid showing disrespect, since it is understood that the more familiar the form of address to a person, the more socially junior or unimportant he must be regarded.[10]

In cultures that are very attuned to status differences among people, such as Japan, Korea, and Indonesia, the language system requires distinctions based on people's degree of social dominance. In Indonesia, for instance,

> The Balinese speak a language which reflects their caste, a tiered system where (like the Javanese) at each level their choice of words is governed by the social relationship between the two people having a conversation.[11]

Intercultural communication is often characterized by an increased tendency to *mis*interpret nonverbal control and status cues. In both the United

States and Germany, for instance, private offices on the top floors and at the corners of most major businesses are reserved for the highest-ranking officials and executives; in France, executives typically prefer an office that is centrally located, in the middle of their subordinates if possible, in order to stay informed and to control the flow of activities. Thus, the French may infer that the Germans are too isolated and the Germans that the French are too easily interrupted to manage their respective organizations well.

Affiliation   Members of a culture use affiliation to interpret the degree of friendliness, liking, social warmth, or immediacy that is being communicated. Affiliation is an evaluative component that indicates a person's willingness to approach or avoid others. Albert Mehrabian suggests that we approach those people and things we like and we avoid or move away from those we do not like.[12] Consequently, affiliative behaviors are those that convey a sense of closeness, communicate interpersonal warmth and accessibility, and encourage others to approach.

Affiliation can be expressed through eye contact, open body stances, leaning forward, close physical proximity, touching, smiling, a friendly tone of voice, and other communication behaviors. Edward Hall has called those cultures that display a high degree of affiliation "high-contact" cultures; those that display a low level are called "low-contact" cultures.[13]

Compared to low-contact cultures, members of high-contact cultures tend to stand closer, touch more, and have fewer barriers such as desks and doors to separate themselves from others. High-contact cultures, which are generally located in warmer climates, include many of the cultures in South America, Latin America, southern Europe, and the Mediterranean region; most Arab cultures; and Indonesia. Low-contact cultures, which tend to be located in colder climates, include the Japanese, Chinese, U.S. Americans, Canadians, and northern Europeans. One explanation for these climate-related differences is that the harshness of cold-weather climates forces people to live and work closely with one another in order to survive, and some cultures have compensated for this forced togetherness by developing norms that encourage greater distance and privacy.[14]

Activation   Activation refers to the ways people react to the world around them. Some people seem very quick, excitable, energetic, and lively; others value calmness, peacefulness, and a sense of inner control. Your perception of the degree of activity that another person exhibits is used to evaluate that person as fast or slow, active or inactive, swift or sluggish, and spirited or deliberate.

Cultures differ in what they consider acceptable and appropriate in a conversation. For instance, among many of the black tribes of southern Africa, loud talking is considered inappropriate. Similarly, among Malaysians,

> Too much talk and forcefulness on the part of an adult speaker is disapproved. . . .
> A terse, harmonious delivery is admired. . . . The same values—of evenness and
> restraint—hold for Malay interpersonal relations generally. Thus Malay village

conversation makes little use of paralinguistic devices such as facial expression, body movement, and speech tone. . . . Malays are not highly emotive people.[15]

Thais, like Malays, often dampen or moderate their level of responsiveness. As John Feig suggests,

> Thais have a tendency to neutralize all emotions; even in a very happy moment, there is always the underlying feeling: I don't want to be too happy now or I might be correspondingly sad later; too much laughter today may lead to too many tears tomorrow.[16]

Iranians tend to have the opposite reaction, as they are often very emotionally expressive in their conversations. Particularly when angry, a man's conversation may consist of behaviors such as "turning red, invoking religious oaths, proclaiming his injustices for all to hear, and allowing himself to be held back."[17]

European Americans are probably near the midpoint of this dimension. Compared to the Japanese, for instance, European Americans tend to be fairly active and expressive in their conversations. As Harvey Taylor suggested,

> An American's forehead and eyebrows are constantly in motion as he speaks, and these motions express the inner feelings behind the words. The "blank," nearly motionless Japanese forehead reveals very little of the Japanese person's inner feelings to the American (but not necessarily to the Japanese). Therefore the American feels that the Japanese is not really interested in the conversation or (worse yet) that the Japanese is hiding the truth.[18]

Compared to Jordanians, Iranians, African Americans, and Latinos, however, European Americans are passive and reserved in conversational expressiveness.

It is useful once again to remind you that all beliefs, values, and cultural norms lie on a continuum. How a particular characteristic is displayed or perceived in a specific culture is interpreted against the culture with which it is being compared. Thus it is possible for an African American to seem very active and emotionally expressive to the Japanese but quite calm and emotionally inexpressive to the Kuwaitis.

THE MAINTENANCE OF FACE IN INTERPERSONAL RELATIONSHIPS

A very important concept for understanding interpersonal communication among people from different cultures is that of face, or the public expression of the inner self. Erving Goffman defined *face* as the favorable social impression that a person wants others to have of him or her.[19] Face therefore involves a claim for respect and dignity from others.

The definition of *face* suggests that it has three important characteristics. First, face is *social*. This means that face is not what an individual thinks of him- or herself but rather how that person wants others to regard his or her worth. Face therefore refers to the public or social image of an individual that

CULTURE CONNECTIONS

An amusing but revealing example of how this [face] is achieved occurs in one popular Chinese television program aired in Taiwan. The program, roughly similar to the American program, "The Love Connection," allows a contestant to choose among five potential dating partners. However, in the Chinese version, the four contestants who are not chosen are matched with dating partners from the audience at the conclusion of the program! Since each of the pairs of contestants is given a chance to express appreciation for their "date," everyone's *mien-tzu* [face] is protected.

Source: Hui-Ching Chang and G. Richard Holt, "A Chinese Perspective on Face as Inter-Relational Concern," *The Challenge of Facework,* ed. Stella Ting-Toomey (Albany: State University of New York Press, 1994): 128–129.

is held by others. Face, then, always occurs in a relational setting. Since it is social, one can only gain or lose face through actions that are known to others. The most heroic deeds, or the most bestial ones, do not affect a person's face if they are done in complete anonymity. Nor can face be claimed independent of the social perceptions of others. For instance, the statement "No matter what my teachers think of me, I know I am a good student," is not a statement about face. Since face has a social component, a claim for face would only occur when the student conveys to others the idea that teachers should acknowledge her or his status as a good student. In this sense, the concept of *face* is only meaningful when considered in relation to others in the social network.[20] Consequently, it differs from such psychological concepts as self-esteem or pride, which can be claimed for oneself independently of others and can be increased or decreased either individually or socially.

Second, face is an *impression,* which may or may not be shared by all, that may differ from a person's self-image. People's claims for face, therefore, are not requests to know what others actually think about them; instead, they are solicitations from others of favorable expressions about them. To maintain face, people want others to act toward them with respect, regardless of their "real" thoughts and impressions. Thus, face maintenance involves an expectation that people will act as though the others are appreciated and admired.

Third, face refers only to the *favorable* social attributes that people want others to acknowledge. Unfavorable attributes, of course, are not what others are expected to admire. However, cultures may differ in the behaviors that are highly valued, and they may have very different expectations, or norms, for what are considered to be desirable face behaviors.

Types of Face Needs

Penelope Brown and Stephen Levinson extended Goffman's ideas by proposing a universal model of social politeness.[21] They pointed out that, regardless of their culture, all people have face and a desire to maintain and even gain more of it. Face is maintained through the use of various politeness rituals in social interactions, as people try to balance the competing goals of task efficiency and relationship harmony.[22] Brown and Levinson also proposed an important distinction between two types of face needs: negative and positive. *Negative face* is the need to avoid being hindered or impeded by others in order to act independently. *Positive face* is the need to be treated as a desirable person who is respected and approved. In the following example, the emphasis on face needs and politeness rituals helps to explain the strategic choices that are available in requesting a favor.

> A college student who wanted to borrow a classmate's notes typically would not ask for them baldly ("Lend me your notes, would you?"), but more frequently would ask in a manner that paid attention either to a person's negative face-wants ("Would it be at all possible for me to borrow your notes for just an hour? I'll xerox them and get them back to you right away.") or positive ones ("Jim, good friend, how would you like the opportunity to do a big favor for little old me? Can I borrow your notes?").[23]

In a modification and extension of Brown and Levinson's ideas, Tae-Seop Lim suggests that there are actually three kinds of face needs.[24] The first is similar to what Brown and Levinson call negative face, and it involves the need for control. The others are both related to what Brown and Levinson call positive face, but Lim differentiates between two types of positive face needs: approval and admiration. We now describe these three universal face needs for control, approval, and admiration.

The Need for Control   Control face is concerned with individual requirements for freedom and personal authority. It is related to people's need for others to acknowledge their individual autonomy and self-sufficiency. As Lim suggests, it involves people's

> image that they are in control of their own fate, that is, they have the virtues of a full-fledged, mature, and responsible adult. This type of face includes such values as "independent," "in control of self," "initiative," "mature," "composed," "reliable," and "self-sufficient." When persons claim these values for themselves, they want to be self-governed and free from others' interference, control, or imposition.[25]

The claim for control face, in other words, is embodied in the desire to have freedom of action.

The Need for Approval   Approval face is concerned with individual requirements for affiliation and social contact. It is related to people's need for others to acknowledge their friendliness and honesty. This type of face is similar to what the Chinese call *lien*, or the integrity of moral character, the loss of which makes it impossible for a person to function appropriately within a social group. As Hsien Chin Hu relates,

> A simple case of *lien*-losing is afforded by the experience of an American traveller in the interior of China. In a little village she had made a deal with a peasant to use his donkey for transportation. On the day agreed upon the owner appeared only to declare that his donkey was not available, the lady would have to wait one day. Yet he would not allow her to hire another animal, because she had consented to use his ass. They argued back and and forth first in the inn, then in the courtyard; a crowd gathered around them, as each stated his point of view over and over again. No comment was made, but some of the older people shook their heads and muttered something, the peasant getting more and more excited all the time trying to prove his right. Finally he turned and left the place without any more arguments, and the American was free to hire another beast. The man had felt the disapproval of the group. The condemnation of his community of his attempt to take advantage of the plight of the traveller made him feel he had "lost *lien*."[26]

Lien is maintained by acting with good *jen*, the Chinese term for "man." As Francis Hsu explains,

> when the Chinese say of so-and-so "*ta pu shih jen*" (he is not *jen*), they do not mean that this person is not a human animal; instead they mean that his behavior in relation to other human beings is not acceptable."[27]

Hsu regards the term *jen* as similar in meaning to the Yiddish term *mensh*, which refers to a good human being who is kind, generous, decent, and upright. Such an individual should therefore be admired for his or her noble character. As Leo Rosten says of this term,

> It is hard to convey the special sense of respect, dignity, approbation, that can be conveyed by calling someone "a real *mensh*." . . . The most withering comment one might make on someone's character or conduct is: "He is not (did not act like) a *mensh*." . . . The key to being "a real *mensh*" is nothing less than—character: rectitude, dignity, a sense of what is right, responsible, decorous. Many a poor man, many an ignorant man, is a *mensh*.[28]

Thus approval face reflects the desire to be treated with respect and dignity.

The Need for Admiration   Admiration face is concerned with individual needs for displays of respect from others. It is related to people's need for others to acknowledge their talents and accomplishments. This type of face is similar to what the Chinese call *mien-tzu*, or prestige acquired through success and social standing. One's *mien-tzu*

> is built up through high position, wealth, power, ability, through cleverly establishing social ties to a number of prominent people, as well as through avoidance of acts that would cause unfavorable comment . . . All persons growing up in any community have the same claim to *lien*, an honest, decent "face"; but their *mien-tzu* will differ with the status of the family, personal ties, ego's ability to impress people, etc.[29]

Thus admiration face involves the need for others to acknowledge a person's success, capabilities, reputation, and accomplishments.

Facework and Interpersonal Communication

The term *facework* refers to the actions people take to deal with their own and others' face needs. Everyday actions that impose on another, such as requests, warnings, complements, criticisms, apologies, and even praise, may jeopardize the face of one or more participants in a communicative act. Ordinarily, say Brown and Levinson,

> people cooperate (and assume each other's cooperation) in maintaining face in interaction, such cooperation being based on the mutual vulnerability of face. That is, normally everyone's face depends on everyone else's being maintained, and since people can be expected to defend their faces if threatened, and in defending their own to threaten others' faces, it is in general in every participant's best interest to maintain each others' face.[30]

The degree to which a given set of actions may pose a potential threat to one or more aspects of people's face depends on three characteristics of the relationship.[31] First, the potential for face threats is associated with the control dimension of interpersonal communication. Relationships in which there are large power or status differences among the participants have a great potential for people's actions to be interpreted as face-threatening. Within a large organization, for instance, a verbal disagreement between a manager and her employees will have a greater potential to be perceived as face-threatening than will an identical disagreement among employees who are equal in seniority and status.

Second, face-threat potential is associated with the affiliation dimension of interpersonal communication. That is, relationships in which participants have a large social distance, and therefore less social familiarity, have a great potential for actions to be perceived as face-threatening. Thus, very close family members may say things to one another that they would not tolerate from more distant acquaintances. Note, however, that the increased face-threat potential associated with more distant relationships only holds for what are sometimes referred to as "inside" relationships, where there is at least some degree of familiarity or perceived association among the individuals; "outside" relationships, where strangers have no formal connection to one another but are, for example, simply waiting in line at the train station, the taxi stand, or the bank, may sometimes be seen as an exception to this general principle.[32] As Ron Scollon and Suzie Wong Scollon suggest, "Westerners often are struck with the contrast they see between the highly polite and deferential Asians they meet in their business, educational, and governmental contacts and the rude, pushy, and aggressive Asians they meet on the subways of Asia's major cities."[33] At many train stations in the People's Republic of China, for example, people are not in the midst of members of their own community, so the drive to preserve face and act with proper behavior is much lower. Passengers usually wait in waiting rooms until the attendant moves a barrier and they can cross the area between them and the train. The competition is quite fierce as passengers rush toward the train with their luggage, and they have little regard for the safety of other passengers. Often, fellow travelers are injured by luggage, knocked to the ground, or even pushed between the platform and the train, where they fall to the tracks.[34]

Third, face-threat potential is related to culture-specific evaluations that people make. That is, cultures may make unique assessments about the degree to which particular actions are inherently threatening to a person's face. Thus, certain actions within one culture may be regarded as face-threatening, whereas those same actions in another culture may be regarded as perfectly acceptable. In certain cultures, for instance, passing someone a bowl of soup with only one hand, or with one particular hand, may be regarded as an insult and therefore a threat to face; in other cultures, however, those same actions are perfectly acceptable.

Stella Ting-Toomey suggests that cultural differences in individualism-collectivism and in high-context versus low-context communication preferences affect the facework behaviors that people are likely to use. In individualist and in low-context cultures, preserving one's own face is more important than maintaining the face of others, because it is vital that individual autonomy is preserved. Consequently, direct, dominating, and controlling face-negotiation strategies are common, and there is a low degree of sensitivity to the face-threatening capabilities of particular messages. Conversely, in collectivist and in high-context cultures, the mutual preservation of face is extremely important, because it is vital that people be approved and admired by others. Therefore, indirect, obliging, and smoothing face-negotiation strategies are common, direct confrontations between people are avoided, and ordinary communication messages are seen as having a great face-threatening potential.[35]

Facework and Intercultural Communication

Competent facework, which lessens the potential for specific actions to be regarded as face-threatening, encompasses a wide variety of communication behaviors. These behaviors may include apologies, excessive politeness, the narration of justifications or excuses, displays of deference and submission, the use of intermediaries or other avoidance strategies, claims of common ground or the intention to act cooperatively, or the use of implication or indirect speech. The specific facework strategies a person uses, however, are shaped and modified by his or her culture. For instance, the Japanese and U.S. Americans have very different reactions when they realize that they have committed a face-threatening act and would like to restore the other's face. The Japanese prefer to adapt their messages to the social status of their interaction partners and provide an appropriate apology. They want to repair the damage if possible, but without providing reasons that explain or justify their original error. Conversely, U.S. Americans would prefer to adapt their messages to the nature of the provocation and provide verbal justifications for their initial actions. They may use humor or aggression to divert attention from their actions but do not apologize for their original error.[36]

As another example of culture-specific differences in facework behaviors, consider the comments that are commonly appended to the report cards of high school students in the United States and in China. In the United States, evaluations of high school students include specific statements about students' strengths and weaknesses. In China, however, the high school report cards that are issued at the end of each semester never criticize the students directly; rather, teachers use indirect language and say "I wish that you would make more progress in such areas as . . ." in order to save face while conveying his or her evaluations.[37]

Facework is a central and enduring feature of all interpersonal relationships. Facework is concerned with the communication activities that help to create, maintain, and sustain the connections between people. As Robyn Penman says,

> Facework is not something we do some of the time, it is something that we unavoidably do all the time—it is the core of our social selves. That it is called face and facework is curious but not critical here. What is critical is that the mechanism the label stands [for] seems to be as enduring as human social existence. In the very act of communicating with others we are inevitably commenting on the other and our relationship with them. And in that commenting we are maintaining or changing the identity of the other in relationship to us.[38]

IMPROVING INTERCULTURAL RELATIONSHIPS

Competent interpersonal relationships among people from different cultures do not happen by accident. They occur as a result of the knowledge and perceptions people have about one another, their motivations to engage in meaningful interactions, and their ability to communicate in ways that are regarded as appropriate and effective. To improve these interpersonal relationships, then, it is necessary to learn about and thereby reduce uncertainty about people from other cultures, to share oneself with those people, and to handle the inevitable differences in perceptions and expectations.

Learning About People from Other Cultures

The need to know, to understand, and to make sense of the world is a fundamental necessity of life. Without a world that is somewhat predictable and

CULTURE CONNECTIONS

What are some of the main pitfalls to avoid whenever you're doing business?

- Asking questions about a foreigner's personal life. Executives in Europe and the Far East like to keep their private lives quite separate from their business lives.
- Plunging into discussions on a first-name basis. It's always smart to let your foreign contacts make the first move in this respect.
- Failing to patiently develop a solid relationship. Instead of watching the clock, invest time—say, over a long lunch—to cement closer ties.
- Arriving without a gift when it's appropriate to give one. Carefully research when to give a gift and what kind of present will best fit the occasion.

Source: "Executive Etiquette While Abroad" *T & E* [American Express Newsletter] 7(4), (April 1990): 1.

that can be interpreted in a sensible and meaningful way, humankind itself would not survive.

We have already suggested in Chapter 6 that both individuals and cultures can differ in their need to reduce uncertainty and in the extent to which they can tolerate ambiguity and, therefore, in the means they select to adapt to the world. The human need to learn about others, to make sense of their actions, and to understand their beliefs, values, and behaviors has typically been studied under the general label of *uncertainty reduction theory*.[39] This theory explains both the degree of interpersonal attraction that people have for one another and the likelihood that they will seek additional information from one another. In the sections that follow, we will describe the causes, components, and consequences of uncertainty reduction behaviors and some strategies for reducing uncertainty in interpersonal relationships.

Causes of Uncertainty Reduction   Three conditions are related to uncertainty reduction behaviors: your expectations about future interactions with other people, the degree to which other people exhibit behaviors that deviate from your expectations, and the incentive value or potential rewards that relationships with other people may have for you. The first condition is closely related to the information or knowledge component of intercultural competence, the second is related to the emotional or motivation component, and the third is related to both the knowledge and motivation components.

The first condition is your *expectations about future interactions* with another person. If you believe that you are very likely to interact with some person on future occasions, the degree to which you can live with ambiguity and insufficient information about that person will be low, and your need for more knowledge about that person will be high. Conversely, if you do not expect to see and talk with someone again, you will be more willing to remain uncertain about her or his motives and intentions, and you will therefore not attempt to seek out any additional information. This person will continue to be a stranger. Strangers are people with whom you do not expect to interact again, acquaintances are people with whom you expect to interact occasionally on a casual or superficial level, and friends and family are people with whom you expect to interact over a lengthy period of time. Uncertainty reduction theory suggests that sojourners and immigrants who know they will be interacting in a new culture for a long period of time will be more likely to try to reduce their uncertainty about how and why people behave than will a tourist or temporary visitor.

The second condition is the *degree of deviance* that the other person exhibits. Deviant behaviors are those that are not typically expected because they are inconsistent with the common norms that govern particular social situations. When a person acts deviantly, your level of uncertainty about that person increases because he or she is far less predictable to you. Conversely, when a person conforms to your expectations by behaving in a predictable way, your level of uncertainty about that person decreases. A person who behaves in deviant and unexpected ways is often disliked and is regarded as interpersonally unattractive, whereas one who conforms to others' expectations and is therefore predictable is often most liked and preferred. In intercultural communication, it is extremely likely that the other person will behave "deviantly" or differently from what you might expect. Thus, uncertainty about people from other cultures will typically be high.

The third condition, *incentive value*, refers to the perceived likelihood that the other person can fulfill various needs that you have, give you some of the resources that you want, or provide you with certain rewards that you desire. If a person's incentive value is high—that is, if the other person has the potential to be very rewarding to you—your need to find out more about that person will be correspondingly high. As you might expect, a high incentive value also increases the degree to which a person will be preferred or viewed as interpersonally attractive. Of course, the needs or rewards that people might want vary widely; the incentive value of a given person is related to his or her ability to provide status, affection, information, services, goods, money, or some combination of these resources.[40]

One form of incentive value that has been widely investigated is the perceived similarity of the other person. The *similarity-attraction hypothesis* suggests that we like and are attracted to those whom we regard as comparable to ourselves in ways that we regard as important. Conversely, we are unlikely to be attracted to those who are very different from us. This hypothesis implies that, at least in the initial stages of intercultural encounters, the dissimilarities created by cultural differences may inhibit the development of new interpersonal relationships.

Components of Uncertainty Reduction   There are two broad components of uncertainty reduction behaviors: tolerance for ambiguity and level of uncertainty. The former refers to an individual's willingness or ability to live with uncertainty, to cope with change, and to contend with vague and imprecise information. As we suggested, tolerance for ambiguity is influenced by expectations about future interactions; if you think you will have to interact with someone in the future, your tolerance for ambiguity will be lower than if you never expect to meet that person again.

Tolerance for ambiguity is also influenced by culture. In Chapter 6, when we discussed Hofstede's value dimensions, we suggested that cultures differ in the extent to which they prefer or can cope with uncertainty. It should now be obvious that Hofstede's uncertainty avoidance dimension is related to what is here being referred to as tolerance for ambiguity, but the two concepts differ in two very important ways. First, they have opposite meanings; an increase in uncertainty avoidance corresponds to a decrease in tolerance for ambiguity. Second, there is a difference in the level of analysis to which each term is applied. Hofstede's dimension refers to the culture as a whole, whereas tolerance for ambiguity is a psychological concept that refers to particular individuals within a culture. Indeed, it might be useful to think of a culture's level of uncertainty avoidance as representing the typical or average level of intolerance for ambiguity that the individuals in that culture commonly experience.

The second component of uncertainty reduction behaviors refers to a person's level or amount of uncertainty; that is, the extent to which a person lacks the knowledge, information, and ability to predict the intentions and behaviors of another. We have already seen that the level of uncertainty is very high when dealing with people who act in deviant or unexpected ways, and that such deviance may lead to unfavorable social perceptions. Because intercultural communication involves people from dissimilar cultures, their behaviors are likely to violate each other's expectations. Consequently, there is always the possibility that fear, distrust, and similar negative emotions may prevail, particularly in the early stages of the relationship. Often, but not always, the negative emotions can be overcome, usually when the interaction has the potential to be highly rewarding.

Consequences of Uncertainty Reduction   The consequences of uncertainty reduction behaviors that are applicable to intercultural communication can be grouped under two general labels: informational consequences and emotional consequences. Informational consequences result from the additional knowledge that has been gained about other people, including facts or inferences about their culture; increased accuracy in the judgments made about their beliefs, values, and norms; and an increased degree of confidence that they are being perceived accurately.

Emotional consequences may include increased levels of self-disclosure, heightened interpersonal attraction, increases in intimacy behaviors, more frequent nonverbal displays of positive emotions, and an increased likelihood that future intercultural contacts will be favorable. Of course, these positive outcomes all presume that the reduction in uncertainty about another person results in an increase in positive feelings, which is not necessarily the case. However, in intercultural encounters, negative perceptions frequently occur because of unchallenged cultural assumptions. As we have seen, the perception that a person is acting in a deviant way (as defined by one's own cultural expectations) will often lead to decreased interpersonal attraction.

Strategies for Reducing Uncertainty   To behave both appropriately and effectively in an intercultural encounter, you must make an accurate assessment about many kinds of information: the individual characteristics of the person with whom you interact, the social episodes that are typical of the particular setting and occasion, the specific roles that are being played within the episode, the rules of interaction that govern what people can say and do, the setting or context within which the interaction occurs, and the cultural patterns that influence what is regarded as appropriate and effective. Thus, uncertainty is not reduced for its own sake, but occurs every day for strategic purposes. As Charles R. Berger suggested,

> To interact in a relatively smooth, coordinated, and understandable manner, one must be able both to predict how one's interaction partner is likely to behave, and, based on these predictions, to select from one's own repertoire those responses that will optimize outcomes in the encounter.[41]

The three general types of strategies used to gain information about other people, and thus to reduce the level of uncertainty, can be characterized as passive, active, and interactive. Passive strategies involve quiet and surreptitious observation of another person to learn how he or she behaves. Active strategies include efforts to obtain information about another person by asking others or structuring the environment to place the person in a situation that provides the needed information. Interactive strategies involve actually conversing with the other person in an attempt to gather the needed information.

As you might expect, there are large cultural differences in the types of strategies that are used to reduce uncertainty in intercultural encounters. For example, European Americans are more likely than their Japanese counterparts to ask questions and to self-disclose as a way to obtain information about another person.[42]

Sharing Oneself with People from Other Cultures

The human tendency to reveal personal information about oneself and to explain one's inner experiences and private thoughts is called *self-disclosure*. Self-disclosure occurs among people of all cultures, but there are tremendous

Couples from diverse cultural backgrounds sometimes approach self-disclosure and conflict resolution differently. *(Copyright © Myron W. Lustig & Jolene Koester.)*

cultural differences in the breadth, depth, valence, timing, and targets of self-
disclosing events.

The *breadth* of self-disclosing information refers to the range of topics
that are revealed, and European Americans tend to self-disclose about more
topics than do members of most other cultures. For example, Tsukasa Nishida
found that European Americans discussed a much wider range of topics that
were related to the self (such as health and personality) with strangers than
did Japanese; also, Japanese had far more self-related topics than did European
Americans that they would never discuss with others.[43] Ghanaians tend to
self-disclose about family and background matters, whereas U.S. Americans
self-disclose about career concerns.[44] In contrast,

> Chinese culture takes a conservative stand on self-disclosure. For a Chinese, self-
> centered speech would be considered boastful and pretentious. Chinese tend to
> scorn those who often talk about themselves and doubt their motives when they
> do so. Chinese seem to prefer talking about external matters, such as world

events. For Americans, self-disclosure is a strategy to make various types of relationships work; for Chinese, it is a gift shared only with the most intimate relatives and friends.[45]

The *depth* of the self-disclosing information refers to the degree of "personalness" about oneself that is revealed. Self-disclosure can reveal superficial aspects ("I like broccoli") or very private thoughts and feelings ("I'm afraid of my father"). Of the many cultures that have been studied, European Americans are among the most revealing self-disclosers. European Americans disclose more than African Americans, who in turn disclose more than Mexican Americans.[46] European Americans also disclose more than the British,[47] French,[48] Germans, Japanese,[49] and Puerto Ricans.[50]

Valence refers to whether the self-disclosure is positive or negative, and thus favorable or unfavorable. Not only do European Americans disclose more about themselves than do members of many other cultures, but they are also more likely to provide negatively valenced information. Compared to many Asian cultures, for example, European Americans are far less concerned with issues of "face" and are therefore more inclined to share information that may not portray them in the most favorable way.

Timing refers to when the self-disclosure occurs in the course of the relationship. For European Americans, self-disclosure in new relationships is generally high because the participants share information about themselves that the others do not know. A person's name, hometown, employment or educational affiliations, and personal interests are all likely to be shared in initial interactions. As the relationship progresses, the amount of self-disclosure diminishes because the participants have already learned what they need to know to interact appropriately and effectively. Only if the relationship becomes more personal and intimate will the amount of self-disclosure again begin to increase. But the timing of the self-disclosure process can be very different in other cultures. For example, Native Americans typically reveal very little about themselves initially because they believe that too much self-disclosure at that stage is inappropriate. A similar pattern may be found among members of Asian cultures.

Target refers to the person to whom self-disclosing information is given. Among European Americans, spouses are usually the targets of a great deal of self-disclosure, and mutual self-disclosure is widely regarded as contributing to an ideal and satisfactory marriage.[51] The breadth and depth of self-disclosure among other European American family members is much less frequent. Other cultures have different patterns. Among the Igbos of Nigeria, for instance, age is used to determine the appropriate degree of self-disclosure among interactants, younger interactants being expected to self-disclose far more than their older counterparts. As a cultural norm, when elder Igbos are in an initial encounter with someone who is younger, they have the right to inquire about the young person's background, parents, hometown, and similar information that may ultimately lead to contact with distant relatives or old friends.

CULTURE CONNECTIONS

But then there is another word, or phrase, worth learning: *Mai pen rai*. In conversation, *mai pen rai* is a richer "no problem" or "never mind," a kind of verbal shrug. Beyond conversation, the phrase speaks volumes. It means that clashes are dealt with in something other than the Western, head-on way. In a year spent in a Thai newsroom, I never heard an angry voice, or a slamming door. "We recognize problems when they arrive, not before"—that line, with a smile, from a chief advisor to the prime minister.

Source: "Buddhist Ritual," *Vis à Vis,* March 1990: 56.

Handling Differences in Intercultural Relationships

Conflict in interpersonal relationships is a major nemesis for most people. Add the complications of different cultural backgrounds and problems in managing conflict can become even more severe. Stella Ting-Toomey's work on why, when, what, and how conflict varies can provide some direction for managing intercultural conflict.[52]

Ting-Toomey's work uses Edward Hall's distinction between high-context and low-context cultures, which are discussed more fully in Chapter 6. Briefly, high-context cultures emphasize nonverbal and implicit code systems in which messages are covert and reactions are reserved. Interpersonal bonds are enduring, and there are distinct ingroups and outgroups. High-context cultures are very traditional, often with little incentive for innovation and change. Low-context cultures emphasize explicit code systems, in which the details of messages are plainly verbalized and reactions are explicitly articulated. The bonds between people are fragile, and because people belong to many different groups that often change, membership in ingroups and outgroups is very flexible. Low-context cultures are therefore often characterized by rapid innovation and change.

Conflict may involve either task or instrumental issues. Task issues are concerned with how to do something or how to achieve a specific goal, whereas instrumental issues are concerned with personal or relationship problems such as hostility toward another person. The distinction therefore focuses on conflict about ideas versus conflict about people.

Ting-Toomey believes that people in high- and low-context cultures define and respond to conflict differently. In high-context cultures, people are more likely to merge task and instrumental concerns, and conflict is therefore likely to be seen as personal. To shout and scream publicly, thus displaying the conflict to others, threatens everyone's face to such an extreme degree

Table 10.1   CHARACTERISTICS OF CONFLICT IN HIGH- AND LOW-CONTEXT CULTURES

Questions	High-Context Cultures	Low-Context Cultures
Why?	Expressively oriented (person-centered)	Instrumentally oriented (task- or issue-centered)
	Integration of conflict and conflict parties	Dichotomy between conflict and conflict parties
When?	Group-oriented	Individual-oriented
	Violations of group expectations create conflict potentials	Violations of individual expectations create conflict potentials
What?	Concealing	Revealing
	Indirect, nonconfrontational attitude	Direct, confrontational attitude
	Face and relationship orientation	Action- and solution-orientation
How?	Implicit communication codes	Explicit communication codes

Source: Adapted from Stella Ting-Toomey, "Toward a Theory of Conflict and Culture," *Communication, Culture, and Organizational Processes,* ed. William B. Gudykunst, Lea P. Stewart, and Stella Ting-Toomey (Beverly Hills, CA: Sage, 1985), 82.

that such behavior is usually avoided at all costs. In contrast, individuals in low-context cultures are more likely to separate the task and the instrumental dimensions. Thus, they are able to express their agitation and anger (perhaps including shouting and strong nonverbal actions) about an issue and then joke and socialize with the other person once the disagreement is over. It is almost as if once the conflict is resolved, it is completely forgotten.

Because there is a great deal of volatility and variability in people's behaviors in low-context cultures, there is often considerable potential for conflict. Because people are encouraged to be individualistic, their behaviors are not as predictable as they would be in high-context and collectivistic cultures. Also, because expectations are individually based rather than group-centered, there is always the possibility that the behavior of any one person will violate the expectations of another, possibly producing conflict.

Cultures also shape attitudes toward conflict. In high-context cultures, which value indirectness and ambiguity, conflicts and confrontations are typically avoided. Thus, rather than trying to resolve the problem directly, people in high-context cultures will attempt to maintain the external smoothness of the relationship. In low-context culture, which are more likely to be "doing" or activity-oriented cultures, people's approach to conflict will be action-oriented. That is, the conflict precipitates actions, and the conflict is explicitly revealed and named. Table 10.1 summarizes the differences that Ting-Toomey describes in approaches to conflict among high- and low-context cultures.

CULTURE CONNECTIONS

Korean interpersonal relationships operate on the principle of harmony. Maintaining a peaceful, comfortable atmosphere is more important than attaining immediate goals or telling the absolute truth. Koreans believe that to accomplish something while causing unhappiness or discomfort to individuals, is to accomplish nothing at all. If relationships are not kept harmonious, it is difficult, if not impossible, to work toward any goal. All cultures value how its members feel emotionally, but few cultures value it as much as Koreans do. To Koreans, to put greater emphasis on efficiency, honesty or some other form of moral integrity is to be cold and unfeeling.

Source: Sonja Vegdahl Hur and Ben Seunghwa Hur, *Culture Shock! Korea* (Singapore: Times Books International, 1988) 34.

A very important concept for understanding how people from different cultures handle conflict is that of face, which we discussed earlier in this chapter. In conflicts, in particular, face is very likely to be threatened, and all participants are vulnerable to the face-threatening acts that can occur.

The actions of people in conflict can include attempts to save face for themselves, others, or all participants. Members of high-context cultures are likely to deal with face threats such as conflicts by selecting strategies that smooth over their disagreements and allow them to maintain the face of both parties, that is, mutual face-saving. As Ringo Ma suggests, however, such strategies do not simply ignore the conflicting issues; after all, conflicts do get resolved in high-context cultures. Rather, nonconfrontational alternatives are used to resolve differences. Often, for instance, a friend of those involved in the conflict, or an elderly person respected by all, will function as an unofficial intermediary who attempts to preserve the face of each person and the relationship by preventing rejection and embarrassment.[53] Members of low-context cultures, conversely, are likely to deal with face threats in a direct, controlling way. It is important to their sense of self to maintain their own face, to take charge, to direct the course of action, and in so doing to protect their own dignity and self-respect even at the expense of others.[54]

Imagine a scene involving two employees assigned to an important and high-tension project. Perhaps they are operating under serious time constraints, or perhaps the lives of many people depend on their success. Inevitably, disagreements about how to approach the assignment, as well as the specifics of the assignment itself, are likely to occur. Now assume that one employee is from a high-context culture such as Korea and the other is from a low-context culture such as the United States. The difficulties inherent in completing their assignment will probably be increased by the great differences in their approaches to the problems that will arise. Each person's attempt to maintain face may induce the other to make negative judgments and evaluations. Each person's attempt to cope with the conflict and accomplish the task may produce even more conflict. As Ting-Toomey suggests, these differences will need to be addressed before the work can be accomplished successfully.

INTERPERSONAL RELATIONSHIPS AND INTERCULTURAL COMPETENCE

Intercultural competence in interpersonal relationships requires knowledge, motivation, and skill in using verbal and nonverbal codes, as described in previous chapters. In addition, it requires behaviors that are appropriate and effective for the different types and dimensions of interpersonal relationships described in this chapter.

Competence in intercultural relationships requires that you understand the meanings attributed to particular types of interpersonal relationships. Whom should you consider to be a stranger, an acquaintance, a friend, or a family member? What expectations should you have for people in these categories? What clues do people from other cultures offer about their expectations for you? Your expectations about the nature of interpersonal relationships affect how you assign meaning to other people's behaviors.

Your willingness to understand the face needs of people from other cultures and to behave appropriately in order to preserve and enhance their sense of face is critical to your intercultural competence. Always consider a person's need to maintain a favorable face in her or his interactions with others. Perceptions of autonomy, approval, and respect by others are important, but you must meet these face needs with facework that is appropriate to the other's cultural beliefs.

Your expectations about self-disclosure, obtaining information about others, and handling disagreements will not, in all likelihood, be the same as those of people from other cultures. Competence in developing and maintaining intercultural relationships requires knowledge of differences, a willingness to consider and try alternatives, and the skill to enact alternative relational dynamics.

SUMMARY

People in an intercultural relationship may have very different expectations about the preferred nature of their social interactions. The types of interpersonal relationships, including those among strangers, acquaintances, friends, romantic partners, and family members, may also vary greatly across cultures.

Interpersonal relationships can be interpreted along the three dimensions of control, affiliation, and activation. The control dimension provides interpretations about status or social dominance. The affiliation dimension indicates the degree of friendliness, liking, and social warmth that is being communicated. The activation dimension is concerned with interpersonal responsiveness.

The concept of face refers to the positive social impressions that people want to have and would like others to acknowledge. Face includes the need for autonomy or individual freedom of action, approval or inclusion in social groups, and admiration or respect from others because of one's accomplishments. The need for facework depends on the control and affiliation dimensions of interpersonal communication, and on culture-specific judgments about the extent to which certain actions inherently threaten one's face.

To improve intercultural relationships, you must learn about people from other cultures and thereby reduce the degree of uncertainty. Sharing yourself in appropriate ways with people from other cultures and learning to use culturally sensitive ways to handle the differences and disagreements that may arise are additional ways to improve intercultural relationships.

11
CHAPTER

Episodes, Contexts, and Intercultural Interactions

There is a repetitiveness to everyday communication experiences that helps to make them understandable and predictable. The recurring features of these common events, which we call social episodes, allow you to anticipate what people may do, what will likely happen, and what variations from the expected sequence of events could mean.

SOCIAL EPISODES IN INTERCULTURAL RELATIONSHIPS

People undertake intercultural relationships in predictable ways. In this section we describe how communication experiences are grouped into common events. Our point is that people's interactions are structured by their participation in events that are quite predictable and routine.

The Nature of Social Episodes

Think about how your daily life is structured. If you are like most people, there is a great deal of predictability in what you do each day and even with whom you do it. If you are attending a college or university, much of your life is taken up with such activities as attending class, studying, talking with a classmate in the cafeteria, working at a job, going shopping, meeting a friend after work, attending a party, and eating dinner. These are the kinds of structures in your life that we refer to as *social episodes,* that is, interaction sequences that are repeated over and over again. Not only do these social episodes recur, their structure is also very predictable. The individuals who participate in these episodes generally know what to expect from others and what others expect from them. It is almost as if there were an unwritten script that tells you roughly what to say, whom to say it to, and how to say it.

Take the example of going to class. You probably attend class in a room filled with chairs, or tables with chairs, that face the front of the room. When you take a seat, you put your notebooks and other texts on the floor or under the desk. You keep your chair oriented in the way all the other chairs are oriented. The room is arranged so that you can look at the teacher, and there is a clearly marked space in the front of the room for the teacher to stand or sit. When you enter the classroom, you never consider taking that spot. You expect the teacher, when she or he walks into the room, to do so. You do not expect the teacher to walk into the room and take the chair next to you.

If you get to class early enough, you might engage in small talk with another student. There are fairly predictable topics you might discuss, depending on how well you know each other. You probably talk about the class, whether you have done the reading, how your work is going, and the assignments. You might talk about the teacher and analyze his or her strengths and weaknesses. You might talk about the weather, the latest sports scores, or other common topics.

You expect the teacher to give a lecture or in some other way provide a sense of structure for the class. You take notes if the teacher gives a lecture, trying to summarize the key points. If you talk to a classmate while the teacher is lecturing, you whisper rather than talk in a loud voice. If the teacher did not enact the behaviors you expect for the person playing the part of "teacher," you might complain about it to others. Similarly, if one of your fellow classmates did not follow the expected behaviors for "being a student," you might think there was something wrong.

The purpose of this extended example is to underscore our point that much of what people do is made up of social episodes, which are repetitive, predictable, and routine behaviors that form the structure of their interactions with others. These social episodes provide information about how to interpret the verbal and nonverbal symbols of the interactants. The meanings of the symbols are understood because of the context in which they are given. Because those who participate in a social episode usually have the same understanding about what is to take place, they usually know how to behave, what to say, and how to interpret the actions and intentions of others.

In social episodes that include intercultural interactions, however, those involved may—and in all likelihood will—have very different expectations and interpretations about people's behaviors and intentions. As the interaction becomes more and more ambiguous, the expected behaviors that pattern

CULTURE CONNECTIONS

It is interesting to compare what happens in France and in the United States in the supermarket when the store is crowded, with a long line in front of the cash register and a long wait. In France, in most cases, one quickly shows signs of impatience, by raising one's eyes to the ceiling with an exasperated expression, by taking on an exhausted look, by stiffening or clamming up, or by exchanging with others glances of complicity. But one does not speak to others—all is expressed through body movements. At most, one might protest, "grumble" out loud while looking at one's neighbor, but without speaking to him directly. One simply makes him an accomplice against the cashier, the store, the system, those who are "going too far." In the United States, the situation is completely different. One turns to one's neighbors; people strike up rather general conversations, help each other pass the time, and joke about the situation—even sympathize with the cashier—and, when they finally get to the register, encourage the person there with a few kind words. I've seen strangers show each other family photos, exchange advice, recipes, or useful addresses, compare pregnancies and births, all just as calmly as if they were talking about the quality of a product or the use of an unusual vegetable in one's shopping cart. Most of all I've seen them joke around a lot. A French woman who heard me speaking French to a friend I had met in the supermarket introduced herself to us, gave us her address and telephone number, and invited us to come see her if we were passing by the city in which she lived. Then, just before leaving us, she apologized for her behavior by saying, "Excuse me for having come up to you like that, but I heard you speaking French. I've become very American, you know. . . ."

Source: Raymonde Carroll, *Cultural Misunderstandings: The French–American Experience* (Chicago: The University of Chicago Press, 1987) 31.

the social episode also become more unpredictable and problematic. Though your culture teaches you to interpret the meanings and behaviors in social episodes in particular ways, other cultures may provide their members with very different interpretations of these same experiences.

Components of Social Episodes

There are five components of social episodes, each of which influences intercultural communication: cultural patterns, social roles, rules of interaction, interaction scenes, and interaction contexts.

CULTURE CONNECTIONS

We were married in a traditional Navajo ceremony. My family entered the hogan first, bearing gifts for my wife's family and a saddle: a sign that I was ready to make a new home. Then my wife's family entered the hogan carrying corn mush prepared by her grandmother. White cornmeal, representing the woman's family, was mixed with the male's yellow cornmeal and set in a wedding basket. My wife and I grabbed fingerfuls of mush and ate them, and we were married. Two lives combined into one. Navajos say it is a new life.

Source: *Hemispheres,* November 1993: 73. Excerpted from *A Circle of Nations.*

Cultural Patterns   Cultural patterns are shared judgments about what the world is and what it should be, and widely held expectations about how people should behave. The patterns of a culture's beliefs and values, described in Chapters 5 and 6, permeate the ways in which members of a culture think about their world.

Cultural patterns are like tinted glasses that color everything people see and to which they respond. The episodes that are used to structure people's lives—attending class, eating dinner, playing with a friend, going to work, talking with a salesperson—are certainly common to many cultures. But the interpretations that are imposed on these behaviors vary greatly, depending on the cultural patterns that serve as the lens through which the social episodes are viewed. Tamar Katriel, for example, describes a common episode in middle-class Israeli life called *mesibot kiturim,* or "griping party." She argues that, while these griping parties might occur in other cultures, they are particularly important in Israel and reflect a communally oriented cultural pattern.[1]

Joseph Forgas and Michael Bond found that Hong Kong Chinese and Australian students, although leading superficially very similar lives—going to classes, studying, and so on—perceived various social episodes very differently. The perceptions of the Chinese students reflected values and cultural patterns associated with that culture's emphasis on community, the collective good, and acceptance of authority. The Australian students saw the same episodes in terms of self-confidence, competition, and the pleasure they might receive from the interactions in which they participated.[2]

Social Roles   A social role is a set of expected behaviors associated with people in a particular position. Common roles that exist in most cultures include student, mother, father, brother, sister, boss, friend, service person, employee, sales clerk, teacher, manager, soldier, woman, man, and mail carrier. The role that you take in a particular social episode strongly suggests to you the way in which you should act. If you are participating in an episode of a boss giving an employee a performance review, you would expect to behave very differently if you were the employee rather than the boss. If another person is upset about the comments of a co-worker, your response would be influenced by the particular role you play in relationship to the upset person. Are you in the role of friend, relative, or employer? Your answer to the question will definitely affect how you respond to the person's concerns. In many episodes you play clearly defined roles that give you guidance about what you should say to the other person and even how you should say it. Furthermore, the role you are playing is matched by the roles of others in the episode. You have expectations for yourself based on your roles and you also have expectations for others based on their roles.

The expectations for appropriate behavior for the roles of student and teacher are quite apparent in the example at the beginning of this section. However, appropriate behaviors for these roles will vary greatly among cultures. In many Asian cultures it is not acceptable to ask a teacher questions or to whisper to another student. Students are expected to stand up when the teacher enters the room and again when the teacher leaves the room. The students would never call a teacher by his or her first name but only by a formal title.

The role of friends also varies greatly from culture to culture. As discussed in Chapter 10, European Americans have a tendency to call a lot of people "friends," and they often separate their friends into different categories based on where the friendship is established. They might have friends at work, friends from their neighborhoods, and friends from clubs or organizations to which they belong. Many of these friendships are fairly transitory and might last only as long as people work for the same organization or live in the same neighborhood. When the place in which the friendship is conducted is no longer shared in common, the friendship no longer exists in any active sense. In many other cultures, people may have fewer friends, but these friendships are often maintained for longer periods of time.

The importance of this discussion to your participation in intercultural communication should be obvious. Even though you may think you are fulfilling a particular role (such as that of student, friend, house guest, or customer), the expectations of the role may vary widely between your culture and the culture in which you are interacting. There are also sets of rules that generally govern the interactions among people in an episode. Some of these rules are related to specific roles, but others are simply norms or guides to govern behavior.

Rules of Interaction   Rules of interaction provide a predictable pattern or structure to social episodes and give relationships a sense of coherence.[3] Rules of interaction are not written down somewhere, nor are they typically shared verbally. Instead, they operate at the level of unwritten, unspoken expectations. Most of the time, people are not even consciously aware of the rules that govern a social episode until they are broken. Think about the various kinds of rules, for example, that govern the interactions at a wedding. In addition to the various roles (bride, groom, parents, bridesmaids, groomsmen, and guests), there are a host of rules embedded in the different types of weddings that occur. A wedding invitation from a U.S. American couple that is engraved on heavy linen paper and announces a candlelight ceremony at dusk suggests something about the rules governing what a guest should wear and how a guest should act. In contrast, a photocopied invitation on colored paper announcing that pizza and beer will be served following the ceremony suggests a very different set of rules. As B. Aubrey Fisher indicates,

> Virtually every social relationship has rules to determine what is appropriate and what is inappropriate for that relationship. For some relationships, the most important rules can be found in a larger social context. Meet someone at a church social, and you will probably conform to rules appropriate to interpersonal communication in a church. For other relationships, the important rules are created during the process of interaction. After you get to know someone, you are more likely to be innovative and to do something "different."[4]

Rules of interaction include such diverse aspects as what to wear, what is acceptable to talk about, the sequence of events, and the artifacts that are part of the event. In France, for instance, you would never talk about your work at a dinner party, even if all of the people there were in some way connected to the same place of work. Among most U.S. American businesspeople, however, it is commonplace to expect talk about business at a dinner table. An invitation to a dinner party can mean that immediately upon arrival, you will be given the meal and only after you have eaten will you sit and talk leisurely with your hosts; or the invitation may mean that you must spend a substantial period of time before a meal is served in having drinks and talking with your hosts. Do you bring gifts such as flowers, wine, or candy? If so, are there particular artifacts that are taboo, such as wine or other forms of alcohol in Saudi Arabia or chrysanthemums in Italy (which are only given at a funeral)? The rules of interaction provide culture-specific instructions about what should and should not occur in particular social episodes.

Interaction Scenes   Interaction scenes are made up of the recurring, repetitive topics that people talk about in social conversations. Most conversations are organized around these ritualized and routinized scenes, which are the chunks of conversational behavior adapted to the particular circumstances.

Kathy Kellermann describes a standard set of interaction scenes that are commonly used by college students in U.S. universities when engaged in informal conversations. As Figure 11.1 indicates, Kellermann's research suggests that interaction scenes are organized into subsets, so that the scenes in subset 1 come before those in subset 2, and so on; however, within a particular subset, no specific order of scenes exists. Consequently, an informal conversation among acquaintances might include such topics as a ritualized greeting ("Hello!"), a reference to the other person's health ("How are you?"), a reference to the present situation, a discussion of the weather, a comment on people known in common, other common interests, a positive evaluation of the

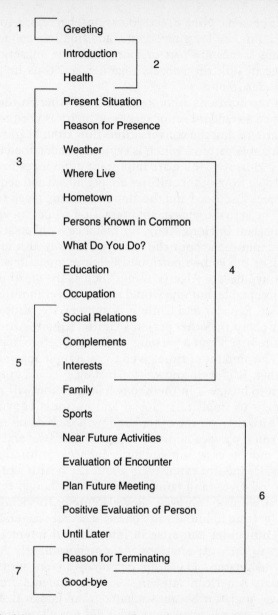

1
- Greeting
- Introduction
- Health

2

3
- Present Situation
- Reason for Presence
- Weather
- Where Live
- Hometown
- Persons Known in Common

4

- What Do You Do?
- Education
- Occupation

5
- Social Relations
- Complements
- Interests
- Family
- Sports

6
- Near Future Activities
- Evaluation of Encounter
- Plan Future Meeting
- Positive Evaluation of Person
- Until Later

7
- Reason for Terminating
- Good-bye

Figure 11.1 Typical interaction scenes. (*Source:* Kathy Kellermann, "The Conversation MOP: II. Progression Through Scenes in Discourse" *Human Communication Research 17* (1991): 388.

other person ("Nice to see you again!"), a reason for terminating the conversation ("I'm late for a meeting"), and finally a good-bye sequence.[5] Notice that certain scenes are part of more than one subset; these scenes function as a bridge to link the subsets together and thus help the conversation to flow from idea to idea.

Conversations among people from other cultures have a similar structure. That is, a standard set of scenes or topics is used to initiate and maintain conversations, and the conversations flow from beginning to end in a more-or-less predictable pattern, which is typically understood and followed by the interactants. However, there are important differences in the ways the conversations of people from other cultures are organized and sequenced, including the types of topics discussed and the amount of time given to each one.

The actual topics in an interaction scene can vary widely from one culture to another. In Hong Kong, for instance, conversations among males often include inquiries about the other person's health and business affairs. In Denmark or the French portion of Belgium, questions about people's incomes are to be avoided. In Algeria, topics such as the weather, health, or the latest news are acceptable, but one would almost never inquire about female family members. In Ecuador and Chile it is appropriate, almost obligatory, to inquire politely about the other person's family. Among Africans, a person is expected to inquire first about a person's well-being before making a request.

The amount of time given to each topic may also vary from one culture to another. It is well known, for instance, that European Americans like to get down to business in their conversations and will typically avoid elaborate sequences of small talk. Social and business conversations among the Saudis and Kuwaitis, on the other hand, will include far more elaborate greeting rituals, some phrases actually being repeated several times before the conversation moves on to subsequent sequences. Similarly, when Africans meet they typically inquire extensively about the health and welfare of each other's parents, relatives, and family members. Although the Japanese do not typically repeat words or phrases, they also prefer to spend considerably more time in the "getting to know you" phase of social conversations.

Difficulties can arise in intercultural interactions when the participants differ in their expectations. At a predominantly African American university in Washington, D.C., for example, an encounter took place between an African American student; African students from Tanzania, Nigeria, and Kenya; and Caribbean students from Jamaica, Trinidad, and Tobago. The African American student, who did not share the others' expectations about the need for elaborate greeting rituals before making a simple request, walked into the graduate assistant's office to inquire about the time. "Hi! Does anyone know what time it is?" he asked, without any formal greetings. No one responded. After a few moments, he repeated his question, apparently frustrated. The African and Caribbean students looked up but continued with their work without responding. At this point the Nigerian student, who realized that the problems were due to incompatible expectations, responded to the first student's question. The student thanked him and left the room.

CULTURE CONNECTIONS

After hanging his coat Somdali turned to greet the others. When we had come in they had just glanced at us and resumed their conversation. The African way of entering the company of others is for the newcomer to announce himself by greeting first. It is the "umthakathi" (wizard) who arrives unseen.

Source: Norman Hodge, ed., *To Kill A Man's Pride, and Other Stories from Southern Africa* (Johannesburg: Ravan Press, 1984) 226.

When the African American had gone, the other students wondered aloud why the Nigerian had answered the question. "He has no respect," one of them remarked. "How could he walk into the room and ask about the time without greeting anyone?" another argued. Interestingly, both the African American and the other students were simply attempting to conform to their own expectations about the appropriate behaviors in an interaction scene involving strangers who are making requests.

Interaction Contexts   Interaction contexts are the settings or situations within which social episodes occur. Interaction contexts impose a "frame" around social episodes by helping people to determine what specific actions should mean, what behaviors are expected, and how to act competently in a particular interaction.

Dean Barnlund captures the importance of interaction contexts: "The streets of Calcutta, the avenues of Brasilia, the Left Bank of Paris, the gardens of Kyoto, the slums of Chicago, and the canyons of lower Manhattan provide dramatically different backgrounds for human interaction."[6] An afternoon conversation at a crowded sidewalk café and an evening of candlelight dining in a private salon will differ in the kinds of topics that are covered and in the interpretations that are made about the meanings of certain phrases or glances.

The meanings assigned to particular behaviors can differ dramatically as different definitions of the context are imposed. As John Condon says about differences in male-female relationships in the United States and Mexico,

> There are meanings to be read into settings and situations which must be learned if one is to avoid misunderstandings and even unpleasant experiences. A boss who invites his secretary out for a drink after work may or may not have ulterior motives in either country. However, the assumption that this was a romantic overture would be far more common in Mexico City than in New York or Los Angeles.[7]

Participating in a social evening at a friend's home is often a context in which intercultural communication occurs. Think about all of the expectations that govern behaviors in social settings. How do you respond to these episodes when the participants have different rules about what should occur? *(Copyright © B. Bachmann/The Image Works.)*

The interaction context influences interpersonal relationships in many obvious ways. As Donald Klopf so poignantly illustrates, knowledge of the interaction context often provides important information about the meanings that are intended and the kinds of communication that are possible:

> I wanted to see her one more time before leaving Hong Kong. So I called her at work and she agreed to lunch. Near her office was a traditional *dim sum* restaurant. Sounded good to me; *dim sum* literally means "to touch the heart" and she had done that to me. What a mistake! Noisy?! The place was bedlam. The waitresses shouted out their wares—some sixty to seventy *dim sum* choices. We shared a table with a couple of tourists who griped about the food, and everything else. Crowded, every steno around must have decided on a *yam cha* meal today. Words of endearment didn't seem appropriate there. "Let's go next door to the Lau Ling Bar," I suggested, "for our black tea." Quiet and refined, it was the proper site to touch the heart, and I think I did.[8]

CONTEXTS FOR INTERCULTURAL COMMUNICATION

U.S. Americans are increasingly being asked to participate in social episodes within three specific contexts that we would like to highlight: health care, education, and business. Each provides an important and recurring meeting ground where people from many cultures converge and interact. We now describe in greater detail the particular importance and challenge of these three contexts.

The Health-Care Context

In Chapter 1 we indicated that the need for intercultural competence arises, in part, because of the increased cultural mixing that has occurred across national boundaries and within the United States itself. In the health-care context, this need presents itself to doctors, nurses, counselors, and other health-care workers, as well as to patients and their families. As Gary L. Kreps and Elizabeth N. Kunimoto indicate, "it is becoming increasingly common to encounter foreign-born and foreign-educated health care providers working in American hospitals, and as the American population becomes more multicultural there are increasing numbers of foreign-born individuals seeking health care."[9]

Health-care professionals have responded to this intercultural imperative by including courses that are designed to increase intercultural communication skills within their professional training and development programs. The nursing profession, for instance, has developed both a specialization in "transcultural nursing" and a new professional organization, the Transcultural Nursing Society.[10] Textbooks and training materials are now readily available to assist nursing students in their academic preparations for intercultural communication challenges, as courses in transcultural nursing are standard offerings in many nursing degree programs.[11] Indeed, as a prerequisite to their certification, many health-care providers are asked to demonstrate their competence in interacting with diverse cultural groups.[12]

All participants in the health-care context—from the providers to the patients and their families—bring with them their own cultural patterns and expectations about what constitutes appropriate and effective medical care. These cultural patterns often lead to very clear expectations about the right and wrong ways to treat illnesses and help people—expectations that are not necessarily shared by those from other cultures.

We suggested in Chapter 5 that cultural patterns provide the lenses through which people come to understand their world. Cultural patterns affect how people make sense of many aspects of the health-care setting: the meanings that people give to health and illness, the causes of diseases, the means to prevent illnesses, appropriate cures, and the types of individuals most qualified to provide the care and attempt the cure.

There are three general approaches to beliefs about health that cultures might adopt to explain issues of illness and wellness: magico-religious, holistic, and biomedical.[13] These three approaches bear a strong resemblance to elements in the cultural patterns we described in Chapters 5 and 6.

In the *magico-religious approach,* health and illness are closely linked to supernatural forces. Health and illness are caused by mystical forces, typically outside of human control, and a person's health is therefore at the mercy of the powerful forces of good and evil. Sometimes illnesses occur because of transgressions or improper actions; the restoration of health is therefore a gift, or even a reward, for proper conduct. Within this approach, health and illness are usually seen as anchored in or related to the whole community, rather

CULTURE CONNECTIONS

Today, as we approach the year 2000, Western medicine views the body essentially as a machine, an exceedingly complex mechanism that can be understood, modified and repaired. Specificity is the tradition's greatest asset: our physicians work best when they can identify and eliminate a disease-causing agent that originates outside the body, and our surgeons are unsurpassed in dealing with acute trauma. Health is defined in strictly clinical terms by physicians. The fate of the spirit is relegated to religious specialists who have little to say about their followers' physical well-being.

For most societies around the world today, priest and physician are still one. The state of the body is inseparable from the condition of the spirit. Sickness is disruption, imbalance, the manifestation of malevolent forces in the flesh. Health is a state of balance, of harmony, and in most cultures it is something holy. Accordingly, healers act on two levels at once. Physical ailments are treated with herbal baths and massage, the administration of medicinal plants, isolation of the patient in a sacred place, and in some traditions an animal sacrifice so that the patient may return to the earth a gift of life's vital energy.

For the Native American shaman the vehicle to the gods is the sweat lodge. The Huichol people of the American Southwest ingest peyote. Tibetan healers mediate their patients' fates by ritually transforming themselves into deities. African priests also become gods, demonstrating their power by handling burning embers. In the high Andes of Peru, healers diagnose ailments by reading coca leaves, a practice reserved for those who have survived a lightning strike. With no rigid separation between the sacred and the secular, every act of the healer becomes a prayer for the entire community, every ritual a form of collective preventive medicine.

Western medicine tends to dismiss the ideas that lie at the heart of traditional healing—ideas concerning the spiritual realm, mind-body interactions, the interplay among humanity, the environment and the cosmos—for they don't fit readily into its scientific model. Yet there is a growing recognition that the mysteries of health and healing cannot be separated from the totality of the human experience.

Source: Wade Davis, "The Power to Heal," *Newsweek*, September 24, 1990: 39–40.

than to a specific individual. The actions of one person, then, dramatically affect others. Treatments for illnesses within this framework are directed toward soothing or removing problematic supernatural forces, rather than toward something organic within the individual. Such treatments are performed by healers, who are best equipped to deal with both the spiritual and the physical worlds. Some African cultures, for example, believe that illness is caused by demons and evil spirits.[14] Many Asian cultures also believe in the supernatural as an important source of illness.[15] Within the United States, cultural groups with many members who share such beliefs include various Latino cultures and African Americans.

In the *holistic approach*, humans desire to maintain a sense of harmony with the forces of nature. Illnesses occur when organs in the body (such as the heart, spleen, lungs, liver, and kidneys) are out of balance with some aspect of nature. There is thus a great emphasis on the prevention of illness by maintaining a sense of balance and good health. Good health, however, means more than just an individual's biological functioning. Rather, it includes her or his relationship to the larger social, political, and environmental circumstances. Some diseases, for instance, are thought to be caused by external climatic elements such as wind, cold, heat, dampness, and dryness. Native Americans, for example, often define health in terms of a person's relationship to nature; health occurs if a person is in harmony with nature, whereas sickness occurs because a principle of nature has been violated. A common distinction within this approach is a contrast among both foods and diseases as either hot or cold. The classification of a disease as hot or as cold links it both to a diagnosis and to a treatment.[16] A common metaphor within the Chinese culture, the ancient principle of *yin* and *yang*, captures the essence of this distinction; everything in the universe is either positive or negative, cold or hot, light or dark, male or female, plus or minus, and so on, and people should have a harmonious balance between these opposing forces in their approach to all of life's issues.

In the *biomedical approach*, people are thought to be controlled by biochemical forces. Good health is achieved by knowing which biochemical reactions to set in motion. Disease occurs when a part of the body breaks down, resulting in illness or injury. Treatments are provided by doctors and nurses, who fix the biochemical problem affecting the "broken part," thus making the body healthy again. This approach is closely linked to the European American cultural pattern and has had a major influence on the development of the health-care system in the United States. Indeed, the biomedical approach is so dominant within the United States that it is sometimes very difficult for individuals—providers and patients alike—to act competently in and adapt themselves to alternative cultural patterns.[17]

Cultural patterns are also very important in defining who should be treated as a patient. The health-care system in the United States has typically focused solely on the individual patient as the source of the medical problem in need of a cure. Yet many cultures in the United States are more collectivist and group-oriented, and this difference can be the basis for serious problems and misunderstandings. Cultures that value the community or the extended family, for instance, may influence people's willingness to keep important health-care appointments. Navajo women, for example, who often give priority to family members' needs, have been known to forego clinic appointments when someone from the extended family stops in to visit and ask for help.[18] Likewise, competent treatment for Latino patients may require the involvement and agreement of other family members.[19]

The responsibilities of family members in the health-care context differ widely across cultures. Among the Amish communities in the United States,

CULTURE CONNECTIONS

The Mien people believe the hospital is haunted. At night, the spirits of the dead rove the corridors like a poisonous wind. In their minds, the hospital is a forbidding forest of restless souls and muffled cries.

In their language, there is no word for cancer. Or antibiotics. They don't believe in surgery. Or "bad news." They believe in herbal remedies, in bodily humors, in animal sacrifice and tribal shamans—in appeasement. They believe illness is caused by evil spirits, by ancestral transgressions, by ineluctable destiny. With no philosophic immune system, so to speak, they are resigned to their mortality, however premature. . .

Since sickness is perceived as a communal affliction, often the entire Mien clan will attempt to crowd into the hospital room to witness the proceedings. In grave cases, even the shaman might appear to perform a rite.

Source: Bob Sylva, "In Any Language: Hope," *Sacramento Bee,* May 1993.

for example, the family includes a large, extended group, with adult members of the extended family having obligations and responsibilities to children other than their own biological ones. Hospital rules that give rights and responsibilities only to members of the immediate family pose challenges when an Amish child is hospitalized. The large number of people who expect to make lengthy visits to the child may prove difficult for the medical staff.[20] Similarly, when suggesting health-care intervention strategies for Pacific Islanders and Hawaiians, experts recommend focusing on the entire family, rather than just the identified patient, in order to be effective.[21]

Of course, intercultural difficulties may occur when the family's ideas about the appropriate course of treatment differ from those of the medical staff. A Latino teenager, for example, was hospitalized on an oncology unit. Problems occurred when his family took him home for a day but did not follow the medical rules for such visits. He ate forbidden foods, did not return to the hospital at the specified time, and generally did not follow other aspects of his treatment. The medical team was upset with the family because their patient suffered a setback. The parents, however, knew that their son had only a limited time to live and wanted him to be with his family and enjoy what little time he had. Only the skilled intervention of an interculturally competent nurse, who was able to understand both cultures' points of view, prevented a head-on clash.[22]

Medical examinations can themselves be the source of intercultural difficulties, as cultures differ in their expectations about modesty and bodily dis-

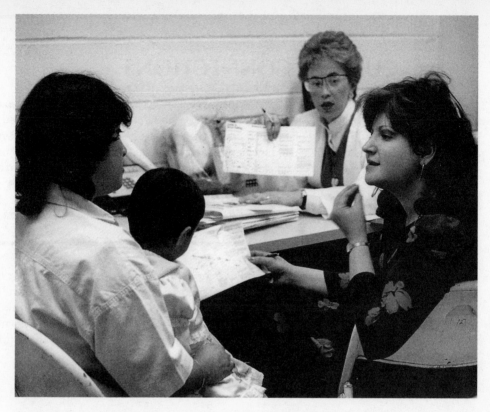

The complexities of health care delivery in this intercultural interaction also includes translating to and from Spanish and English. *(Copyright © R. Sidney/The Image Works.)*

plays. In some cultures, for instance, role requirements governing appropriate behaviors for women do not permit undressing for an examination by male physicians or nurses. Among many Latina women, for example, there are strong social taboos against showing the body to others; disrobing for a medical examination may be embarrassing and difficult.[23]

Because of cultural differences in interaction rules, interviews between caregivers and patients, a basic component of the health-care context, can be another source of intercultural problems. Latinos and Arabs, for example, may engage in extensive small talk before indicating their reasons for the medical interview. Interviews with Native Americans may be punctuated with extensive periods of silence. Medical interviewers may consider such small talk or silence a "waste of time" rather than a vital component of the person's cultural pattern that affects his or her comfort level and willingness to proceed with the interview.[24] Similarly, direct and explicit discussions with many Asians and Asian Americans may pose serious threats to their face, and the use of indirection or other face-saving strategies may be preferred.[25]

CULTURE CONNECTIONS

A Nigerian psychiatrist told me that, when a psychiatric clinic was first set up in a rural district of Nigeria to treat the mentally ill, the family invariably accompanied the sufferer and insisted upon being present at the patient's interview with the psychiatrist. The idea that the patient might exist as an individual apart from the family, or that he might have personal problems which he did not want to share with them, did not occur to Nigerians who were still living a traditional village life.

Source: Anthony Storr, *Solitude: A Return to the Self* (New York: Free Press, 1988) 78.

Cultural patterns can have a powerful effect on the treatment of illnesses. Consider the case of a nurse or pharmacist who instructs a patient to "take three pills a day at mealtime" and expects that the patient will take one pill at each of three meals. Patients who come from cultures that do not separate their day into three major meal times may instead take all three pills simultaneously at the one large meal every day.[26]

The Educational Context

In Chapter 1 we described the U.S. educational system as one that increasingly requires competent intercultural communication skills from its participants. As students, parents, professionals, or ordinary citizens, you will inevitably be challenged to communicate interculturally in the educational context.

Teachers, students, parents, school administrators, and other staff bring their culture's beliefs, values, and norms with them when they enter the educational context. Cultural differences may lead to dissimilarities in expectations about competent behaviors for students and teachers, the best ways to learn, how classroom activities should be structured, how behaviors should be regulated, how teachers should teach, and the importance of education itself. While we will not describe all of the ways in which cultural differences affect the classroom, we do want to emphasize the effects of your own cultural patterns on your ability to communicate competently in this increasingly intercultural educational context.

Think for a moment about the classroom experiences you have had. Did they encourage students to work cooperatively in groups? Or were classroom activities designed for students to work alone, succeeding or failing on their individual merits?

Recall from Chapter 5 that Stewart and Bennett's taxonomy of cultural differences describes variations among cultures in their orientations to the self. Similarly, Hofstede's taxonomy in Chapter 6 describes differences along the individualism-collectivism dimension. Choices on these dimensions influence how students and teachers approach education. Cultures that define the self through identification with the family or other groups will prefer different approaches to education than will those that value the self and are, therefore, more individualistic in their orientation.

Cultural patterns directly affect preferred ways to learn in the classroom. Latino children, whose culture teaches the importance of family and group identities, are more likely to value cooperativeness than competitiveness.[27] Because Native American cultural patterns emphasize the group, harmony with nature, and circularity, children from that culture often respond better to learning approaches that are noncompetitive, holistic, and cooperative.[28] European American children, in contrast, often prefer learning approaches that emphasize competition, discrete categories for information, and individual achievement.

Even the value of education itself differs from one culture to another. For Thais and Filipinos, education affects the family's status and social standing. By excelling in school, therefore, children bring honor to their families while preparing for future successes that will further enhance the family stature. Education is thus a family concern, rather than an individual achievement.[29]

Cultural preferences concerning social orientations are very important in creating expectations within the educational context. Native American children often prefer more holistic learning styles, in contrast to the European American preference for categorization.[30] Those who prefer a more hierarchical relationship between individuals will structure the relationship between student and teacher with greater status differences. Within many Asian and Asian American cultures, for instance, teachers are highly revered and respected. Students and parents would not openly and directly question the authority and statements of a teacher. The expectations for teachers within these cultures is usually for a great deal of formality.

Many teachers in the United States, using the European American preference for informality, may offend and shock the parents of their students whose cultural backgrounds prescribe more formality to the teacher role. Many U.S. university professors, for instance, who allow their students to call them by their first names in a reflection of the European American penchant for informality, report that some of their students express discomfort with this kind of informality because it suggests disrespect.

How students participate in the classroom also varies greatly across cultures. Because of the basic rules for interaction that are taught within their culture, some Native American children have a difficult time asking straightforward questions and looking directly at the teacher.[31] Similarly, many Native American and Asian American students may be unwilling to volunteer, speak out, or raise problems or concerns unless the teacher specifically calls on them by name. Questions for clarification are rarely asked of the teacher directly; to do so might be regarded as a challenge to the teacher's authority and could threaten his or her face should the answer not be known.

Students from other cultures who go to school in the United States sometimes find it difficult to adapt to the verbal style expected of them. Con-

These educators and their students work in the educational setting to bridge cultural differences in expectations about appropriate and effective communication. *(Copyright © Antman/The Image Works and Copyright © M. Siluk/The Image Works.)*

versely, when U.S. students study overseas, they often experience similar difficulties in understanding the cultural expectations related to the educational context.[32] Yet a willingness to speak in class is a communication characteristic highly valued by European American teachers and students, whose cultural framework celebrates individual achievement and responsibility. To students from cultures that emphasize the collective good and the maintenance of face, however, such behaviors in the classroom are too competitive, as they disrupt the group's harmony and separate people from one another.

Turn-taking within the classroom is also governed by cultural expectations. Watch how teachers in your various classes regulate the flow of conversations and contributions. A teacher has a particular set of expectations about who speaks in the classroom as well as when and how they speak. Is it acceptable for students to talk amongst themselves? How loudly can they talk to each other? How long can a private conversation continue before the teacher asks for it to stop? How do students get permission to speak in class? All of these classroom behaviors, which are crucial to how teachers evaluate their students and how students evaluate teachers and classroom environments, are grounded in cultural expectations.

Differences in communication style are also present in the classroom. African American children, whose culture emphasizes the development of verbal skills and expressiveness, may be affected in their classroom interactions with a European American teacher:

> In both verbal and nonverbal language, they [African American children] are more theatrical, show greater emotion, and demonstrate faster responses and higher energy. . . . African-American speakers are more animated, more persua-

CULTURE CONNECTIONS

Dealing with cultural diversity is high on the agenda of almost every campus in the United States.

As scholars from Australia, we can vouch for the fact that multiculturalism is no less a burning issue where we come from.

Source: Mary Kalantzis and William Cope, "Multiculturalism May Prove to be the Key Issue of Our Epoch." *The Chronicle of Higher Education,* November 4, 1992.

sive, and more active in the communication process. They often are perceived as confrontational because of this style. On the other hand, the school, and most Anglo-American teachers, are more oriented toward a passive style, which gives the impression that the communicator is somewhat detached, literal, and legalistic in use of the language. Most African-American students find this style distancing and dissuasive.[33]

Responses to a classroom mistake are also strongly influenced by one's culture. The cultural imperative for maintaining face, as described in Chapter 10, affects whether students are willing to say when they do not understand something and how teachers should handle questioning and classroom discussion.

Even the need for the customary parent-teacher conferences may not make much sense to parents from cultures in which there is no expectation that parents will play an active role in decisions about their children's education.[34] Many Middle Eastern parents, for instance, expect their children will do well in school. Thus, when the children actually do well,

> there is generally less overt praise or material reward than is common in the United States; children are doing what is expected of them. However, when children do not do well, parents may present a variety of attitudes including denial, blaming the school, blaming the child, and feeling ashamed.[35]

Similar expectations exist among many Asian and Asian-American parents. A teacher's request for a routine conference, therefore, may be met with a sense of skepticism or a deep concern that the family may have been dishonored by a disobedient child. Because of face-saving needs, the parents may even assume that the exact nature of this problem will not be stated explicitly but must be discerned through a clever analysis and interpretation of the teacher's subtle clues. The teacher's bland statements that their child behaves well are therefore regarded as merely a social politeness. Not wanting to heep unlimited praise on the child for fear of setting false expectations, the teacher may unwittingly provide the parents with just the sort of high-context hints and generalities about the child's faults and weaknesses that they will interpret as an indication of a deeper and more difficult problem in need of correction.

The admonition to understand one's own cultural background is excellent advice for educators at all levels—from preschool to graduate school. Teachers and administrators need to recognize that their culture creates expectations for how classrooms should operate and how students should behave. Another suggestion to improve competence in the classroom is to use varied approaches to the presentation of classroom material.[36]

While the following example focuses on Native Americans, it is equally true of students from a variety of cultural backgrounds. It illustrates the importance of the educational context and the potential for both permanent and harmful consequences as a result of interactions within that context.

> When many young Native American children enter the classroom, they frequently find themselves in foreign environments where familiar words, values, and lifestyles are absent. As the classroom activities and language become increasingly different from the familiar home environment, the students suffer a loss of self-confidence and self-esteem, a loss that is sometimes irreparable.[37]

The Business Context

The business context is increasingly intercultural. Commerce and trade are global and affect our daily lives. Look at your possessions and you will see ample evidence of the products and people that have crossed national and cultural boundaries. People, however, are the key ingredients in the intercultural business world.

Throughout most people's working lives, they will be within an intercultural business context; customers, co-workers, supervisors, and subordinates may all come from cultures that differ from their own. Unfortunately, many U.S. employees have been poorly prepared for these intercultural assignments. U.S. managers, for instance, who have been on temporary overseas assignments for U.S. multinational corporations, are far more likely to fail in their missions and to return home prematurely than are their Japanese or European counterparts. Whereas over one-half of the West European and three-fourths of the Japanese firms have failure rates that are under 5 percent, a majority of U.S. multinational corporations have failure rates in the 10 to 20 percent range.[38] The underlying problem, experts agree, is top management's ethnocentricity and its corresponding failure to provide adequate preparation and rewards for these intercultural assignments.[39] Even within corporations and small businesses that are wholly owned and operated in the United States, there is an enormous degree of commerce and connection with people from a

Work settings are increasingly culturally diverse, providing opportunities to improve intercultural competence. *(Copyright © Nita Winter/The Image Works.)*

variety of cultural backgrounds, again creating the need to communicate competently in the intercultural business context.

The taxonomies offered in Chapters 5 and 6 suggest that cultures vary in their interpretations about what constitutes appropriate and effective business communication. Cultural patterns influence how people approach a negotiation, the factors that motivate people, and the customary business practices.[40]

Bookstores regularly stock reference materials that provide insights into specific cultures and suggest some of the do's and don'ts of conducting business with individuals from those cultures.[41] Only recently has there been more formal research on communication within the business setting; to date, the overwhelming bulk of this research has been on Japanese business practices and how U.S. Americans should do business with the Japanese.[42] Most of these discussions contrast the cultural patterns of the Japanese with those of European Americans. In Table 11.1, Alan Goldman illustrates some of these key differences in expectations for business negotiations when U.S. Americans interact with the Japanese. Among the Japanese, who value group loyalty and age, advancement is based on seniority, there is a longer-term approach to negotiating, and the formation and nurturance of longer-lasting business relationships are extremely important. Interpersonal communication is likely to be indirect, conciliatory in tone, and formal. Often an intermediary is used,

Table 11.1   JAPANESE AND WESTERN ORGANIZATIONAL BEHAVIOR AND PROTOCOL

Japanese Protocol	Western Protocol
1. Generalist workers	Specialist workers
2. Advancement by seniority	Advancement by accomplishment
3. Private, prescribed channels for grievances	Public arenas for grievances and disputes
4. Publicly conciliatory	Publicly more argumentative
5. Organizational relationships are highest priority	Tasks/goals are highest priority
6. Long-term organizational agendas	Shorter-term organizational agendas
7. Primarily vertical upward and horizontal communication	More vertical downward communication
8. Clear distinction between *tatemae* and *honne*	Less distinction between surface communication and true intentions
9. Accessible informal channels for manager-employee communication	More formalized channels for manager-employee communication
10. Decision making via complete consensus	Decision making via majority vote or designated leaders
11. *Amae* (interdependence) crucial in intra- and interorganizational communication (e.g., *keiretsus*)	*Amae* less pronounced and not publicly sanctioned (e.g., antitrust legislation)
12. Strong dependencies (*giri*) and commitments between organizations and employees	Less binding, more flux in commitments between organizations and employees
13. Organizational security via lifetime employment in large MNOs	More turnover, less security; layoffs, firings
14. Close workplace proxemics	More individualized work spaces
15. Ritualized, restricted formal codes for interaction	More informal; less restricted codes
16. Interactions more situationally bound	Interactions more ideologically bound
17. Valuing of intuitive, nonverbal communication (*haragei*)	Values analytical logic over intuitive communication
18. More reliance on face-to-face communication	Greater use of print communication

Source: Alan Goldman, "Strategic Arenas of Interaction with Japanese Multinationals: Organizational Negotiations, Proxemic and Performance Protocols",1992.

the real decision making occurs privately and away from the actual negotiations, the negotiating teams make group decisions, and all team members are expected to present a united front.

In the United States and in other Western countries where individual achievement is valued, advancements occur because of accomplishments, there is a shorter-term and results-oriented approach to negotiating, and a high priority is placed on getting the job done and accomplishing task-related

CULTURE CONNECTIONS

John Grisham's novel "The Firm," Stephen King's thrillers, Eric Carle's "The Very Hungry Caterpillar," and Brian Weiss's "Many Lives, Many Masters" are all popular books in English—and now brisk sellers in Spanish.

At least three large United States bookstore chains—New York-based Barnes & Noble, Waldenbooks Inc., based in Stamford, Conn., and Landover, MD.-based Crown Books—are increasingly stocking shelves in selected stores with Spanish-language titles. These chains have discovered new profits in a previously ignored market of more than 17 million US Spanish speakers.

Source: Patricia Horn, "US Book Industry Learns a New Language," *The Christian Science Monitor,* March 8, 1994: 8.

objectives. Interpersonal communication is typically direct, confrontational, face-to-face, and informal. Negotiating teams are willing to make decisions and concessions in the public negotiation setting, where individuals within the team may disagree publicly with one another. One individual is usually given the authority to make decisions that are binding on all.[43]

Japanese work organizations are an extension of the family hierarchy. That is,

> presidents are "family heads," executives "wise uncles," managers "hard-working big brothers," workers "obedient and loyal children." American workers employed in Japanese-managed companies do not see themselves as "loyal and obedient children" and instead hold traditional American values of individualism, competitiveness, and social mobility.[44]

Even the seating arrangements and protocol during Japanese negotiations are highly prescribed. Tables are never round in such business settings, and the expression "head of the table" is meaningless. Rather, as Figure 11.2 indicates, the two sides sit opposite one another, with the power position in the middle of each side. The power seat is flanked by advisors and, if necessary, an interpreter. Next come information suppliers and note takers, followed by other interested parties and junior people, who are closest to the door. Contrary to the usual practice in the United States, the power seat is not necessarily occupied by the most senior person present. Rather, whoever is most knowledgeable about the specific discussion topic takes the power seat and is designated as the company's official spokesperson for this aspect of the negotiations. At the conclusion of the business meeting, ritualistic thank-you's are uttered while all are still seated, both sides arise simultaneously and begin bowing, and the power person from the host company is expected to stay with the "guests" until they are outside the premises and are able to depart.[45]

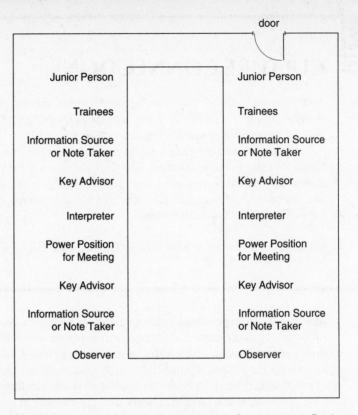

Figure 11.2 Conference Table Seating Arrangements for Japanese Business Negotiations. (*Source:* Adapted from Richard H. Reeves-Ellington, "Using Cultural Skills for Cooperative Advantage in Japan," *Human Organization 52 [1993]:* 209.)

Such differences in role expectations and in the rules for interactions between Japanese and U.S. American businesspeople are not confined to meetings that take place in Japan, nor are they limited to negotiations among teams from different organizations. Young Yun Kim and Sheryl Paulk found that communication problems and misunderstandings occurred within a Japanese-owned company in the United States because of the Japanese preference for indirectness and the U.S. preference for directness.[46]

The extended Japanese examples point to issues that may be major sources of difficulty for businesspeople working with their counterparts from other cultures. For instance, cultures have different patterns for the flow or pacing of business negotiations. In the initial stages of a negotiation, German business managers may ask numerous questions about technical details. In Scandinavia, there is a great deal of initial frankness and a desire to get right down to business. Among the French, however, the early emphasis is on laying out all aspects of the potential deal. In contrast, many Italian and Asian managers may use these same initial stages to get to know the other person by talking about subjects other than the business deal. Likewise, preliminaries in Spain may take several days.[47]

In many cultures, it is vital that businesspeople establish cordial interpersonal relationships and maintain them over time. The assumption that it is possible to have a brief social exchange that will produce the degree of understanding necessary to establish a business agreement is simply incorrect. In many African cultures, friendship takes precedence over business. Similarly, most Middle Easterners extend their sociability to business meetings, where schedules are looser and the first encounter is only for getting acquainted and not for business.[48] A similar regard for establishing social relationships as a prelude to doing business is common in China, Japan, and Korea.[49] In Columbia and other Latin American countries, achieving objectives by using interpersonal connections to obtain jobs, contracts, supplies, and other contacts—that is, giving and receiving personal favors to create an interdependent network of relationships—is regarded very positively.[50] Similar customs exist in India and elsewhere.

Chinese businesspeople will likely have to check with their superiors before making any real decisions. In Chinese organizations, superiors are expected to participate in many decisions that U.S. managers might routinely delegate to subordinates. The Chinese process of consulting the next higher level in the hierarchy often continues up the bureaucratic ladder to the very top of the organization. Thus, autonomy that is expected and rewarded in the United States may be regarded as insubordination in China.[51]

The Chinese concept of legal or contractual agreements also differs from the U.S. concept. In the United States, of course, a business contract is binding and is expected to be implemented precisely as agreed. In China, however, contracts are regarded more as statements of intent than as promises of performance. Therefore, they are binding only if the circumstances and conditions that were in effect when the contract was signed are still present when the contract should be implemented.[52]

Reward systems to motivate employees to give their best efforts similarly vary from one culture to another. In Mexico, for instance, though the individual is valued, people are not motivated by the same external actions and individual achievements that are typical of U.S. Americans. Thus production contests and "employee of the month" designations would not necessarily work to motivate a Mexican employee. Rather, Mexicans often prefer formality and emphasize status differences in business, whereas European Americans prefer informality and minimal status differences.[53] Chinese managers do not provide their subordinates with the detailed performance appraisal that is customary in many U.S. firms. Feedback on failures and mistakes, for instance, is often withheld, which allows subordinates to save face and maintain their sense of esteem for future tasks within the organization. Similarly, while decisions to approve or reject specific requests or proposals may be communicated clearly by Chinese managers, justifications for such decisions are often vague or omitted in an effort to protect the face of the employees. In a business negotiation involving Chinese and U.S. Americans, therefore, attempts

Success in business endeavors now requires an ability to persuade culturally different others. *(Copyright © Rhoda Sidney/The Image Works.)*

by the U.S. team to insist on explanations for Chinese decisions may communicate a lack of respect and a failure to acknowledge the Chinese attempts at face maintenance.

Another area in which cultural differences will likely affect the business context is gender expectations. Cultures differ in their prescriptive roles for men and women, and in many cultures women are unlikely to have managerial or supervisory positions in business. Women from the United States may have to make careful adjustments in order to be interculturally competent in the business setting.[54]

In Korea, the most important concept when doing business, and indeed the most important concern for all Korean interpersonal relationships, is that of *kibun*. *Kibun* refers to an individual's personal harmony, pleasurable inner feelings, positive state of mind, sense of pride, and dignity. In Korean relationships, keeping *kibun* in good order takes precedence over virtually all other considerations. In the business context, people must maintain a harmonious atmosphere that enhances the *kibun* of all, for to damage people's *kibun* may irreparably damage interpersonal relationships and create lifelong enemies.[55] Koreans believe that maintaining *kibun* is more important than attaining immediate goals, accomplishing task-related objectives, or telling the absolute truth. That is,

> *Kibun* enters into every aspect of Korean life. Knowing how to judge the state of other people's *kibun,* how to avoid hurting it, and keeping your own *kibun* in a satisfactory state are important skills. . . . For example, a Korean's *kibun* is damaged when his subordinate does not show proper respect, that is, by not bowing soon enough, not using honorific words, not contacting the superior within an appropriate period of time, or worse, handing something to him with the left hand. Most of these rules of etiquette are well known to Koreans, and while they are often difficult or cumbersome to remember, they must be heeded to avoid hurting *kibun.*[56]

To cope with cultural differences in the business context, Charles R. Bantz describes the lessons he learned from working in a multicultural research team engaged in a long-term project spanning several years and several continents. Bantz recommends that more efforts should be devoted to gathering information about the multiple perspectives that will inevitably be present; maintaining flexibility and a willingness to adapt to differing situations, issues, and needs; building social relationships as well as task cohesion; and clearly identifying and emphasizing mutual long-term goals.[57]

EPISODES, CONTEXTS, AND INTERCULTURAL COMPETENCE

Recall from Chapter 3 that interaction contexts are a component of intercultural competence related to the associations between two people interacting in specific settings. The discussion in this chapter on social episodes and interaction contexts elaborates on these important ideas.

Just as a picture hung on the wall has a frame around it, each intercultural encounter is surrounded or defined by a cultural frame. Competence in intercultural communication requires understanding the nature of this cultural frame.

People frame their intercultural encounters by the definitions or labels they give to particular social episodes. The activities in which you interact are chunked or grouped into social episodes that are influenced by your cultural patterns, roles, rules, interaction scenes, and interaction contexts. A social episode that to you is "small talk with a classmate" may be taken as "an offer of friendship" by another person. What is to you a businesslike episode of "letting off steam with a co-worker about one of her mildly irritating habits" may be viewed as a "public humiliation." Do not assume that what you regard as appropriate social roles and sensible rules of interaction will necessarily be comfortable or even acceptable to another.

SUMMARY

Social episodes are the repetitive, predictable, and routine behaviors that form the structure of one's interactions with others. Social episodes are made up of cultural patterns, social roles, rules of interaction, interaction scenes, and interaction contexts. People frame intercultural interactions by the expectations they have for particular social episodes.

Three specific social contexts—health care, education, and business—have become prominent meeting grounds where people from many cultures converge and interact. Each context was described in some detail to illustrate the importance of intercultural competence in everyday experiences.

FIVE

12

Obstacles to Intercultural Competence

In previous chapters we explained how the components of culture can affect intercultural competence. These components include cultural patterns, code systems, and cultural variations in interpersonal relationships. In this chapter we consider another important component: obstacles that arise because of the particular characteristics of people or specific aspects of situations. We begin with two puzzles that have perplexed those who study the effects of intercultural contacts.

The first puzzle about individuals engaged in intercultural contact, such as students studying abroad and Peace Corps volunteers, concerns the obvious differences in how people adjust. Some who live in the midst of another culture thrive; they establish satisfying relationships with others, accomplish their tasks, and enjoy the new culture. Others are miserable, have difficulty achieving their goals, and find the new culture a constant irritant. In the same way, even in the United States there are people who dislike the cultural diversity around them and find it difficult to work and live with people who are culturally different, while others are able to interact comfortably with members of the diverse cultures that make up the U.S. population. Variations in individual personality traits and attitudes may explain these disparate responses.

The second puzzle is similar to the first, but it deals with nations and entire cultural groups rather than with individuals. In some nations, different cultures can live together in relative harmony, with little tension between members of the cultural groups; yet in other nations, tensions between members of different cultures repeatedly erupt into physical violence, resulting in a loss of life and damage to property.

In this chapter, we explore those characteristics of persons and situations that seem to have the greatest effects on intercultural contact. We begin with a brief review and description of the role of culture in creating a stable and nonthreatening world, as well as the unpredictability that characterizes many intercultural situations.

CULTURE, PREDICTABILITY, AND OBSTACLES TO INTERCULTURAL COMPETENCE

In Chapter 2, we defined culture as a learned set of shared perceptions about beliefs, values, and norms that affect the behaviors of a relatively large group of people. We also pointed out that culture really exists in people's minds, but that the consequences of culture—shared interpretations about beliefs, values, and norms—can be seen in people's behaviors. Shared interpretations, or what we have called cultural patterns, provide guidelines about how people should behave, and they indicate what to expect in interactions with others. In other words, a culture's shared interpretations create predictability and stability in people's lives. Cultural similarity allows people to reduce uncertainty and to know what to expect when interacting with others.

Interaction only within one's own culture produces a number of obvious benefits. Because the culture provides predictability, it reduces the threat of the unknown. When something or someone that is unknown or unpredictable enters a culture, the culture's beliefs, values, and norms tell people how to interpret and respond appropriately, thus reducing the perceived threat of the intrusion. Cultural patterns also allow for automatic responses to stimuli; in essence, cultural patterns save people time and energy.

Intercultural communication, by definition, means that people are interacting with at least one culturally different person. Consequently, the sense of security, comfort, and predictability that characterizes communication with culturally similar people is lost. The greater the degree of interculturalness, the greater the loss of predictability and certainty. Assurances about the accuracy of interpretations of verbal and nonverbal messages are lost.

Terms that are often used when communicating with culturally different people include *unknown, unpredictable, ambiguous, weird, mysterious, unexplained, exotic, unusual, unfamiliar, curious, novel, odd, outlandish,* and *strange.* As you read this list, consider how the choice of a particular word might also reflect a particular attitude. What characteristics, attitudes, and knowledge allow individuals to respond more competently to the threat of dealing with cultural differences? What situations heighten the perception of threat among members of different cultural groups?

OBSTACLES TO INTERCULTURAL COMPETENCE WITHIN PEOPLE

Three features in the way humans process information present obstacles to intercultural competence. First, as cognitive psychologists have repeatedly demonstrated, people impose a pattern on their world by organizing the stimuli that bombard their senses into conceptual categories. Every waking moment, people are presented with literally hundreds of different perceptual stimuli. Therefore, it becomes necessary to simplify the information by selecting, organizing, and reducing it to less complex forms. That is, to comprehend stimuli, people organize them into categories, groupings, and patterns. As a child, you might have completed a drawing by connecting numbered dots. Emerging from the lines was the figure of an animal or a familiar toy. Even though its complete form was not drawn, it was relatively easy to identify. This kind of recognition occurs simply because human beings have a tendency to organize perceptual cues to impose meaning, usually by using familiar, previous experiences.

Second, humans simplify the processing and organizing of information from the environment by identifying certain characteristics as belonging to certain categories of persons and events. For example, a child's experiences with several dogs that growled and snapped are likely to result in a future reaction to other dogs as if they will also growl and snap. The characteristics of particular events, persons, or objects, once experienced, are often assumed to be typical of similar events, persons, or objects. Though these assumptions are sometimes accurate, often they are not. Not all dogs necessarily growl and snap at young children. Nevertheless, information processing results in a simplification of the world, so that prior experiences are used as the basis for determining both the categories and the attributes of the events.

Please note that we are describing this human tendency in a nonevaluative manner. Its obvious advantage is that it allows people to respond to a variety of perceptual stimuli. Nevertheless, this organization and simplification create some genuine obstacles to intercultural competence because ethnocentrism, stereotypes, prejudice, discrimination, racism, and lack of knowledge and skill can result.

Third, most people tend to think that other people perceive, evaluate, and reason about the world in the same way that they do. In other words, humans assume that other people with whom they interact are like themselves. Indeed, it is quite common for people to draw on their personal experiences to understand the motivations of others. Philip Harris and Robert Moran call this tendency "projective cognitive similarity."[1]

Ethnocentrism

We briefly introduced the concept of ethnocentrism in Chapter 4, where we discussed cultural differences and intercultural competence. All cultures have a strong ethnocentric tendency, that is, the tendency to use the categories of one's own culture to evaluate the actions of others. William G. Sumner, who first introduced the concept of ethnocentrism, defined it as "the view of things in which one's own group is the center of everything, and all others are scaled and rated with reference to it."[2] Sumner illustrates how ethnocentrism works in the following example:

> When Caribs were asked whence they came, they replied, "We alone are people." "Kiowa" means real or principal people. A Laplander is a "man" or "human being." The highest praise a Greenlander has for a European visiting the island is that the European by studying virtue and good manners from the Greenlanders soon will be as good as a Greenlander. Nature peoples call themselves "men" as a rule. All others are something else, but not men. The Jews divide all mankind into themselves and Gentiles—they being the "chosen people." The Greeks and Romans called outsiders "barbarians." Arabs considered themselves as the noblest nation and all others as barbarians. Russian books and newspapers talk about its civilizing mission, and so do the books and journals of France, Germany, and the United States. Each nation now regards itself as the leader of civilization, the best, the freest, and the wisest. All others are inferior.[3]

Because cultures teach people what the world is "really like" and what is "good," people consequently believe that the values of their culture are natural and correct. Thus, people from other cultures who do things differently are wrong.

Ethnocentrism can occur along all of the dimensions of cultural patterns discussed in Chapters 5 and 6. People from individualistic cultures, for instance, find the idea that a person's self-concept is tied to a group unfathomable. To most U.S. Americans the idea of an arranged marriage seems strange at best and a confining and reprehensible limitation on personal freedom at worst.

One area of behavior that quickly reveals ethnocentrism is personal hygiene. For example, U.S. Americans see themselves as the cleanest people on earth. In the United States, bathrooms contain sinks, showers or bathtubs, and toilets, thus allowing the efficient use of water pipes. Given this arrangement, people bathe themselves in close proximity to the toilet, where they urinate and defecate. Described in this way, the cultural practices of the United States may seem unclean, peculiar, and even absurd. Why would people in a so-called modern society place two such contradictory functions next to each other? That sentiment is shared by people from many other cultures, who consider the U.S. arrangement to be unclean and unhealthy.

Our point here is that what is familiar and comfortable inevitably seems the best, right, and natural way of doing things. Ethnocentrism then becomes an obstacle to intercultural competence.

CULTURE CONNECTIONS

An encounter with other cultures can lead to openness only if you can suspend the assumption of superiority, not seeing new worlds to conquer, but new worlds to respect. When young women arrived in Iran as the American wives of Iranian Muslims, they often came with assumptions of superiority, but their actual positions required sensitivity and adaptation, more like adopted children than like explorers arriving to claim new territory.

Source: Mary Catherine Bateson, *Composing a Life* (New York: Atlantic Monthly Press, 1989).

Stereotyping

Journalist Walter Lippmann first introduced the term *stereotyping* to refer to a selection process that is used to organize and simplify perceptions of others.[4] Stereotypes are a form of generalization about some group of people. When people stereotype others, they take a category of people and make assertions about the characteristics of all people who belong to that category. The consequence of stereotyping is that the vast degree of differences that exists among the members of any one group may not be taken into account in the interpretation of messages.

To illustrate how stereotyping works, read the following list: college professors, surfers, Marxists, Democrats, bankers, New Yorkers, Californians. Probably, as you read each of these categories, it was relatively easy for you to associate particular characteristics and traits with each group. Now imagine that a person from one of these groups walked into the room and began a conversation with you. In all likelihood you would associate the group's characteristics with that specific individual.

Your responses to this simple example illustrate what typically occurs when people are stereotyped.[5] First, someone identifies an outgroup category—"they"—whose characteristics differ from those in one's own social ingroup. Next, the perceived dissimilarities between the groups are enlarged and accentuated, thereby creating differences that are clearer and more distinct. By making sharper and more pronounced boundaries between the groups, it becomes more difficult for individuals to move from one group to another.[6] Concurrently, an evaluative component is introduced, whereby the characteristics of the outgroup are negatively judged; that is, the outgroup is regarded as wrong, inferior, or stigmatized as a result of given characteristics. Finally, the group's characteristics are attributed to all people who belong to the group, so

The members of this Venezuelan family are spending time in their home. Study the picture carefully and monitor your reactions. *(Copyright © Myron W. Lustig & Jolene Koester.)*

that a specific person is not treated as a unique individual but as a typical member of a category.

Categories that are used to form stereotypes about groups of people can vary widely, and they might include the following:

- Regions of the world (Asians, Arabs, South Americans, Africans)
- Countries (Kenya, Japan, China, France, Great Britain)
- Regions within countries (northern Indians, southern Indians, U.S. Midwesterners, U.S. Southerners)
- Cities (New Yorkers, Parisians, Londoners)
- Cultures (English, French, Latino, Russian, Serbian, Yoruba, Mestizo, Thai, Navajo)
- Race (African, Caucasian)

- Religion (Muslim, Hindu, Buddhist, Jewish, Christian)
- Age (young, old, middle-aged, children, adults)
- Occupations (teacher, farmer, doctor, housekeeper, mechanic, architect, musician)
- Relational roles (mother, friend, father, sister, brother)
- Physical characteristics (short, tall, fat, skinny)
- Social class (wealthy, poor, middle class)

This list is by no means exhaustive. What it should illustrate is the enormous range of possibilities for classification and simplification. Consider your own stereotypes of people in these groups. Many may have been created by direct experience with only one or two people from a particular group. Others are probably based on second-hand information and opinions, output from the mass media, and general habits of thinking; they may even have been formed without any direct experience with individuals from the group. Yet many people are prepared to assume that the stereotype is an accurate representation of all members of a specific group.

Stereotypes can be inaccurate in a three ways.[7] First, as we have suggested, stereotypes often are assumed to apply to all or most of the members of a particular group or category, resulting in a tendency to ignore differences among the individual members of the group. This type of stereotyping error is called the *out-group homogeneity effect* and results in a tendency to regard all members of a particular group as much more similar to one another than they actually are.[8] Arab Americans, for instance, complain that other U.S. Americans often hold undifferentiated stereotypes about members of their culture. Albert Mokhiber laments that

> If there's problem in Libya we're all Libyans. If the problem is in Lebanon we're all Lebanese. If it happens to be Iran, which is not an Arab country, we're all Iranians. Conversely, Iranians were picked on during the Gulf War as being Arabs. Including one fellow who called in who was a Polynesian Jew. But he looked like what an Arab should look like, and he felt the wrath of anti-Arab discrimination. Nobody's really free from this. The old civil rights adage says that as long as the rights of one are in danger, we're all in danger. I think we need to break out of our ethnic ghetto mentality, all of us, from various backgrounds, and realize that we're in this stew together.[9]

A second form of stereotype inaccuracy occurs when the group average, as suggested by the stereotype, is simply wrong or inappropriately exaggerated. This type of inaccuracy occurs, for instance, when Germans are stereotypically regarded as being very efficient, or perhaps very rigid, when they may actually be less efficient or less rigid than the exaggerated perception of them would warrant.

A third form of stereotype inaccuracy occurs when the degree of error and exaggeration differs for positive and negative attributes. For instance, imagine that you have stereotyped a culture as being very efficient (a positive attribute) but also very rigid and inflexible in their business relationships (a negative attribute). If you tend to overestimate the prevalence and importance of the culture's positive characteristics, such as its degree of efficiency, while simultaneously ignoring or underestimating its rigidity and other negative characteristics, you would have a "positive valence inaccuracy." Conversely, a "negative valence inaccuracy" occurs if you exaggerated the negative attributes while ignoring or devaluing its positive ones. This latter condition, often called "prejudice," will be discussed in greater detail below.

The problems associated with using stereotyping as a means of understanding individuals is best illustrated by identifying the groups to which you belong. Think about the characteristics that might be stereotypically assigned to those groups. Determine whether the characteristics apply to you or to others in your group. Some of them may be accurate descriptions; many, however, will be totally inaccurate, and you would resent being thought of in that way. Stereotypes distort or hide the individual. Ultimately, people may become blind to the actual characteristics of the group because not all stereotypes are accurate. Most are based on relatively minimal experiences with particular individuals.

Stereotype inaccuracy can lead to errors in interpretations and expectations about the behaviors of others. Interpretation errors occur because stereotypes are used not only to categorize specific individuals and events but also to judge them. That is, one potentially harmful consequence of stereotypes is that they provide inaccurate labels for a group of people, which are then used to interpret subsequent ambiguous events and experiences involving members of those groups. As Ziva Kunda and Bonnie Sherman-Williams note,

> Consider, for example, the unambiguous act of failing a test. Ethnic stereotypes may lead perceivers to attribute such failure to laziness if the actor is Asian but to low ability if the actor is Black. Thus stereotypes will affect judgments of the targets' ability even if subjects base these judgments only on the act, because the stereotypes will determine the meaning of the act.[10]

Because stereotypes are sometimes applied indiscriminately to members of a particular culture or social group, they can also lead to errors in one's expectations about the future behaviors of others. Stereotypes provide the basis

CULTURE CONNECTIONS

A great many people think they are thinking when they are merely rearranging their prejudices.

Source: Attributed to William James, U.S. American philosopher (1842–1920).

for estimating, often inaccurately, what members of the stereotyped group are likely to do. Most disturbingly, stereotypes will likely persist even when they are repeatedly disconfirmed by members of the stereotyped group. Once a stereotype has taken hold, members of the stereotyped group who behave in nonstereotypical ways will be expected to compensate in their future actions in order to "make up for" their atypical behavior. Even when some individuals from a stereotyped group repeatedly deviate from expectations, they may be regarded as exceptions or as atypical members of their group. Indeed, stereotypes may remain intact, or may even be strengthened, in the face of disconfirming experiences; those who hold the stereotypes often expect that the other members of the stereotyped social group will be even *more* likely to behave as the stereotype predicts, in order to "balance out" or compensate for the "unusual" instances that they experienced. That is, stereotypes encourage people to expect future behaviors that compensate for perceived inconsistencies, and thus allow people to anticipate future events in a way that makes it unnecessary to revise their deeply held beliefs and values.[11]

The process underlying stereotyping is absolutely essential for human beings to function. Some categorization is necessary and normal. Indeed, there is survival value in the ability to make accurate generalizations about others, and stereotypes function as mental "energy-saving devices" to help make those generalizations efficiently.[12] However, intercultural competence requires an ability to move beyond stereotypes and to respond to the individual. Previous experiences should be used only as guidelines or suggested interpretations rather than as hard and fast categories.

Prejudice

Prejudice refers to negative attitudes toward other people that are based on faulty and inflexible stereotypes. Prejudiced attitudes include irrational feelings of dislike and even hatred for certain groups, biased perceptions and beliefs about the group members that are not based on direct experiences and firsthand knowledge, and a readiness to behave in negative and unjust ways toward members of the group. Gordon Allport, who first focused scholarly attention on prejudice, argued that prejudiced people ignore evidence that is inconsistent with their biased viewpoint, or they distort the evidence to fit their prejudices.[13]

The strong link between prejudice and stereotypes should be obvious. Prejudiced thinking is dependent on stereotypes and is a fairly normal phenomenon. To be prejudiced toward a group of people sometimes makes it easier to respond to them. We are not condoning prejudice or the hostile and violent actions that may occur as a result. We are suggesting that prejudice is a universal psychological process; all people have a propensity for prejudice toward others who are unlike themselves. For individuals to move beyond prejudicial attitudes and for societies to avoid basing social structures on their

CULTURE CONNECTIONS

There is a direct relationship between national chauvinism and racial and cultural chauvinism. In one case, the person who is narrow-minded at best, bigoted at worst, says: "I don't like and anyway I'm superior to all of those folks in those foreign countries." In the other case, the persons says: "I don't like and anyway I'm superior to all of these Hispanic, Asian, African, and Native Americans who have invaded *my* America."

There is a definitive rise in blatant expressons of racism, anti-Semitism, and biased incidents against recent immigrants to our nation. Any expression of bigotry is reprehensible and must be combatted.

Source: Johnnetta R. Cole, "International Education: Broadening the Base of Participation," Speech given at the 43rd International Conference on Educational Exchange, Charleston, South Carolina, November 1990.

prejudices about groups of people, it is critical to recognize the prevalence of prejudicial thinking.

What functions does prejudice serve? We have already suggested that the thought process underlying prejudice includes the need to organize and simplify the world. Richard Brislin describes four additional benefits, or what he calls functions, of prejudice.[14] First, he suggests that prejudice satisfies a *utilitarian* or adjustment function. Displaying certain kinds of prejudice means that people receive rewards and avoid punishments. For example, if you express prejudicial statements about certain people, other people may like you more. It is also easier to simply dislike and be prejudiced toward members of other groups because they can then be dismissed without going through the effort necessary to adjust to them. Another function that prejudice serves is an *ego-defensive* one; it protects self-esteem. For example, people who are unsuccessful in business may be prejudiced toward groups whose members are successful. Still another advantage of prejudicial attitudes is the *value-expressive* function. If people believe that their group has certain qualities that are unique, valuable, good, or in some way special, their prejudicial attitudes toward others is a way of expressing those values. Finally, the *knowledge function* is described by Brislin as prejudicial attitudes that people hold because of their need to have the world neatly organized and boxed into categories. This function takes the normal human proclivity to organize the world to an extreme. The rigid application of categories and the prejudicial attitudes assigned to certain behaviors and beliefs provide security and increase predictability. Obviously, these functions cannot be neatly applied to all instances of prejudice. Nor are people usually aware of the specific reasons for

CULTURE CONNECTIONS

"My mother is Vietnamese, and my father is African American. People have stereotypes about me. They think, she's Asian: she's smart, she doesn't need help. Or she's a black girl: she's likely to get pregnant."
    —Monica Watkins, 18, San Leandro, California

Source: Kristen Golden, "What Do Girls See?" *Ms.* 10(6) (May/June 1994): 56.

their prejudices. For each person, prejudicial attitudes may serve several functions.

Discrimination

Whereas *prejudice* refers to people's attitudes or mental representations, the term *discrimination* refers to the behavioral manifestations of that prejudice. Thus discrimination can be thought of as prejudice "in action."

Discrimination can occur in many forms. From the extremes of segregation and apartheid to biases in the availability of housing, employment, education, economic resources, personal safety, and legal protections, discrimination represents unequal treatment of certain individuals solely because of their membership in a particular group.

Teun van Dijk has conducted a series of studies of people's everyday conversations as they discussed different racial and cultural groups. Van Dijk concludes that when individuals make prejudicial comments, tell jokes that belittle and dehumanize others, and share negative stereotypes about others, they are establishing and legitimizing the existence of their prejudices and are laying the "communication groundwork" that will make it acceptable for people to perform discriminatory acts.[15]

Racism

One obstacle to intercultural competence to which we want to give special attention is racism. Because racism often plays such a major role in the communication that occurs between people of different races or ethnic groups, it is particularly important to understand how and why it occurs.

I BELIEVE THAT THERE WILL ULTIMATELY one race: HUMAN
BE A CLASH BETWEEN THE OPPRESSED AND THOSE one future: OURS
WHO DO THE OPPRESSING... A CLASH BETWEEN THOSE WHO WANT FREEDOM
JUSTICE AND EQUALITY FOR EVERYONE AND THOSE WHO WANT TO
CONTINUE THE SYSTEM OF EXPLOITATION. I BELIEVE THAT THERE WILL
BE THAT KIND OF CLASH, BUT I DON'T THINK IT WILL BE BASED
ON THE COLOUR OF THE SKIN. - MALCOLM X

transcend racism

Racism is a force that individuals and social systems must grapple with. *(Copyright © Myron W. Lustig & Jolene Koester.)*

The word *racism* itself can evoke very powerful emotional reactions, especially for those who have felt the oppression and exploitation that stems from racist attitudes and behaviors. For members of the African American, Asian American, Native American, and Latino cultures, racism has created a social history shaped by prejudice and discrimination.[16] For individual members of these groups, racism has resulted in the pain of oppression. To those who are members of cultural groups that have had the power to oppress and exploit others, the term *racism* often evokes equally powerful thoughts and emotional reactions that deny responsibility for and participation in racist acts and thinking. In this section, we want to introduce some ideas about racism that illuminate the reactions of both those who have received racist communication and those who are seen as exhibiting it.

Robert Blauner has described racism as a tendency to categorize people who are culturally different in terms of their physical traits such as skin color, hair color and texture, facial structure, and eye shape.[17] Dalmas Taylor offers a related approach that focuses on the behavioral components of racism. Taylor defines racism as the cumulative effects of individuals, institutions, and cultures that result in the oppression of ethnic minorities.[18] Taylor's approach is useful in that it recognizes that racism can occur at three distinct levels: individual, institutional, and cultural.

At the individual level, racism is conceptually very similar to prejudice. Individual racism involves beliefs, attitudes, and behaviors of a given person toward people of a different racial group.[19] Specific European Americans, for example, who believe that African Americans are somehow inferior, exemplify individual racism. These attitudes can sometimes be changed by positive contact and interaction between members of the two groups. Yet as the preceding discussion of prejudice suggests, people with prejudicial beliefs about others often distort new information to fit their original prejudices.

At the institutional level, racism is the exclusion of certain people from equal participation in the society's institutions solely because of their race.[20] Institutional racism is built into such social structures as the government, schools, and industry practices. It leads to certain patterns of behaviors and responses to specific racial or cultural groups that allow those groups to be systematically exploited and oppressed. For example, institutional racism has precluded both Jews and African Americans from attending certain public schools and universities, and at times it has restricted their participation in particular professions.[21]

At the cultural level, racism denies the existence of the culture of a particular group,[22] for example, the denial that African Americans represent a unique and distinct culture that is separate from both European American culture and all African cultures. Cultural racism also involves the rejection by one group of the beliefs and values of another, such as the "negative evaluations by whites of black cultural values."[23]

Though racism is often used synonymously with *prejudice* and *discrimination*, the social attributes that distinguish it from these other terms are oppression and power. Oppression refers to "the systematic, institutionalized mistreatment of one group of people by another."[24] Thus racism is the tendency by groups in control of institutional and cultural power to use it to keep members of groups who do not have access to the same kinds of power at a disadvantage. Racism oppresses entire groups of people, making it very difficult, and sometimes virtually impossible, for their members to have access to political, economic, and social power.[25]

Forms of racism vary in intensity and degree of expression, with some forms far more dangerous and detrimental to society than others. The most extreme form of racism is *old-fashioned racism*. Here, members of one group openly display obviously bigoted views about those from another group. Judgments of superiority and inferiority are commonplace in this kind of racism, and there is a dehumanizing quality to it. African Americans and other cultural groups in the United States have often experienced this form of racisim from other U.S. Americans.

In *symbolic racism*, the form currently prevalent in the United States, members of one group believe that their traditional values, such as individualism and self-reliance, are threatened by members of another group. Fears that the outgroup will achieve economic or social success, with a simultaneous loss of economic or social status by the ingroup, typify this form of racism. In many parts of the United States, for instance, this type of racism has been directed toward Asians and Asian Americans who have achieved economic success.

Tokenism as a form of racism occurs when individuals do not perceive themselves as prejudiced because they make small concessions to, while holding basically negative attitudes toward, members of the other group. Tokenism is the practice of reverse discrimination, in which people go out of their way to favor a few members of another group in order to maintain their own self-concepts as individuals who believe in equality for all. While such behaviors may increase a person's esteem, they may also decrease the possibilities for more meaningful contributions to intercultural unity and progress.

Aversive racism, like tokenism, occurs when individuals who highly value fairness and equality among all racial and cultural groups nevertheless have negative beliefs and feelings about members of a particular race, often as a result of childhood socialization experiences. Individuals with such conflicting feelings may restrain their overt racist behaviors, but they may also avoid close contact with members of the other group and may express their underlying negative attitudes subtly, in ways that appear rational and that can be justified on the basis of some factor other than race or culture. Thus the negativity of aversive racists "is more likely to be manifested in discomfort, uneasiness, fear, or avoidance of minorities rather than overt hostility."[26] An individual at work, for instance, may be polite but distant to a co-worker from another culture but may avoid that person at a party they both happen to attend.

Genuine likes and dislikes may also operate as a form of racism. The cultural practices of some groups of people can form the basis for a prejudicial attitude simply because the group displays behaviors that another group does not like. For example, individuals from cultures that are predominantly vegetarian may develop negative attitudes toward those who belong to cultures that eat meat.

Finally, the least alarming form of racism, and certainly one that everyone has experienced, is based on the *degree of unfamiliarity* with members of other groups. Simply responding to unfamiliar people may create negative attitudes because of a lack of experience with the characteristics of their group. The others may look, smell, talk, or act differently, all of which can be a source of discomfort and can form the basis for racist or prejudicial attitudes.

Lack of Knowledge, Motivation, and Skill

In the closing section of each chapter we have discussed the development of competence in intercultural communication. The critical importance of knowledge, motivation, and skill has been a major theme. Although we do not want to repeat guidelines already discussed, we do wish to stress once again the very important role these elements play in overcoming the obstacles to competent intercultural communication.

Ethnocentrism, stereotyping, prejudice, discrimination, and racism are so familiar and comfortable that overcoming them requires a commitment both to learning about other cultures and to understanding one's own. A willingness to explore various cultural experiences without prejudgment is necessary. An ability to behave appropriately and effectively with culturally different others, without invoking prejudiced and stereotyped assumptions, is required. Although no one can completely overcome the obstacles to intercultural competence that naturally exist, the requisite knowledge, motivation, and skill can certainly help to minimize the negative effects of prejudice and discrimination.

The intercultural challenge for all of us now living in a world where interactions with people from different cultures are common features of daily life is to be willing to grapple with the consequences of prejudice, discrimination, and racism at the individual, social, and institutional levels. Because "prejudice" and "racism" are such emotionally charged concepts, it is sometimes very difficult to comment on their occurrence in our interactions with others. Individuals who believe that they have perceived discriminatory remarks and actions often feel that they cannot risk the resentment of their co-workers, fellow students, teachers, or service providers that would likely occur should they demand interactions that do not display prejudice against them. Conversely, those who do not regard themselves as having prejudiced or racist attitudes and who believe they never behave in discriminatory ways are horrified to learn that others might interpret their attitudes as prejudiced and their actions as discriminatory. While discussions about prejudice, discrimination, and racism can lead to a better understanding of the interpersonal dynamics that arise as individuals seek to establish mutually respectful relationships, they can just as easily lead to greater divisions and hostilities between people. The challenge for interculturally competent communicators is to contend with the pressing but potentially inflammatory issues of prejudice and discrimination in a manner that is both appropriate and effective.

OBSTACLES TO INTERCULTURAL COMPETENCE WITHIN SETTINGS

As part of the socialization process, people are taught to identify themselves with particular groups. People in all cultures, for example, are taught to identify with their families. As part of the family socialization process, individuals may also be taught to view themselves as belonging to a racial, ethnic, or cultural group. As the child becomes a teenager and then an adult, the development of vocational and avocational interests creates new groups with which to identify. "Baseball player," "ballet dancer," or "scientist" may become important labels to describe the self.

Another feature of socialization is that people are taught about groups to which they do not belong, and they often learn that certain groups should be avoided. This tendency to identify as a member of some groups, called *ingroups*, and to distinguish these ingroups from *outgroups*, is so prevalent in human thinking that it has been described as a universal human tendency.[27] The very process of mentally labeling another person as a member of an outgroup creates possible situational obstacles to intercultural competence. Sort-

CULTURE CONNECTIONS

The Vietnamese woman waded with her children in the dark green waters, seining fish. It could have been the Mekong. Instead, it was a city lake in Riverside. Immigrants carry into their new world habits from the old.

These habits often do not suit their new surroundings. Children more readily adapt, but they often disappoint their parents doing so: They give up the mother tongue and marry outsiders. Subsequent generations find little solace in their "modernity"—they have no sense of a past. So rivalries develop between clans, creeds and cultures, as each ethnocentric circle defines a form of life that's theirs.

Source: David Glidden, "America's Challenge: Getting Along with Each Other," *Los Angeles Times,* June 9, 1991: M6.

ing people into the categories of "part of my group" or "not part of my group" levels the differences that exist within "my group," overlooks variations among outgroup members, and devalues the latter.

Related to the distinction between ingroup and outgroup membership is the concept of *social identity*. Henri Tajfel, who first introduced the idea, suggested that self-concept is built on both an individual's personal and social identity.[28] Personal identity is based on the unique perceptions that a person has about his or her attributes. Social identity is formed from the identification process that results from membership in particular groups. That is, a person takes on the characteristics and concerns of the group as part of his or her self-identity. Thus, the characteristics of the group, rather than the personal and unique attributes of the individuals who form the group, become the basis of intercultural communication. Ingroup and outgroup distinctions, along with social identity, can form powerful barriers to intercultural competence.

Intercultural Contact

Many people believe that positive attitudes toward members of other groups are fostered by creating the opportunity for personal contact. Indeed, this assumption provides the rationale for numerous international exchange programs for high school and college students. There are also international "sister city" programs, wherein a U.S. city pairs itself with a city from another country and encourages the residents of both cities to visit with and stay in one another's homes. Sometimes, of course, intercultural contact does overcome the obstacles of cultural distance, and positive attitudes between those involved do result.

Unfortunately, there is a great deal of historical and contemporary evidence to suggest that contact between members of different cultures does not always lead to good feelings. In fact, under many circumstances such contact only reinforces negative attitudes or may even change a neutral attitude into a negative one. For instance, tourists in other countries are sometimes repelled by the inhabitants, and immigrants to the United States have not always been accepted by the communities into which they have settled. In some communities and among some people, there is still much prejudice and negative feeling between European Americans and African Americans.

The factors that lead to cordial and courteous interactions among people from different cultural groups are very complicated. One factor, that of access to and control of institutional and economic power, strongly influences attitudes between members of different cultures.

Dominance and Subordination Between Groups   Not all groups within a nation, region, or continent have equal access to sources of institutional and economic power. When cultures share the same political, geographic, and economic landscapes, some form of a status hierarchy often develops. Groups of people who are distinguished by their religious, political, cultural, or ethnic identity often struggle among themselves for dominance and control of the available economic and political resources.

Recent examples include the events in eastern Europe. Yugoslavia, for instance, is a country that was held together for decades by a strong and repressive dictator. Now the country is in a virtual civil war because the Serbians and Croatians, which are the major cultural groups, have historically felt animosity toward each other and are unable to work cooperatively to maintain a nation-state. Similarly, the loss of control by the Soviet Union's central government, coupled with economic hardships and political turmoil, has resulted in outbreaks of violence between members of cultural groups sharing the same territory. In the United States, racial tensions between African Americans and European Americans have resulted in numerous incidents. Immigrants from various parts of the world have experienced open hostility, and sometimes violent reactions, from people who live in areas where they have settled. When these kinds of competitive tensions characterize the political and economic setting in which individuals from differing cultures interact, intercultural communication is obviously affected.

A cultural group that has primary access to institutional and economic power is often characterized as *dominant* or as the *majority*. As we indicated in Chapter 1, we find these terms imprecise when describing cultural groups in the United States. Now, however, we choose to use the term *dominant* to refer to institutional and economic power.

Scholars have given considerable attention to the influence of dominant and subordinate group membership on interpersonal and intercultural communication processes.[29] The results of their investigations suggest that there is a very interesting set of relationships among the factors that affect these interactions. For instance, members of dominant cultures will often devalue the language styles of subordinate cultural members and judge the "correctness" of their use of preferred speech patterns. In some cases, members of subordinate cultures will try to accommodate or adapt their speech to that of the dominant culture. In other circumstances, they will very deliberately emphasize their group's unique speech characteristics when they are in the presence of people from the dominant culture.

As we discussed in Chapter 7, special forms of language, including jargon, argot, and accents, are often used to signal identification among members of the subordinate group and to indicate a lack of submission to the dominant group. Similarly, members of the dominant group are likely to retain the special characteristics of their language, including preferences for certain words, accents, and linguistic patterns, and may therefore devalue the linguistic patterns of others. For example, there are instances in which European Americans have devalued the use of Black Standard English.[30] However, as we also noted earlier, when the status of two cultures is perceived by their members to be similar, language differences often result in positive attitudes between them.[31]

Attitudes Between Cultural Members   Our focus in this section is on the attitudes that form among cultures that have frequent contact with one another. In his classic study, Amir describes four conditions that are likely to lead to positive attitudes as a result of intercultural communication: (1) There is support from the top; that is, a person who is in charge, or who is recognized as an authority, organizes and supports the intercultural contact. (2) Those involved have a personal stake in the outcome, so that interactions are regarded as personal rather than casual. (3) The intercultural contacts are pleasing and pleasant. (4) All parties benefit from the contact; that is, members of both cultures have common goals or view the interaction as allowing them to achieve their own individual goals.[32]

Recent investigations suggest that four additional factors also affect attitudes and outcomes. One is the strength of identification that the members of a culture have for their cultural group. Do the individuals in an encounter think of the person with whom they are interacting as a unique individual, or do they view that person primarily as a representative of a different cultural group? Similarly, do the interactants view themselves as unique individuals or as representatives of particular cultural groups? One study finds that the outcomes of intercultural encounters depend on the extent to which cultural identities are seen as an important component of people's interpersonal identities.[33] Identification with their culture increases if they have a relatively high status within the group, as well as if the bonds to their culture are strong and all their friends and social networks are associated with it.

Intercultural communication outcomes are also affected by the degree of perceived threat. If the members of a culture believe that certain fundamental aspects of their cultural identity—such as their language and special charac-

Contrast the difference between your own culture and the culture of those in the picture. How difficult would it be for you to communicate competently in this setting? Some will find it very difficult, others comparatively easy, depending on the distance between your culture and the one pictured. *(Copyright © René Burri, Magnum.)*

teristics—are threatened, they are likely to increase their identification with their culture, and intercultural contacts are less likely to be favorable. Even groups that are in the majority sometimes see the presence of people from other cultures as threatening. For example, consider the perceived threat and consequent reactions of U.S. Americans to immigrants who are willing to work for a lower wage.

Another factor is the degree of typicality with which the other interactants are viewed. That is, participants in intercultural encounters make a judgment about the degree to which specific individuals are typical or atypical of their culture, which in turn influences the positive or negative character of their attitudes. More important, typicality affects the likelihood that experiences with one member of a culture are generalized to other members of that culture.[34] For example, if someone is viewed as unique and unrepresentative of the typical members of a culture, a positive experience with that individual will not necessarily result in positive attitudes toward other people from the same cultural group.

The nature of the interactants' cultural stereotypes is another factor in intercultural contacts. Miles Hewstone and Howard Giles propose that these stereotypes are used as filters to assess the behaviors of members of other groups.[35] They also suggest that if a person does not conform to the cultural stereotype in some important way, that person is dismissed as atypical. Consequently, negative stereotypes toward the culture can persist even when

CULTURE CONNECTIONS

So much has happened in these past 14 years. I find it so hard to believe so much time has passed since my life and the lives of my family changed so radically. It seems like only yesterday that my family and I set foot on American soil to begin our new lives.

I am often asked about my impressions of life here in the United States. But I find it more interesting to reflect on the expectations or impressions which I held about the United States before I came here. The contrast between what is reality and what is fiction can at times be amazing.

"The United States is heaven. You will find eternal happiness and peace in this new land." These were the words that so many of us heard in our homeland about the United States. Thoughts of a land so rich that they could build a bridge of gold were instilled in us. We believed these things. We had to. Living in a country plagued with war, starvation, and death, we needed to believe that there was such a utopian place called America.

Because of these false impressions, many Southeast Asians became disillusioned and disappointed when they arrived in America. Feelings of abandonment, along with their problems such as language, prejudice, and clashing values, made them overly critical of their new homeland.

After arriving at Camp Pendleton, I thought life here was simple and there was a lot of free time to just play. As a child only 10 years old, I didn't realize all of this "play time" was simply a transition period we had to spend in the camps. The reality was yet to start.

Soon enough, we found our permanent home in Modesto, California. This is when my perceptions of life here began to change rapidly. I was placed in an American school that was not equipped to handle this new influx of refugees. The language problem was the first major ordeal which I had to overcome. Looking back, I

there are positive and favorable interactions with a member of the culture.

In any intercultural communication, then, obstacles to competence may exist in the strength and importance of the cultural identities among those communicating. Contact between members of different cultures is influenced by local conditions that heighten suspicion and concern and that promote strong identification with one's own cultural group.

Differences Between Cultures

The degree of difference between the people involved in an intercultural interaction is another potential obstacle to intercultural competence. Assume, for

now realize that my young age was to my advantage because it allowed me to master English more quickly. But my first few years in school were very traumatic. Besides the normal "growing up" problems, I had to deal with learning to communicate in a strange language.

Problems in communciation had to be tackled right away. When a friend tried to communicate with me, I would resort to using hand gestures or "the guessing game." Most of the time, the meaning received was the opposite of what I was trying to say. For example, once during a lunch, a friend asked me for my cookie. Not understanding what she had said, I simply shook my head. She thought I didn't want the cookie so she proceeded to take it. I thought she was rude and pushy.

Problems with the new language did not go away as I began to learn how to speak English. Often I was laughed at because of the way I pronounced certainwords. This made me embarrassed, and I avoided speaking to Americans. At times, I got so frustrated that I wished I were back in Viet Nam again.

In America, I stood out in many ways. Not only was my language problem a barrier between my peers and me, but my physical features were also very difficult from that of many Americans. I remember some of my new friends out of curiosity wanting to touch my almond-shaped eyes and olive-colored skin. Unfortunately, my differences were not always perceived with curiosity. There were those who hated me simply because of my differences. Prejudice is one thing the idealists forgot to tell us about when they spoke of this "utopia."

One of my most painful and ongoing ordeals which I, and most refugees, have faced is one of clashing cultural values. Coming from a different culture and having to adapt to another culture can have its own advantages. But when two cultures rarely meet because one is more conservative than the other, it can create many conflicts and jumbled messages.

Source: My-Lien Dinh, "The Bridge of Gold," *Passages,* ed. Katsuyo K. Howard (Fresno: California State University, Southeast Asian Student Services, 1990).

example, that three people—one each from Brazil, Spain, and Denmark—are typical representatives of their culture's preferences. The taxonomies of cultural patterns described in Chapters 5 and 6 could be used to map the differences in their cultural characteristics. In the Hofstede taxonomy, for instance, the Brazilian could be described as being about average on the masculinity-femininity dimension and having a strong preference for power distance, uncertainty avoidance, and collectivism; the Spaniard, who is similar to the Brazilian, is about average on individualism-collectivism and has a preference for power distance, uncertainty avoidance, and femininity; and the Dane, who differs greatly from both the Brazilian and the Spaniard, is very individualistic and is also very low on power distance, uncertainty avoidance, and masculin-

Which way to Athens? Are we going toward Navplion or Neapolis? The fatigue associated with communication in an unfamiliar language can sometimes be overwhelming. *(Copyright © Myron W. Lustig & Jolene Koester.)*

ity. The cultural distance between the Brazilian and the Spaniard is quite modest, whereas that between them and the Dane is very large. Therefore, the Dane would probably interpret the world very differently than would the Brazilian or the Spaniard. Built into every intercultural communication, then, is an obstacle of enormous consequence: the degree of cultural distance between the interactants. If the distance between the cultures is small, as in the case of the Brazilian and the Spaniard, it poses less of a hindrance. But if the distance between cultures is very large, as in the case of the Brazilian and the Dane, the skills and attitudes of the individual communicators will be severely tested.

Incompatible Goals

In any intercultural interaction, the incompatibility of the participants' goals is a potential obstacle to intercultural competence. For example, a tourist might want to take home "bargains," whereas a shopkeeper might want to make a great deal of money. The businessperson in another country might want to negotiate the deal quickly and go home, whereas the hosts might want to establish harmonious personal relationships before discussing any business. People have particular goals, both personal and professional. Those with whom you interact will have their own goals and objectives, which may not be compatible with yours.

Culture Shock or Acculturation

Sustained intercultural contact that requires total immersion in another culture may produce a phenomenon that has sometimes been called *culture shock*. The anthropologist Kalvero Oberg, who coined the term, describes some of the reasons why it occurs:

> Culture shock is precipitated by the anxiety that results from losing all our familiar signs and symbols of social intercourse. These signs or cues include the thousand and one ways in which we orient ourselves to the situations of daily life: when to shake hands and what to say when we meet people, when and how to give tips, how to give orders to servants, how to make purchases, when to accept and when to refuse invitations, when to take statements seriously and when not. Now these cues, which may be words, gestures, facial expressions, customs, or norms, are acquired by all of us in the course of growing up and are as much a part of our culture as the language we speak or the beliefs we accept. All of us depend for our peace of mind and our efficiency on hundreds of these cues, most of which we are not consciously aware.[36]

That is, culture shock is said to occur when people must deal with a barrage of new perceptual stimuli that are difficult to interpret because the cultural context has changed. Things taken for granted at home require virtually constant monitoring in the new culture to assure some degree of understanding. The loss of predictability, coupled with the fatigue that results from the need to stay consciously focused on what would normally be taken for granted, produces the negative responses associated with culture shock. These can include

> excessive washing of the hands; excessive concern over drinking water, food, dishes, and bedding; fear of physical contact with attendants or servants; the absent-minded, far-away stare (sometimes called the "tropical stare"); a feeling of helplessness and a desire for dependence on long-term residents of one's own nationality; fits of anger over delays and other minor frustrations; delay and outright refusal to learn the language of the host country; excessive fear of being cheated, robbed, or injured; great concern over minor pains and eruptions of the skin; and finally, that terrible longing to be home, to be able to have a good cup of coffee and a piece of apple pie, to walk into that corner drugstore, to visit one's relatives, and in general, to talk to people who really make sense.[37]

Often associated with culture shock are the U-curve and W-curve hypotheses of cultural adjustment. In the U-curve hypothesis, the initial intercultural contacts are characterized by a positive, almost euphoric, emotional response. As fatigue mounts and culture shock sets in, however, the individual's responses are more and more negative, until finally a low point is reached. Then, gradually, the individual develops a more positive attitude and the new culture seems less foreign, until a positive emotional response once again occurs.

The U-curve hypothesis has been extended to the W-curve, which includes the person's responses to her or his own culture upon return. It posits that a second wave of culture shock, which is similar to the first and has been called *re-entry shock*, may occur when the individual returns home and must

CULTURE CONNECTIONS

Many people talk a lot about "cultural shock," but no one I've heard has come close to really describing the complete emotional disruption which accompanies cultural transition. In a very real sense, all the convenient cultural cushions we have become so accustomed to having around are in one moment totally dislodged. You're left flat on your back with only that *within* you for support. "Alone in the wilderness"—inadequate description. For alone you certainly are not, though in unfamiliar terrain, you are. Not alone. For you are continually surrounded by people. Every action is under scrutiny for you are *indeed* a very strange intrusion. Yet, still very alone in the sense that you lack anyone to emphathize with your discomfort and disorientation. There is nothing lonelier than the feeling that there is no one with whom you can communicate; that no one understands your problems and that even when you talk with someone, though he may understand you, he really doesn't understand *you*. Everything except that people still eat, sleep, talk, laugh, cry, and defecate is strange and different.

Source: David Wallender, "Excerpts from a Volunteer's Journal," *The Bridge,* Fall 1977: 4.

readapt to the once taken-for-granted practices that can no longer be followed without question.[38] Some returnees to the United States, for instance, have difficulties with the pace of life, the relative affluence around them, and the seemingly superficial values espoused by the mass media. Others are frustrated when their co-workers and friends seem uninterested in their intercultural experiences, which may have changed them profoundly, but instead want simply to fill them in on "what they missed." Such reentry problems, of course, are not confined to U.S. Americans who have been to another culture.[39] Japanese school-age children who returned from living in English-speaking countries, for instance, have identified readjustment problems because of their differences from their peers, the precise expectations for their behaviors in school, their reduced proficiency in the Japanese language, and their interpersonal styles.[40] One girl had to dye her hair black because it had lightened from the sun. Another had to remind herself continually, "I shouldn't be different from others; I should do the same as others in doing anything."[41]

Though initially regarded as plausible, the U-curve and the W-curve hypotheses do not provide sufficiently accurate descriptions of the acculturation process. They do not account, for instance, for those whose experiences remain favorable, for those who fail to adapt and return home prematurely, or for those whose level of discomfort changes little during the adjustment period. Rather, there seem to be a variety of possible adjustment patterns that individuals could experience, depending on their particular circumstances.

The Myriad of unfamiliar sights, sounds and smells contribute to the phenomenon called culture shock. *(Copyright © Myron W. Lustig & Jolene Koester.)*

The pattern of adjustment varies widely from one individual to the next, and therefore no single pattern can be said to characterize the typical adjustment process.[42]

The term *culture shock* can now be seen to describe a pattern in which the individual has severe negative reactions on contact with another culture. Such extreme responses, however, in which the person's knowledge, motivation, and skills are initially insufficient to cope with the strangeness of a new culture, are among many likely reactions. We therefore prefer the more general term *acculturation* to refer to the pattern of adaptation and accommodation that results from people's contact experiences with another culture. As many theorists have suggested, it is through acculturation that personal transformation from cultural contact takes place.[43]

SUMMARY

This chapter has discussed the obstacles that operate within people and situations to impede the development of intercultural competence. Ethnocentrism, stereotyping, prejudice, discrimination, and racism occur because of the human need to organize and streamline the processing of information. When people assume that these "thinking shortcuts" are accurate representations, intercultural competence is impaired.

The situational obstacles to intercultural competence are based on normal human tendencies to view ourselves as members of a particular group and to view others as not belonging to that group. Attitudinal and behavioral outcomes of contact between people from different cultures are heavily influenced by status, power, and economic differences. Situational obstacles are a reminder that all relationships take place within a political, economic, social, and cultural context. The degree of difference between the cultures can also create an obstacle. Finally, the ability to communicate competently will be mediated by the level of adjustment to a new cultural setting. Adaptation to changes in verbal and nonverbal codes, as well as to differences in the beliefs, values, norms, and preferred ways to conduct human relationships, can create culture shock, an extreme instance of the kind of fatigue that people might experience in coping with the unpredictability of a new culture.

13
CHAPTER

The Potential for Intercultural Competence

It should be clear that we are personally committed to understanding the dynamics of culture and its effects on interpersonal communication. William Shakespeare suggested that the world is a stage filled with actors and actresses, but they come from different cultures and they need to coordinate their scripts and actions in order to accomplish their collective purposes. The image of a multicultural society is one that we firmly believe will characterize most people's lives as the twentieth century ends and the twenty-first century begins. Intercultural communication will become far more commonplace in people's day-to-day lives and the communication skills that lead to the development of intercultural competence will be a necessary part of people's personal and professional lives.

It should also be clear that intercultural communication is a complex and challenging activity. Intercultural competence, although certainly attainable in varying degrees, will elude everyone in at least some intercultural interactions. Nevertheless, we hope that in addition to the challenges of intercultural interaction, this book also reminds you of the joys of discovery that can occur when interacting with people whose culture differs from your own.

In this chapter we turn our attention to some final suggestions for enhancing your intercultural competence. First we discuss some tools for intercultural interactions, then we explore some of their possible consequences to both individuals and cultures, and we conclude with a discussion of ethical issues.

BASIC TOOLS FOR IMPROVING INTERCULTURAL COMPETENCE

In the preceding chapters we described how various aspects of culture affect interpersonal communication. We suggested some ways for you to increase your intercultural competence by using your knowledge, motivation, and skills to deal appropriately and effectively with differences in cultural patterns, verbal codes, nonverbal codes, and the developmental differences in interpersonal relationships. We now offer two additional tools to overcome some of the obstacles described in Chapter 12. These tools will help you improve your interpersonal interactions and will facilitate the development of intercultural relationships.

The BASICs of Intercultural Competence

The Behavioral Assessment Scale for Intercultural Competence (BASIC), developed by Jolene Koester and Margaret Olebe,[1] is based on work done originally by Brent Ruben and his colleagues.[2] A very simple idea provides the key to understanding how to use these BASIC skills: What you actually do, rather than your internalized attitudes or your projections of what you might do, is what others use to determine whether you are interculturally competent. The BASIC skills are a tool for examining people's communication behaviors—yourself included—and in so doing provides a guide to the very basics of intercultural competence.

Eight categories of communication behavior are described in the BASIC instrument, each of which contributes to the achievement of intercultural competence (see Table 13.1). As each of the categories is described, mentally assess your own ability to communicate. Do you display the behaviors necessary to achieve intercultural competence? From what you now know about intercultural communication, what kinds of changes might make your behavior more appropriate and effective?

Before we describe each of the BASIC skills, we would like to emphasize that the BASIC descriptions of behaviors are culture-general. That is, in most cultures the types of behaviors that are described are used by their members to make judgments of competence. But within each culture there may be, and in all likelihood will be, different ways of exhibiting these behaviors.

Display of Respect   Although the need to display respect for others is a culture-general concept, within every culture there are specific ways to show respect and there are specific expectations about those to whom respect should be shown. What constitutes respect in one culture, then, will not necessarily be so regarded in another culture.

Respect is shown through both verbal and nonverbal symbols. Language

Table 13.1   THE BASICS OF INTERCULTURAL COMPETENCE

Display of Respect	The ability to show respect and positive regard for another person.
Orientation to Knowledge	The terms people use to explain themselves and the world around them.
Empathy	The capacity to behave as though you understand the world as others do.
Task Role Behavior	Behaviors that involve the initiation of ideas related to group problem-solving activities.
Relational Role Behavior	Behaviors associated with interpersonal harmony and mediation.
Interaction Management	Skill in regulating conversations.
Tolerance for Ambiguity	The ability to react to new and ambiguous situations with little visible discomfort.
Interaction Posture	The ability to respond to others in descriptive, nonevaluative, and nonjudgmental ways.

that can be interpreted as expressing concern, interest, and an understanding of others will often convey respect, as will formality in language, including the use of titles, the absence of jargon, and an increased attention to politeness rituals. Nonverbal displays of respect include showing attentiveness through the position of the body, facial expressions, and the use of eye contact in prescribed ways. A tone of voice that conveys interest in the other person is another vehicle by which respect is shown. The action of displaying respect increases the likelihood of a judgment of competence.

Orientation to Knowledge   Orientation to knowledge refers to the terms people use to explain themselves and the world around them. A competent orientation to knowledge occurs when people's actions demonstrate that all experiences and interpretations are individual and personal rather than universally shared by others.

Many actions exhibit people's orientation to knowledge, including the specific words that are used. Among European Americans, for instance, declarative statements that express personal attitudes or opinions as if they were facts, and an absence of qualifiers or modifiers, would show an ineffective orientation to knowledge:

- "New Yorkers must be crazy to live in that city."
- "Parisians are rude and unfriendly."
- "The custom of arranged marriages is barbaric."
- "Every person wants to succeed—it's human nature."

In contrast, a competent intercultural communicator acknowledges a personal orientation to knowledge, as illustrated in the following examples:

- "I find New York a very difficult place to visit and would not want to live there."

Despite many cultural differences, BASIC skills can be used to develop competence in interpersonal communication. These Viennese citizens can communicate interculturally. *(Copyright © Myron W. Lustig & Jolene Koester.)*

- "Many of the people I interacted with when visiting Paris were not friendly or courteous to me."
- "I would not want my parents to arrange my marriage for me."
- "I want to succeed at what I do and I think most people do."

At least some of the time, all people have an orientation to knowledge that is not conducive to intercultural competence. In learning a culture, people develop beliefs about the "rightness" of a particular way of seeing events, behaviors, and people. It is actually very natural to think, and then to behave, as if your personal knowledge and experiences are universal. Intercultural competence, however, requires an ability to move beyond the perspective of your cultural framework.

Empathy   Individuals who are able to communicate an awareness of another person's thoughts, feelings, and experiences are regarded as more competent in intercultural interactions. Alternatively, those who lack empathy, and who therefore indicate little or no awareness of even the most obvious feelings and thoughts of others, will not be perceived as competent. Empathetic behaviors include verbal statements that identify the experiences of others and nonverbal codes that are complementary to the moods and thoughts of others.

It is necessary to make an important distinction here. Empathy does not mean "putting yourself in the shoes of another." It is both physically and psychologically impossible to do so. However, it is possible for people to be sufficiently interested and aware of others that they appear to be putting themselves in others' shoes. The skill we are describing here is the capacity to *behave as if one understands the world as others do.* Of course, empathy is not just responding to the tears and smiles of others, which may, in fact, mean something very different than your cultural interpretations would suggest. Although empathy does involve responding to the emotional context of another person's experiences, tears and smiles are often poor indicators of emotional states.

Interaction Management   Some individuals are skilled at starting and ending interactions among participants and at taking turns and maintaining a discussion. These management skills are important because through them all participants in an interaction are able to speak and contribute appropriately. In contrast, dominating a conversation or being nonresponsive to the interaction is detrimental to competence. Continuing to engage people in conversation long after they have begun to display signs of disinterest and boredom, or ending conversations abruptly may also pose problems.

Interaction management skills require knowing how to indicate turn-taking both verbally and nonverbally. The example in Chapter 9 between Athabaskans and English-speaking Canadians illustrates just how difficult this very simple-sounding behavior can be.

Task Role Behavior   Because intercultural communication often takes place where individuals are focused on work-related purposes, appropriate task-related role behaviors are very important. Task role behaviors are those that contribute to the group's problem-solving activities, for example, initiating new ideas, requesting further information or facts, seeking clarification of group tasks, evaluating the suggestions of others, and keeping a group on task. The difficulty in this important category is the display of culturally appropriate behaviors. The key is to recognize the strong link to a culture's underlying patterns and to be willing to acknowledge that tasks are accomplished by cultures in multiple ways. Task behaviors are so intimately entwined with cultural expectations about activity and work that it is often difficult to respond appropriately to task expectations that differ from one's own. What one culture defines as a social activity, another may define as a task. For example, socializing at a restaurant or a bar may be seen as a necessary prelude to conducting of a business negotiation. Sometimes that socializing is expected to occur over many hours or days, which surprises and dismays many European Americans, who believe that "doing business" is separate from socializing.

Relational Role Behavior   Relational role behaviors concern efforts to build or maintain personal relationships with group members. These behaviors may include verbal and nonverbal messages that demonstrate support for others and that help to solidify feelings of participation. Examples of competent rela-

CULTURE CONNECTIONS

The new *mestiza* copes by developing a tolerance for contradictions, a tolerance for ambiguity. She learns to be an Indian in Mexican culture, to be Mexican from an Anglo point of view. She learns to juggle cultures. She has a plural personality, she operates in a pluralistic mode—nothing is thrust out, the good the bad and the ugly, nothing rejected, nothing abandoned. Not only does she sustain contradictions, she turns the ambivalence into something else.

Source: Gloria Anzaldúa, *Borderlands/La Frontera: The New Mestiza* (Spinsters/Aunt Lute, 1987).

tional role behaviors include harmonizing and mediating conflicts between group members, encouraging participation from others, general displays of interest, and a willingness to compromise one's position for the sake of others.

Tolerance for Ambiguity   Tolerance for ambiguity concerns a person's responses to new, uncertain, and unpredictable intercultural encounters. Some people react to new situations with greater comfort than others. Some are extremely nervous, highly frustrated, or even hostile toward the new situations and those who may be present in them. Those who do not tolerate ambiguity well may respond to new and unpredictable situations with hostility, anger, shouting, sarcasm, withdrawal, or abruptness.

Others view new situations as a challenge; they seem to do well whenever the unexpected or unpredictable occurs, and they quickly adapt to the demands of changing environments. Competent intercultural communicators are able to cope with the nervousness and frustrations that accompany new or unclear situations, and they are able to adapt quickly to changing demands.

Interaction Posture   Interaction posture refers to the ability to respond to others in a way that is descriptive, nonevaluative, and nonjudgmental. Although the specific verbal and nonverbal messages that express judgments and evaluations can vary from culture to culture, the importance of selecting messages that do not convey evaluative judgments is paramount. Statements based on clear judgments of rights and wrongs indicate a closed or predetermined framework of attitudes, beliefs, and values, and they are used by the evaluative, and less competent, intercultural communicator. Nonevaluative and nonjudgmental actions are characterized by verbal and nonverbal messages based on descriptions rather than on interpretations or evaluations.

Description, Interpretation, and Evaluation

We have approached the study of intercultural competence by looking at the elements of culture that affect interpersonal communication. There is, however, a tool that allows people to control the meanings they attribute to the verbal and nonverbal symbols used by others. The tool is based on the differences in how people think about, and then verbally speak about, the people with whom they interact and the events in which they participate.

The interaction tool is called *description, interpretation,* and *evaluation.* It starts with the assumption that, when most people process the information around them, they use a kind of mental shorthand. Because people are taught what symbols mean, they are not very aware of the information they use to form their interpretations. In other words, when people see, hear, and in other ways receive information from the world around them, they generally form interpretations and evaluations of it without being aware of the specific sensory information they have perceived. For example, students and teachers alike often comment about the sterile, institutional character of many of the classrooms at universities. Rarely do these conversations detail the specific perceptual information on which that interpretation is based. Rarely does someone say, for instance, "This room is about 20 by 40 feet in size, the walls are painted a cream color, there is no artwork on the walls, it is lit by eight fluorescent bulbs, and the floors are cream-colored tiles with multiple pieces of dirt." Yet when students and professors say that their classroom is "sterile, institutional-looking, and unattractive," most people who have spent a great deal of time in such rooms have a fairly accurate image of the classroom. Similarly, if a friend is walking toward you, you might say, "Hi! What's wrong? You look really tired and upset." That kind of comment is considered normal, but if you said instead, "Hi! Your shoulders are drooping, you're not standing up straight, and you are walking much slower than usual," it would be considered strange. In both examples, the statements considered to be normal are really interpretations and evaluations of sensory information the individual has processed.

The skill we are introducing trains you to distinguish among statements of description, interpretation, and evaluation. These statements can be made about all characteristics, events, persons, or objects. A statement of description details the specific perceptual cues and information a person has received, without judgments or interpretations—in other words, without being distorted by opinion. A statement of interpretation provides a conjecture or hypothesis about what the perceptual information might mean. A statement of evaluation indicates an emotional or affective judgment about the information.

Often, the interpretations people make of perceptual information are very closely linked to their personal evaluation of that information. Any description can have many different interpretations; but because most people think in a mental shorthand, they are generally aware of only the interpretation that immediately comes to mind, which they use to explain the event. For exam-

Use the skill of description, interpretation, and evaluation to understand this scene involving French teenagers. *(Mark Antman/The Image Works.)*

ple, teachers occasionally have students who arrive late to class. A statement of description about a particular student engaging in this behavior might be as follows:

- Kathryn arrived ten minutes after the start of the class.
- Kathryn also arrived late each of the previous times the class has met.

Statements of interpretation, which are designed to explain Kathryn's behavior, might include some of the following:

- Kathryn doesn't care very much about this particular class.
- Kathryn is always late for everything.
- Kathryn has a job on the other side of campus and is scheduled to work until ten minutes before this class. The person who should relieve her has been late, thus not allowing Kathryn to leave to be on time for class.

- Kathryn is new on campus this semester and is misinformed about the starting time for the class.

For each interpretation, the evaluation can vary. If the interpretation is "Kathryn doesn't care very much about this class," different professors will have differing evaluations:

- I am really offended by that attitude.
- I like a student who chooses to be enthusiastic about only classes she really likes.

The interpretation a person selects to explain something like Kathryn's behavior influences the evaluation that is made of that behavior. In people's everyday interactions, distinctions are rarely made among description, interpretation, and evaluation. Consequently, people deal with their interpretations and evaluations as if these were actually what they saw, heard, and experienced.

The purpose of making descriptive statements when you are communicating interculturally is that they allow you to identify the sensory information that forms the basis of your interpretations and evaluations. Descriptive statements also allow you to consider alternative hypotheses or interpretations. Interpretations, although highly personal, are very much affected by underlying cultural patterns. Sometimes when you engage in intercultural communication with specific persons or groups of people for an extended period of time, you will be able to test the various interpretations of behavior that you are considering. By testing the alternative interpretations, it is also possible to forestall the evaluations that can negatively affect your interactions. Consider the following situation, and notice how differences among description, interpretation, and evaluation affect John's intercultural competence:

> John Richardson has been sent by his U.S.-based insurance company to discuss, and possibly to sell, his company's products with an Argentinean company that has expressed great interest in them. His secretary has set up four appointments with key company officials. John arrives promptly at his first appointment, identifies himself to the receptionist, and is asked to be seated. Some 30 minutes later he is ushered into the offices of the company official, who has one of his employees in the office with whom he is discussing another issue. John is brought into the office of his second appointment within a shorter period of time, but the conversation is constantly disrupted by telephone calls and drop-in visits from others. At the end of the day, John is very discouraged; he calls the home office and says, "This is a waste of time; these guys aren't interested in our products at all! I was left cooling my heels in their waiting rooms. They couldn't even give me their attention when I got in to see them. There were constant interruptions. I really tried to control myself, but I've had it. I'm getting on a plane and coming back tomorrow."

John would be better off if he approached this culturally puzzling behavior by separating his descriptions, interpretations, and evaluations. By doing so, he might choose very different actions for himself. Descriptive statements might be:

- My appointments started anywhere from 15 to 30 minutes later than the time I scheduled them.
- The people with whom I had appointments also talked to other company employees when I was in their offices.
- The people with whom I had appointments accepted telephone calls when I was in their offices.

Interpretations of this sensory information might include the following:

- Company officials were not interested in talking with me or in buying my company's products.
- Company officials had rescheduled my appointments for a different time, but they neglected to tell my secretary about the change.
- In Argentina, attitudes toward time are very different than they are in the United States; although appointments are scheduled for particular times, no one expects that people will be available at precisely that time.
- In Argentina it is an accepted norm of interaction between people who have appointments with each other to allow others to come into the room, either in person or by telephone, to ask their questions or to make their comments.

These interpretations suggest very different evaluations of John's experiences. His frustration with the lack of punctuality and the lack of exclusive focus on him and his ideas may still be a problem even if he selects the correct cultural interpretation, which is that in Argentina time is structured and valued very differently than it is in the United States. But by considering other interpretations, John's evaluations and his actions will be more functional, as he might say the following:

- I don't like waiting around and not meeting according to the schedule I had set, but maybe I can still make this important sale.
- Some of the people here are sure interesting and I am enjoying meeting so many more people than just the four with whom I had scheduled appointments.

The tool of description, interpretation, and evaluation increases your choices for understanding, responding positively to, and behaving appropriately with people from different cultures. The simplicity of the tool makes it available in any set of circumstances and may allow the intercultural communicator to suspend judgment long enough to understand the symbols used by the culture involved.

OUTCOMES OF INTERCULTURAL CONTACT

Both fictional and nonfictional accounts of intercultural contacts are replete with references to individual and cultural changes as a consequence. References are made to people who "go native" or who retain their own cultural

CULTURE CONNECTIONS

An interesting problem surfaced at an educational conference yesterday. Thirty-five "foreign experts" and the headsirs from their assigned schools met to resolve apprehensions. A concern of several of the headsirs was that the foreigners in their villages would not observe proper etiquette in treatment of the lower castes. What was supposed to be a meeting designed to help bridge cultural gaps got off to the wrong start, with some volunteers proselytizing about democracy.

This raises an interesting dilemma. What do you do as a culturally sensitive development worker when elements of the system you are trying to be sensitive to are basically abhorrent to your own values? People who are wonderfully tolerant when it comes to religion seem to have a little more trouble with the caste issue. The women in the group make no bones whatsoever about their intentions to enlighten Nepali women to the possibilities of change from their present subordinate status. It seems easy. We're right and they're wrong.

But what if the Nepalis came over to the U.S. and started telling Iowa beef farmers that it was wrong to kill cows? Or what if the Saudi Arabians came and told women in New York that it was wrong for them to drive cars? Is this what is meant by cultural imperialism? A "culturally sensitive" development worker is beginning to seem a contradiction in terms.

Source: Barbara J. Scot, The Violet Shyness of their Eyes: Notes from Nepal" (Corvallis, OR: CALYX Books, 1993, p. 64).

identity by using only their original language and living in cultural ghettos. During the height of the British Empire in India, for example, many British officials and their families tried to recreate the British lifestyle in India, in a climate not conducive to tuxedos and fancy dresses, with layers and layers of slips and decorative fabrics. References are also made to those who seem to adjust or adapt to life in the new culture.

It is generally accepted that intercultural communication creates stress for most individuals. In intercultural communication, the certainty of one's own cultural framework is gone, and there is a great deal of uncertainty about what other code systems mean. Individuals who engage in intercultural contacts for extended periods of time will respond to the stress in different ways. Most will find themselves incorporating at least some behaviors from the new culture into their own repertoire. Some take on the characteristics, the norms, and even the values and beliefs of another culture willingly and easily. Others resist the new culture and retain their old ways, sometimes choosing to spend time in enclaves populated only by others like themselves. Still others simply find the problems of adapting to a new culture intolerable, and leave if they can.

CULTURE CONNECTIONS

Calling attention to the idea that their ways are not your ways is the right of your host. You are the outsider. Your calling attention to differences, even in little things, can create awkwardness, sometimes tension or embarrassment. But if *they* call attention to differences, it will usually be in the form of a compliment—especially if your host should come across with the *big* one: "Most Americans don't do it the way we do—you're different." It can be fun to hear this, especially in reference to something no one ever told you—something you noticed and figured out for yourself.

My first experience with the *mandi* of Indonesia was of this sort. As it turned out, there was no one to observe, but there were plenty of clues all around. My host had handed me a towel and invited me to "cool off . . . take as long as you want." He pointed outside to a little shed attached to the house. I nodded and headed for the shed. Inside I found a waist-high cubic concrete tub filled with water, a pair of hooks high on one wall, and a floor covered with wooden slats and slightly tilted toward a low spot where a sizable drain hole was covered with a small square of metal screening. Now what?

Was I supposed to get in that tub? In spite of the extremely hot and sultry weather, I didn't relish the idea of climbing into such a large tub of unheated water. Furthermore, whoever had installed the pipe (yes, there was only one) had positioned the faucet almost directly over the center of the tub. How could you get in and out with that thing in the middle? I was confused and not at all comfortable, so I did what uncomfortable, confused people do—I found a scapegoat: stupid Indonesian plumbers. And, as usual, that helped in no way whatsoever—except to remind me that "stupid locals" is an outsider's cover-up for his or her own ignorance.

So I looked around some more. This time two more things came into view: There was a plastic sauce pan with a long handle. Could it be an oversize dipper? And a small plastic box was perched on a crosspiece of the wall frame some distance from the tub. What was in it? Aha! soap; but why so far from the tub?

While all this observing and thinking was going on I got out of my clothes. Although I wasn't sure what to do next, I didn't imagine that Indonesians could keep as clean and neat as they do by daily face-washing. And with my pants in hand, I looked for a place to put them. The hooks high on the wall! Indonesians come in fairly short sizes, so I wondered at the height of the hooks. But, unlike my long-legged problem in many an American bathroom, the cuffs weren't going to get wet here, I thought. And then it began to fall into place.

Standing right there on the slatted floor was where my "shower" was to take place. The dipper was my shower, the tub was my ample reservoir, and the faucet was to refill the reservoir when I was through. At least all those ideas fit together.

It seemed to be a reasonable set of hypotheses. If I could just confirm any one part of it, I'd give it a try. The reservoir idea—why not just work directly from the faucet? I turned it. A trickle. More turns. Still a trickle. Never could you shower with that little flow. But over time, it would accumulate in the reservoir and you could have plenty to shower with. Further, as the cold tap water stood in the tub it would be warmed to a more pleasant temperature.

Fingers in the water. Right. Exactly the temperature to refresh without inducing a heart attack on this steamy day.

Here we go. The dipper. A half-cup down the left arm. A bit of soap. The water ran to the floor-slats and headed across to the drain. Aha! The open-air plumbing does work, after all. A little more water this time, and again.

Suddenly a childhood reading experience flashed into mind. Was it Kipling in India? Stevenson on his visits to Polynesia? I had read them all. (Childhood reading and my Great Aunt Mabel had got me into all of this in the first place.) I recalled the writer singing at the top of his voice as he splashed (yes, that was the word), splashed, and "threw water everywhere" (yes!). So I tried it. First the singing, then the splashing. And a bit more of each until the whole household could hear that I had found one of the profound pleasures of Indonesia, the *mandi*.

In the process I discovered why the clothes hooks are high on the wall. When the celebration of elemental values of life came to an end, I rebuttoned the not-too-wet essentials and emerged. My host was grinning from ear to ear.

"You've used a *mandi* before, I gather," he said with a slight bow.

"No, but it doesn't take me long to learn."

"I should have explained it to you, but I didn't know if you needed me to."

Here's an important point: I could have asked. Perhaps I should have asked. Indeed, I would have asked if it had remained a mystery after I had taken a good look. But I didn't need to, and even if I had done something fundamentally wrong—even had I climbed bodily into the tub and displaced two hundred pounds of water, my host would have accepted it. I was an outsider. My ways were not his ways. But he wouldn't have been quite so delighted that I could enjoy *his* ways even without being told.

And then came the reward: "Did you turn on the faucet when you finished?" he asked.

"Yes," I replied. "It likely will take thirty minutes or so to replace what I used from the tub."

"Yes, about that. I'll turn it off after awhile. Do you know you are the first American ever to visit us who knew to leave the water running?" And his smile became even warmer.

Source: Ted Ward, *Living Overseas* (The Free Press, 1984) 107–109.

People's reactions may also change over time. That is, the initial reactions of acceptance or rejection often shift as increased intercultural contacts produce different kinds of outcomes. As we suggested in Chapter 12, such changes in the way people react to intercultural contacts are called *acculturation*.

Acculturation

Words such as *assimilation, adjustment, adaptation,* and even *coping* are used to describe how individuals respond to their experiences in other cultures. Many of these terms refer to how people from one culture react to prolonged contact with those from another. Over the years, different emotional overtones have been attached to these terms. To some people, for instance, *assimilation* is a negative outcome; to others it is positive. Some consider *adjustment* to be "good," whereas for others it is "bad."

We offer an approach that allows you to make your own value judgment about what constitutes the right kind of outcome. We believe that competent adjustment to another culture will vary greatly from situation to situation and from person to person. We have used the broader term of *acculturation* to characterize these adjustments because it subsumes various forms of cultural or individual adaptation.

Acculturation, which is "culture change that results from continuous, firsthand contact between two distinct cultural groups,"[3] has been described as

> the process by which individuals change their psychological characteristics, change the surrounding context, or change the amount of contact in order to achieve a better fit (outcome) with other features of the system in which they carry out their life.[4]

Note that this definition suggests that when individuals acculturate they learn how to "fit" themselves into the situation. Again remember that different individuals and different groups will make the fit in different ways.

Acculturation includes physical, biological, and social changes. Physical changes occur because people are confronted with new physical stimuli—they eat different food, drink different water, live in different climates, and reside in different kinds of housing. When people are exposed to a new culture, they may undergo actual physical or biological changes. People deal with new viruses and bacteria; new foods cause new reactions and perhaps even new allergies. Prolonged contact between groups results in intermarriage, and the children of these marriages are born with a mixture of the genetic features of the people involved. Social relationships change with the introduction of new people. Outgroups may become bonded with the ingroups, for example, in opposition to the new outgroup members. Such changes may also cause individuals to define themselves in new and different ways.[5]

Alternatively, the culture itself might change because of the influences of people from other cultures. The French, for example, have raised concerns

CULTURE CONNECTIONS

Arthur Ashe talking to graduates of the State University College in Brockport, NY said "Cultural diversity is like a marriage. You have to work at it."

Source: San Diego Union, May 22, 1990; C2.

about the effects of the English language on their own language and culture. Traditional societies have sometimes expressed this distress about the Westernization or urbanization of their cultures.

The Acculturation Process   As we noted in the previous chapter, early efforts to describe the acculturation process resulted in the U-curve and the W-curve hypotheses. We now know that those hypotheses describe some people's experiences but certainly not everyone's. Recent efforts to describe the acculturation process suggest a more complex set of patterns. Daniel J. Kealey found that the U-curve was an accurate description of the acculturation process for only about 10 percent of the individuals he studied; the majority experienced little change (30 percent remained highly satisfied, 10 percent stayed moderately satisfied, and 15 percent maintained a low level of satisfaction throughout); and another 35 percent had an extremely low level of satisfaction initially but improved continuously for the duration of their intercultural assignment.[6] Interestingly, many in this latter group, which experienced the most severe adjustment stress, eventually became the most competent in their ability to function in another culture.

There is also ample evidence to suggest that the acculturation process has multiple dimensions or factors associated with it. For example, Mitchell R. Hammer, William B. Gudykunst, and Richard L. Wiseman have suggested that intercultural effectiveness consists of three such dimensions: the ability to deal with psychological stress, skill in communicating with others both effectively and appropriately, and proficiency in establishing interpersonal relationships.[7] Colleen Ward and her colleagues have identified just two dimensions of acculturation: psychological and sociocultural. The former is similar to Hammer et al.'s first dimension and the latter seems to combine the remaining two.[8] Similarly, Guo-Ming Chen found that communicator adaptability and interaction with others were major positive contributors to international students' ability to cope with adjustment difficulties in the United States.[9]

Despite such distinctions, however, the acculturation process has usually been viewed as a single "package" of related features that all follow the same

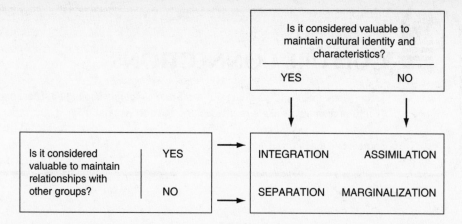

Figure 13.1 Forms of acculturation. (*Source:* John W. Berry, Uichol Kim, and Pawel Boski, "Psychological Acculturation of Immigrants," *Cross-cultural Adaptation: Current Approaches,* ed. Young Yun Kim and William B. Gudykunst [Newbury Park, CA: Sage, 1988.]

trajectory of change for a given individual. Perhaps, however, a separate pattern of change might characterize each dimension of acculturation. Thus, for instance, the adjustment pattern to the pace of life may differ from the adjustment pattern to the culture's expectations regarding the use of indirection in language.

Types of Acculturation   Answers to two important questions shape the response of individuals and groups to prolonged intercultural contact, thus producing different acculturation outcomes. The first issue is whether it is considered important to maintain one's cultural identity and to display its characteristics. The second question involves whether people believe it is important to maintain relationships with the outgroups.[10]

Assimilation occurs when it is deemed relatively unimportant to maintain one's original cultural identity but it is important to establish and maintain relationships with other cultures. The metaphor of the United States as a melting pot, which envisions many cultures giving up their individual characteristics to build the new, homogenized cultural identity of the United States, illustrates the choice described in Figure 13.1 as assimilation. Assimilation means taking on the new culture's beliefs, values, and norms.

When an individual or group retains its original cultural identity while seeking to maintain harmonious relationships with other cultures, *integration* occurs. Countries such as Switzerland, Belgium, and Canada, with their multilingual and multicultural populations, are good examples. Integration produces distinguishable cultural groups that work cooperatively to ensure that the society and the individuals continue to function well. Both integration and assimilation promote harmony and result in an appropriate fit of individuals and groups to the larger culture.

When individuals or groups do not want to maintain positive relationships with members of other groups, the outcomes are starkly different. If a culture does not want positive relationships with another culture and if it also wishes to retain its cultural characteristics, *separation* may result. If the separation occurs because the more politically and economically powerful culture does not want the intercultural contact, the result of the forced separation is called *segregation*. The history of the United States provides numerous examples of segregation in its treatment of African Americans. If, however, a nondominant group chooses not to participate in the larger society in order to retain its own way of life, the separation is called *seclusion*. The Amish are a good example of this choice.

When individuals or groups neither retain their cultural heritage nor maintain positive contacts with the other groups, *marginalization* occurs. This form of acculturation is characterized by confusion and alienation. The choices of marginalization and separation are reactions against other cultures. The fit these outcomes achieve in the acculturation process is based on battling against, rather than working with, the other cultures in the social environment.[11]

For purposes of simplification, Figure 13.1 suggests that each of the questions must be answered as wholly "yes" or "no." In reality, however, people could choose a variety of points between these two extremes. The French, for example, while certainly not isolationists, have raised concerns about the effects of the English language on their own language and culture. Similarly, traditional societies have sometimes been distressed about the Westernization or urbanization of their cultures while simultaneously expressing a desire for increased contact and trade.

Becoming an Interculturally Competent Communicator

Obviously, not all individuals acculturate similarly. Some find the daily challenges of responding to another culture to be too stressful and overwhelming. If possible, such individuals will choose to return to their culture of origin; if they cannot do so, various kinds of maladaptive adjustments, or even mental illnesses, can occur.

At the opposite extreme, and of particular interest to us, are those individuals who move easily among many cultures. Such people generally have a profound respect for many varied points of view and are able to understand others and to communicate appropriately and effectively with people from a variety of cultures. Such individuals are able to project a sense of self that transcends any particular cultural group.

Young Yun Kim and Brent Ruben use the term *intercultural transformation* to describe the process by which individuals move beyond the thoughts, feelings, and behaviors of their initial cultural framework to incorporate other cultural realities. The process can be described as follows:

> The process of becoming intercultural—of personal transformation from cultural to intercultural—is a process of growth beyond one's original cultural conditioning. One consequence of extensive communication experiences and the subsequent internal transformation is the development of a cultural identity that is far

CULTURE CONNECTIONS

We have to face the fact that either all of us are going to die together or we are going to live together, and if we are to live together we have to talk.

Source: Attributed to Eleanor Roosevelt.

from being "frozen." An intercultural person's cultural identity is characteristically open to further transformation and growth. This does not mean that a highly intercultural person's identity is culture-free or cultureless. Rather, it is not rigidly bound by membership to any one particular culture. . . . A second consequence [of an intercultural transformation]. . . . is a cognitive structure that enables a broadened and deepened understanding of human conditions and cultural differences and a view of things that are larger than any one cultural perspective. . . . The increased cognitive depth and breadth is, in turn, likely to facilitate corresponding emotional and behavioral capacities as well.[12]

Interculturally competent communicators integrate a wide array of culture-general knowledge into their behavioral repertoires, and they are able to apply that knowledge to the specific cultures with which they interact. They are also able to respond emotionally and behaviorally with a wide range of choices in order to act appropriately and effectively within the constraints of each situation. They have typically had extensive intercultural communication experiences, and they have learned to adjust to alternative patterns of thinking and behaving.

THE ETHICS OF INTERCULTURAL COMPETENCE

Those who attempt to achieve intercultural competence must face a number of ethical dilemmas. It is imperative to explore the following issues to become aware of the choices that are made all too often without due consideration and reflection.

There are three key ethical dilemmas. The first is summarized in the adage "When in Rome, do as the Romans do." The second asks if it is possible to judge a particular belief, value, or norm as morally reprehensible. If so, when and under what circumstances? Stated in a slightly different way, if all cultures have differing beliefs, values, and norms, does that mean that there are no true rights and wrongs? The third dilemma relates to the consequences of intercultural contacts. Are they necessarily positive for individuals and their societies? In other words, should all intercultural contacts be encouraged?

Sojourners to other cultures often face ethical dilemmas in terms of values and behavior.

When in Rome. . . .

A fundamental issue confronting those who are in the midst of another culture is a decision about how much they should change their behaviors to fit the beliefs, values, and norms of those with whom they interact. Is it the responsibility of the visitors, newcomers, or sojourners to adjust their behaviors to the cultural framework of the host culture, or should members of the host culture adjust their communication and make allowances for the newcomers and strangers?

The old adage "When in Rome, do as the Romans do," which clearly places the responsibility for change on the newcomer, offers a great deal of wisdom. Behaviors that conform to cultural expectations show respect for the other culture and its ways. Conformity with common cultural practices also allows the newcomer to interact with and to meet people from the host culture on some kind of genuine basis. Respecting differences in verbal and non-verbal codes means that the ethical intercultural communicator takes responsibility for learning as much about these codes as is possible and reasonable. Naturally, what is possible and reasonable will vary, depending on a range of circumstances.

CULTURE CONNECTIONS

I try to encourage students to always think in terms of three cultures, their own and at least two others—not one other, because they could too easily reduce true human diversity to a single dimension of difference, us and them. . . .

Source: Mary Catherine Bateson, *Composing a Life* (New York: Atlantic Monthly Press, 1989).

Sometimes it is difficult for people to change their behaviors to match cultural patterns that contradict their own beliefs and values. For example, many European American women, whose actions are based on the values of freedom and equality, may find it difficult to respond positively to the Saudi Arabian cultural practices that require women to wear veils in public and to use male drivers or chaperones. The ethical dilemma that intercultural communicators face is the decision about how far to go in adapting their behaviors to another culture. Should people engage in behaviors that they regard as personally wrong or difficult? At what point do people lose their own sense of self, their cultural identities, and their moral integrity? One of the challenges and delights of intercultural communication is in discovering the boundaries and touchstones of one's own moral perspective while simultaneously learning to display respect for other ways of dealing with human problems.

Another perspective from which to explore the ethical issues embedded in the adage is that of the "Romans." A common point of view, often expressed by U.S. Americans about those who have recently immigrated to the United States or who still retain many of the underlying patterns of their own culture, is that since these people now live in the United States, they should adapt to its cultural ways. The same comments are often made about students from other countries who come to the United States to study.

We ask you to consider the experiences of those people who immigrate to or study in another country. Perhaps you are such a person. Or perhaps your parents or grandparents did so. Not all immigrants or students have so freely chosen the country where they now reside. Large numbers of people migrate from one country to another because of political, military, and economic upheavals in their own country, which makes living and learning there nearly impossible. For many, the choice to leave is juxtaposed against a choice to die, to starve, or to be politically censored. We also ask you to consider how difficult it must be for people to give up their culture. Remember how fundamental your cultural framework is, how it provides the logic for your behavior and view of the world. How easy would it be for you if you were forced into new modes of behavior? Assimilation into another culture is difficult.

Are Cultural Values Relative or Universal?

A second ethical issue confronting the intercultural communicator is whether it is ever acceptable to judge the people of a culture when their behaviors are based on a radically different set of beliefs, values, and norms. Are there any values that transcend the boundaries of cultural differences? Are there any universally right or wrong values?

A culturally relativistic point of view suggests that every culture has its own set of values and that judgments can be made only within the context of the particular culture. Most people do not completely subscribe to this view, partly because it would lead to a lack of any firm beliefs and values on which to build a sense of self-identity.

David Kale argues that there are two values that transcend all cultures. First, the human spirit requires that all people must struggle to improve their world and to maintain their own sense of dignity, always within the context of their own particular culture. Thus Kale suggests that "the guiding principle of any universal code of intercultural communication, therefore, should be to protect the worth and dignity of the human spirit."[13] The second universal value is a world at peace. Thus, all ethical codes must recognize the importance of working toward a world in which people can live at peace with themselves and one another.[14]

Ethical intercultural communicators continually struggle with the dilemmas presented by differences in cultural values. The tensions inherent in seeking to be tolerant of differences while holding firmly to one's own critical cultural values must always be reconciled. Kale's suggestions for responding ethically to cultural differences in values are excellent starting points for the internal dialogue that all competent intercultural communicators must conduct.

Do the Ends Justify the Means?

The final ethical dilemma we wish to raise concerns these questions: Should all intercultural contacts be encouraged? Are the outcomes of intercultural contacts positive? Are all circumstances appropriate for intercultural contact? In short, do the ends justify the means?

We have been shamelessly enthusiastic about the potential benefits and delights of intercultural interaction. Nevertheless, certain outcomes may not necessarily be justified by the means used to obtain them. Tourism, for example, can sometimes create an ethical dilemma. Although it often provides economic benefits for those living in the tourist destination and allows people from one culture to learn about another, it can also produce serious negative consequences. In some popular tourist destinations, for instance, the tourists actually outnumber the native population, and tourists may consume natural resources at a greater rate than they can be replaced.

Some of the following questions must be confronted:

CULTURE CONNECTIONS

A West German group was surprised when it departed its charter flight at Goa, India.

The plane was met by an ad-hoc army of professors, Catholic nuns and local businessmen, armed with leaflets and placards.

"Go home," one of the protest signs said. "Mass tourism is destroying our society."

The incident in Goa was not an isolated one, said Virginia Hadsell, founder of the small California group known as the North American Coordinating Center for Responsible Tourism.

"It's beginning to happen all over," she added, "anywhere a fragile ecosystem and infrastructure are threatened by hordes of invading tourists."

For a while last year, Bhutan closed its borders to tourists in an attempt to protect the "religious integrity" of its shrines and temples. And Bermuda has limited the number of cruise ships that can visit its harbors.

"People need to think hard about what happens when people from the 'First World' go to the Third World, when the haves visit the have-nots," Hadsell said. "Most Americans have no intention to harm the culture they visit. They're just not aware of the local etiquette, and they need to learn."

This past winter, more than 20 million people from wealthy countries spent their holiday dollars in the Third World. But tourism's sizable economic benefit can corrupt a culture and destroy the environment.

Source: Peter S. Greenberg, "California Group Seeks to Increase the Cultural Sensitivity of Tourists," *Sacramento Bee*, July 29, 1990: T4.

- Is it ethical to go to another country, for whatever reason, if you are naive and unprepared for cultural contact?
- Should intercultural contacts be encouraged for those who speak no language but their own?
- Should those who are prejudiced seek out intercultural contacts?
- Is it ethical to send missionaries to other countries?
- Is it acceptable to provide medical assistance to help a culture resist a disease, when in providing the assistance you may destroy the very infrastructure and nature of the indigenous culture?
- Is it justifiable for the sojourner from one culture to encourage a person from another culture to disregard his or her own cultural values?

There are no simple answers to any of these questions, but the competent intercultural communicator must confront these ethical dilemmas.

CULTURE CONNECTIONS

It was a transforming experience. I saw ways of life I would never have seen had I remained within the comfortable domain of my provincial Midwestern upbringing. For the first time, I learned to think of someone besides myself, to consider that there is no single way of observing a problem or answering a troubling question. I discovered that without the mutual tolerance and respect of other people's cultures, there is no possibility for harmony in our world.

I'm convinced that what I learned overseas as a Peace Corps volunteer was fairly typical. Yes, there were others who had difficult assignments, but few will deny that their gains were greater than their losses. Would they do it again? You bet, on a moment's notice, as some already have and others plan to do once lives now immersed in families and careers have taken another turn.

Source: Charles A. Larson, "The Value of Volunteering," *Newsweek,* July 22, 1991: 10–11.

Ethics—Your Choices

We have offered few specific answers to these ethical dilemmas because every person must provide his or her own response. In the context of your own experiences and your own intercultural interactions, therefore, you must resolve the ethical dilemmas that will inevitably occur in your life. Kale provides four principles to guide you as you develop your own personal code of ethics. Ethical communicators should:

- Address people of other cultures with the same respect that they would like to receive themselves.
- Try to describe the world as they perceive it as accurately as possible.
- Encourage people of other cultures to express themselves in their unique natures.
- Strive for identification with people of other cultures.

SUMMARY

Two tools can be used to improve intercultural competence. The first is provided in the culture-general concepts of the Behavioral Assessment Scale for Intercultural Competence (BASIC). Such concepts include the ability to display respect, a recognition that knowledge is personal rather than universal, an empathic sense about the experiences of others that results in behaviors appropriate to those experiences, the ability to manage interactions with others,

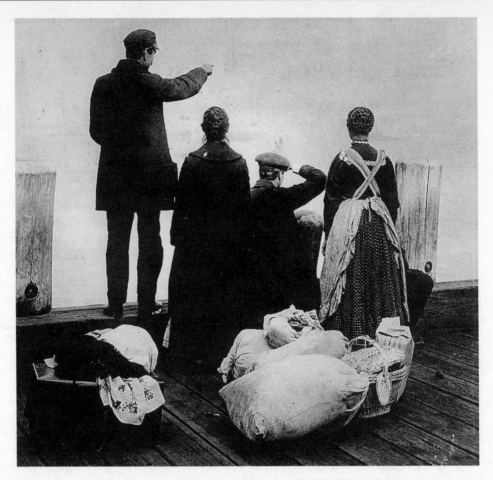

These 1912 immigrants are looking toward a new life as U.S. Americans. Their great-grandchildren must live in a multicultural world that demands competent intercultural communication skills. *(Library of Congress.)*

skills in enacting appropriate task and relational role behaviors, the capacity to tolerate uncertainty without anxiety, and a nonevaluative posture toward the beliefs and actions of others. Within each culture there will be culturally specific ways of behaving that are used to demonstrate these competencies.

The second tool is to distinguish among the techniques of description, interpretation, and evaluation. This tool encourages communicators to describe the sensory information they receive and then to construct alternative interpretations about their perceptions by making correspondingly different evaluations.

When one cultural group lives near other cultural groups, various forms of acculturation occur. The desire to maintain both an identification with the culture of origin and positive relationships with other cultures influence the type of acculturation that is experienced. Intercultural transformation occurs

CULTURE CONNECTIONS

It is time for the preachers, the rabbis, the priests and pundits, and the professors to believe in the awesome wonder of diversity so that they can teach those who follow them. It is time for parents to teach young people early on that in diversity there is beauty and there is strength. We all should know that diversity makes for a rich tapestry, and we must understand that all the threads of the tapestry are equal in value no matter their color; equal in importance no matter their texture.

Source: Maya Angelou, *Wouldn't Take Nothing For My Journey Now* (New York: Random House Inc., 1993) 124.

when people are able to move beyond the limits of their own cultural experiences to incorporate the perspectives of other cultures into their own interpersonal interactions.

Ethical issues in the development of intercultural competence concern questions about whose responsibility it is to adjust to a different culture, issues about right and wrong, and the degree to which all intercultural contacts should be encouraged.

CONCLUDING REMARKS

We began this book with a sense of optimism, but also with a deep concern about the pressing need for intercultural communication competence. On this, the threshold of the twenty-first century, such competence is an essential attribute for personal survival, professional success, national harmony, and international peace. The challenge of living in a multicultural world is the need to transcend the unpredictability of intercultural interactions, to cope with the accompanying fears that such interactions often engender, and to feel joy and comfort in the discovery of cultural variability.

Our focus has been on the interpersonal hurdles—the person-to-person problems—that arise in coping with the realities of cultural diversity. We commend and encourage all who have struggled to adapt to the multicultural nature of the human landscape. Inclusion of others is the means to a better future, so we must "reconstitute the inner circle"[15] by celebrating and acknowledging cultural differences in all aspects of life.

The need for an intercultural mentality to match our multicultural world, the difficulties inherent in the quest of such a goal, the excitement of the challenges, and the rewards of the successes are summarized in the words of Troy Duster:

There is no longer a single racial or ethnic group with an overwhelming numerical and political majority. Pluralism is the reality, with no one group a dominant force. This is completely new; we are grappling with a phenomenon that is both puzzling and alarming, fraught with tensions and hostilities, and yet simultaneously brimming with potential and crackling with new energy. Consequently, we swing between hope and concern, optimism and pessimism about the prospects for social life among people from differing racial and cultural groups.[46]

We urge you to view this book and each intercultural experience as steps in a lifelong commitment to competence in intercultural communication. Intercultural competence is, in many ways, an art rather than a science. Our hope is that you will use your artistic talents to make the world a better place in which people from all cultures can live and thrive.

Notes

CHAPTER 1

1. Catharine R. Stimpson, "A Conversation, Not a Monologue," *Chronicle of Higher Education*, March 16, 1994, B1.
2. Mark E. Mendenhall, Edward Dunbar, and Gary R. Oddou, "Expatriate Selection, Training, and Career-Pathing: A Review and Critique," *Human Resource Management* 26 (1987): 331–345.
3. President's Commission on Foreign Language and International Studies (Washington, DC: Department of Health, Education, and Welfare, 1979) 1.
4. *Educating for Global Competence: The Report of the Advisory Council for International Education Exchange*, (Washington, DC: Council for International Exchange, August 1988) 3–4.
5. "Green Light for Growth: Xerox Bets on a New Generation of Digital Office Equipment," *U.S. News & World Report*, August 15, 1994: 48.
6. Jolene Koester, *A Profile of the U.S. Student Abroad* (New York: Council on International Exchange, 1985); Jolene Koester, *A Profile of the U.S. Student Abroad: 1984 and 1985* (New York: Council on International Exchange, 1987).
7. "More Study-Abroad Programs Available to U.S. Students, IIE Report Shows," *Higher Education & National Affairs*, American Council on Education, June 13, 1994: 4.
8. Paul Desruisseaux, "A Foreign-Student Record," *Chronicle of Higher Education*, December 1, 1993, A42; "Foreign Enrollment Still Increasing," *Higher Education & National Affairs*, American Council on Education, June 13, 1994: 4.
9. Cathy Lynn Grossman, "More Foreign Visitors Destined for the U.S.," *USA Today*, May 23, 1994, D1.
10. Robert Shuter, "The Centrality of Culture," *Southern Communication Journal*, 55 (1990): 241.
11. William A. Henry III, "Beyond the Melting Pot," *Time*, April 9, 1990: 28.
12. Frank Clifford, "Asian, Latino Numbers Soar in U.S. Census," *Los Angeles Times*, March 11, 1991, A1, A24.
13. "America's Changing Face," *Newsweek*, September 10, 1990: 47.
14. "For 14%, English it isn't," *San Diego Union-Tribune*, April 28, 1991, A1, A25.

15. Tony Bizjak, "383 million Americans by 2020?" *Sacramento Bee,* December 4, 1992, A1, A24.

16. Antonia Pantoja and Wilhelmina Perry, "Cultural Pluralism: A Goal to Be Realized," *Voices from the Battlefront,* ed. Marta Moreno Vega and Cheryll Y. Greene (Trenton, NJ: Africa World Press, 1993) 136.

17. "Classrooms of Babel," *Newsweek,* February 11, 1991: 56–57.

18. Ruby Modesto, "Envisioning California," Speech presented at the Envisioning California Conference, Sacramento, March 1991.

19. "Classrooms of Babel" 57.

20. "U.S. Schools to Be One-Third Minority by 1995, Study Says," *Sacramento Bee,* September 13, 1991, A8.

21. "By '95, Minority Graduates to Be Majority in State, Study Says," *San Diego Union,* September 23, 1991, A42.

22. "1992 Enrollment by Race at 3,300 Institutions of Higher Education," *Chronicle of Higher Education Almanac,* February 23, 1994, A31.

23. Christopher Shea, "Women and Minorities Led the Way in a Year of Slow Enrollment Growth," *Chronicle of Higher Education,* January 26, 1994, A32.

24. Ann M. Morrison and Mary Ann Von Glinow, "Women and Minorities in Management," *American Psychologist* 45 (1990): 200–208.

25. Tom Mathews, "Quotas," *Newsweek* December 31, 1990: 29.

26. The melting pot metaphor for U.S. cultural diversity was popularized by Israel Zangwell's play of 1908, *The Melting Pot.* The idea was anticipated over a hundred years earlier in Crèvecoeur's description of America: "Here individuals of all nations are melted into a new race of men, whose labors and posterity will one day cause great changes in the world." See J. Hector St. John Crèvecoeur, *Letter from an American Farmer* (New York: Albert and Charles Boni, 1782/1925) 55; Israel Zangwell, *The melting pot. Drama in four acts.* (New York: Arno Press, 1908/1975).

27. See Rodolfo O. de la Garza, Louis DeSipio, F. Chris Garcia, John Garcia, and Angelo Falcon, *Latino Voices: Mexican, Puerto Rican, & Cuban Perspectives on American Politics* (Boulder: Westview Press, 1992).

28. James Diego Vigil, *From Indians to Chicanos: The Dynamics of Mexican American Culture* (Prospect Heights, IL: Waveland Press, 1980) 1.

29. Mark Z. Barabak, "Differences Found Among U.S. Hispanics," *San Diego Union,* August 30, 1991, A2.

30. Juan L. Gonzales, Jr., *Racial and Ethnic Groups in America* (Dubuque, IA: Kendall/Hunt, 1990) 199.

31. Earl Shorris, "The Latino vs. Hispanic Controversy," *San Diego Union-Tribune,* October 29, 1992, B11. See also Earl Shorris, *Latinos: A Biography of the People* (New York: W. W. Norton, 1992); Earl Shorris, "Latinos: The Complexity of Identity," *Report on the Americas* 26 (1992): 19–26.

32. Michael L. Hecht and Sidney Ribeau, "Sociocultural Roots of Ethnic Identity: A Look at Black America," *Journal of Black Studies,* 21 (1991): 501–513.

33. Dwight Conquergood, "Rethinking Ethnography: Towards a Critical Cultural Politics," *Communication Monographs,* 58 (1991): 186.

34. See, for example, Mary Kalantzis and William Cope, "Multiculturalism May Prove to Be the Key Issue of Our Epoch," *Chronicle of Higher Education,* November 4, 1992, B3, B5.

35. Renato Rosaldo, *Culture & Truth: The Remaking of Social Analysis* (Boston: Beacon Press, 1989): 28.

CHAPTER 2

1. See Frank E. X. Dance, "The 'Concept' of Communication," *Journal of Communication* 20 (1970): 201–210: Frank E. X. Dance and Carl E. Larson, *The Functions of Human Communication* (New York: Holt, Rinehart & Winston, 1976) Appendix A.
2. Alfred L. Kroeber and Clyde Kluckhohn, *Culture: A Critical Review of Concepts and Definitions* (Cambridge, MA: Harvard University Press, 1952).
3. E. B. Tylor, "The Science of Culture," *Culture and Consciousness: Perspectives in the Social Sciences*, ed. Gloria B. Levitas (New York: George Braziller, 1967) 47.
4. Harry C. Triandis, *The Analysis of Subjective Culture* (New York: Wiley, 1972) 4. See also Marshall R. Singer, "Culture: A Perceptual Approach" *Intercultural Communication: A Reader*, 4th ed., ed. Larry A. Samovar and Richard E. Porter (Belmont, CA: Wadsworth, 1985) 62–69.
5. Geert Hofstede, *Cultures and Organizations: Software of the Mind* (London: Mc-Graw-Hill, 1991).
6. Donal Carbaugh, " 'Soul' and 'Self': Soviet and American Cultures in Conversation," *Quarterly Journal of Speech* 79 (1993): 182; see also Donal Carbaugh, "Intercultural Communication," *Cultural Communication and Intercultural Contact*, ed. Donal Carbaugh (Hillsdale, NJ: Lawrence Erlbaum, 1990) 151–175.
7. Donal Carbaugh, "Comments on 'Culture' in Communication Inquiry," *Communication Reports* 1 (1988): 38–41.
8. See Mary Jane Collier and Milt Thomas, "Cultural Identity: An Interpretive Approach," *Theories in Intercultural Communication*, ed. Young Yun Kim and William B. Gudykunst (Newbury Park, CA: Sage, 1988) 99–120; Gerry Philipsen, *Speaking Culturally: Explorations in Social Communication* (Albany: State University of New York Press, 1992).
9. Collier and Thomas 103.
10. William Wetherall, "Ethnic Ainu Seek Official Recognition," *Japan Times*, January 25–31, 1+. Rpt. in *Ethnic Groups*, Vol. 4, ed. Eleanor Goldstein. (Boca Raton, FL: Social Issues Resources Ser., 1994), art. no. 62.

CHAPTER 3

1. The idea that the degree of heterogeneity among participants distinguishes intercultural from intracultural communication, and thereby results in a continuum of "interculturalness" of the communication, was first introduced by L. E. Sarbaugh, *Intercultural Communication* (Rochelle Park, NJ: Hayden Book Company, 1979).
2. For a more detailed discussion of the relationships among these terms, see Molefi Kete Asante and William B. Gudykunst, eds., *Handbook of Intercultural Communication* (Newbury Park, CA: Sage, 1989) 7–13.
3. For a discussion of the concept and measurement of communicative competence, see Arthur P. Bochner and Clifford W. Kelly, "Interpersonal Competence: Rationale, Philosophy, and Implementation of a Conceptual Framework," *Speech Teacher* 23 (1974): 279–301; Myron W. Lustig and Brian H. Spitzberg, "Methodological Issues in the Study of Intercultural Communication Competence," *Intercultural Communication Competence*, ed. Richard L. Wiseman and Jolene Koester (Newbury Park, CA: Sage, 1993): 153–167; Charles Pavitt, "The Ideal Communicator as the Basis for Competence Judgments of Self and Friend," *Com-*

munication Reports, 3 (1990): 9–14; Brian H. Spitzberg, "Communication Competence as Knowledge, Skill, and Impression," *Communication Education* 32 (1983): 323–329; Brian H. Spitzberg, "Issues in the Study of Communicative Competence," *Progress in Communication Sciences* (1987): 1–46; Brian H. Spitzberg, "Communication Competence: Measures of Perceived Effectiveness," *A Handbook for the Study of Human Communication*, ed. Charles H. Tardy (Norwood, NJ: Ablex, 1988) 67–105; Brian H. Spitzberg, "Issues in the Development of a Theory of Interpersonal Competence in the Intercultural Context," *International Journal of Intercultural Relations* 13 (1989): 241–268; Brian H. Spitzberg, "An Examination of Trait Measures of Interpersonal Competence," *Communication Research* 3 (1991): 22–29; Brian H. Spitzberg, "The Dark Side of (In)Competence," *The Dark Side of Interpersonal Communication*, ed. William R. Cupach and Brian H. Spitzberg, (Hillsdale, NJ: Erlbaum, 1994): 25–49; Brian H. Spitzberg and Claire C. Brunner, "Toward a Theoretical Integration of Context and Competence Research," *Western Journal of Speech Communication* 55 (1991): 28–46; Brian H. Spitzberg and William R. Cupach, *Handbook of Interpersonal Competence Research* (New York: Springer-Verlag, 1989); Brian H. Spitzberg and William R. Cupach, *Interpersonal Communication Competence* (Beverly Hills, CA: Sage, 1984); Brian H. Spitzberg and Michael L. Hecht, "A Component Model of Relational Competence," *Human Communication Research* 10 (1984): 575–599; John Wiemann, "Explication and Test of a Model of Communicative Competence," *Human Communication Research* 3 (1977): 195–213; John M. Wiemann and Philip M. Backlund, "Current Theory and Research in Communicative Competence," *Review of Educational Research* 50 (1980): 185–99; John M. Wiemann and James J. Bradic, "Metatheoretical Issues in the Study of Communicative Competence," *Progress in Communication Sciences* 9 (1988): 261–284.

4. Brian H. Spitzberg, "Communication Competence: Measures of Perceived Effectiveness," *A Handbook for the Study of Human Communication*, ed. Charles H. Tardy (Norwood, NJ: Ablex, 1988): 67–105.

5. For more thorough reviews, see Mary Jane Collier, "Cultural and Intercultural Communication Competence: Current Approaches and Directions for Future Research," *International Journal of Intercultural Relations* 13 (1989): 287–302; Mitchell R. Hammer, "Intercultural Communication Competence," *Handbook of Intercultural Communication*, ed. Molefi Kete Asante and William B. Gudykunst (Newbury Park, CA: Sage, 1989) 247–260; Judith N. Martin, "Intercultural Communication Competence: A Review," *Intercultural Communication Competence*, ed. Richard L. Wiseman and Jolene Koester (Newbury Park, CA: Sage, 1993): 16–29; Brent D. Ruben, "The Study of Cross-Cultural Competence: Traditions and Contemporary Issues," *International Journal of Intercultural Relations* 13 (1989): 229–240.

6. Hiroko Abe and Richard Wiseman, "A Cross-cultural Confirmation of the Dimensions of Intercultural Effectiveness," *International Journal of Intercultural Relations* 7 (1983): 53–67; Mitchell R. Hammer, "Behavioral Dimensions of Intercultural Effectiveness: A Replication and Extension," *International Journal of Intercultural Relations* 11 (1987): 65–88; Mitchell R. Hammer, William B. Gudykunst, and Richard C. Wiseman, "Dimensions of Intercultural Effectiveness: An Exploratory Study," *International Journal of Intercultural Relations* 2 (1978): 382–393; Judith N. Martin, "The Relationships Between Student Sojourner Perceptions of Intercultural Competencies and Previous Sojourn Experience," *In-*

ternational Journal of Intercultural Relations 11 (987): 337–355; Judith N. Martin and Mitchell R. Hammer, "Behavioral Categories of Intercultural Communication Competence: Everyday Communicators' Perceptions," *International Journal of Intercultural Relations* 13 (1989): 303–332.

7. Judith N. Martin and Mitchell R. Hammer, "Behavioral Categories of Intercultural Communication Competence: Everyday Communicators' Perceptions," *International Journal of Intercultural Relations* 13 (1989): 303–332; Brent D. Ruben, "Assessing Communication Competence for Intercultural Adaptation," *Group and Organization Studies* 1 (976): 334–354; Brent D. Ruben, Lawrence R. Askling, and Daniel J. Kealey, "Cross-cultural Effectiveness," *Overview of Intercultural Training, Education and Research, Vol. 1: Theory,* ed. David Hoopes, Paul B. Pedersen, and George W. Renwick (Washington DC: Society for Intercultural Education, Training and Research, 1977) 92–105; Brent D. Ruben and Daniel J. Kealey, "Behavioral Assessment of Communication Competency and the Prediction of Cross-Cultural Adaptation," *International Journal of Intercultural Relations* 3 (1979): 15–47.

8. Harry C. Triandis, "Culture Training, Cognitive Complexity, and Interpersonal Attitudes," *Readings in Intercultural Communication, Vol. II,* ed. David Hoopes (Pittsburgh: Regional Council for International Education, 1973) 55–67.

9. William R. Cupach and T. Todd Imahori, "Identity Management Theory: Communication Competence in Intercultural Episodes and Relationships," *Intercultural Communication Competence,* ed. Richard L. Wiseman and Jolene Koester (Newbury Park, CA: Sage, 1993): 112–131; T. Todd Imahori and Mary L. Lanigan, "Relational Model of Intercultural Communication Competence," *International Journal of Intercultural Relations* 13 (1989): 269–286.

10. Fathi S. Yousef, "Human Resource Management: Aspects of Intercultural Relations in U.S. Organizations," *Intercultural Communication: A Reader,* 5th ed., ed. Larry A. Samovar and Richard E. Porter (Belmont, CA: Wadsworth, 1988) 175–182.

11. See, for example, John T. Masterson, Norman H. Watson, and Elaine J. Cichon, "Cultural Differences in Public Speaking," *World Communication* 20 (1991): 39–47.

12. Jolene Koester and Margaret Olebe, "The Behavioral Assessment Scale for Intercultural Communication Effectiveness," *International Journal of Intercultural Relations* 12 (1988): 233–246; Margaret Olebe and Jolene Koester, "Exploring the Cross-cultural Equivalence of the Behavioral Assessment Scale for Intercultural Communication," *International Journal of Intercultural Relations* 13 (1989): 333–347.

CHAPTER 4

1. Gustav Ichheiser, *Appearances and Realities: Misunderstanding in Human Relations* (San Francisco: Jossey-Bass, 1970) 8.

2. J. M. Roberts, *The Pelican History of the World,* rev. ed. (London: Penguin Books, 1987) 511.

3. David McCullough, 1994 Commencement Address at the University of Pittsburgh, qtd. in *Chronicle of Higher Education,* June 8, 1994, B2.

4. Geert Hofstede, *Culture's Consequences: International Differences in Work-Related Values* (Beverly Hills, CA: Sage, 1980).

5. See William Calvin, *The Ascent of Mind: Ice Age Climates and the Evolution of Intelligence* (New York: Bantam Books, 1990); Frank D. Roylance, "Humans May Owe Their Big Brains to Ice Age," *Sacramento Bee*, January 2, 1990, D4.

6. Derek F. Roberts, *Climate and Human Variability* (Menlo Park, CA: Cummings, 1978).

7. Peter A. Andersen, "Explaining Intercultural Differences in Nonverbal Communication," *Intercultural Communication: A Reader*, ed. Larry A. Samovar and Richard E. Porter (Belmont, CA: Wadsworth, 1988) 272–281; Edward T. Hall, *The Hidden Dimension* (Garden City, NY: Doubleday, 1966); Miles L. Patterson, *Nonverbal Behavior: A Functional Perspective* (New York: Springer-Verlag, 1983).

8. Peter A. Andersen, Myron W. Lustig, and Janis F. Andersen, "Changes in Latitude, Changes in Attitude: The Relationship Between Climate and Interpersonal Communication Predispositions," *Communication Quarterly* 38 (1990): 291–311.

9. Marshall R. Singer, *Intercultural Communication: A Perceptual Approach* (Englewood Cliffs, NJ: Prentice Hall, 1987) 168.

10. H. Weiss, M. A. Courty, W. Wetterstrom, F. Guichard, L. Senior, R. Meadow, and A. Curnow, "The Genesis and Collapse of Third Millenium North Mesopotamian Civilization," *Science*, 261 (1993): 995–1004.

11. Joel Achenbach, "Then the Climate Changed and Put Greenland on Ice," *San Diego Union-Tribune*, May 17, 1994, E2.

12. Charlotte Evans, "Barbed Wire, the Cutting Edge in Fencing," *Smithsonian* 22 (4) (July 1991): 72–78, 80, 82–83.

13. See Clayton Jones, "Cultural Crosscurrents Buffet the Orient," *Christian Science Monitor*, December 8, 1993, 11, 13; Sheila Tefft, "Satellite Broadcasts Create Stir Among Asian Regimes," *Christian Science Monitor*, December 8, 1993, 12–13.

14. Daniel L. Hartl, *Our Uncertain Heritage: Genetics and Human Diversity*, 2nd ed. (New York: Harper & Row, 1985).

15. Sandra Scarr, A. J. Pakstis, S. H. Katz, and W. B. Barker, "Absence of Relationship Between Degree of White Ancestry and Intellectual Skills Within a Black Population," *Human Genetics* 39 (1977): 69–86; Sandra Scarr and Richard A. Weinberg, "I.Q. Test Performance of Black Children Adopted by White Families," *American Psychologist* 31 (1976): 726–739; Richard A. Weinberg, Sandra Scarr, and Irwin D. Waldman, "The Minnesota Transracial Adoption Study: A Follow-up of IQ Test Performance at Adolescence," *Intelligence* 16 (1992): 117–135. See also Thomas J. Bouchard Jr., David T. Lykken, Matthew McGue, Nancy Segal, and Auke Tellegen, "Sources of Human Physiological Differences: The Minnesota Study of Twins Reared Apart," *Science* 250 (1990): 223–228.

16. Michael Winkelman, *Ethnic Relations in the U.S.: A Sociohistorical Cultural Systems Approach*, (Minneapolis: West, 1993): 67–68.

17. Cary Quan Gelernter, "Racial Realities," *Seattle Times/Post-Intelligencer*, January 15, 1989, K1+. Rpt. in *Ethnic Groups*, Vol. 4., ed. Eleanor Goldstein. (Boca Raton, FL: Social Issues Resources Ser., 1994), art. no. 83.

18. Linda Vigilant, Mark Stoneking, Henry Harpending, Kristen Hawkes, and Allan C. Wilson, "African Populations and the Evolution of Human Mitochondrial DNA," *Science* 253 (1991): 1503–1507.

19. For discussions of race and ethnicity as social and political distinctions rather than as a genetic one, see: Richard D. Alba, *Ethnic Identity: The Transformation of White America* (New Haven: Yale University Press, 1990); Martha E. Bernal and George P. Knight, *Ethnic Identity: Formation and Transmission Among Hispanics and Other Minorities* (Albany: State University of New York Press, 1993);

Stephen Cornell, *The Return of the Native: American Indian Political Resurgence* (New York: Oxford University Press, 1988); Ellis Cose, *A Nation of Strangers: Prejudice, Politics, and the Populating of America* (New York: William Morrow, 1992); Yen Le Espiritu, *Asian American Panethnicity: Bridging Institutions and Identities* (Philadelphia: Temple University Press, 1992); Susan E. Keefe and Amado M. Padilla, *Chicano Ethnicity* (Albuquerque: University of New Mexico Press, 1987); Susan Olzak, *The Dynamics of Ethnic Competition and Conflict* (Stanford, CA: Stanford University Press, 1992); Michael Omi and Howard Winant, *Racial Formation in the United States: From the 1960s to the 1980s* (New York: Routledge & Kegan Paul, 1986); Felix M. Padilla, *Latino Ethnic Consciousness: The Case of Mexican Americans and Puerto Ricans in Chicago* (Notre Dame, IN: University of Notre Dame Press, 1985); Mary C. Waters, *Ethnic Options: Choosing Identities in America* (Berkeley: University of California Press, 1990).

20. Jonathan Tilove, "Racial Identity in U.S. Is a Mix of Politics, Fashion and Genetics," *Houston Chronicle*, April 26, 1992, 8A+. Rpt. in *Ethnic Groups*, Vol. 4, ed. Eleanor Goldstein. Boca Raton, FL: Social Issues Resources Ser., 1994, art. no. 48. See also Scott Thybony, "Against All Odds, Black Seminole Won Their Freedom," *Smithsonian*, August, 1991: 90–101.
21. See, for instance, Richard J. Herrnstein and Charles Murray, *The Bell Curve: Intelligence and Class Structure in American Life*, (New York: Free Press, 1994).
22. See Richard L. Worsnop, "Native Americans," *CQ [Congressional Quarterly] Researcher*, May 8, 1992: 387–403. Rpt. in *Ethnic Groups*, Vol. 4, ed. Eleanor Goldstein. (Boca Raton, FL: Social Issues Resources Ser., 1994), art. no. 52.
23. Singer.

CHAPTER 5

1. Milton Rokeach, *Beliefs, Attitudes, and Values: A Theory of Organization and Change* (San Francisco: Jossey-Bass, 1969).
2. Elisabeth Bumiller, *May You Be the Mother of a Hundred Sons* (New York: Fawcett Columbine, 1990) 11.
3. Milton Rokeach, *The Nature of Human Values* (New York: Free Press, 1973); Milton Rokeach, "Value Theory and Communication Research: Review and Commentary," *Communication Yearbook 3*, ed. Dan Nimmo (New Brunswick, NJ: Transaction, 1979) 7–28.
4. Florence Rockwood Kluckhohn and Fred L. Strodtbeck, *Variations in Value Orientations* (Evanston, IL: Row, Peterson, 1960).
5. Edward C. Stewart, *American Cultural Patterns: A Cross-Cultural Perspective* (Pittsburgh: Regional Council for International Education, 1971); Edward C. Stewart and Milton J. Bennett, *American Cultural Patterns: A Cross-Cultural Perspective*, Revised Edition (Yarmouth, ME: Intercultural Press, 1991). For a general approach to U.S. American cultural patterns, see Esther Wanning, *Culture Shock: USA* (Singapore: Times Books, 1991).
6. John C. Condon and Fathi Yousef, *An Introduction to Intercultural Communication* (Indianapolis, IN: Bobbs-Merrill, 1975). Two excellent resources with thorough descriptions of the cultural patterns of U.S. American cultural groups are Don C. Locke, *Increasing Multicultural Understanding: A Comprehensive Model*

(Newbury Park, CA: Sage, 1992) and Eleanor W. Lynch and Marci J. Hanson, *Developing Cross-Cultural Competence: A Guide for Working with Young Children and Their Families* (Baltimore: Paul Brookes Publishing Co., 1992).

7. Jack L. Daniel and Geneva Smitherman, "How I Got Over: Communication Dynamics in the Black Community," *Quarterly Journal of Speech* 62 (1976): 32.

8. See, for example, Ringo Ma, "The Role of Unofficial Intermediaries in Interpersonal Conflicts in the Chinese Culture," *Communication Quarterly*, 40 (1992): 269–278.

9. Mary Jane Collier, Sidney A. Ribeau, and Michael L. Hecht, "Intracultural Communication Rules and Outcomes Within Three Domestic Cultures," *International Journal of Intercultural Relations* 10 (1986): 452. Also see Mary Jane Collier, "A Comparison of Conversations Among and Between Domestic Cultural Groups: How Intra- and Intercultural Competencies Vary," *Communication Quarterly* 36 (1988): 122–144.

10. Daniel and Smitherman 29.

11. Daniel and Smitherman 31.

12. Jamake Highwater, *The Primal Mind* (New York: New American Library, 1981).

13. Melvin Delgado, "Hispanic Cultural Values: Implications for Groups," *Small Group Behavior* 12 (1981): 75.

14. Daniel and Smitherman 29.

CHAPTER 6

1. Edward T. Hall, *Beyond Culture* (Garden City, NY: Anchor, 1977).

2. Geert Hofstede, *Culture's Consequences: International Differences in Work-Related Values* (Beverly Hills, CA: Sage, 1980); Geert Hofstede, *Cultures and Organizations: Software of the Mind* (London: McGraw-Hill, 1991).

3. Hofstede's total sample included about 117,000 respondents. Of these, 29,000 people were surveyed again several years later to assess response consistency. However, the actual data analyses reported by Hofstede were based on the average scores (means) obtained in each of the surveyed countries. Thus the sample size for the information reported here was 53; each sample (country or region) score was based on an aggregate of the individual scores obtained.

4. Joseph P. Forgas and Michael H. Bond, "Cultural Influences on the Perception of Interaction Episodes," *Personality and Social Psychology Bulletin* 11 (1985): 75–88; Geert Hofstede and Michael H. Bond, "Hofstede's Culture Dimensions: An Independent Validation using Rokeach's Value Survey," *Journal of Cross-Cultural Psychology* 15 (1984): 417–433.

5. Hui-Ching Chang and G. Richard Holt, "More Than Relationship: Chinese Interaction and the Principle of *Kuan-Hsi*," *Communication Quarterly* 39 (1991): 268.

6. See Harry C. Triandis, *The Analysis of Subjective Culture* (New York: Wiley, 1972); C. Harry Hui and Harry C. Triandis, "Individualism-Collectivism: A Study of Cross-Cultural Researchers," *Journal of Cross-Cultural Psychology* 17 (1986): 225–248.

7. Data from 22 countries are reported in: Chinese Culture Connection, "Chinese Values and the Search for Culture-Free Dimensions of Culture," *Journal of Cross-Cultural Psychology* 18 (1987): 143–164. Data on the People's Republic of China,

which were added to the survey after the initial publication of results, can be found in Geert Hofstede, *Cultures and Organizations: Software of the Mind* (London: McGraw-Hill, 1991), 166.

8. Hofstede, *Cultures and Organizations*, 164–166.

9. We draw on the following sources for the ideas presented: Chang and Holt, "More Than Relationship," 251–271; Guo-Ming Chen and Jensen Chung, "The Impact of Confucianism on Organizational Communication," *Communication Quarterly* 42 (1994): 93–105; Raymond Dawson, *Confucius* (New York: Hill and Wang, 1982); Geert Hofstede and Michael Harris Bond, "The Confucius Connection: From Cultural Roots to Economic Growth," *Organizational Dynamics*, 16 (1988): 5–21; Sonja Vegdahl Hur and Ben Seungwa Hur, *Culture Shock! Korea* (Singapore: Times Books International, 1988) 34–45; June Ock Yum, "Korean Philosophy and Communication," *Communication Theory: Eastern and Western Perspectives*, ed. D. Lawrence Kincaid (San Diego: Academic Press, 1987) 71–86; June Ock Yum, "The Practice of *Uye-Ri* in Interpersonal Relationships," *Communication Theory: Eastern and Western Perspectives*, ed. D. Lawrence Kincaid (San Diego: Academic Press, 1987) 87–100; June Ock Yum, "The Impact of Confucianism on Interpersonal Relationships and Communication Patterns in East Asia," *Communication Monographs* 55 (1988): 374–388. For an alternative view on the centrality of Confucian values to East Asian cultures, see Hui-Ching Chang and G. Richard Holt, "The Concept of *Yuan* and Chinese Interpersonal Relationships," *Cross-Cultural Interpersonal Communication*, ed. Stella Ting-Toomey and Felipe Korzenny (Newbury Park, CA: Sage, 1991) 28–57.

10. Hui-Ching Chang and G. Richard Holt, "More than Relationship: Chinese Interaction and The Principle of *Kuan-Hsi*," *Communication Quarterly* 39 (1991): 253–254.

11. Donald Dale Jackson, " 'Behave like your actions reflect on all Chinese,' " *Smithsonian*, February, 1991: 115.

12. Yum, "The Practice of *Uye-Ri*," 94.

13. Hofstede, *Cultures and Organizations*, 164.

14. Geert Hofstede and Michael Harris Bond, "The Confucius Connection: from Cultural Roots to Economic Growth," *Organizational Dynamics* 16 (1988): 19.

CHAPTER 7

1. Charles F. Hockett, "The Origin of Speech," *Human Communication: Language and Its Psychobiological Bases* (*Readings from Scientific American*) (San Francisco: W. H. Freeman, 1982) 5–12.

2. No, it isn't just that *tka* begins with two consonant sounds. *Spring* begins with three such sounds. For an interesting discussion of the rules of language, see Steven Pinker, *The Language Instinct: How the Mind Creates Language* (New York: HarperCollins, 1994).

3. Roger Brown, *Social Psychology* (New York: Free Press, 1965); quoted in Donald W. Klopf, *Intercultural Encounters: The Fundamentals of Intercultural Communication* (Englewood, CO: Morton, 1987) 137.

4. Wen Shu Lee, "On Not Missing the Boat: A Processual Method for Inter/cultural Understanding of Idioms and Lifeworld," *Journal of Applied Communication Research* 22 (1994): 141–161.

5. Christiane F. Gonzalez, "Translation," *Handbook of International and Intercultural Communication,* ed. Molefi Kete Asante and William B. Gudykunst (Newbury Park, CA: Sage, 1989) 484.

6. For an example of the kinds of translation problems that occur in organizations with a multilingual work force, see Stephen E. Banks and Anna Banks, "Translation as Problematic Discourse in Organizations," *Journal of Applied Communication Research,* 19 (1991) 223–241. See also Henriette W. Langdon, *The Interpreter Translator Process in the Educational Setting* (Sacramento, CA: Resources in Special Education, California State University with the California Department of Education, 1994).

7. Eugene A. Nida, *Toward a Science of Translating* (Leiden: E. J. Brill, 1964).

8. Lee Sechrest, Todd L. Fay, and S. M. Zaidi, "Problems of Translation in Cross-cultural Communication," *Intercultural Communication: A Reader,* 5th ed., ed. Larry A. Samovar and Richard E. Porter, (Belmont, CA: Wadsworth, 1988) 253–262.

9. There is some evidence that as early as the fifteenth century an Asian scholar named Bhartvhari, in a work entitled *Vahyapidan,* argued that speech patterns are determined by social contexts.

10. Edward Sapir, quoted in Benjamin Lee Whorf, *Language, Thought, and Reality* (Cambridge, MA: MIT Press, 1956) 134.

11. For a thorough summary and discussion of the experimental research in psychology investigating the validity of the linguistic determinism hypothesis, see: Curtis Hardin and Mahzarin R. Banaji, "The Influence of Language on Thought," *Social Cognition* 11 (1993): 277–308; Earl Hunt and Franca Agnoli, "The Whorfian Hypothesis: A Cognitive Psychology Perspective," *Psychological Review* 98 (1991): 377–389.

12. Whorf suggested there may be about 7 words for snow, though the actual number is closer to 12. Over time and numerous retellings of this example, however, the number of words claimed to represent forms of snow has increased dramatically, typically to the 17–23 range; the *New York Times* once cavalierly referred to 100 different words. See Geoffrey K. Pullum, *The Great Eskimo Vocabulary Hoax, and Other Irreverent Essays on the Study of Language* (Chicago: University of Chicago Press, 1991); "The melting of a Mighty Myth," *Newsweek,* July 22, 1991: 63.

13. Richard W. Brislin, Kenneth Cushner, Craig Cherrie, and Mahealani Yong, *Intercultural Interactions: A Practical Guide* (Beverly Hills, CA: Sage, 1986) 276.

14. John C. Condon and Fathi S. Yousef, *An Introduction to Intercultural Communication* (Yarmouth, ME: Intercultural Press, 1975) 182.

15. Michael Cole and Sylvia Scribner, *Culture and Thought: A Psychological Introduction* (New York: Wiley, 1974) 2.

16. Eleanor Rosch Heider and Donald C. Olivier, "The Structure of the Color Space in Naming and Memory for Two Languages," *Cognitive Psychology* 3(1972): 337–354.

17. For a more complete discussion of the evidence on variations in vocabulary of the color spectrum, see Cole and Scribner 45–50; Thomas M. Steinfatt, "Linguistic Relativity: Toward a Broader View," *Language, Communication, and Culture: Current Directions,* ed. Stella Ting-Toomey and Felipe Korzenny (Newbury Park, CA: Sage, 1989) 35–75.

18. Stephen W. Littlejohn, *Theories of Human Communication,* 4th ed. (Belmont, CA: Wadsworth, 1992) 209.

19. Li-Rong Lilly Cheng, *Assessing Asian Language Performance: Guidelines for Evaluating Limited-English-Language Proficient Students* (Rockville, MD: Aspen, 1987) 8.

20. For an interesting discussion of the difficulties that Mandarin speakers might have in using English pronouns appropriately, see Stephen P. Banks, "Power Pronouns and Intercultural Understanding," *Language, Communication, and Culture: Current Directions*, eds. Stella Ting-Toomey and Felipe Korzenny (Newbury Park, CA: Sage, 1989) 180–198.
21. Michael Dorris, *The Broken Cord* (New York: Harper & Row, 1989) 2.
22. See Earl Hunt and Franca Agnoli, "The Whorfian Hypothesis: A Cognitive Psychology Perspective," *Psychological Review* 98 (1991): 377–389.
23. Wilma M. Roger, *National Foreign Language Center Occasional Papers* (Washington, DC: Johns Hopkins University Press, February 1989).
24. Studies of the relationship of language and intercultural communication are often conducted under the rubric of "intergroup behavior" or "intergroup communication." See, for example, John C. Turner and Howard Giles, eds., *Intergroup Behavior* (Chicago: University of Chicago Press, 1981).
25. Henri Tajfel, "Social Categorization, Social Identity, and Social Comparison," *Differentiation Between Social Groups*, ed. Henri Tajfel (London: Academic Press, 1978).
26. Howard Giles and Patricia Johnson, "The Role of Language in Ethnic Group Relations," *Intergroup Behavior*, ed. John C. Turner and Howard Giles (Chicago: University of Chicago Press, 1981) 199–243.
27. Joshua A. Fishman, "Language and Ethnicity," *Language, Ethnicity, and Intergroup Relations*, ed. Howard Giles (London: Academic Press, 1977) 15–58.
28. William B. Gudykunst, "Cultural Variability in Ethnolinguistic Identity," *Language, Communication, and Culture: Current Directions*, ed. Stella Ting-Toomey and Felipe Korzenney (Newbury Park, CA: Sage, 1989) 223.
29. Rèal Allard and Rodrique Landry, "Subjective Ethnolinguistic Vitality Viewed as a Belief System," *Journal of Multilingual and Multicultural Development* 7 (1986): 1–12.
30. Howard Giles and Arlene Franklyn-Stokes, "Communicator Characteristics," *Handbook of International and Intercultural Communication*, ed. Molefi Kete Asante and William B. Gudykunst (Newbury Park, CA: Sage, 1989) 117–144.
31. Nancy F. Burroughs and Vicki Marie, "Communication Orientations of Micronesian and American Students," *Communication Research Reports* 7 (1990): 139–146.
32. Ellen Bouchard Ryan, Howard Giles, and Richard J. Sebastian, "An Integrative Perspective for the Study of Attitudes Toward Language Variation," *Attitudes Toward Language Variation: Social and Applied Contexts*, ed. Ellen Bouchard Ryan and Howard Giles (London: Edward Arnold, 1982) 1.
33. Michael L. Hecht, Mary Jane Collier, and Sidney Ribeau, *African American Communication: Ethnic Identity and Cultural Interpretation* (Newbury Park, CA: Sage, 1993) 84–89.
34. John R. Edwards, *Language Attitudes and Their Implications Among English Speakers*, ed. Ellen Bouchard Ryan and Howard Giles (London: Edward Arnold, 1982) 22.
35. E. Hope Bock and James H. Pitts, "The Effect of Three Levels of Black Dialect on Perceived Speaker Image," *Speech Teacher* 24 (1975): 218–225.
36. For an excellent summary of research on the effect of accent and dialect variations among ethnic groups, see Giles and Franklyn-Stokes. A recent study on the interaction between accented speech and the speaker's status can be found in Diane M. Badzinski, "The Impact of Accent and Status on Information Recall and Perception Information," *Communication* 5 (1992): 99–106.
37. Edwards 22–27.

38. Richard Rodriguez, *Hunger of Memory: The Education of Richard Rodriguez* (Toronto: Bantam Books, 1982) 14–16.

39. Hecht, Collier, and Ribeau 90.

40. Abdelala Bentahila, *Language Attitudes Among Arabic-French Bilinguals in Morocco* (London: Multilingual Matters, 1983) 27–65.

CHAPTER 8

1. Peter A. Andersen, "Consciousness, Cognition, and Communication," *Western Journal of Speech Communication* 50 (1986): 87–101; Peter A. Andersen, John P. Garrison, and Janis F. Andersen, "Implications of a Neurophysiological Approach for the Study of Nonverbal Communication," *Human Communication Research* 6 (1979): 74–89.

2. Albert E. Scheflen, "On Communication Processes," *Nonverbal Behavior: Applications and Cross-cultural Implications*, ed. Aaron Wolfgang (New York: Academic Press, 1979) 1–16.

3. Sheila J. Ramsey, "Nonverbal Behavior: An Intercultural Perspective," *Handbook of Intercultural Communication*, ed. Molefi Kete Asante, Eileen Newmark, and Cecil A. Blake (Beverly Hills, CA: Sage, 1979) 111.

4. Edward T. Hall, *The Silent Language* (Garden City, NY: Doubleday, 1959).

5. Charles Darwin, *The Expression of Emotions in Man and Animals* (New York: Appleton, 1872).

6. Michael Argyle, *Bodily Communication* (New York: International Universities Press, 1975) 95.

7. Paul Ekman and Wallace V. Friesen, "Constants Across Cultures in the Face and Emotion," *Journal of Personality and Social Psychology*, 17 (1971): 124–129. Paul Ekman and Wallace V. Friesen, *Unmasking the Face* (Englewood Cliffs, NJ: Prentice Hall, 1975). Alan J. Fridlund, Paul Ekman, and Harriet Oster, "Facial Expressions of Emotion: Review of Literature, 1970–1983," *Nonverbal Behavior and Communication*, 2nd ed., ed. Aron W. Siegman and Stanley Feldstein (Hillsdale, NJ: Lawrence Erlbaum, 1987) 143–224.

8. Robert Ardrey, *The Territorial Imperative: A Personal Inquiry into the Animal Origins of Property and Nations* (New York: Atheneum, 1966).

9. Judith N. Martin, Mitchell R. Hammer, and Lisa Bradford, "The Influence of Cultural and Situational Contexts on Hispanic and Non-Hispanic Communication Competence Behaviors," *Communication Quarterly* 42 (1994): 160–179.

10. Robert G. Harper, Arthur N. Wiens, and Joseph D. Matarazzo, *Nonverbal Communication: The State of the Art* (New York: Wiley, 1978).

11. Sharon Ruhly, *Intercultural Communication*, 2nd ed. (Chicago: Science Research Associates, 1982) 23–26.

12. John C. Condon and Fathi S. Yousef, *Intercultural Communication* (Indianapolis, IN: Bobbs-Merrill, 1975) 122.

13. Ray Birdwhistell, *Kinesics and Context: Essays on Body Motion Communication* (Philadelphia: University of Pennsylvania, 1970) 34.

14. Aaron Wolfgang, "The Teacher and Nonverbal Behavior in the Multicultural Classroom," *Nonverbal Behavior: Applications and Cultural Implications*, ed. Aaron Wolfgang (New York: Academic Press, 1979) 167.

15. Joseph A. DeVito, *Messages: Building Interpersonal Communication Skills* (New York: Harper & Row, 1990) 218.

16. Paul Ekman and Wallace V. Friesen, "The Repertoire of Nonverbal Behavior: Categories, Origins, Usage, and Coding," *Semiotica* 1 (1969): 49–98.

17. Tom Brosnahan, *Turkey: A Travel Survival Kit*, 2nd ed. (Victoria, Australia: Lonely Planet, 1988) 27.

18. Paul Ekman, Wallace V. Friesen, and Phoebe Ellsworth, *Emotion in the Human Face: Guidelines for Research and an Integration of Findings* (New York: Pergamon, 1972).

19. See Klaus R. Scherer and Harald G. Wallbott, "Evidence for Universality and Cultural Variation of Differential Emotion Response Patterning," *Journal of Personality and Social Psychology* 66 (1994): 310–328.

20. James A. Russell, "Is There Universal Recognition of Emotion from Facial Expression? A Review of the Cross-Cultural Studies," *Psychological Bulletin* 115 (1994): 102–141; James A. Russell, "Culture and the Categorization of Emotion," *Psychological Bulletin* 110 (1991): 426–450.

21. Michael Harris Bond, "Emotions and Their Expressions in Chinese Culture," *Journal of Nonverbal Behavior* 17 (1993): 245–262.

22. Marianne LaFrance and Clara Mayo, "Racial Differences in Gaze Behavior During Conversations: Two Systematic Observational Studies," *Journal of Personality and Social Psychology* 33 (976): 547–552.

23. Edward T. Hall, *The Hidden Dimension* (Garden City, NY: Doubleday, 1966).

24. Edward T. Hall and Mildred Reed Hall, *Understanding Cultural Differences* (Yarmouth, ME: Intercultural Press, 1990) 12.

25. Hall and Hall, 180.

26. Hall and Hall 10.

27. Stanley E. Jones and A. Elaine Yarbrough, "A Naturalistic Study of the Meanings of Touch," *Communication Monographs* 52 (1985): 19–56.

28. Nancy M. Henley, *Body Politics: Power, Sex, and Nonverbal Communication* (Englewood Cliffs, NJ: Prentice Hall, 1977).

29. Hall and Hall 11.

30. Dean Barnlund, "Communication Styles in Two Cultures: Japan and the United States," *Organizational Behavior in Face-to-Face Interaction*, eds. Adam Kendon, Richard M. Harris, and Mary Ritchie Key (The Hague: Mouton, 1975) 427–456.

31. Sidney M. Jourard, "An Exploratory Study of Body Accessibility," *British Journal of Social and Clinical Psychology* 5 (1966): 221–231.

32. John Reader, *Man on Earth* (New York: Harper & Row, 1988) 91. Reader's ideas are based on Paul Spencer, *The Samburu: A Study in Gerontocracy in a Nomadic Tribe* (London: Routledge & Kegan Paul, 1968).

33. Reader 163.

34. Edward T. Hall, "The Hidden Dimensions of Time and Space in Today's World," *Cross-cultural Perspectives in Nonverbal Communication*, ed. Fernando Poyatos (Toronto: C. J. Hogrefe, 1988) 151.

35. Hall, *Silent Language*.

36. Hall, *The Silent Language*, 178.

37. Alexander Gonzalez and Philip G. Zimbardo, "Time in Perspective," *Psychology Today* 19 (March 1985): 20–26.

38. Rosita Daskel Albert and Gayle L. Nelson, "Hispanic/Anglo-American Differences in Attributions to Paralinguistic Behavior," *International Journal of Intercultural Relations* 17 (1993): 19–40.

39. Mara B. Adelman and Myron W. Lustig, "Intercultural Communication Problems as Perceived by Saudi Arabian and American Managers," *International Journal of Intercultural Relations* 5 (1981): 349–364; Myron W. Lustig, "Cultural and Communication Patterns of Saudi Arabians," *Intercultural Communication: A Reader*, 5th ed., ed. Larry A. Samovar and Richard E. Porter (Belmont, CA: Wadsworth, 1988) 101–103.

40. William S. Condon, "Cultural Microrhythms," *Interaction Rhythms: Periodicity in Communicative Behavior*, ed. Martha Davis (New York: Human Sciences Press, 1982) 66.

41. Befu, 1975; as quoted in Sheila J. Ramsey, "Nonverbal Behavior" 118.

42. Holley S. Hodgins and Richard Koestner, "The Origins of Nonverbal Sensitivity," *Personality and Social Psychology Bulletin* 19 (1993): 466–473.

43. Anna-Marie Dew and Colleen Ward, "The Effects of Ethnicity and Culturally Congruent and Incongruent Nonverbal Behaviors on Interpersonal Attraction," *Journal of Applied Social Psychology* 23 (1993): 1376–1389.

44. David Matsumoto and Tsutomu Kudoh, "American-Japanese Cultural Differences in Attributions of Personality Based on Smiles," *Journal of Nonverbal Behavior* 17 (1993): 231–243. See also Ann Bainbridge Frymier, Donald W. Klopf, and Satoshi Ishii, "Affect Orientation: Japanese Compared to Americans," *Communication Research Reports* 7 (1990): 63–66; Donald W. Klopf, "Japanese Communication Practices: Recent Comparative Research," *Communication Quarterly* 39 (1991): 130–143.

CHAPTER 9

1. Robert B. Kaplan, "Cultural Thought Patterns in Intercultural Education" *Language Learning* 16 (966): 15.

2. Laurie G. Kirszner and Stephen R. Mandell, *Writing: A College Rhetoric*, 2nd ed. (New York: Holt, Rinehart & Winston, 1988) 185, 188.

3. Kaplan.

4. Satoshi Ishii, "Thought Patterns as Modes of Rhetoric: The United States and Japan," *Intercultural Communication: A Reader*, 4th ed., ed. Larry A. Samovar and Richard E. Porter (Belmont, CA: Wadsworth, 1985) 97–102.

5. Yamuna Kachru, "Writers in Hindi and English," *Writing Across Languages and Cultures: Issues in Contrastive Rhetoric*, ed. Alan C. Purvis (Newbury Park, CA: Sage, 1988) 109–137.

6. Arpita Misra, "Discovering Connections," *Language and Social Identity*, ed. John L. Gumperz (Cambridge: Cambridge University Press, 1982) 57–71.

7. Linda Wai Ling Young, "Inscrutability Revisited," *Language and Social Identity*, ed. John L. Gumperz (Cambridge: Cambridge University Press, 1982) 72–84.

8. Joy Reid, "A Computer Text Analysis of Four Cohesion Devices in English Discourse by Native and Nonnative Writers," *Journal of Second Language Writing* 1 (1992): 90.

9. J. Hinds, "Reader versus Writer Responsibility: A New Typology," *Writing Across Languages: Analysis of L2 Written Text*, ed. Ulla Connor and Robert B. Kaplan (Reading, MA: Addison-Wesley, 1986) 141–152.

10. Judith Sanders, Robert Gass, Richard Wiseman, and Jon Bruschke, "Ethnic Comparison and Measurement of Argumentativeness, Verbal Aggressiveness, and Need for Cognition," *Communication Reports* 5 (1992): 50–56.

11. James F. Hamill, *Ethno-logic: The Anthropology of Human Reasoning* (Urbana, IL: University of Illinois Press, 1990) 23.

12. Stephen Toulmin, *The Uses of Argument* (Cambridge: Cambridge University Press, 1958). See also Wayne Brockriede and Douglas Ehninger, "Toulmin on Argument: An Interpretation and Application," *Quarterly Journal of Speech* 46 (1960): 44–53; Sonja K. Foss, Karen A. Foss, and Robert Trapp, *Contemporary Perspectives on Rhetoric* (Prospect Heights, IL: Waveland Press, 1985) 77–100.

13. Stephen Toulmin, *Human Understanding, Volume I: The Collective Use and Evolution of Concepts* (Princeton, NJ: Princeton University Press, 1972) 95.

14. Michael Cole and Sylvia Scribner, *Culture and Thought: A Psychological Introduction* (New York: Wiley, 1974) 3.

15. Barbara Johnstone, "Linguistic Strategies for Persuasive Discourse," *Language, Communication, and Culture: Current Directions*, ed. Stella Ting-Toomey and Felipe Korzenny (Newbury Park, CA: Sage, 1989) 139–156.

16. John C. Condon, *Good Neighbors: Communicating with the Mexicans* (Yarmouth, ME: Intercultural Press, 1985).

17. S. B. Lubman, "Negotiations in China: Observations of a Lawyer Communicating with China," ed. R. A. Kapp (Chicago: Intercultural Press, 1983).

18. Johnstone.

19. John T. Masterson, Norman H. Watson, and Elaine Cichon, "Cultural Differences in Public Speaking," *World Communication* 20 (1991): 39–47.

20. Patricia A. Sullivan, "Signification and African-American Rhetoric: A Case Study of Jesse Jackson's 'Common Ground and Common Sense' Speech," *Communication Quarterly* 41 (1993): 1–15.

21. D. Lawrence Kincaid, "Communication East and West: Points of Departure," *Communication Theory: Eastern and Western Perspectives*, ed. D. Lawrence Kincaid (San Diego: Academic Press, 1987) 337.

22. Akira Tsujimura, "Some Characteristics of the Japanese Way of Communication," *Communication Theory: Eastern and Western Perspectives*, ed. D. Lawrence Kincaid (San Diego: Academic Press, 1987) 115–126.

23. Donald W. Klopf, *Intercultural Encounters: The Fundamentals of Intercultural Communication*, 2nd ed. (Englewood Cliffs, NJ: Morgan, 1991) 181.

24. June Ock Yum, "Korean Philosophy and Communication," *Communication Theory: Eastern and Western Perspectives*, ed. D. Lawrence Kincaid (San Diego: Academic Press, 1987) 79.

25. Yum 83.

26. Peter Nwosu, "Negotiating with the Swazis," *Howard Journal of Communication* 1 (1988): 148.

27. Aino Sallinen-Kuparinen, James C. McCroskey, and Virginia P. Richmond, "Willingness to Communicate, Communication Apprehension, Introversion, and Self-Reported Communication Competence: Finnish and American Comparisons," *Communication Research Reports* 8 (1991): 55–64.

28. Keith H. Basso, " 'To Give Up on Words': Silence in Western Apache Culture," *Cultural Communication and Intercultural Contact*, ed. Donal L. Carbaugh (Hillsdale, NJ: Lawrence Erlbaum, 1990) 303–320.

29. Basso 308.

30. See, for example, Donal L. Carbaugh, ed., *Cultural Communication and Intercultural Contact* (Hillsdale, NJ: Lawrence Erlbaum, 1990).

31. Klopf.

32. William B. Gudykunst and Stella Ting-Toomey, *Culture and Interpersonal Communication* (Newbury Park, CA: Sage, 1988) 99–116.

33. Thomas Kochman, "Force Fields in Black and White," *Cultural Communication and Intercultural Contact,* ed. Donal Carbaugh (Hillsdale, NJ: Lawrence Erlbaum, 1990) 193–194.

34. Melanie Booth-Butterfield and Felecia Jordan, "Communication Adaptation Among Racially Homogeneous and Heterogeneous Groups," *Southern Communication Journal* 54 (1989): 265.

35. Ronald Scollon and Suzanne Wong-Scollon, "Athabaskan-English Interethnic Communication," *Cultural Communication and Intercultural Contact,* ed. Donal Carbaugh (Hillsdale, NJ: Lawrence Erlbaum, 1990) 270.

36. Scollon and Wong-Scollon 273.

CHAPTER 10

1. John Paul Feig, *A Common Core: Thais and Americans,* rev. Elizabeth Mortlock (Yarmouth, ME: Intercultural Press, 1989) 50.

2. John C. Condon, *Good Neighbors: Communicating with the Mexicans* (Yarmouth, ME: Intercultural Press, 1985).

3. Daniel Perlman and Beverley Fehr, "The Development of Intimate Relationships," *Intimate Relationships: Development, Dynamics, and Deterioration,* ed. Daniel Perlman and Steven Duck (Newbury Park, CA: Sage, 1987) 13–42.

4. Michael L. Hecht, Mary Jane Collier, and Sidney A. Ribeau, *African American Communication: Ethnic Identity and Cultural Interpretation* (Newbury Park, CA: Sage, 1993).

5. Mary Jane Collier, "Cultural Background and the Culture of Friendships: Normative Patterns," Paper presented at the Annual Conference of the International Communication Association, San Francisco, May 1989. See also Mary Jane Collier, "Conflict Competence within African, Mexican, and Anglo American Friendships," *Cross-Cultural Interpersonal Communication,* ed. Stella Ting-Toomey and Felipe Korzenny (Newbury Park, CA: Sage, 1991) 132–154.

6. Ge Gao, "Stability of Romantic Relationships in China and the United States," *Cross-Cultural Interpersonal Communication,* ed. Stella Ting-Toomey and Felipe Korzenny (Newbury Park, CA: Sage, 1990) 99–115.

7. Irene I. Blea, *Toward A Chicano Social Science* (New York: Praeger, 1988).

8. Don C. Locke, *Increasing Multicultural Understanding: A Comprehensive Model* (Newbury Park, CA: Sage, 1992) 55.

9. Lin Yutang, *The Chinese Way of Life* (New York: World Publishing, 1972) 78.

10. William D. Wilder, *Communication, Social Structure and Development in Rural Malaysia: A Study of Kampung Kuala Bera* (London: Athlone Press, 1982) 107.

11. Joe Cummings, Susan Forsyth, John Noble, Alan Samagalski, and Tony Wheelan, *Indonesia: A Travel Survival Guide* (Berkeley, CA: Lonely Planet Publications, 1990) 321.

12. Albert Mehrabian, *Silent Messages* (Belmont, CA: Wadsworth, 1971).

13. Edward T. Hall, *The Hidden Dimension* (Garden City, NY: Doubleday, 1966).

14. Peter A. Andersen, Myron W. Lustig, and Janis F. Andersen, "Changes in Latitude, Changes in Attitude: The Relationship Between Climate and Interpersonal Communication Predispositions," *Communication Quarterly* 38 (1990): 291–311.

15. Wilder 105.

16. Feig 41.
17. William O. Beeman, *Language, Status, and Power in Iran* (Bloomington: Indiana University Press, 1986) 86.
18. Harvey Taylor, "Misunderstood Japanese Nonverbal Communication," *Gengo Seikatsu* (Language Life), 1974; quoted in Helmut Morsbach, "The Importance of Silence and Stillness in Japanese Nonverbal Communication: A Cross-cultural Approach," *Cross-cultural Perspectives in Nonverbal Communication,* ed. Fernando Poyatos (Toronto: C. J. Hogrefe, 1988) 206.
19. See Erving Goffman, *Interaction Ritual: Essays on Face-to-Face Behavior.* (Garden City, NY: Anchor Books, 1967).
20. David Yau-fai Ho, "On the Concept of Face," *American Journal of Sociology,* 81 (1976): 867–884.
21. Penelope Brown and Stephen Levinson, "Universals in Language Use: Politeness Phenomena," *Questions and Politeness: Strategies in Social Interaction,* ed. Esther N. Goody (Cambridge: Cambridge University Press, 1978) 56–289; Penelope Brown and Stephen Levinson, *Politeness: Some Universals in Language Use* (Cambridge: Cambridge University Press, 1987). Though Brown and Levinson's ideas have been criticized on several points, the portion of their ideas expressed here are generally accepted. For a summary of the criticisms, see: Karen Tracy and Sheryl Baratz, "The Case for Case Studies of Facework," *The Challenge of Facework: Cross-Cultural and Interpersonal Issues,* ed. Stella Ting-Toomey (Albany: State University of New York Press, 1994) 287–305.
22. Greg Leichty and James L. Applegate, "Social-Cognitive and Situational Influences on the Use of Face-Saving Persuasive Strategies," *Human Communication Research,* 17 (1991): 451–484.
23. Tracy and Baratz 288.
24. We have modified Lim's terminology and concepts somewhat but draw on his overall conception. See Tae-Seop Lim, "Politeness Behavior in Social Influence Situations," *Seeking Compliance: The Production of Interpersonal Influence Messages,* ed. James Price Dillard (Scottsdale, AZ: Gorsuch Scarisbrick, 1990) 75–86; Tae-Seop Lim, "Facework and Interpersonal Relationships," *The Challenge of Facework: Cross-Cultural and Interpersonal Issues,* ed. Stella Ting-Toomey (Albany: State University of New York Press, 1994) 209–229; Tae-Seop Lim and John Waite Bowers, "Facework: Solidarity, Approbation, and Tact," *Human Communication Research* 17 (1991): 415–450.
25. Lim 211
26. Hsien Chin Hu, "The Chinese Concepts of 'Face'," *American Anthropologist* 46 (1944): 45–64.
27. Francis L. K. Hsu, "The Self in Cross-Cultural Perspective," *Culture and Self: Asian and Western Perspectives,* ed. Anthony J. Marsella, George DeVos, and Francis L. K. Hsu (New York: Tavistock, 1985) 33.
28. Leo Rosten, *The Joys of Yiddish* (New York: McGraw-Hill, 1968) 234.
29. Hu 61–62.
30. Brown and Levinson 66.
31. Brown and Levinson; see also Robert T. Craig, Karen Tracy, and Frances Spisak, "The Discourse of Requests: Assessment of a Politeness Approach," *Human Communication Research,* 12 (1986): 437–468.
32. Ron Scollon and Suzie Wong Scollon, "Face Parameters in East-West Discourse," *The Challenge of Facework: Cross-Cultural and Interpersonal Issues,* ed. Stella Ting-Toomey (Albany: State University of New York Press, 1994) 133–157.

33. Scollon and Scollon 137.

34. Lijuan Stahl, "Face-Negotiation," unpublished manuscript (San Diego: San Diego State University, 1993) 12–13.

35. See Stella Ting-Toomey, "Toward a Theory of Conflict and Culture," *Communication, Culture, and Organizational Processes,* ed. William B. Gudykunst, Lea P. Stewart, and Stella Ting-Toomey (Beverly Hills, CA: Sage, 1985) 71–86; Stella Ting-Toomey, "Intercultural Conflict Styles: A Face-Negotiation Theory," *Theories in Intercultural Communication,* ed. Young Yun Kim and William B. Gudykunst (Newbury Park, CA: Sage, 1988) 213–235; Stella Ting-Toomey, "Intergroup Diplomatic Communication: A Face-Negotiation Perspective," *Communicating for Peace,* ed. Felipe Korzenny and Stella Ting-Toomey (Newbury Park: Sage, 1990) 75–95; Stella Ting-Toomey and Beth-Ann Cocroft, "Face and Facework: Theoretical and Research Issues," *The Challenge of Facework: Cross-Cultural and Interpersonal Issues,* ed. Stella Ting-Toomey (Albany: State University of New York Press, 1994) 307–340.

36. Dean C. Barnlund, "Apologies: Japanese and American Styles," *International Journal of Intercultural Relations,* 14 (1990): 193–206; William R. Cupach and T. Todd Imahori, "Managing Social Predicaments Created by Others: A Comparison of Japanese and American Facework," *Western Journal of Communication* 57 (1993): 431–444; William R. Cupach and T. Todd Imahori, "A Cross-Cultural Comparison of the Interpretation and Management of Face: U.S. American and Japanese Responses to Embarrassing Predicaments," *International Journal of Intercultural Relations,* 18 (1994): 193–219; Naoki Nomura and Dean Barnlund, "Patterns of Interpersonal Criticism in Japan and the United States," *International Journal of Intercultural Relations,* 7 (1983): 1–18; Kiyoko Sueda and Richard L. Wiseman, "Embarrassment Remediation in Japan and the United States," *International Journal of Intercultural Relations,* 16 (1992): 159–173.

37. Stahl 14.

38. Robyn Penman, "Facework in Communication: Conceptual and Moral Challenges," *The Challenge of Facework: Cross-Cultural and Interpersonal Issues* ed. Stella Ting-Toomey (Albany: State University of New York Press, 1994) 21.

39. Our discussion of uncertainty reduction theory is based on many sources, including the following: Charles R. Berger, "Communicating Under Uncertainty," *Interpersonal Processes: New Directions in Communication Research,* ed. Michael E. Roloff and Gerald R. Miller (Newbury Park, CA: Sage, 1987) 39–62; Charles R. Berger and James J. Bradac, *Language and Social Knowledge: Uncertainty in Interpersonal Relations* (London: Edward Arnold, 1982); Charles R. Berger and Richard J. Calabrese, "Some Explorations in Initial Interaction and Beyond: Toward a Developmental Theory of Interpersonal Communication," *Human Communication Research* 1 (1975): 99–112; Glen W. Clatterbuck, "Attributional Confidence and Uncertainty in Initial Interaction," *Human Communication Research* 5 (1979): 147–157; William Douglas, "Uncertainty, Information-Seeking, and Liking During Initial Interaction, *Western Journal of Speech Communication* 54 (1990): 66–81; William B. Gudykunst, "The Influence of Cultural Similarity, Type of Relationship, and Self-Monitoring on Uncertainty Reduction Processes," *Communication Monographs* 52 (1985): 203–217; William B. Gudykunst, Elizabeth Chua, and Alisa J. Gray, "Cultural Dissimilarities and Uncertainty Reduction Processes," *Communication Yearbook 10,* ed. Margaret McLaughlin (Beverly Hills, CA: Sage, 1984) 456–469; William B. Gudykunst and Tsukasa Nishida, "Individual and Cultural Influences on Uncertainty Reduction," *Communication Monographs* 51 (1984): 23–36; William B. Gudykunst, Seung-Mock

Yang, and Tsukasa Nishida, "A Cross-cultural Test of Uncertainty Reduction Theory: Comparisons of Acquaintances, Friends, and Dating Relationships in Japan, Korea, and the United States," *Human Communication Research* 11 (1985): 407–455; Kathy Kellermann and Rodney Reynolds, "When Ignorance Is Bliss: The Role of Motivation to Reduce Uncertainty in Uncertainty Reduction Theory," *Human Communication Research* 17 (1990): 5–75; Sally Planalp and James M. Honeycutt, "Events That Increase Uncertainty in Personal Relationships," *Human Communication Research* 11 (1985): 593–604; Sally Planalp, Diane K. Rutherford, and James M. Honeycutt, "Events That Increase Uncertainty in Personal Relationships II: Replication and Extension," *Human Communication Research* 14 (1988): 516–547; Michael Sunnafrank, "Predicted Outcome Value During Initial Interactions: A Reformulation of Uncertainty Reduction Theory," *Human Communication Research* 13 (1986): 3–33.

40. Edna B. Foa and Uriel G. Foa, "Resource Theory: Interpersonal Behavior as Exchange," *Social Exchange: Advances in Theory and Research*, ed. Kenneth Gergen, Martin S. Greenberg, and Richard H. Willis (New York: Plenum Press, 1980) 77–101.

41. Berger 41.

42. Gudykunst and Nishida.

43. Tsukasa Nishida, "Sequence Patterns of Self-Disclosure Among Japanese and North American Students," Paper presented at the Conference on Communication in Japan and the United States, Fullerton, CA, March, 1991.

44. Judith A. Sanders, Richard L. Wiseman, and S. Irene Matz, "A Cross-cultural Comparison of Uncertainty Reduction Theory: The Cases of Ghana and the United States," Paper presented to the Annual Conference of the International Communication Association, San Francisco, May 1989.

45. Changsheng Xi, "Individualism and Collectivism in American and Chinese Societies," *Our Voices: Essays in Culture, Ethnicity, and Communication*, ed. Alberto González, Marsha Houston, and Victoria Chen (Los Angeles: Roxbury Publishing, 1994) 155.

46. Robert Littlefield, "Self-Disclosure Among Some Negro, White, and Mexican-American Adolescents," *Journal of Counseling Psychology* 21 (1974) 133–136.

47. Sidney Jourard, "Self-Disclosure Patterns in British and American College Females, *Journal of Social Psychology* 54 (1961): 315–320.

48. Stella Ting-Toomey, "Intimacy Expressions in Three Cultures: France, Japan, and the United States," *International Journal of Intercultural Relations* 15 (1991): 29–46.

49. Dean Barnlund, *Public and Private Self in Japan and the United States: Communicative Styles of Two Cultures* (Tokyo: Simul Press, 1975); Ting-Toomey, "Intimacy Expressions."

50. Sidney Jourard, *Self-Disclosure: An Experimental Analysis of the Transparent Self* (New York: Wiley, 1971).

51. George Levinger and David J. Senn, "Disclosure of Feelings in Marriage," *Merrill Palmer Quarterly* 13 (1987): 237–249.

52. Our discussion of managing conflict draws on a number of works, including Ting-Toomey, "Conflict and Culture"; Stella Ting-Toomey, "Conflict Styles in Black and White Subjective Cultures," *Current Research in Interethnic Communication*, ed. Young Yun Kim (Beverly Hills, CA: Sage, 1986); Ting-Toomey, "Face Negotiation Theory."

53. Ringo Ma, "The Role of Unofficial Intermediaries in Interpersonal Conflicts in the Chinese Culture," *Communication Quarterly* 40 (1992): 269–278.

54. Ting-Toomey, "Face Negotiation Theory."

CHAPTER 11

1. Tamar Katriel, *Communal Webs: Communication and Culture in Contemporary Israel* (Albany, NY: State University of New York Press, 1991) 35–49.

2. Joseph P. Forgas and Michael H. Bond, "Cultural Influences on the Perception of Interaction Episodes," *Journal of Cross-Cultural Psychology*, 11 (1985): 75–88.

3. Robert T. Craig and Karen Tracy, *Conversational Coherence: Form, Structure, and Strategy* (Beverly Hills, CA: Sage, 1983); Susan B. Shimanoff, *Communication Rules: Theory and Research* (Beverly Hills, CA: Sage, 1980).

4. B. Aubrey Fisher, *Interpersonal Communication: Pragmatics of Human Relationships* (New York: Random House, 1987) 59.

5. Kellermann calls these interaction scenes "Memory Organization Packets" (MOPs). Our description of her research is based on the following: Kathy Kellermann, "The Conversation MOP II: Progression Through Scenes in Discourse," *Human Communication Research* 17 (1991): 385–414; Kathy Kellermann, "The conversation MOP: A model of Pliable Behavior," *The Cognitive Bases of Interpersonal Communication*, ed. Dean E. Hewes (Hillsdale, NJ: Erlbaum, in Press); Kathy Kellerman and Tae-Seop Lim, "The Conversation MOP: III. Timing of Scenes in Discourse," *Journal of Personality and Psychology* 54 (1990): 1163–1179.

6. Dean Barnlund, *Interpersonal Communication: Survey and Studies* (Boston: Houghton Mifflin, 1968) 512.

7. John C. Condon, *Good Neighbors: Communicating with the Mexicans* (Yarmouth, ME: Intercultural Press, 1985) 34.

8. Donald W. Klopf, *Intercultural Encounters: The Fundamentals of Intercultural Communications* (Englewood, CO: Morton, 1987) 23–24.

9. Gary L. Kreps and Elizabeth N. Kunimoto, *Effective Communication in Multicultural Health Care Settings* (Thousand Oaks, CA: Sage, 1994) 5.

10. For a more detailed discussion of other professional opportunities in transcultural nursing, see Margaret M. Andrews, "Cultural Perspectives on Nursing in the 21st Century," *Journal of Professional Nursing* 8 (1992): 7–15.

11. See, for example, Joyceen S. Boyle and Margaret M. Andrews, *Transcultural Concepts in Nursing Care* (Glenview, IL: Scott, Foresman, 1989); Susan M. Dobson, *Transcultural Nursing: A Contemporary Imperative* (London: Scutari Press, 1991); Geri-Ann Galanti, *Caring for Patients from Different Cultures: Case Studies from American Hospitals* (Philadelphia: University of Pennsylvania Press, 1991); Joyce Newman Giger and Ruth Elaine Davidhizar, eds., *Transcultural Nursing: Assessment and Intervention* (St. Louis: Mosby Year Book, 1991); Janice M. Morse, ed., *Issues in Cross-Cultural Nursing* (New York: Churchill Livingstone, 1988); Janice M. Morse, ed., *Cross-Cultural Nursing: Anthropological Approaches to Nursing Research* (Philadelphia: Gordon and Breach, 1989); Cheryl L. Reynolds, *Madeleine Leininger: Cultural Care Diversity and Universality Theory* (Newbury Park, CA: Sage, 1993); Jean Uhl, ed., *Application of Cultural Concepts to Nursing Care: Proceedings of the Ninth Annual Transcultural Nursing Conference, Scottsdale, Arizona, September, 1993* (Salt Lake City: Transcultural Nursing Society, 1984).

12. Kathryn Hopkins Kavanagh and Patricia H. Kennedy, *Promoting Cultural Diversity* (Newbury Park, CA: Sage, 1992) 28.

13. Boyle and Andrews 26–36.

14. Rachel E. Spector, *Cultural Diversity in Health and Illness*, 3rd ed. (Norwalk, CT: Appleton-Lange, 1991) 190.

15. Sam Chan, "Families with Asian Roots," *Developing Cross-Cultural Competence: A Guide for Working with Young Children and Their Families*, ed. Eleanor W. Lynch and Marci J. Hanson (Baltimore: Paul H. Brookes Publishing Co., 1992) 223.

16. Chan 222.

17. For a discussion of these issues, see Kavanaugh and Kennedy 22–24.

18. Ursula M. Wilson, "Nursing Care of American Indian Patients," *Ethnic Nursing Care: A Multicultural Approach*, ed. Modesta Soberano Orque, Bobbie Bloch, and Lidia S. Ahumada Monroy (St. Louis: C.V. Mosby, 1983) 277.

19. Joan Kuipers, "Mexican Americans," *Transcultural Nursing: Assessment and Intervention*, ed. Joyce Newman Giger and Ruth Elaine Davidhizar (St. Louis: Mosby Year Book, 1991) 192–194.

20. Boyle and Andrews 151–155.

21. Noreen Mokuau and Pemerika Tauili'ili, "Families with Native Hawaiian and Pacific Island Roots," *Developing Cross-Cultural Competence: A Guide for Working with Young Children and Their Families*, ed. Eleanor W. Lynch and Marci J. Hanson (Baltimore: Paul Brookes Publishing Co., 1992) 313.

22. Kavanagh and Kennedy 37. See also Kuipers.

23. Kuipers 188.

24. Kuipers 189. See also Kavanagh and Kennedy; Wilson 277.

25. Chan 241.

26. Boyle and Andrews 55.

27. Maria E. Zuniga, "Families with Latino Roots," *Developing Cross-Cultural Competence: A Guide for Working with Young Children and Their Families*, ed. Eleanor W. Lynch and Marci J. Hanson (Baltimore: Paul Brookes Publishing Co., 1992) 151–179.

28. Jennie R. Joe and Randi Suzanne Malach, "Families with Native American Roots," *Developing Cross-Cultural Competence: A Guide for Working with Young Children and Their Families*, ed. Eleanor W. Lynch and Marci J. Hanson (Baltimore: Paul Brookes Publishing Co., 1992) 108; Cornel Pewewardy, "Toward Defining A Culturally Responsive Pedagogy for American Indian Children: The American Indian Magnet School," *Multicultural Education for the Twenty-First Century, Proceedings of the Second Annual Meeting, National Association for Multicultural Education, February 13–16th, 1992*, ed. Carl A. Grant (Morristown, NJ: Paramount Publishing, 1992) 218.

29. See Sam Chan, "Families with Pilipino Roots," *Developing Cross-Cultural Competence: A Guide for Working with Young Children and Their Families*, ed. Eleanor W. Lynch and Marci J. Hanson (Baltimore: Paul Brookes Publishing Co., 1992) 276.

30. Jennie R. Joe and Randi Suzanne Malach, "Families with Native American Roots," *Developing Cross-Cultural Competence: A Guide for Working with Young Children and Their Families*, ed. Eleanor W. Lynch and Marci J. Hanson (Baltimore: Paul Brookes Publishing Co., 1992) 108. See also Pewewardy.

31. Joe and Malach 110.

32. Jolene Koester and Myron W. Lustig, "Communication Curricula in the Multicultural University," *Communication Education* 40 (1991): 250–254.

33. Barbara J. Shade and Clara A. New, "Cultural Influences on Learning: Teaching Implications," *Multicultural Education: Issues and Perspectives*, ed. James A. Banks and Cherry A. McGee Banks, 2nd ed. (Boston: Allyn and Bacon, 1993) 320.

34. Leonard Davidman with Patricia T. Davidman, *Teaching with a Multicultural Perspective: A Practical Guide* (New York: Longman, 1994) 43.

35. Virginia Shirin Sharifzadeh, "Families with Middle Eastern Roots," *Developing Cross-Cultural Competence: A Guide for Working with Young Children and Their Families,* ed. Eleanor W. Lynch and Marci J. Hanson (Baltimore: Paul Brookes Publishing Co., 1992) 341.

36. Davidman with Davidman xi.

37. Joe and Malach 109.

38. Rosalie L. Tung, "Expatriate Assignments: Enhancing Success and Minimizing Failure," *Academy of Management Executive* 1 (1987): 117–126.

39. Gary Oddou and Mark Mendenhall, "Expatriate Performance Appraisal: Problems and Solutions," *International Human Resource Management,* ed. Mark Mendenhall and Gary Oddou (Boston: PWS-Kent, 1991) 364–374; Rosalie Tung and Edwin L. Miller, "Managing in the Twenty-First Century: The Need for Global Orientation," *Management International Review* 30 (1990): 5–18.

40. JC. Bruno Teboul, Ling Chen, and Lynn M. Fritz, "Intercultural Organizational Communication Research in Multinational Organizations," *Communicating in Multinational Organizations,* ed. Richard L. Wiseman and Robert Shuter (Thousand Oaks, CA: Sage, 1994) 12–29.

41. See, for example: John A. S. Abecasis-Phillips, *Doing Business with the Japanese* (Lincolnwood, IL: NTC Business Books, 1994); Roger E. Axtell, *The Do's and Taboos of Hosting International Visitors* (New York: Wiley, 1990); Gerald F. Cavanagh, *American Business Values,* 3rd ed. (Englewood Cliffs, NJ: Prentice Hall, 1990); Chin-Ning Chu, *The Asian Mind Game: Unlocking the Hidden Agenda of the Asian Business Culture: A Westerner's Survival Manual* (New York: Rawson Associates, 1991); Boye Lafayette De Mente, *How to Do Business with the Japanese,* 2nd ed. (Lincolnwood, IL: NTC Business Books, 1993); Farid Elashmawi and Philip R. Harris, *Multicultural Management: New Skills for Global Success* (Houston: Gulf, 1993); Christopher Engholm, *When Business East Meets Business West: The Guide to Practice and Protocol in the Pacific Rim* (New York: Wiley, 1991); Edward T. Hall and Mildred Reed Hall, *Hidden Differences: Doing Business with the Japanese* (Garden City, NY: Anchor Press, 1987); Timothy Harper, *Cracking the New European Markets* (New York: Wiley, 1992); Philip R. Harris and Robert T. Moran, *Managing Cultural Differences,* 3rd ed. (Houston: Gulf Publishing Co., 1991); Michael Johnson and Robert T. Moran, *Robert T. Moran's Cultural Guide to Doing Business in Europe,* 2nd ed. (Oxford: Butterworth-Heinemann, 1992); Christer Jonsson, *Communication in International Bargaining* (London: Pinter, 1990); Dennis Laurie, *Yankee Samurai: American Managers Speak Out About What It's Like to Work for Japanese Companies in the U.S.* (New York: HarperCollins, 1992); Candace Bancroft McKinniss and Arthur Natella, Jr., *Business in Mexico: Managerial Behavior, Protocol, and Etiquette* (New York: Haworth Press, 1994); Robert T. Moran, *Getting Your Yen'$ Worth: How to Negotiate with Japan, Inc.* (Houston: Gulf, 1985); Robert T. Moran, Philip R. Harris, and William G. Stripp, *Developing the Global Organization: Strategies for Human Resource Professionals* (Houston: Gulf, 1993); Robert T. Moran and William G. Stripp, *Dynamics of Successful International Business Negotiations* (Houston: Gulf, 1991); Mary O'Hara-Devereaux and Robert Johansen, *Globalwork: Bridging Distance, Culture, and Time* (San Francisco: Jossey-Bass, 1994); Sondra Snowdon, *The Global Edge: How Your Company Can Win in the International Marketplace* (New York: Simon and Schuster, 1986); Sondra B. Thiederman, *Profiting in America's Multicultural Marketplace:*

How to Do Business Across Cultural Lines (New York: Lexington Books, 1991); I. William Zartman, ed., *International Multilateral Negotiation: Approaches to the Management of Complexity* (San Francisco: Jossey-Bass, 1994).

42. Robert Shuter and Richard L. Wiseman, "Communication in Multinational Organizations: Conceptual, Theoretical, and Practical issues," *Communicating in Multinational Organizations*, ed. Richard L. Wiseman and Robert Shuter (Thousand Oaks, CA: Sage, 1994) 3–11.

43. Alan Goldman, "Communication in Japanese Multinational Organizations," *Communicating in Multinational Organizations*, ed. Richard L. Wiseman and Robert Shuter (Thousand Oaks, CA: Sage, 1994) 49–59.

44. William I. Gordon, "Organizational Imperatives and Cultural Modifiers," *Business Horizons* 27 (1984): 81.

45. Richard H. Reeves-Ellington, "Using Cultural Skills for cooperative Advantage in Japan," *Human Organization* 52 (1993): 203–215.

46. Young Yun Kim and Sheryl Paulk, "Interpersonal Challenges and Personal Adjustments: A Qualitative Analysis of the Experiences of American and Japanese Co-Workers," *Communicating in Multinational Organizations*, ed. Richard L. Wiseman and Robert Shuter (Thousand Oaks, CA: Sage, 1994) 117–140. See also Alan E. Omens, Stephen R. Jenner, and James R. Beatty, "Intercultural Perceptions in United States Subsidiaries of Japanese Companies," *International Journal of Intercultural Relations* 11 (1987): 249–264; David W. Shwalb, Barbara J. Shwalb, Delwyn L. Harnisch, Martin L. Maehr, and Kiyoshi Akabane, "Personal Investment in Japan and the U.S.A.: A Study of Worker Motivation," *International Journal of Intercultural Relations* 16 (1992): 107–124.

47. Alex Blackwell, "Negotiating in Europe," *Hemispheres* (July, 1994) 43+.

48. Harris and Moran.

49. De Mente; Engholm.

50. Lecia Archer and Kristine L. Fitch, "Communication in Latin American Multinational Organizations," *Communicating in Multinational Organizations*, ed. Richard L. Wiseman and Robert Shuter (Thousand Oaks, CA: Sage, 1994) 75–93.

51. Cindy P. Lindsay and Bobby L. Dempsey, "Ten Painfully Learned Lessons About Working in China: The Insights of Two American Behavioral Scientists," *Journal of Applied Behavioral Science* 19 (1983): 265–276.

52. Lindsay and Dempsey.

53. Harris and Moran.

54. See, for example, Christalyn Branner and Tracey Wilson, *Doing Business with Japanese Men: A Woman's Handbook* (Berkeley: Stone Bridge Press, 1993).

55. Harris and Moran 418.

56. Sonja Vegdahl Hur and Ben Seunghwa Hur, *Culture Shock! Korea* (Singapore: Times Books International, 1988) 34.

57. Charles R. Bantz, "Cultural Diversity and Group Cross-Cultural Team Research," *Journal of Applied Communication Research* 21 (1993): 1–20.

CHAPTER 12

1. Philip R. Harris and Robert T. Moran, *Managing Cultural Differences*, 3rd ed. (Houston: Gulf, 1991) 59.

2. William G. Sumner, *Folkways* (Boston: Ginn, 1940) 27.

3. Sumner.

4. Walter Lippman, *Public Opinion* (New York: Harcourt, Brace, 1922) 25.

5. See Carl Friedrich Graumann and Margret Wintermantel, "Discriminatory Speech Acts: A Functional Approach," *Stereotyping and Prejudice: Changing Conceptions*, ed. Daniel Bar-Tal, Carl F. Graumann, Arie W. Kruglanski, and Wolfgang Stroebe (New York: Springer-Verlag, 1989) 183–204.

6. Henri Tajfel, *Differentiation Between Social Groups: Studies in the Social Psychology of Intergroup Relations* (New York: Academic Press, 1978).

7. See Charles M. Judd and Bernadette Park, "Definition and Assessment of Accuracy in Social Stereotypes," *Psychological Review*, 100 (1993): 109–128.

8. Marilynn B. Brewer, "Social Identity, Distinctiveness, and In-Group Homogeneity," *Social Cognition*, 11 (1993): 150–164; E. E. Jones, G. C. Wood, and G. A. Quattrone, "Perceived Variability of Personal Characteristics in In-Groups and Out-Groups: The Role of Knowledge and Evaluation," *Personality and Social Psychology Bulletin*, 7 (1981): 523–528; Charles M. Judd and Bernadette Park, "Out-Group Homogeneity: Judgments of Variability at the Individual and Group Levels," *Journal of Personality and Social Psychology*, 54 (1988): 778–788; P. W. Linville and E. E. Jones, "Polarized Appraisals of Out-Group Members," *Journal of Personality and Social Psychology*, 38 (1980): 689–703; Brian Mullen and L. Hu, "Perceptions of Ingroup and Outgroup Variability: A Meta-Analytic Integration," *Basic and Applied Social Psychology*, 10 (1989): 233–252; Thomas M. Ostrom, Sandra L. Carpenter, Constantine Sedikides, and Fan Li, "Differential Processing of In-Group and Out-Group Information," *Journal of Personality and Social Psychology*, 64 (1993): 21–34.

9. David Barsamian, "Albert Mokhiber: Cultural Images, Politics, and Arab Americans," *Z Magazine*, May 1993: 46–50. Rpt. in *Ethnic Groups*, Vol. 4. Ed. Eleanor Goldstein. Boca Raton, FL: Social Issues Resources Ser., 1994), art. no. 73.

10. Ziva Kunda and Bonnie Sherman-Williams, "Stereotypes and the Construal of Individuating Information," *Personality and Social Psychology Bulletin*, 19 (1993): 97.

11. John J. Seta and Catherine E. Seta, "Stereotypes and the Generation of Compensatory and Noncompensatory Expectancies of Group Members," *Personality and Social Psychology Bulletin*, 19 (1993): 722–731.

12. C. Neil Macrae, Alan B. Milne, and Galen V. Bodenhausen, "Stereotypes as Energy-Saving Devices: A Peek Inside the Cognitive Toolbox," *Journal of Personality and Social Psychology* 66 (1994): 37–47.

13. Gordon W. Allport, *The Nature of Prejudice* (New York: Macmillan, 1954).

14. Richard W. Brislin, *Cross-cultural Encounters: Face-to-Face Interaction* (New York: Pergamon, 1981) 42–49.

15. Teun A. van Dijk, *Communicating Racism: Ethnic Prejudice in Thought and Talk* (Newbury Park, CA: Sage, 1987).

16. For a discussion of the effects of racism on various groups of people, see *Racism in America: Opposing Viewpoints*, ed. William Dudley and Charles Cozic (San Diego: Greenhaven, 1991).

17. Robert Blauner, *Racial Oppression in America* (New York: Harper & Row, 1972) 112.

18. Dalmas A. Taylor, "Race Prejudice, Discrimination, and Racism," *Social Psychology*, ed. A. Kahn, E. Donnerstein, and M. Donnerstein (Dubuque, IA: Wm. C. Brown, 1984); cited in Phyllis A. Katz and Dalmas A. Taylor, "Introduction," *Eliminating Racism: Profiles in Controversy*, ed. Phyllis A. Katz and Dalmas A. Taylor (New York: Plenum, 1988) 6.

19. Katz and Taylor 7.
20. Blauner.
21. James M. Jones, "Racism in Black and White: A Bicultural Model of Reaction and Evolution," *Eliminating Racism: Profiles in Controversy,* ed. Phyllis A. Katz and Dalmas A. Taylor (New York: Plenum, 1988) 130–131.
22. Jones 118–126.
23. Katz and Taylor 7.
24. Jenny Yamoto, "Something about the Subject Makes It Hard to Name," *Race, Class, and Gender in the United States: An Integrated Study,* 2nd ed., ed. Paula S. Rothenberg (New York: St. Martin's, 1992) 58.
25. For discussions of racism and prejudice, see: Benjamin P. Bowser, Gale S. Auletta, and Terry Jones, *Confronting Diversity Issues on Campus* (Newbury Park, CA: Sage, 1994); John C. Brigham, "College Students' Racial Attitudes," *Journal of Applied Social Psychology* 23 (1993): 1933–1967; Richard W. Brislin, "Prejudice and Intergroup Communication," *Intergroup Communication,* ed. William B. Gudykunst (London: Edward Arnold, 1986) 74–85; Brislin (1981), 42–49; Charles E. Case, Andrew M. Greeley, and Stephan Fuchs, "Social Determinants of Racial Prejudice," *Sociological Perspectives* 32 (1989): 469–483; Samuel L. Gaertner and John F. Dovidio, "The Aversive Form of Racism," *Prejudice, Discrimination and Racism: Theory and Research,* ed. John F. Dovidio and Samuel L. Gaertner (New York: Academic, 1986) 61–89; David Milner, "Racial Prejudice," *Intergroup Behavior,* ed. John C. Turner and Howard Giles (Chicago: Univ. of Chicago, 1981) 102–143; Albert Ramirez, "Racism toward Hispanics: The Culturally Monolithic Society," *Eliminating Racism: Profiles in Controversy,* ed. Phyllis A. Katz and Dalmas A. Taylor (New York: Plenum, 1988) 137–157; David O. Sears, "Symbolic Racism," *Eliminating Racism: Profiles in Controversy,* ed. Phyllis A. Katz and Dalmas A. Taylor (New York: Plenum, 1988) 53–84; Key Sun, "Two Types of Prejudice and Their Causes," *American Psychologist* 48 (1993): 1152–1153; Ian Vine, "Inclusive Fitness and the Self-System: The Roles of Human Nature and Sociocultural Processes in Intergroup Discrimination," *The Sociobiology of Ethnocentrism: Evolutionary Dimensions of Xenophobia, Discrimination, Racism, and Nationalism,* ed. Vernon Reynolds, Vincent Falger, and Ian Vine (London: Croom Helm, 1987) 60–80.
26. Brigham 1934.
27. Marilyn Brewer and Donald T. Campbell, *Ethnocentrism and Intergroup Attitudes* (New York: Wiley, 1976).
28. Henri Tajfel, *Differentiation Between Social Groups* (London: Academic Press, 1978); Henri Tajfel, *Human Groups and Social Categories: Studies in Social Psychology* (Cambridge: Cambridge University Press, 1981).
29. For summaries of these studies, see William B. Gudykunst, ed., *Intergroup Communication* (London: Edward Arnold, 1986); Ellen Bouchard Ryan and Howard Giles, eds., *Attitudes Toward Language Variation: Social and Applied Contexts* (London: Edward Arnold, 1982).
30. Cynthia Gallois, Arlene Franklyn-Stokes, Howard Giles, and Nikolas Coupland, "Communication Accomodation in Intercultural Encounters," *Theories in Intercultural Communication,* ed. Young Yun Kim and William B. Gudykunst (Newbury Park, CA: Sage, 1988) 157–188.
31. William B. Gudykunst, "Intercultural Contact and Attitude Change: A Review of Literature and Suggestions for Future Research," *International and Intercultural Communication Annual,* ed. Nemi C. Jain (Falls Church, VA: Speech Communication Association, 1977) 1–15.

32. Y. Amir, "Contact Hypothesis in Ethnic Relations," *Psychological Bulletin* 71 (1969): 319–343.

33. Gallois et al.

34. Miles Hewstone and Rupert Brown, "Contact Is Not Enough: An Intergroup Perspective on the 'Contact Hypothesis,' " *Contact and Conflict in Intergroup Encounters*, ed. Miles Hewstone and Rupert Brown (Oxford: Basil Blackwell, 1986) 1–44.

35. Miles Hewstone and Howard Giles, "Social Groups and Social Stereotypes in Intergroup Communication: A Review and Model of Intergroup Communication Breakdown," *Intergroup Communication*, ed. William B. Gudykunst (London: Edward Arnold, 1986) 10–26.

36. Kalvero Oberg, "Cultural Shock: Adjustment to New Cultural Environments," *Practical Anthropology* 7 (1960): 176.

37. Oberg.

38. Michael Brein and Kenneth H. David, "Intercultural Communication and the Adjustment of the Sojourner," *Psychological Bulletin,* 76 (1971): 215–230; J. Gullahorn and J. E. Gullahorn, "An Extension of the U-Curve Hypothesis," *Journal of Social Issues,* 14 (1963): 33–47; Daniel J. Kealey, "A Study of Cross-Cultural Effectiveness: Theoretical Issues, Practical Applications," *International Journal of Intercultural Relations,* 13 (1989): 387–428; Otto Klineberg and W. Frank Hull, *At a Foreign University: An International Study of Adaptation and Coping* (New York: Praeger, 1979); Jolene Koester, "Communication and the Intercultural Reentry: A Course Proposal," *Communication Education* 23 (1984): 251–256; Judith N. Martin, "The Intercultural Reentry: Conceptualizations and Suggestions for Future Research," *International Journal of Intercultural Relations* 8 (1984): 115–134.

39. See, for instance, Sarah Brabant, C. Eddie Palmer, and Robert Gramling, "Returning Home: An Empirical Investigation of Cross-Cultural Reentry," *International Journal of Intercultural Relations* 14 (1990): 387–404.

40. Walter Enloe and Philip Lewin, "Issues of Integration Abroad and Readjustment to Japan of Japanese Returnees," *International Journal of Intercultural Relations* 11 (1987): 223–248; Louise H. Kidder, "Requirements for Being 'Japanese': Stories of Returnees," *International Journal of Intercultural Relations* 16 (1992): 383–393.

41. Enloe and Lewin 235.

42. Nancy Adler, "Re-Entry: Managing Cross-Cultural Transitions," *Group and Organization Studies,* 6 (1981): 341–356; Austin Church, "Sojourner Adjustment," *Psychological Bulletin* 91 (1982): 540–572; Kealey, Dennison Nash, "The Course of Sojourner Adaptation: A New Test of the U-Curve Hypothesis," *Human Organization,* 50 (1991): 283–286.

43. See, for example, Young Yun Kim and Brent D. Ruben, "Intercultural Transformation: A Systems Theory," *Theories in Intercultural Communication*, ed. Young Yun Kim and William B. Gudykunst (Newbury Park, CA: Sage, 1988) 299–321.

CHAPTER 13

1. Jolene Koester and Margaret Olebe, "The Behavioral Assessment Scale for Intercultural Communication Effectiveness," *International Journal of Intercultural Relations* 12 (1988): 233–246; Margaret Olebe and Jolene Koester, "Exploring the Cross-cultural Equivalence of the Behavioral Assessment Scale for Intercultural

Communication," *International Journal of Intercultural Relations* 13 (1989): 333–347.

2. Brent D. Ruben, "Assessing Communication Competency for Intercultural Adaptation," *Group and Organization Studies* 1 (1976): 334–354; Brent D. Ruben, Lawrence R. Askling, and Daniel J. Kealey, "Cross-cultural Effectiveness," *Overview of Intercultural Training, Education, and Research, Vol. I: Theory*, ed. David S. Hoopes, Paul B. Pedersen, and George W. Renwick (Washington, DC: Society for Intercultural Education, Training and Research, 1977) 92–105; Brent D. Ruben and Daniel J. Kealey, "Behavioral Assessment of Communication Competency and the Prediction of Cross-Cultural Adaptation," *International Journal of Intercultural Relations* 3 (1979): 15–48.

3. John W. Berry, Uichol Kim, and Pawel Boski, "Psychological Acculturation of Immigrants," *Cross-cultural Adaptation: Current Approaches*, ed. Young Yun Kim and William B. Gudykunst (Newbury Park, CA: Sage, 1988) 64.

4. Berry, and Boski 53.

5. Berry, Kim, and Boski.

6. Daniel J. Kealey, "A Study of Cross-Cultural Effectiveness: Theoretical Issues, Practical Applications," *International Journal of Intercultural Relations* 13(1989): 387–428.

7. Mitchell R. Hammer, William B. Gudykunst, and Richard L. Wiseman, "Dimensions of Intercultural Effectiveness: An Exploratory Study," *International Journal of Intercultural Relations* 2 (1978): 382–393.

8. See Colleen Ward and Antony Kennedy, "Locus of Control, Mood Disturbance, and Social Difficulty during Cross-Cultural Transitions," *International Journal of Intercultural Relations* 2 (1992): 175–194; Colleen Ward and Antony Kennedy, "Acculturation and Cross-Cultural Adaptation of British Residents in Hong Kong," *Journal of Social Psychology* 133 (1993): 395–397; Colleen Ward and Wendy Searle, "The Impact of Value Discrepancies and Cultural Identity on Psychological and Sociological Adjustment of Sojourners," *International Journal of Intercultural Relations* 15 (1991): 209–225.

9. Guo-Ming Chen, "Communication Adaptability and Interaction Involvement as Predictors of Cross-Cultural Adjustment," *Communication Research Reports* 9 (1992): 33–41.

10. Berry, Kim, and Boski 66.

11. Berry, Kim, and Boski 71.

12. Young Yun Kim and Brent D. Ruben, "Intercultural Transformation: A Systems Approach," *Theories in Intercultural Communication*, ed. Young Yun Kim and William B. Gudykunst (Newbury Park, CA: Sage, 1988) 313–314.

13. David W. Kale, "Ethics in Intercultural Communication," *Intercultural Communication: A Reader*, 6th ed., ed. Larry A. Samovar and Richard E. Porter (Belmont, CA: Wadsworth, 1991) 423.

14. Kale.

15. Gale S. Auletta and Terry Jones, "Reconstituting the Inner Circle," *American Behavioral Scientist* 34 (1990): 137–152.

16. Troy Duster, "Understanding Self-Segregation on the Campus," *The Chronicle of Higher Education*, September 25, 1991: B2.

Credits

Author Index

Bumiller, Elisabeth, 242, 359

Calabrese, Richard J., 370
Calvin, William, 358
Campbell, Donald T., 377
Campbell, Joseph, 36
Carbaugh, Donal, 34, 235, 355, 367, 368
Carpenter, Sandra L., 376
Carroll, Raymonde, 243, 273
Case, Charles E., 377
Chan, Sam, 373
Chang, Hui–Chang, 136, 145, 254, 360, 361
Chen, Guo–Ming, 341, 361, 379
Chen, Ling, 374
Chen, Victoria, 371
Cheng, Li–Rong L., 362
Christopher, Robert, 219
Chua, Elizabeth, 370
Chung, Jensen, 361
Churchill, Winston, 160
Cichon, Elaine, 367
Clatterbuck, Glen W., 370
Clifford, Frank, 353
Cocroft, Beth–Ann, 370
Cole, Johnetta, 8, 56, 310
Cole, Michael, 225, 362, 667
Collier, Mary J., 111, 355, 360, 363, 364, 368
Condon, John, 102, 192, 225, 245, 279, 359, 362, 364, 366–368, 372
Condon, William, 212
Conquergood, Dwight, 25
Cope, William, 289, 354
Cornell, Stephen, 359
Cose, Ellis, 359
Coskran, Kathleen, 172
Coughlin, Ellen K., 149
Coupland, Nikolas, 377
Courtney, Brian A., 15
Courty, M. A., 358
Cozic, Charles, 376
Craig, Robert T., 369, 372
Crèvecoeur, J. Hector, 354
Cummings, Joe, 368
Cupach, William R., 356, 357, 370
Curnow, A., 358

Dance, Frank E. X., 355
Daniel, Jack, 104, 113, 360
Darwin, Charles, 190, 364
David, Kenneth H., 378
Davidhizar, Ruth E., 372, 373
Davidman, Leonard, 374
Davidman, Patricia, 374
Davis, Wade, 282

Dembling, Sophia, 244
DeSipio, Louis, 354
Desruisseaux, Paul, 353
Devito, Joseph A., 207, 365
Dew, Anna–Marie, 366
Dickey, Christopher, 70
Dillard, James P., 369
Dinh, My–Lien, 321
Donnerstein, Kahn E,, 376
Donnerstein, M., 376
Dorris, Michael, 114, 174, 363
Douglas, William, 370
Dovidio, John F., 377
Duck, Steven, 368
Dudley, William, 376
Dunbar, Edward, 353
Duster, Troy, 379

Edwards, John R., 179, 363
Ehninger, Douglas, 367
Ekman, Paul, 190, 196, 364, 365
Ellsworth, Phoebe, 365
Engholm, Christopher, 374
Enloe, Walter, 378
Erdrich, Louise, 97
Erlbaum, Lawrence, 235, 367, 368
Espiritu, Yen Le, 359
Evans, Charlotte, 358

Falcon, Angelo, 354
Fehr, Beverley, 368
Feig, John P., 368, 369
Feldstein, Stanley, 364
Fisher, B. Aubrey, 371
Fishman, Joshua A., 363
Fitch, Kristine L., 375
Foa, Edna B., 371
Foa, Uriel G., 371
Forgas, Joseph, 274, 360, 372
Forsyth, Susan, 368
Foss, Karen A., 367
Foss, Sonja K., 367
Franklyn–Stokes, Arlene, 363, 377
Fridlund, Alan J., 364
Friesen, Wallace, 196, 364, 365
Fritz, Lynn M., 374
Fuchs, Stephen, 377

Gaertner, Samuel L., 377
Galanti, Geri–Ann, 372
Gallois, Cynthia, 377, 378
Garza de la, Rodolfo O., 354
Garcia, F. Chris, 354
Garcia, John, 354
Ge Gao, 247, 368
Gelernter, Cary Q., 358

Subject Index